Crime and Behaviour

An Introduction to Criminal and Forensic Psychology

Crime and Behaviour

An Introduction to Criminal and Forensic Psychology

Majeed Khader

Nanyang Technological University, Singapore
Home Team Behavioural Sciences Center, Singapore

 **World Scientific**

NEW JERSEY · LONDON · SINGAPORE · BEIJING · SHANGHAI · HONG KONG · TAIPEI · CHENNAI · TOKYO

Published by

World Scientific Publishing Co. Pte. Ltd.
5 Toh Tuck Link, Singapore 596224
USA office: 27 Warren Street, Suite 401-402, Hackensack, NJ 07601
UK office: 57 Shelton Street, Covent Garden, London WC2H 9HE

Library of Congress Cataloging-in-Publication Data
Names: Khader, Majeed, 1966–   author.
Title: Crime and behaviour : an introduction to criminal and forensic psychology /
    Majeed Khader, Ministry of Home Affairs, Singapore & Home Team Behavioural
    Sciences Center, Singapore & Nanyang Technological University, Singapore.
Other titles: Crime and behavior
Description: New Jersey : World Scientific, [2018]
Identifiers: LCCN 2018049593 | ISBN 9789813279339 (hardcover)
Subjects: LCSH: Criminal justice, Administration of--Singapore. | Criminal investigation--
    Singapore. | Crime prevention--Singapore. | Forensic psychology--Singapore.
Classification: LCC HV9960.S56 K43 2018 | DDC 364.3--dc23
LC record available at https://lccn.loc.gov/2018049593

British Library Cataloguing-in-Publication Data
A catalogue record for this book is available from the British Library.

For any available supplementary material, please visit
https://www.worldscientific.com/worldscibooks/10.1142/11244#t=suppl

Desk Editor: Karimah Samsudin

Typeset by Stallion Press
Email: enquiries@stallionpress.com

Printed in Singapore

"The Home Team must continue to recruit the best young officers...
we cannot have a situation where the criminals are smarter and better
resourced than you. If we don't recruit strong officers, with moral
fibre and a sense of purpose, you will go downhill very fast. Criminals
with clever lawyers will run rings around you in court.

We need officers who understand the intricacies of the legal
system, are proficient in forensic analysis, and understand the
psychological aspects of crime and criminality."

Speech by former Minister Mentor, Mr Lee Kuan Yew,
at a Senior Police Officers' Mess dining-in on 17 November 2011.

This book is dedicated to all the men and women in blue in the SPF and
the Home Team, who keep the streets of Singapore safe and secure.

ACKNOWLEDGEMENTS

This book has been a personal endeavour to provide a text for my students. As Singaporeans, they found it limiting to use American, Canadian, and British criminal psychology textbooks, even though much of the theoretical content was still useful. Their laws and contexts differed from ours. I also typically receive one or two emails a week asking about criminal psychology or criminology career prospects. All of these hinted that there was fast growing interest in this subject and that there was a need for local material. Hence, the reason for this book.

Readers should note that I have not been asked to write this for any organisation. I write it because of a conviction that the Singapore model works. The Singapore crime management model is not a perfect one. It need not be. It just needs to be a model that works for most Singaporeans and for Singapore.

I am grateful, however, for the support provided by the Singapore Police and the Ministry of Home Affairs, as this project commenced during a sabbatical I took from work. My present and past leaders have been very supportive of the need to do research. I am thankful towards Mr. Pang Kin Keong, Mr. Leo Yip, Mr. Tan Tee How, Madam Goh Soon Poh, Mr. Phua Kok Keong, Mr. T. Rajakumar, and Mr. Hoong Wee Teck. I am particularly grateful for the guidance of Mr. Benny Lim, who has reminded me to "do it right and do it well".

My past supervisors, Mr. Jerry See, Mr. Loy Chye Meng, Mr. Ng Boon Gay, Mr. Tan Hung Hooi, Mr. Dennis Tang, Mr. Ng Seng

Liang, Mr. Goh Liang Kwang, Mr. Khoo Boon Hui and Mr. Soh Kee Hean have been very supportive and I thank them too.

Starting off as a pioneering police psychologist was not easy. There were no senior psychologists to guide you. Many police officers, however, guided me. I am thankful therefore to Ng Bah Tee, Sri Kanthan, C.V. Gabriel, Mickey Lee, Chan Soo Wah, Simon Suppiah, Ang Hin Kee, and Haffidz Abdul Hamid. To Burhanudeen Haji Hussainar, Goh Tat Boon, Dominique Ngoo, Raymond Tan, Roy Lim, and Osman Bin Mohamad Noor, a heart-warming thanks for discussions on investigative and profiling matters.

To my ever-supportive close friends and police officer colleagues: Devrajan Bala, David Scott Arul, Jarrod Pereira, Daniel Tan, Lee Su Peng, Sekher Warrier, Abdul Jalil, and Gerald Lim, I have been privileged to work alongside with you over these 25 years.

Developing as a psychologist, I learnt much from Singaporean giants and senior colleagues: Associate Professor Fred Long Foo Yee, Mr. Ong Kian Chye, Associate Professor John Elliot, Professor David Chan, Dr. Lyn Chua, Professor Chong Siow Ann, Elizabeth Pang, Susan Sim, and Vivienne Ng.

At Nanyang Technological University, I got warm support from Associate Professor Ringo Ho, Associate Professor Joyce Pang, Professor Annabel Chen, Professor Adrian Raine, Assistant Professor Olivia Choy, Associate Professor Kumar Ramakrishna, Dr. Damien Cheong and Dr. Shashi Jayakumar.

Internationally, Emeritus Professor Rhona Flin, Professor Amina Memon, Professor Ray Bull, Professor Laurence Alison, Professor Rebecca Milne, Master Rachel Spearing, Professor Clive Hollin, Professor Kate Fritzon, Professor Graham Davies, Mr. Lee Rainbow, and Professor Mark Kebbell have been wonderful supportive mentors and friends. Much thanks to my friends at the U.S.-based Society of Police and Criminal Psychology; Dr. Gary Aumiller, Professor Michael Stoloff and Professor JoAnne Brewster. All of you have my deep gratitude.

I also owe much to my colleagues at the Police Psychological Services Division, and Home Team Behavioural Sciences Centre. My deep appreciation to Jeffery Chin, Carolyn Misir, Whistine Chai, Gabriel Ong, Jansen Ang, and Tim Leo, with whom I have had many discussions on crime psychology. Especially, to Neo Loo Seng for his insights on the Terrorism chapter. I must also acknowledge the assistance of my research assistants, Rachel Ng Li En and Loh Ying Hui.

Working with Karimah Samsudin at WSPC has also been a smooth journey, which made this project so much easier. She has been patient, encouraging, and professional in guiding me.

I am thankful for the blessings of my mum Hawa and brothers Firoz and Mohideen. Although he is no longer with us, as I wrote this, I was inspired by what my dad Othmansa Abdul Khader would have said to cheer me on. My children, Tasneem and Raouf, have been my joy. Most importantly, to Tscheng Yee, who has been a source of emotional support, clever ideas, and critical feedback.

PREFACE

"Why does Singapore have a murder rate of 16 to 20 murders a year for a population of over five million? What is working here? Is there a different psyche to the Singaporean?" asked an American friend. I replied that I had not the faintest idea. There have been no major studies conducted on this question. Then he said, "Then, why don't you write about it?" This started the idea for this book.

People joke about Singapore's strict laws. No chewing gum is allowed into the country because it litters the streets. There are fines for different things. There are strict laws for drug use and trafficking. Retail shops are also not allowed to sell alcohol after certain hours. Stand up comedians joke about how everyone in Singapore crosses at the traffic lights and there is little jay walking.

Is crime and disorder low because of these no-nonsense laws? Well, we know from criminology that when you take care of the small things (such as 'broken windows' or vandalism), the bigger things are usually taken care of as well. People get a sense of 'guardianship', or that someone is watching, or that society cares about damage to property.

Still, it would be simplistic to think that strict rules alone matter. We do know that macro factors such as the economy and the rule of law are associated with lower crime. However, mid-level and micro factors such as trust in the police and the courts matter.

When we analyze the Singapore model of crime management, not a lot of it is about the direct application of criminal psychology, since it is a relatively new field. There is, however, a very good understanding of the criminal psyche which has evolved in the Singapore model of policing and criminal justice. It is clear that administrators, policymakers, and ground police officers understand the criminal mind and deterrence issues because if they did not, they would not be able to keep crime rates so low. These issues will be discussed in this book. We do not purport to know all the answers, but this book is a start. Research progresses with time. I hope this spurs more researchers to study these questions further.

In this writing, I have tried to put together some of the ideas and practices we have in Singapore, to cull some of the local and Asian studies on crime, and to provide a rationale for the way we do things. Having said that, I stand on the shoulders of many international criminal psychology and criminology giants, and have drawn on the wealth of material that has developed in the U.K., the U.S., New Zealand, Australia, Canada, Japan, and other parts of the world. We, in Singapore, have never proclaimed to have a monopoly over wisdom. Much of what we have done in Singapore has evolved from innovations from the best practices all over the world.

How is this book different from others? Well, I write as an academic who has also been practicing chiefly as a psychologist: a 'pracademic'.[1] Much of what I have learnt has been shaped by two and half decades of practice and lessons from the excellent professionals I have worked with in Singapore. This means I am drawing from theory, but also from the real world of applying psychology in managing crime.

Who is this book for? I keep in mind three groups: university students, psychologists who want to specialize in forensic and criminal psychology, and law enforcement trainees who will benefit by understanding criminal behaviour. It differs from most books on criminal psychology, which tend to overemphasize theoretical concepts. This book is neither theory-focused nor theory-heavy. It hopes to provide a balanced perspective covering theoretical/academic and practical/applied perspectives.

---

[1] This is a term coined by a close friend Master Rachel Spearing, who teaches at Portsmouth University.

There are several features of this book:

- *It is introductory reading.* This book is not meant to provide a sophisticated analysis of any particular forensic psychology or criminal psychology problem or question (for example, community policing). This is an introductory textbook. References are provided so that readers may follow up on interested material, if they want to.
- *This book has a pedagogical imperative.* Its primary intention is to teach and enable readers to learn. To do this, there are thinking questions, summary points, resources, legal references, and sample essay questions at the end of each chapter.
- *Resources and contacts are provided.* This book is meant to be useful to the reader. For this reason, I have provided many resources for the students, and phone and website details for readers. This is deliberate, even though some reviewers of this book have found this to be unconventional.
- *Toolkits are featured.* For the practitioner, there are toolkits in each chapter. These are recipe-like suggestions for the practitioner who wants to apply knowledge to practice.
- *There are case studies.* Case studies will be provided, offering the university student, junior psychologist or the so inclined police officer with rich real-world examples of criminal behaviour. Most of the time, actual names and details are masked to provide anonymity. I have hidden identifying information, since the world has become smaller and families of offenders reading about the misdeeds of their loved ones do feel upset. We have to respect them.
- *There is a Singaporean and Asian perspective.* This is a valuable perspective for the reader since criminal justice procedures and practices may differ in Singapore and in Asia. For example, Singapore does not have the jury system, and we have strong anti-drugs and anti-terrorism laws. Students who return from overseas exchange courses where they learn about forensic psychology enjoy their training, but often grumble that they cannot relate to the foreign laws and criminal justice context. Furthermore, there are

cultural differences; for instance, victims of crime in Singapore may not always report all of the details to the police out of the shame or embarrassment that they feel, and investigators in Singapore and Asia understand these nuances.

- *This book has a strong bias towards explaining the Singaporean criminal justice system.* I make no excuses for this. The Singapore government has good reasons for doing what it does, even if not all of it is apparent to everyone. The streets are safe and crime is low. It is therefore worth the while, to pen down some possible hypotheses for this positive state of things.

- *This book has a multidisciplinary approach but with a strong focus on psychology.* Psychology does not have a monopoly over the understanding of crime. Hollywood shows such as *Criminal Minds* and *Lie to Me* have made criminal psychology sexy sounding but, in reality, psychologists do not solve crime cases. Police officers do. And prosecutors argue cases in court. So, the approach in this book has been to look at crime from a multidisciplinary perspective, looking into the forensic science, legal, psychology, and the policing aspects of each crime type and criminal case. I have developed this method of analysis because real-life crime solving draws on different perspectives.

- *The structure, scope, and focus of this book.* Being an introductory book, the topic of this book was scoped to cover the criminal justice system, basic theories, deception, interpersonal crimes (sex and violence), terrorism, and responses to crime. I added a final section on forensic psychology that could be applied to legal matters because this may make it clearer to the legal and psychological professions about how psychology might help answer some legal questions. This is an emerging area of collaboration and I wanted to dedicate a small chapter to it. Property crimes, cyber crimes, organised crimes, and white collars crimes were all left out, so as to provide some focus on what is needed for an a introductory training course. Of course, it could be argued that this material could be presented in another way. I do not disagree with that. However, this is the way I have been teaching it and thus far, students seem to like it and I have kept this order for this book.

As a final note, readers should note that the information provided here does not constitute legal nor psychological advice. You should obtain specific legal advice from a lawyer or psychologist before taking any action. I did try to ensure the accuracy of the information on this book and point out available resources at varying points of this book. I hope readers will find this book a useful read. Any errors made in this book are entirely mine and I welcome any feedback you have at majkhader@gmail.com. I do not have a monopoly over wisdom and would be happy to learn from anyone.

All proceeds from the royalties of this book will be given to charities.

Dr. A Majeed Khader
M.Sci. with Distinction (Leicester), Ph.D. (Aberdeen)
Assistant Professor (Adjunct), Nanyang Technological University
Asian Director, Society of Police and Criminal Psychology
Member, Asia-Pacific Association of Threat Assessment Professionals

LIST OF TABLES

LIST OF FIGURES

CONTENTS

CHAPTER 1

INTRODUCTION TO CRIMINAL AND FORENSIC PSYCHOLOGY

"Do you commit crimes because you are a criminal? Or do you become a criminal, when you commit crime?"

Professor Gwen Adshead
Author of *The Criminal Mind: The Relationships between Criminology and Psychology*

1.1 Introduction

Why write another book on criminal behaviour? Are there not enough books on crime already? The main reason for this book, in my view, is that crime is always contextual, happening in a particular place and time, so the Singaporean and Asian picture of crime and our ways of responding may be interesting to the reader. Singapore has been called one of the safest places in the world. The Economist Safe City Index, for instance, ranked Singapore second out of over 60 cities in the world, only behind Tokyo (*The Economist*, 2017). Would it not be interesting to examine why? Is criminal behaviour manifested differently here? Is the manner of managing crime and disorder different from other parts of the world?

Additionally, criminal behaviour itself is facinating for two main reasons: first, crime itself is interesting, with all its juicy facts and nitty-gritty details. Secondly, the human actor behind the crime intrigues us. Who is he? Why did he do it? (it is usually a 'he'). We wonder if we could be capable of such deeds, or if our neighbours are secretly criminals. We get shaken when we discover a crime committed by someone we knew as a child in school or someone we know at work. In this sense, the world of crime immerses us psychologically. Yet, it is not imagined. Crime is real, and it is part of our lives. We yearn to know the 'whys'. This book hopes to explain the 'whys' of criminal motivations and actions. Let's start with some cases, just to get us thinking. Think about the following crimes below and ask yourself why these offenders do what they do. What is their 'psychological makeup'?

Case #1.1: Jeffrey Choi, a Singaporean man, stole a pink brassiere off a clothes rack outside a neighbour's flat. He crept on the floor with the bra in his hands. He sniffed the bra for a while before getting up, putting it in his sling bag and walking away. A neighbour saw him and called '999'. Choi was arrested and taken back to his flat, where police found 155 bras and 151 pairs of panties in his room! They were arranged by size and colour along a chromatic scale. Choi said he had picked them up over the years as he had developed a liking for collecting undergarments. What made him obsessed with undergarments, which are basically cloth? Was it the association with sex? What did he do with them? Where did he hide them?

Case #1.2: Jack Able, an Austrian man, kept his daughter as his sex slave for 24 years in the basement of his house. Elaine was imprisoned from the age of 18 in the cramped 18-square-meters cellar, during which she was raped repeatedly by her father. There were no windows and she could not escape. She gave birth to eight of his children while being held captive, with three of them ending up trapped in the cellar with her! She escaped one day to tell her tales of horror. How could a father do this to his biological daughter? Why did he do this?

Case #1.3: Allen Menzies, a 25-year-old Scottish man, became obsessed with the film *Queen of the Damned* and its main character, the vampire queen Akasha. On the day that he killed his friend, Menzies claimed that his friend had made an insulting remark about Akasha and he had just snapped. He struck his friend on the head at least 10 times with a hammer before stabbing him. He then drank some of his victim's blood and ate part of his skull. Is this a kind of vampirism? Was he mentally ill?

Why do crimes like these occur? Is it nature or nurture? Is it biology that pushes one to be obsessed with underwear? Is it poor parenting? Is it bad friends who teach us about vampirism? Is there too much violence on television and social media?

> **THINKING POINT**
>
> As a mental exercise, list three factors that you think could have contributed to the above crimes, and try to be specific if you can. Entertain different contributing factors — for example, the role played by parents, bad company, unhealthy thinking, genes, biology, building design, lack of CCTV cameras, and so on. Some of the factors are discussed in the later parts of this chapter if you want to get some ideas, but try to figure out some of these on your own.

1.1.1 *What is Crime?*

If we are discussing the 'whys' of criminal behaviour, we must first know what 'crime' is. A formal definition has been provided by Professor Larry J. Siegel who explained that "crime is a violation of societal rules of behaviour as interpreted and expressed by the criminal law, which reflects public opinion, traditional values and the viewpoint of people currently holding social and political power" (Siegel, 2010). This definition discusses 'violations of rules' but also that these rules are reflective of current societal values. Therefore, in the past, there may have been acts, which were not criminalized because society did not deem them serious enough. Some examples would be stalking, marital rape or child abuse which were not criminalized at various points in times in various countries, including Singapore. The question of what makes a behaviour criminal, at a point in time, is a complex one which involves the history and evolution of law, but this is beyond the scope of this book.

Another definition of crime is that, "crime is anything your legislature says it is!" Although simplistic, it is broadly speaking quite true. Criminal law defines what is crime. If your lawmakers say that riding a trishaw in Singapore below 80 miles per hour (mph) or eating *char kuay teow* too slowly is a wrongdoing and thus, a crime, then it would be! However, things are of course more complex. Sometimes, crimes may involve 'acts of omissions', and crime has been defined as 'an act or omission punishable by law' (Muncie and McLaughlin, 2001).

Complicating things even further, legal systems distinguish between crimes and behaviours for which someone can get punished. German law, for instance, distinguishes *Strafrecht* (criminal law) and *Straftaten* (crimes) from what is called *Ordnungswidrigkeitenrecht* (regulations) and *Ordnungswidrigkeiten* (violations) (Weigend, 1988). The American Law Institute's Model Penal Code also distinguishes 'crimes' from 'violations'. Violations include behaviour that legal systems count as rule-breaking (not criminal), such as regulations that are breached. There are many dimensions to what society would consider as behaviours it would frown upon and punish. This variation in definition is not entirely a bad thing, since you do not really want to live in a society where there are hundreds of laws for every misdeed! So, it may not be a bad thing to have some laws and some regulations.

Sometimes, crime is defined in terms of the reactions it invokes. Deviant behaviours evoke reactions from others. Deviance includes behaviours which we can call criminal, but it is broader in scope, and mainstream society considers this odd (Joyce, 2012). However, as they say, 'to be a creep is not criminal'. The issue, however, is about who defines what deviancy is. Is it sections of powerful people in society judging others? The vocal minority? Do the laws represent the people's concerns? Furthermore, what is considered deviant now may not be so in the years to come. For example, many considered those with mental illnesses as deviant and persecuted them, because they were thought to be possessed by demons. Now, we understand mental illnesses a lot more, and are more sympathetic to the predicaments of mentally ill individuals.

Adding to all this complexity, there are crimes that are accepted internationally as wrongful acts that ought to be criminalized. For example, the International Criminal Court is concerned with crimes against humanity, genocide, and war crimes.

Taking these together, it seems that crime is socially constructed. Criminal law and thus crime are not static across time. They change as time marches on and, thus, are based on what society accepts as right or wrong at any point of time. What is 'criminal' depends on where and when (time period) it is committed.

As a student or practitioner of psychology, this causes problems for psychological explanations of criminal behaviour (Durrant, 2013). How can one be a criminal for an act today and not a criminal for the same act tomorrow? Thankfully, these changes in definitions are neither frequent nor drastic. Whatever the case, one way to address these issues is to focus on what everyone would agree to be deviant and anti-social universally across time and space. For example, murder, rape, or stealing is accepted as wrong and criminal in most societies and across most times. Thus, experts have divided crime into *mala in se* (inherently wrong) and *mala prohibita* (wrong by legislation or regulation). Most societies would agree that unwarranted killings are *mala in se*, while prohibited smoking in public areas could be *mala prohibita* (Coomber *et al.*, 2015).

1.2 What *is* Criminal and Forensic Psychology?

As 'psychology' is about the scientific study of people and how people think, feel, and behave, it is relevant in explaining why people commit crimes. '*Criminal and forensic psychology*' is an emerging field of psychology, which involves the use of psychology to advance our understanding of the causes of and the management of crime and legal issues. As this is a rudimentary introductory book, I will be using the terms 'forensic psychology' and 'criminal psychology' interchangeably. In my view, having practiced the field for more than two decades, 'forensic psychology' can be defined as the scientific research and application of psychology as a discipline to criminal justice, civil justice, legal, and courtroom settings. This definition carries a few implications. First, it is both a field of application and research. This means there is a place for it in both industry and academia. Second, it can be applied beyond the fields of criminal law to civil law, legal questions (e.g., child custody issues), and courtroom dynamics (e.g., credibility as a witness, or decision making in court). Thanks to popular television shows and social media, we know about the criminal applications of psychology more than the other areas. Just think of shows and movies such as *Lie to Me*, *Criminal Minds*, *Silence of the Lambs*, and *The Negotiator*. However, criminal psychology is more than that; and in most formal forensic psychology training at the postgraduate level, there is usually discussion on Forensic–Legal Psychology and Courtroom Psychology. Some of the broader issues that may interest us in legal psychology would be the following questions:

- Why do false confessions occur?
- How reliable are eyewitness testimonies for use as evidence in court?
- How do judges make decisions in the courts?
- How can child witnesses be used more effectively in courtroom settings (which can be frightening to children)?

1.2.1 *Working as a Forensic Psychologist*

An often-asked question is: what does it take to be a forensic/criminal psychologist? Well, to work as a forensic psychologist, you will have to first to complete a degree in psychology (usually up to honours level or at least a four-year degree program), after which you will have to complete an accredited master's degree in forensic or forensic–clinical psychology. Some employers will only consider those with postgraduate degrees, while others will employ those with a good Honours degree with plans to send them for postgraduate training later on.

Aspiring students should obtain a specialized degree in forensic psychology if they want to be a specialist in this field. You will usually be trained in criminology, legal psychology, courtroom psychology, how to be an expert witness, risk assessment tools, and crime theory among relevant forensic and legal topics. Police and military officers who are considering a post-graduate training in forensic or investigative psychology can opt to undertake a master's level, PsychD, or Ph.D. programme, where the entry criteria places a heavier focus on their relevant experience as law or security enforcers, and may not require them to have basic degree in psychology (although they would still need a first degree). It is good practice for aspiring forensic psychologists to look up the ethical guidelines of practice in forensic psychology (i.e., you can look up the American Psychology-Law Societies guidelines).

1.2.1.1 *Where do forensic psychologists work?*

Not all psychologists who work in forensic contexts are necessarily forensic psychologists. Many are trained in different aspects of psychology, including occupational, clinical, counselling, and forensic psychology. Sometimes, they work closely with forensic psychiatrists and forensic science specialists or criminologists. Psychologists who work in forensic contexts in Singapore work at the following places:

- *The Police Psychology Services Division* (PPSD) in the Singapore Police Force. Police psychologists work in three main areas that we refer to as the three 'O's:
  - First, applying psychology to enhance police *o*rganizations (e.g., pre-employment screening tests, police leadership assessment, assessing the organizational climate of police units);
  - Secondly, enhancing police *o*perations and investigations (e.g., working in hostage negotiation teams, detection of deception in interviews, developing criminal profiles, morale assessment, supporting victims of crimes; and
  - Finally, providing services for police *o*fficers (services such as peer counselling training, counselling programs, and life-skills building).

Readers interested to find out more about the work of police psychologists should read *Police Psychology in Singapore: The Red Dot Experience* (Khader *et al.*, 2011), *Operations Psychology: The*

Singapore Police Experience (Ang *et al.*, 2011), and *Organisational health in the police: A 3-R approach* (Khader *et al.*, n.d.). Another very comprehensive list would be the *Core Competency and Proficiency Lists*, developed by Joint Committee on Police Psychology Competencies (Corey *et al.*, 2007).

- *The Psychological and Correctional Rehabilitation Department* (PCRD) at the Singapore Prisons Service. Prisons psychologists, working closely with counsellors and case managers, undertake services such as the rehabilitation of prison inmates, the assessment and treatment of inmates, mental resilience work, program evaluation and research, and consultation to operational leaders. Those interested in correctional psychology in Singapore should read *Current Evidence-Based Practices in the Singapore Prison Service* (Leo, n.d.).
- *Psychologists and researchers at the Home Team Behavioural Sciences Centre* (HTBSC) undertake research, training, and consultations related to crisis leadership, offender profiling, terrorism and extremism psychology, criminal psychology, and the psychology of resilience. They undertake these projects to support the training efforts of the Home Team Academy and the policymaking of the Ministry of Home Affairs. The HTBSC organizes the Asian Conference of Criminal and Operations Psychologists every three years in Singapore.
- *Psychologists who work at the immigrations department (ICA Psychological Services Branch)* undertake work such as stress management, peer-support programs, training, studies on deception at the checkpoints, management consultancy, crisis response, operations consultancy, personnel selection, and leadership training.
- Psychologists who work at Central Narcotics Bureau (CNB) Psychological Unit undertake work such as detection of deception training, crisis response, investigations support, and research into the psychology of drug addiction. They also advise on preventive drug education.
- Psychologists at the Singapore Civil Defence Force (SCDF), (*Emergency Behaviour Sciences, and CARE*), undertake work such as stress management, counselling, recruit training, crisis response,

operations consultancy, resilience building, personnel selection, leadership, and deployment support.

- *Psychologists and counsellors with the Singapore Courts.* Counsellors, social workers, and psychologists at the *Counselling and Psychological Services Sections* (CAPS) support the courts in services such as divorce and custody conciliation, brief crisis support counselling, custody evaluation, family violence assessment and counselling, co-mediation with judges, mental health-related training, and crisis intervention.
- *Forensic psychologists at the Ministry of Social and Family Development* (MSF). At the MSF, psychologists are based at the *Clinical and Forensic Psychology Service* (CFPS) division, which oversees several sub-centres of expertise, such as the a) Centre for Trauma and Recovery (CTR), which specializes in the assessment and treatment of children, young persons, and families who have experienced abuse and trauma; b) the Centre for Forensic Mental Health (CFMH), which specializes in the assessment and treatment of high-risk young persons and adults with criminogenic needs; c) the Centre for Research on Rehabilitation and Protection (CRRP); and d) the Centre for Evaluation (CEV). CPFS also conducts local high-impact research and evaluation studies.
- Forensic psychologists at the hospitals, the private sector, and the military. There are a smaller number of psychologists who do forensic psychology work at the hospitals, mainly undertaking services such as the assessment of mental state, risk assessments, and 'fitness to stand trial' assessments. Several forensic psychologists work in the private sector with psychiatrists and lawyers. In many parts of the world, forensic and 'operations' psychologists work in military settings, looking at security assessments and investigations.

There seems to be four main strands of forensic psychology across the world, both in practice and in academia. The two main ones are *'forensic-law enforcement psychology'* (FLEP) and *'forensic-clinical psychology'* (FCP). The next two are in the areas of *'forensic psychology in academia'* and *'forensic-legal psychology'*.

In Singapore, FLEP-oriented psychologists tend to work in the police, immigrations, security departments, and the Home Team Behavioural Sciences Centre. The nature of their work is mainly dealing with police and law enforcement issues, such as crime prevention, criminal profiling, negotiations, crisis response, leadership assessment, personnel selection, psychological inventions for intelligence operations, detection of deception, and victim support. The focus tends towards criminology, investigation support, prevention and enforcement, with some work in specialized personnel assessment and well-being support for law enforcement.

Psychologists in the FCP field work with the psychology department at the prisons service, the narcotics department, the Ministry of Social and Family Development, Courts psychology branch (CAPS), and the Institute of Mental Health (IMH). The nature of work tends to be clinically-oriented, and covers risk assessment, rehabilitation, child abuse, domestic violence, family conferences, and interventions for juvenile offenders, and therapy and treatment of offenders. There is a focus on forensic mental health, and psychologists work closely with social workers, psychiatrists, and the courts. Those interested in pursuing this field should read Dr. Kenji Gwee's paper, *Psychology and psychiatry in Singapore courts: A baseline survey of the mental health landscape in the legal area* (Gwee, 2017). It provides a good outline of the roles that psychologists have played in the Singapore forensic-clinical arena from 1975 to 2014.

The third branch of forensic psychology is *'academic teaching and research'*. This area has not yet been fully developed in Singapore, but there are some modules taught at the undergraduate level at James Cook University (JCU) and the National University of Singapore (NUS). There are also relevant specialized areas being taught, such as criminal and forensic psychology, correctional pscyhology, neuro-criminology, cyber-security, and extremism/terrorism at the Nanyang Technological University (NTU).

The fourth area, *'forensic–legal*[1] *and courtroom psychology'*, is in a state of infancy in Singapore. This refers to the application of psychology to legal questions such as the accuracy of eyewitness accounts, the effects of punishment, investigative interviewing, mediation between

---

[1] See (House of Legal Psychology), http://legalpsychology.eu/index.html, (UC Irvine, Masters of Legal and Forensic Psychology) https://mlfp.soceco.uci.edu/, and Maastrich University Master of Legal Psychology (https://www.maastrichtuniversity.nl/education/master/master-psychology-specialisation-legal-psychology).

conflicting parties, and victims/children as witnesses in court. There is a good degree of work done in the civil law area (e.g., child custody and workplace harassment). This area is expected to grow in the years to come, as the legal profession has been very progressive in adopting a multidisciplinary approach to their work, and has invited several psychologists and psychiatrists to discuss cross-disciplinary issues.

1.2.1.2 *Related disciplines*

Forensic Psychiatry

Forensic psychiatry warrants mention because it has a much longer history, compared to forensic psychology in Singapore. Forensic psychiatry deals with issues arising in the interface between psychiatry and the law. It is concerned with mental illness and criminality; legal tests to define legal insanity; methodologies for the treatment of mental conditions, and perceptions of mental illness among the public (Arboleda-Flores, 2006). In a paper describing the state of forensic psychiatry in Singapore, Chan and Tomita (2013) mentioned that there were 149 registered specialists in psychiatry (in general), which gives a ratio of three psychiatrists per 100,000; with a little under half in the private sector, and the remaining spread out over the Institute of Mental Health (IMH) and the psychiatric departments of six general hospitals. The IMH is the nation's largest hospital and the only tertiary institution for psychiatric care. It has an inpatient capacity consisting of 2,210 beds and has developed clinical departments in early psychosis, addiction medicine, child and adolescent psychiatry, geriatric psychiatry, community psychiatry, and forensic psychiatry. Some excellent reads, although slighted dated now, about forensic psychiatry in Singapore would be *Mental Disorders and the Law* (Kok, Cheang and Chee, 1994) and *Diminished Responsibility: with Special Reference to Singapore* (Kok, Cheang & Chee, 1990).

Forensic Sciences at the Health Sciences Authority (HSA)

This area of work started a long time ago in 1885 when Government Analysts performed analysis of food, medical products, and toxicological specimens. This was extended to include work for the Customs and Police Departments. Over the years, the work became specialized. Presently, the Forensic Medicine Branch includes forensic pathologists, and the department assists the State Coroner by conducting autopsies. Autopsy findings are used as evidence in Coroners' enquiries. The Forensic Biology Section looks at DNA profiling and manages the DNA database. The Forensic Chemistry and Physics Laboratory examines a wide range of crime scene evidence to establish links between a suspect and the crime. It may also look at firearms evidence and trace evidence. The Illicit Drugs Division is concerned with the detection of controlled drugs in Singapore. Finally, the Analytical Toxicology sections looks at drug abuse testing and analyses of drug and poison use (Health Sciences Authority, n.d.).

1.2.1.3 *Principles (Mantras) of effective professional practice*

If you are considering a career as a forensic-criminal psychologist, there are few principles/mantras that I have gathered in the course of my work, which I hope to share here:

- *In the applied world of practice, timeliness of response is more important than perfection of recommendations.* Being timely in your solutions means that policymakers and police officers will be able to use your psychological advice in a timely way. In academia, we take time to deliberate, but in professional practice (or what some would call the 'real world'), we cannot wait too long to solve global problems such as terrorism, crises/disasters, disease, poverty, and crime. Generally, a reasonably informed, 'less than perfect' response that helps understand or solve the problem, even if only partly, is better than a non-response. The only caution here is that you should not do harm in your zest to push something out quickly.
- *'Absence of evidence' is not 'evidence of absence'.* Sometimes, when you undertake research on a new or hard problem — it looks like there is no clear definitive answer. However, you should note that 'absence of evidence' is not the same as 'evidence of absence'. Just because experts have not found a solution *yet*, it does not mean it

cannot be found in the future. The nature of research is that it takes time; you might find that, one day, a solution might be discovered. Research is a marathon and not a sprint. Thirty years ago, academics and researchers did not know how to manage cancer or HIV, but they know more about these conditions today. Imagine if they had given up, saying that nothing works! Do not have let your doubts stop you; strive as a researcher or practitioner to find useful solutions to real world problems.

- *Qualitative research approaches/methods are as good as quantitative ones.* In the field of psychology, it may appear that we are biased. We seem to love quantitative approaches in psychology. Qualitative, single-case studies, however, are just as useful as meta-analyses in understanding real-world phenomena. Students of psychology are often biased against qualitative methods. With qualitative methods, we get a deep understanding of the issue. What is the point of having numbers that we do not really understand? A better way to treat research evidence is with the 'ladder of evidence'. At the lower level of the ladder are case studies, anecdotes, qualitative studies; and at the upper rungs, we have quantitative studies, quasi-experiments, and randomized double-blind trials; and, finally, we have meta-analytic findings at the top rung. Each is important in revealing aspects of the phenomena or issue we are studying. Qualitative approaches give us depth and richness of understanding, while quantitative ones give us comparisons of differences, trends, and the impact of aggregated findings. Deep understanding (qualitative) and measurement (quantitative) are *both* important for science.

- *Quantitative data must be qualitatively interpreted.* We often do not think about this, but quantitative data must be qualitatively interpreted in applied settings. What does it mean when you are rated a '7' for morale (on a 10-point scale and with '1' the lowest point and '10' being the highest point)? Is it good? What if everyone else scored '8'? Then '7' is lower than average and not good. Then again, what does '7' mean in real terms? Does it mean you are good in terms of teamwork or job satisfaction? Numbers do not speak for themselves and instead have to be translated. Therefore, using both qualitative and quantitative research (the 'mixed method') is a good way of doing quality research. Understanding and measurements are both valued concepts in science.

- *'Form'* is as critical as *'substance'* in the applied world. Leaders, politicians, and CEOs (as opposed to first-year undergraduate research participants) may not be interested in your psychological findings, may not cooperate with you, and may resist your exciting ideas. Marketing your psychological findings effectively is important. You will need to learn to persuade if you want apply psychology in the real world. Can you summarize your main idea and talk about it to a curious CEO in two minutes? Senior people have no time for long stories. Also, the same CEO or perhaps a Senior Civil Servant officer will tell you that everything, including counselling and rehabilitation programs, costs money! Thus, you have to demonstrate that it is worth their while to invest in psychological programs and the employment of psychologists. Learn how to market and advocate for that exciting and meaningful idea.

- *There is no perfect data — all forms of data have their limits.* One of my favourite personality psychology experts, Professor David Funder, explained that there are only two types of data — 'bad data' and 'no data'. Perfect data does not exist; do not fool yourself thinking that your approach is the best, no matter what your professor/trainer/supervisor tells you. Every data-gathering approach has its problems. Interviews may be subjective, experiments can lack ecological (real world) validity, meta-analyses over-simplify, and case studies are often just single-case phenomenon. Funder argues that not doing anything at all because of bad data means 'no data' and therefore, no progress. That is worse! Thus, we make do with 'bad data', but appreciate their limitations. This is why, as a general rule, data triangulation and multiple perspectives are valuable in providing a better and accurate picture of things, instead of just one data source. This is true whether in counselling our clients, in assessing leaders, or in forensic interviews of offenders.

- *Psychology does not have monopoly over the understanding of crime; we need multidisciplinary approaches.* The French have a term called *déformation professionnelle,* which is a tendency to look at things from the point of view of one's own profession rather than from a broader perspective. The implication is that deep professional training may result in a distortion of the way one views the world. Hence, there is a danger that the student of criminal psychology may think that all the answers to crime lie within psychology. Well, they do not. The practice of forensic psychology is also informed comprehensively by many disciplines such as the Law, Forensic Sciences, Police Sciences, Sociology, Criminology, and Communication Sciences. While students are expected to be trained in the field of psychology, they ought to read widely and be open to other fields of sciences. Collaboration with other partners and experts is one way of achieving this multidisciplinary analysis. In the chapters to come, you will see that instead of relying on psychology alone, I have adopted a multidisciplinary perspective to offender profiling, which is called the CLIP approach — *C*riminalistics, *L*egal and *L*ocal perspectives, *I*nvestigative perspectives, and *P*sychology.

How can students and readers use these principles and mantras? Some examples of the application of these ideas will be shown in various parts of the chapters in this book. In profiling crimes, for example, while a psychological approach has traditionally been used, the recommended approach by this book is a multidisciplinary one that goes beyond psychology. Also, in interviewing offenders, multiple data sources (e.g., interviews, case file review, talking to significant others, etc.) could help us to better appreciate the offender's needs. These are just some examples of how these mantras can be applied. More will be discussed in the chapters ahead.

1.3 The Criminal Justice System

1.3.1 *Stages in the Criminal Justice Process*

How is crime processed in the system? Well, there are stages. First, a crime occurs when someone commits a criminal act and these crimes are reported. This is the first stage of how crime is processed in the criminal justice system. However, victims of crime do not always report their crimes. Sometimes, victims do not come forward because they perceive that the crime is too trivial, or that the police cannot do anything, or are uninterested. Sometimes, there is fear of reprisal from the offender. Other times, it is too inconvenient to make a police report.[2]

Second, the police or other authorities record these crimes in the next stage. In some developing countries, the police do not record it, so that they can (unethically) save themselves some work. In Singapore, most means of recording crimes these days are computerized and the record remains permanent.

The third stage of processing involves investigation and prosecution after the crime. The prosecution must establish the charge meted out and the presence of two elements at the time of the crime — namely, *actus reus* ('guilty act') and *mens rea* ('guilty mind'). According to Professor Walter Woon, there are four sub-steps involved here. The first sub-step is to find out what happened. This is done by investigatory agencies, e.g., the police. The second sub-step is to ascertain if an offence has been committed and, if so, what offence. Professor Woon explains that this is a legal question. Laypersons are seldom qualified to appreciate the intricacies of Singapore criminal law. In the third sub-step, prosecutors need to ask if the elements of the offence can be proven in court. The prosecution must prove the case against the accused beyond reasonable doubt. It is not for the accused to prove his innocence. The deputy public prosecutor (DPP) has to:

> "...decide whether there is enough evidence that will stand up in court. It is often possible to piece together what happened with a fair degree of certainty. However, there are cases where witnesses will refuse to testify in open court. In other cases, a witness may

---

[2] The system in Singapore where citizens can make electronic police reports probably enhances the chances have someone making a report. They can use https://www. police.gov.sg/e-services/report/police-report.

implicate others when questioned, but when it comes to actually testifying, he will have an attack of selective amnesia. If the DPP thinks that the witnesses cannot be relied on, the prosecution will probably be dropped. If he decides to carry on, there is a chance that the judge may not be convinced beyond reasonable doubt. In that case, the defendant is acquitted. Again, contrary to popular misconception, a verdict of "not guilty" is not synonymous with "innocent". In some cases, it just means that there is a reasonable doubt. Thus, for instance, in a rape case the man may contend that the "victim" consented. The woman may be equally vehement in denying that she did consent. If the judge cannot be sure, then the accused is found "not guilty", even though it may, in fact, have been rape."

Professor Woon says that the last sub-step is asking if there should be a prosecution at all (Woon, 2017).

The fourth stage in this entire process involves the courts and the trial, if the case goes to trial. However, not all cases will go to the trial/court stage, since the person may plead 'guilty'; and when the defendant pleads guilty, there is no trial needed. The defendant will, on occasion, engage his/her own defence lawyer while the State will have its own DPPs to prosecute the case. It should be highlighted here that not all crimes end up in trial in the court of law (unlike what you might see on television).

Finally, if the person were found to be guilty, he or she would be sentenced. You should also note that there is a degree of judgment and discretion regarding which cases should proceed along the stages. This is why not all cases that are reported can be followed up on with an investigation or a prosecution. There is a need to establish which law has been broken and whether there is evidence to proceed. Table 1.1 summarizes the various roles of agents within the criminal justice system. However, as this book is about the application of psychology with the system, the table also illustrates the roles that psychologists play within the system.

Table 1.1: Actors and Roles of Psychologists in the Criminal Justice System

Agency	Personnel	Functions	Role of psychologists
Police; Immigration; Narcotics	Police; Immigration; Narcotics officers	Prevent crime (neighborhood police officer); Arrest and detain suspects, investigate	Police Psychologist Narcotics psychologists (e.g., crime prevention education, behavior analysis/profiling, risk assessment work, program evaluation, etc.)
The Prosecution; The Defence	Government Prosecutors (DPP) and Defence lawyer	Filter out weak cases, keep strong cases, and prepare case for prosecution; Defend the defendant	Legal and court psychology, Forensic-Clinical Psychologists, Forensic Mental Health psychologists (e.g., helping in family conferences for family violence cases, youth offending, reports on risk assessment, IQ, etc.)
Judiciary (Adjudication)	Magistrates; Judges; High Court Judges	Decide on guilt and sentencing	Judiciary (e.g., expert witness reports)
Prisons	Prisons officers	Secure custody; Rehabilitation; Risk Assessment	Prisons psychologists; counsellors (e.g., pre-sentencing reports, risk assessments, etc.)

1.3.1.1 *The 'dark figure' and measuring crime*

Much of what is reported is recorded, and then processed and factored into the official crime rate. Official crime statistics, however useful, are not perfect indicators of the crime level. (Remember the mantra on 'bad data'?) For various reasons, people do not report their victimization. This is known as the 'dark figure'.[3] This is not the fault of law enforcement. People do not report for a variety of reasons. So, in trying to understand the 'dark figure', crime researchers use *offender* and *victim surveys*.

In a typical *offender survey*, a common method is to select a sample from a location and ask respondents (promising anonymity), if they have committed any crimes, but were not caught. For instance, Groth *et al.* (1982) studied hundreds of offenders and discovered that offenders admitted to an average of five or more undetected sexual offences than were known! The main limitation of offender surveys is that they may not tell you everything, or they may make things up and you do not really have a way of checking the accuracy of what they are saying.

Another way of figuring out the dark figure is by using *victim surveys*. The British use the British crime survey, which is developed from the electoral register, and it provides a representative cross-section sample of the population. These surveys are useful to measure concepts such as 'the fear of crime' and 'psychological reactions to crime'. You can appreciate why this is important — sometimes, the fear is worse than the actual incident (which may not have injury)! For example, Resick and Markaway (2013) reported that women who were sexually attacked often report feelings of confusion, fear, and worry, immediately after the attack. They also experienced physical reactions, such as shaking and trembling. These reactions remained high after the first week, and peaked in the third week. Victim surveys, while useful, have their limitations as well. For example, they do not take into account victimless crimes, such as violations of safety and shoplifting. Secondly, when you ask people to recall the event, there is the danger those victims may include irrelevant details and sometimes even make details up.

As a section summary, we conclude that statistics related to crime cannot be perfect measures. There are dark sides to every possible approach. Furthermore, critics have raised the problem of 'abstracted

---

[3] The gap between crime that is reported to the police and crime that is recorded by them is known as the 'grey side' of crime (Joyce, 2012). There are several reasons for this: 1) the police may decide it does not constitute a criminal act; 2) police may feel that it can be responded to with a warning rather than a formal charge, hence it is not recorded; 3) the responding officer may (unprofessionally) decide that recording it may result in paperwork (known as 'cuffing' in the U.K.).

empiricism'. This is the idea that people are biased towards research questions that are amenable to data analysis, fancy statistics, and quantitative methodologies as 'good science', because they are publishable. However, as Young (2011) says, "numbers are signs to be interpreted within specific cultural contexts, figures in themselves do not have any magical objectivity" (2011: 55). This leads to another problem — phenomena, which are not understood or quantified easily, are ignored and dismissed as unimportant (Coomber *et al.*, 2015).

1.4 Organisations within the Criminal Justice System and Related Agencies

Now that we understand the stages of the criminal justice system, let us find out which law enforcement agencies are involved. The main ones are as follows:

Singapore Police Force (SPF)

The Singapore Police Force is the main police agency tasked with maintaining law and order in Singapore.[4] Under the Police Force Act 2004, it is explicitly stated that: "the Police Force shall have the following functions throughout Singapore: (a) to maintain law and order; (b) to preserve public peace; (c) to prevent and detect crimes; (d) to apprehend offenders; and (e) to exercise any other function conferred on it by or under this Act or any other written law". The Singapore Police Force has a heritage almost as old as that of Singapore. There are several major police stations and several specialist departments including Criminal Investigation Department, the Police Coast Guard, the Airport Police Division, and the Special Operations Command.

Central Narcotics Bureau (CNB)

The Central Narcotics Bureau is the main drug enforcement agency in Singapore. Its main aim is to tackle the drug menace and to educate

---

[4] See http://www.police.gov.sg for more information.

the public on the dangers of drug abuse. Drug trafficking is a serious criminal offence which is enforced under the Misuse of Drugs Act. While our drug laws may seem very harsh to observers, it has kept Singaporean streets free from major drug addiction and trafficking.[5]

Singapore Prison Service (SPS)

The Singapore Prisons Service runs prisons and drug rehabilitation centers. The roles and duties of prison officers are spelled out in the Prisons Act[6] (Singapore Statues Online, 2000). Its main roles are the custody, rehabilitation, and aftercare of offenders.[7] SPS has uniformed officers as well as a number of civilian staff, including psychologists, counsellors, and case managers who assist with operations and the rehabilitation of offenders. The SPS has played a major role in reducing overall crime in Singapore. For example, the overall recidivism has been low, with an average of around 22% to 23% in recent years.

A related initiative is the *CARE Network*, which brings together key community and government agencies to promote in-care to aftercare support for ex-offenders. The Network consists of several major community and government organisations responsible for the rehabilitation of ex-offenders.

The Yellow Ribbon Project engages the community in accepting ex-offenders and their families and giving them a second chance at life. SPS works closely with the Singapore Cooperation of Rehabilitative Enterprises or SCORE to ensure the gainful employment and effective reintegration of ex-offenders. The Yellow Ribbon Project was inspired by the popular song, *Tie a Yellow Ribbon Round the Old Oak Tree*, which is based on the real-life tale of an ex-offender's journey to forgiveness. He had written a message to his wife, asking her to show that she had forgiven him by tying a yellow ribbon around the only oak tree in their city square. To his relief, more than a hundred yellow ribbons greeted him on his return.

---

[5] CNB has an excellent preventive drug education portal which is worth looking up at http://www.cnb.gov.sg.

[6] Original Enactment was called the Ordinance 17 of 1933.

[7] See http://www.sps.gov.sg for more details.

Immigrations and Checkpoint Authority

The Immigrations and Checkpoint Authority (ICA) is in charge of immigration, Singapore passports, identity cards, citizen registration (birth and death), permanent residents' services, customs, and issuing permits to foreigners. The ICA oversees the safeguarding of Singapore's borders. It ensures that the movement of people, goods, and conveyances through its checkpoints is legitimate and lawful. ICA reported that there were 1,176 immigration offenders arrested and 90,327 cases of contraband smuggling in 2017. There was also 53 cases of people convicted of entering 'marriages of convenience' in 2017 (Tan, 2018).

Internal Security Department

The Internal Security Department (ISD) addresses security threats such as terrorism and espionage. The ISD monitors and addresses threats from racial tension, domestic counter-terrorism, and international counter-terrorism. Much of what the ISD does is determined by the parameters of the Internal Security Act (ISA), which states that it is "an Act to provide for the internal security of Singapore, preventive detention, the prevention of subversion, (and) the suppression of organized violence against persons and property in specified areas of Singapore..." (Internal Security Act, Chapter 143, Revised Edition, 1985). There will be a greater discussion of ISD's role in preventing and managing terrorism in Chapter 7.

Casino Regulatory Authority

The Casino Regulatory Authority of Singapore (CRA) ensures the smooth regulation, management, and operation of casinos in Singapore. It is concerned with criminal influence on the casinos. It ensures that gaming in a casino is conducted honestly, and that casinos do not cause harm to vulnerable persons and society. The CRA is tasked to take enforcement action against casino operators for breaches of operating conditions (CRA Annual Report, 2015–2016).

Home Team Academy

It is not a natural thing for the police, prisons, fire service, or immigration department in any country to work seamlessly with one another, since they all have their own strong histories, traditions, and cultures. The Home Team Academy (HTA) was thus designed to create a common training ground for various agencies to train together. The HTA conducts training from basic to advanced levels for the uniformed officers and civilians from the police, prisons, immigrations, narcotics, CRA, SCDF, and other relevant agencies. Various subjects are taught, such as Joint Operations, Crisis Leadership, Community Issues, and Terrorism. Its aim is to train officers to operate as one Home Team within the Ministry of Home Affairs. The HTA works closely with many academic institutions, such as the LKY School of Public Policy and INSEAD, to deliver premier leadership courses. The vision of the HTA is to be the Corporate University of the Home Team.

Attorney General Chambers

The Attorney General Chambers is a major entity within the criminal justice system. It has several roles. First, it acts as the main advisor to the government and to the ministries on matters relating to the law. The second role is that of the Public Prosecutor. Under Article 35(8) of the Constitution, the Attorney General has powers to institute, conduct, or discontinue any proceedings for any offence. The third role is that it advises government, ministries, and statutory boards on matters relating to international law. The fourth role is that it is the main law drafting body in Singapore, especially as legislations that are to be introduced in Parliament (Attorney General's Chamber, n.d.).

Interpol Global Complex for Innovation

The Interpol Global Complex for Innovation (IGCI) is an Interpol agency based in Asia (located in Singapore), which looks into cutting-edge research and development for the identification of crime and criminals. It complements the main Interpol headquarters, which is based in Lyons, France. The police, immigration, and security agencies work very closely with the IGCI.

Corrupt Practices Investigation Bureau

The Transparency International Corruption Perceptions Index 2016 ranked Singapore as the seventh least corrupt country in the world! Singapore has maintained its first place in the 2016 Political and Economic Risk Consultancy (PERC) annual survey on corruption. Much of this is due to the work of the Corrupt Practices Investigation Bureau (CPIB), which investigates and prosecutes corruption in the public and private sectors (CPIB Annual Report, 2016). CPIB does preventive work, including conducting outreach programs for younger Singaporeans and school students, as well as participating in international engagements.

Singapore Civil Defence Force

The Singapore Civil Defence Force (SCDF) is the main organization in charge of the provision of emergency services during peacetime and emergency. Although not a formal part of the criminal justice system, it has a part to play in dealing with crises and emergencies in Singapore by providing fire-fighting, rescue, and emergency medical services. Working closely with the police and other enforcement agencies, it implements and enforces regulations on fire safety and civil defence matters.

1.4.1 How are Arrests and Investigations Conducted?

Now that this chapter has discussed the main agencies in the criminal justice system, you might be wondering about the processes involved when someone is arrested and investigated (in Singapore).[8] Here are some (Tok and Turnbull, 2015):

a) *When can you be arrested?* An arrest can be made when a police officer or law enforcer reasonably suspects someone of committing a serious offence such as causing serious hurt, rape, outraging of modesty, drug consumption, or drug trafficking.

---

[8] These points are merely for academic discussion. Please seek the advice of the police or your lawyer if you need actual advice on a crime case.

b) *How is an arrest made?* An arrest is done by informing the alleged offender that they are arrested, and by touching or holding them to prevent their escape. The police will usually provide the reasons for an arrest. You may be handcuffed.

c) *Do you have the right to remain silent?* You may remain silent. However, a negative inference may be drawn against you if you remain silent and do not state your defence, if any, at the earliest possible time.[9]

d) *Can you tell your family or your lawyer?* One can request to make a call to their family or a lawyer telling them of their arrest. However, these requests may be refused, if the police deem that these will interfere with the investigation.

e) *When can you be charged in court?* This is usually after investigations have been carried out.

f) *Who can investigate you?* In Singapore, investigations are usually done by the police, narcotics, immigrations, and agencies that possess investigative powers (e.g., Commercial Affairs Department, Customs officers, etc.) The Investigating Officers (IO) are authorized to order a person to go to a police station for questioning and to make a statement. Usually, they record what is said and require that witnesses sign their statement. Sometimes they may use their powers to search a place and take away things to be used as evidence.

g) *Can you be detained during investigation?* You can be detained for a maximum period of 48 hours from the time of arrest. If the officers want to keep you beyond the 48 hours, they will have to bring you to court. In court, the officer will need to convince the judge on why he needs to detain you further. You may inform the court about any mistreatments or any issue which you disagree with the officer on. If the officer does not further detain you, he

---

[9] In America the officer might say the 'Miranda Warning', which reads 'You have a right to remain silent…and anything you say will be used against you in the court of law…You have the right to consult an attorney before speaking to the police' and if you cannot afford an attorney, one will be appointed for you before any questioning if you wish', and so on. These warnings are quite a complex legal issue and even vary within the states of the U.S. and have variations across countries. Every country has adopted its own provisions, which has suited its own needs.

may release you on 'personal promise' or bail. The police bail is done to ensure you go back to the station on court when you are required to do so. In some cases, bail may not be offered (Tok & Turnbull, 2015).[10] One very useful reference document if you are interested in understanding police procedures is the *Information Booklet on Police Procedures*[11] (updated in 2016) published by the Singapore Police Force.

1.5 How the Judiciary Works

1.5.1 *The Singapore Judicial System*

The function of the judiciary[12] is to administer justice. The Honourable Chief Justice is the Head of the Judiciary. The Judiciary comprises the Supreme Court and the State Courts (previously known as the Subordinate Courts). Judiciary power is vested under the Supreme Court and in the State Courts. The Supreme Court consists of the High Court and the Court of Appeal, and it hears both *criminal* and *civil* cases.

Criminal law deals with acts of purposeful and intentional harm done to individuals, but it has a collective societal angle. For example, if someone molests a young girl, it is harm done directly to this girl, but it also affects the sense of safety that other young girls and their parents may experience; it affects the public sense of safety. Since there is a public safety angle, the State acts to prosecute the offender and protects the victim. In criminal cases, 'PP v. Tan Jet' is read as 'The Public Prosecutor' versus 'Tan Jet' (the accused person). The state is acting for the victim here.[13]

Civil law deals with disputes or acts of harm between private persons. For example, disagreement over a renovation contract, whether an employee was wrongfully sacked from their workplace, or

---

[10] There are 'bailable' and 'non-bailable' offences.

[11] https://www.police.gov.sg.

[12] see http://www.supremecourt.gov.sg for more information.

[13] There is also the Criminal Legal Aid Scheme (CLAS) administered by the Law Society of Singapore (see www.lawsociety.org.sg) for persons facing non-capital charges who are unable to pay for legal counsel.

which of the two parents have custody over their children in divorce cases. Civil cases contain the names of both parties involved. For example, 'Barnabee and Hesham'; there is no 'versus'.

Sometimes, a case may have both civil and criminal angles. Drink driving is a criminal offence, but the claims made to the car damage may be civil in nature.

The 'standards of proof' are higher in criminal than in civil cases. To convict someone of a crime, the prosecution must show that there is proof 'beyond a reasonable doubt' that the person *committed* and *intended* the crime. This gives the accused the benefit of any reasonable doubt and makes it less likely that an innocent person will be wrongfully convicted. Civil cases in comparison must be proven on a 'balance of probabilities' if it is more likely than not that the defendant caused harm (Canadian Superior Courts Judges Associations, 2006).

In Singapore, the High Court hears cases in the first instance as well as cases on appeal cases from the State Courts. The courts would see civil cases where the claim exceeds S$250,000; probate matters if the estate exceeds S$3,000,000; among other types of cases. In criminal cases, the High Court can see all cases but, generally speaking, tries cases where the offences are punishable by death or with imprisonment terms exceed 10 years. The High Court can hear points of law in special cases submitted by a District Court or Magistrate Court. The High Court can reverse decisions from the State Courts, or ask the State Courts to conduct a new trial on the matter, and sees cases on appeal from the State Courts (Supreme Court of Singapore, n.d.).

The Court of Appeal hears appeals on civil and criminal cases from the High Court. The Court of Appeal is presided over by the Chief Justice and is usually made up of three judges.

The State Courts of Singapore comprise the District Courts and Magistrate Court and both can handle criminal and civil matters.

The Coroner's Courts holds inquiries to determine if the crime involved unnatural death.

The Community Court sees some cases involving youthful offenders (aged 16 to 18 years old), offenders with mental disabilities, neighbourhood disputes, and family violence cases, among others.

The Family Justice Courts (FJC) is a body of courts which comprise the Family Division of the High Court, the Family Courts, and the Youth Courts. These Courts will hear cases related to divorce, family violence cases, adoption and guardianship cases, Youth Court cases, applications for deputyship under the Mental Capacity Act, and probate and succession matters. The FJC deals with Administration of Muslim Law Act (Cap. 3); Adoption of Children Act (Cap. 4); Children and Young Persons Act (Cap. 38); Family Justice Act 2014 (Act 27 of 2014); Inheritance (Family Provision) Act (Cap. 138); Maintenance of Parents Act (Cap. 167B); Mental Capacity Act (Cap. 177A); Mental Health (Care and Treatment) Act (Cap. 178A); Wills Act (Cap.352); Women's Charter (Cap. 353); among other important legislation (Family Justice Courts, Singapore, n.d.).

1.5.2 *Laws and the 'The Rule of Law'*

Early humans made laws to regulate behaviours between groups of people. So, if someone breached the law, they would be expelled from the group. Anyone who caused harm to the group was considered an offender (Adshead, 2016). The law and its codes had to be respected in communities. The rule of law is a legal principle that requires everyone, including the government, to obey the law. While the principle is universal, each nation has provisions that take into account special considerations related to its historical and cultural development. As Mr. Lee Kuan Yew aptly puts it:

> "The acid test of any legal system is not the greatness or the grandeur of its ideal concepts, but whether in fact it is able to produce order and justice in the relationships between man and man and between man and the State ..."

Lee Kuan Yew
Founding Prime Minister
Speech At the University of Singapore Law
Society Annual Dinner, 18 January 1962

Prime Minister Lee Hsien Loong also spoke about the importance of the Rule of Law in a speech which defined the issues clearly and is worth quoting:

> "What does the rule of law mean? It means everyone must obey the law, and everyone will be treated equally under the law, whether he is an individual or the Government. Individuals can get redress for their grievances, be it against their peers, persons in high positions, or the Government. It means people trust the courts to hear their cases impartially, and render judgments in accordance with the law and the facts. Justice is accessible to all and wrongdoing is punished firmly and fairly, with mercy and compassion shown to deserving cases. It means a transparent and rational business environment where commerce is governed by transparent, predictable rules and contracts can be enforced and investments protected. It means upholding individual rights and freedoms while carefully balancing them against society's need to maintain law and order, fostering harmony and social cohesion among people of diverse races and religions who call Singapore home. Because we emphasised all these aspects of the rule of law, Singapore distinguished itself from other developing countries, and made it from Third World to First. Internationally, the rule of law among nations is also a vital national interest of a small state like Singapore. We say what we mean, and we mean what we say. We honour agreements we enter into and we expect others to honour agreements they enter into with us. Sometimes we are faulted for being rigid and inflexible — too straight. But it is absolutely critical for our words to count and for us to hold others to what they have undertaken to us. Having a reputation for insisting on these key points is perhaps not a bad thing. The AGC, together with the judiciary, is critical to upholding the rule of law." (Lee, 2017).

The relationship between law and order

We often talk about law and order going together. Which comes first? Our first Prime Minister Lee Kuan Yew remarked, at the opening of the University of Singapore Law Society in 18 January 1962, that "without order, the operation of law is impossible" (Koh, 2016). He explained that "while in established society, law appears to be the precursor of order, in emerging ones wracked by violence and subversion, the reverse was often the case". He explained that "if you allow these shibboleths of law and order to be uttered out of context without reference to the social conditions of disorder, then it spells trouble since in the last analysis, if the state disintegrates, then the rules of all laws must vanish" (Koh, 2016). This point being made is crucial, since the Singapore government pays a lot of attention to the prevention and management of disorder, since it is the foundation upon which laws are based.

1.5.3 *Who Makes the Law?*

Many think that it is the police who create the law. The police, in fact, *enforce* the law that is already made.

There are several 'sources of law' in Singapore and these are: 1) the Singapore Constitution, 2) Common law (sometimes called judge-made law and decisions of judges, as reported in cases), 3) Judicial Precedent (decision of a court), 4) Legislation, 5) English Statues, and 6) Customary Law and Custom (Tan, 1999).

Parliament may create the law based on recommendations by members of parliament, policymakers, and government. They may introduce new laws based on the feedback they receive. Hence, the public may indirectly influence the laws that play out in society. However, this does not mean that laws are created or reviewed based on public pressure. Instead, as the Minister of Law Mr. K. Shanmugam had put it[14]: "It is the task of the Government to decide what is the appropriate legislative provision. And that is the mixture of...what is fair, what is right and also where is the weight of public opinion" (Ng, 2017).

---

[14] http://www.channelnewsasia.com/news/singapore/shanmugam-responds-to-academic-s-comments-on-populism-in-8797788.

There are major areas of law, however, such as contract law, equity, property law, and tort law that are largely judge-made, since these are complex and require deep legal expertise. Judgements handed down by the courts are considered a source of law (Tan, 1999). Most criminal law is statutory and created by Parliament. The general principles of criminal law, as well as the elements and penalties of common criminal offences such as homicide, theft, and cheating, are set out in the Penal Code. The Penal Code does not exhaustively define all the criminal offences applicable in Singapore, and a number of offences are found in other statutes, such as the Arms Offences Act, the Kidnapping Act, the Internal Security Act, the Prevention of Corruption Act, and the Misuse of Drugs Act.

THINKING POINT
How young?

Can young children be criminally responsible if they commit crimes in Singapore?[15]

Those interested in finding out more about the laws in Singapore could read *Know the Law*,[16] which is a useful read and is available from the Singapore Law Society. Another excellent resource would be a book titled *You and The Law* and *Teens and the* Law, produced by the Singapore Association of Women Lawyers.[17] It is a basic introduction to the law in Singapore and an initial reference on where to seek legal help.

The information in Table 1.2, adapted from the Singapore Association of Women Lawyers, is an interesting compilation showing how the law affects us in many ways throughout our lives.

---

[15] Under the Penal Code, Sections 82 and 83: children can actually be held criminally responsible for offences committed from the age of seven. However, children aged older than seven but younger than 12 cannot be held criminally responsible unless they have "attained sufficient maturity of understanding to judge the nature and consequence of [their] conduct on that occasion." However, this particular law is being revised in 2019.

[16] See http://probono.lawsociety.org.sg/Pages/know-the-law-booklet.aspx.

[17] See http://www.sawl.org.sg/books.html.

Table 1.2:   How are You Affected by the Law?

Your age	How the law affects you
Birth	You exist legally and a birth certificate number is given to you.
13	You may work if it does not involve anything dangerous (e.g., part-time), see Employment Act.
Before and at 16	Having sex with a girl under 16 is a serious offence under the Penal Code. You can watch NC-16 movies. You can now be employed in potentially dangerous industrial settings. Before you turn 16, you will be sent to a juvenile court if you did something wrong.
18	A person below 18 is not allowed to buy cigarettes or drink alcohol (Control of Advertisements and Sales of Tobacco). It is an offence to have sex with a person under 18 for money under the Penal Code. You can get married but your parents must agree (Women's Charter). Those below 18 may get married under very special circumstances, with a special license approved by the Minister of Social and Family Development. You can enter into contract with others, buy, or sell shares (Civil Law Act). At 18, you can start a small business or become a director of your own company! Check the legal issues involved, as there are contracts that will be voided by law unless you are 21 (e.g., contracts to lease land for more than a period of three years etc.). You can start learning to drive a car or motorcycle. You can watch M-18 films.
21	Below 21; you are prohibited from entering the Casinos (Casino Control Act). You are now an adult holding full legal responsibilities and an offence may carry a jail term, and you are no longer treated as a young person who may get reformatory training. You can get married without your parents' consent. You can vote (Parliamentary Elections Act). You can make a will according to the Wills Act. You can watch R-21 Films. The age of majority in Singapore is 21 and therefore, in a strict sense, the legal obligation for parents to support their children will cease upon reaching 21.

Source: Adapted from *Teens and the Law* (Singapore Association of Women's Lawyers, 2014).

1.6 Crimes and Criminal Behaviour

Many criminology experts have divided crime into various categories. Table 1.3 shows there could be various subtypes of crime

Table 1.3:   Types of Crimes

Types of crime	Examples
Violent Crimes	Murder, Rape, Sexual Assault, Violent Assault
Property Crimes and sub-types	Housebreaking, Theft, Shoplifting, Robbery, Internet Extortion, Car Theft Robbery
Transnational Organized Crimes[18]	Triads, Loan Sharking, Drug Trafficking, Human Trafficking, Money Laundering, Firearms Trafficking, Illegal Gambling, Counterfeit Goods, Wildlife and Cultural Property Smuggling
Terrorism and Extremism	Religious Terrorism, Eco-Terrorism, Right Wing Terrorism
White Collar Crimes	Money Laundering, Corruption, Credit Card Fraud, Embezzlement, Insider Trading, Insurance Fraud, Charities Fraud, Tax Evasion
Cyber Crimes	Identity Theft, Child Pornography, Cyber stalking, Social Engineering, Hacking, Ransomware, Malware

1.6.1 *Crimes Trends in Singapore*

Crime rates in Singapore are generally low when compared to crime in other parts of the world. See Table 1.4 for statistics on the crime rates in Singapore. Although no one really knows the exact reason for these low crime rates, this is probably due to factors such as the respect for the rule of law, efficient policing, efficient government and judiciary, strong laws, a strong political system, a healthy thriving economy, and a population base that appreciates how crime and

---

[18] The FBI defines transnational organized crime groups are "self-perpetuating associations of individuals who operate, wholly or in part, by illegal means and irrespective of geography. They constantly seek to obtain power, influence, and monetary gains... These groups protect their activities through corruption, violence, international commerce, complex communication mechanisms, and an organizational structure exploiting national boundaries." (https://www.fbi.gov/investigate/organized-crime).

disorder are managed in Singapore. In fact, Minister for Law and Home Affairs, Mr. K. Shanmugam writes about the state of low crime and sense of safety in a paper titled *The Rule of Law*, published in the *Singapore Journal of Legal Studies*, saying that:

> "Children can take public transport on their own; women can travel alone almost anywhere, anytime. Our crime rates are much lower than other major cities in the world — for example, we had 16 homicides in 2011, or 0.3 cases per 100,000 population. This is all the more remarkable given that we have a smaller number of police officers per unit population (about 250 per 100,000 population) than many other cities. Living in an almost crime-free environment is something Singaporeans take for granted, when it is something enjoyed by few cities in the world. All this is a result of our approach to law and order".

Table 1.4: Major Offences in Singapore by Frequency

Type of offence	2011	2012	2013	2014	2015	2016	2017
Overall crime	31,508	31,015	29,984	32,196	33,608	32,964	32,773
Crimes against persons	3,969	3,824	3,822	4,237	4,130	4,374	4,527
Violent/Serious property	443	389	418	538	299	248	218
Housebreaking	706	598	543	350	333	285	328
Theft and related	18,314	18,476	17,075	16,784	15,645	14,127	13,495
Commercial	3,880	3,507	3,947	5,615	8329	8379	8566
Miscellaneous	4,196	4,221	4,179	4,672	4872	5551	5639

Source: https://www.police.gov.sg/news-and-publications/statistics.

THINKING POINT
Crime Statistics (See Table 1.4)

a. Of all types of crime, which crime type is the largest in terms of proportion and can you guess why?
b. Which crime type is slowly emerging as an issue of concern?
c. Which crime type is falling?

The *concern with commercial crimes and scams*

At the time of writing, traditional crime types appear to be stabilizing but commercial crimes appear to be rising. This should not be surprising, given the rising affluence of Singaporeans and Singapore over the years. As we will explain later from the criminal's perspective, if there is more, there is more to take from others. For example, cheating cases involving e-commerce and scams such as credit-for-sex and Internet love scams saw the largest increase.

- E-commerce saw an increase of 508 cases (+30.5%), from 1,665 cases in 2014 to 2,173 cases in 2015. The total sum cheated was approximately $1.76 million, and the largest amount swindled was approximately $50,000.
- Online scams targeting buyers increased by 437 cases (+30.1%), from 1,450 cases in 2014 to 1,887 cases in 2015. The total sum cheated was approximately $1.34 million.
- There was also an increase of 1,137 cases (+1,723%) in credit-for-sex scams, from 66 cases in 2014 to 1,203 cases in 2015. The total sum cheated was approximately $2.9 million, with the largest amount at approximately $74,000.
- Internet love scams were still on the rise, with an increase of 185 cases (+93.4%), from 198 cases in 2014 to 383 cases in 2015. The total sum cheated was approximately $12 million, with the largest amount at approximately $528,000 (Singapore Police Force, n.d.).

Shown below are some examples of scam victims who have reported their cases:

Case #4: *Case study of Credit for Sex Scam*[19]

"A girl added from WeChat, and we had a short chat. She said she was from Taiwan and came to Singapore to study. And she provides sexual services to people. And she sent me her photos and asked if I would like to have the service. I said yes, and she said before that, a friend of her will need to call me to make sure that I'm not a police. After a

---

[19] https://scamalert.sg/types-of-scams/credit-for-sex-scam/post/post/388-taiwanese-girl-offering-sex-conned-me-of-$1,200.

while, the person called me, asked me few questions and then asked me to go AXS machine to get the Alipay Purchase Card. At first, he asked me to buy the purchase card that worth S$200, and asked me to key in the email address that he provided to me earlier. And so I did without any doubt or suspicious feelings. But after that, he said need to get another purchase card which worth S$1,000, and I was so stupid at that time, I purchased the S$1,000, and also key in the same email address. After that he said the girl is on the way and he hung up the card. After five minutes, he called again and said need to pay another S$500 for deposit and at this moment which is already too late I guess? I feel suspicious and hung up the phone. Now I feel so dumb and stupid to get scam by those people, I'm blaming myself for being too stupid because of "sex". The purchase card receipts are with me, but I think it is impossible for me to refund back the money I guess? Sigh." [sic]

Case #5: Case of Internet love scam[20]

"This chap Sam GOH sent a friend request for friendship. Within 10 days, started declaring he wanted a relationship. Claimed he is from Australia, divorced nine years ago and has two grown up kids in USA. Sent me a pic of his meal with the brand [of well-known coffee shop in Singapore] which is not available in Sydney. First lie. Chatted on WhatsApp +61XXXXXX and +XXXXXX. After 10 days chatting he declared he wanted a relationship. ...Then he said he had to go to Jacksonville, Florida to settle a property left by his deceased father. Called me and saw the call was registered as Jacksonville...then he sent whole lot of photos of the house, inside out...and I googled all the photos and found he ripped if off from the Internet...houses from U.K. Claimed property is worth US$6.5 million and he had to settle the property tax of 10% of the house value. Second Lie. Thought he is safe until he sent me a passport copy of himself and I can tell it is a fake. Third Lie. Why bother lying unless there is a reason behind it. Then he said his worker is coming to Singapore and asked me to help

---

[20] Adapted from https://scamalert.sg/ https://www.afp.gov.au/careers/graduate-program/eligibility-qualifications-and-business-area/counter-terrorism-scams/internet-love-scam/post/post/45-well-made-up-lies-almost-led-me-to-fall-prey-to-man-looking-for-love.

him settle down. His worker told me his shipment back to Australia requires S$6,500 and this guy Goh asked me to settle it on his behalf. I wanted to trust him, but from the lies he concorted about the house and the passport photos ... I believe I met a SCAMMER... The scam is very meticulated and well planned... Anyone could have fallen for this. When I told him I do not have the money to loan him, he did not respond to me further. I strongly believe this is a scam." [sic]

> **THINKING POINT**
>
> Study the incidents earlier and think about why the scams had worked in the first case. What were the psychological and behavioural mechanisms of 'persuasion'? What contextual or situational factors could be involved? How can we prevent victims from falling prey to crime?[21]

1.7 Theories of Criminal Behaviour

This next section discusses crime theories. There have been, however, volumes of books papers and literature on crime theories written by many experts. It would be redundant to repeat the major theories here. Readers who are keen to have a deeper theoretical understanding should do well to read *Understanding Crime: Theory and Practice* by Thomas Winfree Jr. and Howard Abadinsky (2003); *Forensic Psychology: Crime, Justice, Law and Interventions* by Graham Davies and Anthony Beech (2012); and *An Introduction to Criminal Psychology* by Russil Durrant (2013). Most of my students get very frustrated reading through all the theories and approaches because there are many. Therefore, my approach here is to distil some of the major approaches and conclude the section with a summary of major

---

[21] The SPF has responded by setting up a special task force to address this issue since October 2017. Some solutions included freezing the account of local scam beneficiaries to cut the flow of funds to foreign scam syndicates. More than 200 money mules were also investigated and about S$1 million from 300 accounts were seized. Another solution was to work closely with regional police agencies (Aw, 2018).

and micro variables that explain criminality, and to provide some references at the end for those who want to read further.

However, before we dive into some of these theories, an important concept to appreciate is the 'risk' and 'protective' factors involved in criminal offending. Broadly speaking, a *risk factor* is anything that increases the probability that a person will suffer harm (e.g., use of drugs or alcohol, or having a dysfunctional family), while a *protective factor* is something that decreases the potential harmful effect of a risk factor (e.g., having a stable relationship with someone or having employment). Protective factors offset the onset of offending via four main processes: reducing risk, reducing negative chain reactions, establishing self-esteem and self-efficacy, and opening up opportunities (Rutter, 1987). Do bear these in mind as we discuss the various theories.

Study the following Table 1.5. What are the main causes for criminal behaviour in your view? Rank the most important risk and protective factors.

One way to remember these factors is to use the mnemonic 'Some Men Find Psychology Boring', 'SMFPB', or 'Situational, Macro-Sociological, Family, Psychological, and Biological Factors'. Let us discuss each of these approaches further.

Table 1.5: What Causes Crime? (Activity)

Causes of crime	Your ranking of importance for each?
Situational and environmental factors (e.g., environmental design, lack of protection in place, no surveillance)	
Macro sociological factors (e.g., unemployment, poverty)	
Family and developmental factors (e.g., conduciveness of the home environment, absent parenting, poor supervision by parents, child abuse)	
Psychological factors (e.g., impulsiveness, low empathy)	
Biological factors (e.g., genes, brain injuries, chromosomes)	

Source: Adapted from Durrant, (2013).

1.7.1 *Situational and Environmental Theories*

The physical environment influences criminality, and there are three important theories that have suggested this:

Rational Choice Theory

According to the rational choice theory, developed by Professors Derek Cornish and Ronald Clarke, offenders seek maximum reward (profit) when they think about committing a crime. The theory explains that offenders calculate the perceived benefits and the costs of offending (Lersch, 2007). For instance, the young offender may believe that the customs officer at the airport will not discover his illegal goods being smuggled into the country and thinks that the costs of getting caught (short jail term) is much less than the benefits he would get from bringing in these goods (e.g., a large sum of money). He therefore commits the crime. This thinking explains why some drug mules[22] are prepared to risk their lives — i.e., they believe that the benefits (payment) they will receive are far greater than the costs (of being caught). This is an interesting perspective, since the offender is engaging in cost–benefit analysis. The question remains then; how does the design of situation come into play? Experts explain that the decision to offend in the first place is psychologically determined, while the final decision of whether or not to offend against a particular target is situationally determined together with a cost–benefit calculation. "Should I choose to break into this house or that house?", for example, is a rational choice involving a cost–benefit calculation.

Routine Activities Theory

Developed by Professors Lawrence Cohen and Marcus Felso, the routine activity theory explains that for a crime to occur, there needs

---

[22] A mule is someone who smuggles illegal goods such as drugs across a border. Smugglers use mules to reduce the risk of getting caught themselves. Methods of smuggling include hiding the goods in vehicles or using the body as a container.

to be: 1) a motivated offender; 2) a suitable target; and 3) the absence of an available guardian (this may be a parent, teacher, community supervisor, or maybe CCTV). This explains why people may steal expensive mobile phones or laptops left unattended. Cohen and Felson emphasized that everyday citizens taking notice of each other and surrounding properties were the most effective guardians. The idea here is to design situations and environments where there are guardians, and to reduce accessibility to targets.

Broken Windows Theory

This theory by James Q. Wilson and George L. Kelling published in *The Atlantic* in March 1982 explains how less serious crimes, untended areas in our neighbourhoods, littering, and signs of disorder decrease neighbourhood residents' willingness to enforce social order which, in turn, leads to more serious crime. The point is that if there is a broken window which remains unfixed for some time, it suggests that no one bothers, no one is watching, and no one cares. This in turn leads the offender to commit more crimes.

To quote the writing of the authors:

"We suggest that "untended" behavior also leads to the breakdown of community controls. A stable neighborhood of families who care for their homes, mind each other's children, and confidently frown on unwanted intruders can change, in a few years or even a few months, to an inhospitable and frightening jungle. A piece of property is abandoned, weeds grow up, a window is smashed. Adults stop scolding rowdy children; the children, emboldened, become more rowdy. Families move out, unattached adults move in. Teenagers gather in front of the corner store. The merchant asks them to move; they refuse. Fights occur. Litter accumulates. People start drinking in front of the grocery; in time, an inebriate slumps to the sidewalk and is allowed to sleep it off. Pedestrians are approached by panhandlers. At this point it is not inevitable that serious crime will flourish or violent attacks on strangers will occur."

Therefore, if we do not attend to the smaller things, we invite bigger problems to come along! Hence, there is a need to fix relatively smaller and minor crimes like graffiti, littering, small damages to property, and deviance.

1.7.2 *Macro Sociological Theories*

Social Disorganization Theory

This theory explains that the structures in society are related to the amount of crime in the society. The more unstructured and disorderly the society is, the greater the amount of crime. High levels of poverty and unemployment, poor economy, and poorly functioning school and community groups are suggestive of poor social organization, and this can fester greater levels of crime. In many macro level studies, it is clear that a good economy can reduce crime rate across countries from two angles — first, because people become busier with work (work is a protective factor); and second, economic growth often goes hand-in-hand with social structures and the rule of law, which are conducive to lower crime rates.

General Strain Theory

Th General Strain Theory (GST) explains that everyone in society has some material and non-material goals that they want to achieve, but are unable to because they lack the opportunities, or may have poor family and peer support (e.g., bad family and anti-social peers are clear risk factors). Thus, they resort to crime, achieving their goals in a negative way. Robert Agnew developed the GST in 1992 (Agnew & Brezina, 2010). The GST focuses on a broad range of strains, including the inability to achieve a variety of goals, the loss of valued possessions, and negative treatment by others.

Social Control Theories

Social control theories explain why people obey rules and accept social control (as opposed to other theories that explain why people break the rules). These theories explain that crime is thrilling, fun, and personally reinforcing to those who commit it, and if it were not for the controls and checks in society, most people would commit crime (Hirschi, 1969). Crime occurs when there is a lack of social controls to stop it, such as the 'social bonds' of marriage[23] and employment (Hirschi, 1969). These controls may also be family, schools, and religious organizations, and may also refer to internal self-controls. In neighbourhoods where controls are poor, more crime occurs.

Deterrence Theory

Deterrence theory explains that crime will depend on the certainty, swiftness, and severity of punishment for a crime. This punishment is carried out by the state. Here, the idea is that deterrence works when people refrain from actions for fear of negative consequences. They are also deterred when the calculated costs of punishment seem more than the benefits of a criminal or deviant act.[24] There are in fact two types of deterrence. *General deterrence* is the deterrence the punishment has on other potential offenders. *Specific deterrence* is the effect punishments have on reducing re-offending in punished offenders (Blackburn, 1993).

Labelling Theory

This theory looks into the sources of labelling, how criminals are labelled, and the effect that labels have on individuals. The main idea here is that being labelled a criminal affects an individual negatively, reducing their self-image, and fostering a criminal career (Blackburn, 1994).

1.7.3 *Family and Developmental Factors*

This is usually discussed as *Developmental Criminology*, and it refers to studies about a) the development of offending from 'womb to

---

[23] This idea is consistent because we know that relationships and employment can be 'protective' (the opposite of risk factor) and they prevent one from getting into or continuing a life of criminality.

[24] This is related to rational choice theory.

tomb'; b) the influence of risk and protective factors across different ages; and c) the effects of life events on the course of human development (Farrington, Loeber & Welsh, 2010).

The literature is rife with material discussing the impact of broken homes and children coming from divorced or single parent families. This is true to some extent, since there are studies which show that children from single parent families are more likely to engage in crime (Bank *et al.*, 1993). However, single parents tend to have single income, more emotional difficulties, and more mental health problems. It is therefore simplistic to attribute delinquency entirely to single parenting itself. Supporting this idea further was the research by Rutter (1971) who showed that the loss of a parent by death, thereby turning the family into a single parent family, does not contribute to delinquency.

Professor David Farrington and other researchers made the following observations about the development of offending and the related risk and protective factors (Farrington, 2010):

(a)   Age and street crime are linked. For many, criminal offending peaked from 15 to 19 years of age. Street crime occurs largely during adolescence, and offenders desist from crime as they age. Most youth do not commit crime;

(b)   For a smaller group of individuals who start earlier to commit more offences, they tend to have a longer offending career. For this group, there is continuity in anti-social and criminal behaviour across the life span;

(c)   The age–crime curve has been observed with males and females, but declines faster for females;

(d)   Unlike the patterns seen in street crimes, crimes related to occupations and making profits (i.e., fraud and embezzlement) start in adulthood because people tend to steal from workplaces;

(e)   A small number of individuals are responsible for the majority of crimes;

(f)   Offenders are versatile and commit a variety of offences;

(g)   Adolescents commit crimes with others, while adults commit crimes alone;

(h) Important 'risk factors' relate to individual characteristics, family, school, and community environments;

(i) Employment, marriage, and having children are related to criminal desistance, and are therefore 'protective'; and

(j) As people age, they are less likely to commit crime on average.

Professor Terry Moffitt, who discussed the 'two-trajectories' theory of Life Course Persistent (LCP) and Adolescent Limited (AL) offenders, developed another interesting theory (Moffitt, 1993). LCP offenders begin to behave anti-socially early in childhood and continue this behaviour into adulthood. They start early at age four, engage in 'acting-out' behaviours, and tend to have Attention Deficit Hyperactivity Disorder (ADHD) and learning disorders. As they grow up, they are left out by their peers and parents, and often end up in violent situations and homes for children, which makes their developmental risk factors even worse. AL offenders, on the other hand, exhibit anti-social behaviour only during adolescence, start offending around 18 years old, and while they attempt to imitate the LCPs, they often drop their deviant or rebellious ways when they go on to education or seek employment.

Putting these factors together, it seems that poor parenting skills, quarrels at home, child maltreatment, low socioeconomic status, broken homes, and anti-social parents seem to be common risk factors linked to delinquency (Table 1.6). As Table 1.6 shows, it is not just family factors, but also other factors that come together to contribute to delinquency and crime. On the other hand, as the right-most column shows, there are also protective factors that reduce and mitigate the chances that a young person may get into a life of crime.

Supportive parenting and good parental supervision are protective. These factors are listed out and presented earlier.

Think of the factors shown in Table 1.6 and analyze if these are programmable or changeable factors. For example, some factors are static and cannot be changed, i.e., being born as a male. Others, on the hand, are factors that can be changed (i.e., they are dynamic) such as the teenagers' exposure to substances such as drugs and alcohol.

Table 1.6:   Risk and Protective Factors of Delinquency and Crime

	Risk factors		
	Early onset (Ages 6 to 11)	Late onset (Ages 12 to 15)	Protective factors
Individual factors	Drug, alcohol, and substance use Anti-social attitudes Being Male Aggression** Hyperactive Exposure to violence on media (TV and the Internet) Dishonesty	Drug, alcohol and substance use Anti-social attitudes Restlessness Inability to concentrate in school or work Risk-taking Aggression Being Male Physical violence Low IQ	Having a high IQ Being female Positive social orientation Intolerant attitude towards deviance and crime
Family factors	Low socioeconomic status Anti-social parents Harsh, lax, or inconsistent parenting Abusive parents Negligent parents Broken home	Low socioeconomic status Poor parent–child relationship Harsh or lax discipline Poor parental supervision Broken home Family conflict**	Warm supportive relationships with parents or other adults Parents' positive perception of peers Parental monitoring
School factors	Poor attitude towards school Poor performance	Poor attitude Poor performance Academic failure	Commitment to school and school activities
Peer and friendships	Weak social ties with others Anti-social peers	Weak social ties Anti-social peers Gang membership	Friends who are good role models and engage in conventional behaviour
Community		Neighbourhood crime Neighbourhood is disorganized	

Note: **Males only.
Source: Office of Surgeon General (2001). Youth Violence: A Report of the Surgeon General. Washington, DC: U.S. Department of Health and Human Services, Office of the Secretary, Office of Public Health and Science, Office of the Surgeon General. Retrieved from www.surgeongeneral.gov/library/youthviolence.

1.7.4 *Psychological Factors*

Personality and personal characteristics

What are the psychological and personality factors involved in offending? As early as in the 1900s in the U.K., famous criminologist Charles Goring in his study, *The English Convict*, looked at 96 traits of each of more than 3,000 English convicts, and found that 'fraudulent offenders' were egotistic, and 'violent offenders' were marked by hot/violent temper, and often had mental illnesses and suicidal tendencies (Driver, 1957).

Studies by Professor Hans Eysenck believed that the personality factor called 'psychoticism' resulted in people being insensitive and cruel. Other traits such as impulsivity, risky thinking, and sensation seeking may play a role (Eysenck and Gudjonsson, 1989). These factors are not very surprising if you consider that self-regulation and self-control are important factors contributing to criminal behaviour. Self-control is related to many aspects of our lives, including self-control in schools, during national service, in relationships, and in workplace settings. Individuals with poor self-control sometimes have problems managing alcohol use, gambling habits, and appropriate medical drug use.

Another area of personality and crime is the psychopathic offender, which was mainly studied by American psychiatrist Hervey M. Cleckley and Canadian psychologist Robert D. Hare. Some of the characteristics of psychopaths include a lack of empathy and guilt, impulsiveness, irresponsibility, pathological lying, manipulativeness, superficial charm, glibness, and a failure to learn from experiences (Hare, 1980). Table 1.7 illustrates how they are categorized into different domains. Hare developed an assessment tool called the Psychopathy Checklist (Revised) (Hare, 2003) to measure this.

Table 1.7:   Features of the Psychopathy and the Main Domains

Interpersonal	Affective	Lifestyle	Antisocial
Glib	Lack of remorse and guilt	Stimulation seeking	Poor behavior controls
Grandiose sense of self/self-worth	Callous lack of empathy	Impulsivity	Early behavior problems
Pathological lying	Failure to accept responsibility	Irresponsible	Juvenile delinquency
Conning and manipulation	Shallow affect	Parasitic orientation	Revocation of conditional release
Superficial charm		Unrealistic goals	Criminal versatility

Source: Adapted from Robert D. Hare, Hare Psychopathy Checklist (Revised), (2nd edition).

Hare and Neumann (2010) explained that psychopathic offenders are disproportionately represented in the criminal justice system. These offenders find it very easy to victimize the vulnerable, and to use intimidation and violence as tools to achieve power and control over others. Their impulsivity and poor behavioural controls may result in reactive forms of aggression, but other features (e.g., lack of empathy, shallow emotions, etc.) make it easy for them to engage in aggression and violence that is more predatory, premeditated, instrumental, or cold-blooded. A good body of research has developed in recent years showing the relationship between psychopathy and violence (see meta-analyses by Campbell *et al.*, 2009).

Intelligence and cognitive abilities

Is there a link between criminality and intelligence? Charles Goring (1913) found a strong relationship between 'defective intelligence' and criminality. Famous early studies by Glueck and Glueck (1934, 1950) found that delinquents had lower IQs than non-delinquents. The big question, however, was whether lower IQ was a consequence of social circumstances, such as poverty or unemployment, rather than indicative of actual intelligence.

Years later, in a controversial book, *The Bell Curve,* Richard Herrnstein and Charles Murray (Herrnstein and Murray, 1994) made the case for a link between low IQ and criminality. They argued that since the mid-1990s, most offenders in prisons appeared to have an IQ of about 91 to 93 (the average IQ being about 100). They made the point that high IQ might be a protective factor preventing criminal behaviour. The critique of this was that IQ and Socioeconomic Status (SES) appeared highly correlated. So, the question is, are we really measuring intelligence or are measuring SES when we say that IQ is connected to criminal behaviour? Questions remain unanswered. First, does low intelligence result in criminality and how *exactly* does this happen? Second, does low intelligence result in poor academic performance, which is, in turn, associated with crime proneness? It must furthermore be recognized that some offenders possess very high IQ scores, especially those involved in organized and corporate crimes (Canter, 2008).

Learning behaviors

Edwin Sutherland, a sociologist (Sutherland and Cressey, 1974), makes interesting points about how criminality can be learnt though one's interactions with others. He says that a) criminal behaviour is learnt; b) learning is through association with others (that is why being with anti-social peers is a risk factor for criminality); c) learning takes place in close groups (e.g., gangs, families, friends, and terror networks); d) the learning revolves around how to commit certain crimes but also developing attitudes, values, and motives. For example, a rapist might learn from his peers that girls who wear miniskirts were "asking for it and want sex"; e) the learning experience will vary person to person; f) the process of learning is no different from other kinds of learning experiences. In a nutshell, criminality can be learnt from others, especially friends and family.

Lack of empathy

This refers to a person's inability to see something from another person's perspective and the inability to respond to their feelings. Sarason (1968) suggested that delinquents were lacking in empathy and social skills. Expression of empathy serves as an inhibitor of negative interactions and helps facilitate positive ones. Research evidence demonstrates that responding to another individual with empathy decreases one's potential for acting aggressively (Feshbach, 1982).

Cognitive scripts and narratives

A 'script' is the details of how someone should behave in a certain social context. A person who is convinced that aggression is a part of life and living is more likely to have hostile and aggressive scripts (Canter, 2008). Research has looked at 'inner narratives' that criminals may have. This is the concept that offenders have of themselves, and this may be played out in roles implicitly or explicit. For example, criminals may see themselves as a 'hero', 'victim', 'professional', or 'adventurer' (Canter, 2008). Narrative analysis has been used in a number of other studies on cocaine use (Copes *et al.*, 2008), drug dealing (Sandberg, 2009), white-collar crime (Klenowski *et al.*, 2011), street violence (Brookman *et al.*, 2011), terrorism (Sandberg, 2013), and violence (Brookman, 2015).

Mental disorders

There has been research that suggests that people with psychotic disorders offend because of their symptoms, mainly because of their delusions and hallucinations. The issue is often the persecutory nature of their delusions, and because they perceive situations and persons as threatening (Arsenault *et al.*, 2000). Research relating to mentally disordered offenders in the U.K. suggested that most had schizophrenia (61%), personality disorders (45%), while a minority had affective disorders (12%) and mental retardation (10%) (Harty *et al.*, 2004). This is a complex area of study in forensic psychology, and is beyond the scope of an introductory book. Interested readers, however, should look into relevant forensic psychological issues such as the "unfitness to plead" (i.e., whether the defendant can defend himself, understand the substance of evidence against him, and follow the court proceedings), the "insanity defence" (i.e., the question being asked here is the defendant's state of mind at the time of offence) and "diminished responsibility" (i.e., whether the defendant has abnormality of mind which impaired their mental responsibility for their acts). In Singapore, one relevant legislation in this regard is the Mental Health (Care and Treatment) Act 2008. Under the Act, a designated medical practitioner at the Institute of Mental Health (IMH) may sign a form which allows the involuntary admission of an individual suffering from a mental illness into the hospital for treatment for up to 72 hours. This is helpful for patients who are mentally ill and at psychiatric risk, but decline voluntary treatment.

'Criminogenic needs': The 'Central Eight'

In an impactful book titled *The Psychology of Criminal Conduct* (fifth edition), Professors Andrews and Bonta (2010) discussed the "Central Eight", which is the idea of eight criminogenic risk and need factors. We call them the 'Eight A-Ls' (think of 8 ALvins), and they are shown in Table 1.8.

Table 1.8:   The Central Eight

4 'A's	4 'L's
Anti-social behaviour	Lack of happiness and stability in relationships, marriage
Anti-social personality	Lack of stability in employment, achievement
Anti-social attitudes	Lack of prosocial leisure
Anti-social peers	Lifestyle of alcohol, drugs

The 4 'A's are:

- *Anti-social behavior:* History of involvement in a number of anti-social acts in a variety of settings;
- *Anti-social personality:* Anti-social personality disorder is characterized by a pervasive pattern of disregard for and violation of the rights of others. Those with anti-social personality tend to have a personality

style which can be irresponsible, aggressive, and violent, impulsive, and may fail to conform to social norms and laws (this includes features such as being impulsive, pleasure seeking, aggressive, hostile, and irritable);

- *Anti-social attitudes and cognitions:* Attitudes, values, beliefs, and rationalization of thinking to justify criminal actions. Offenders generally exhibit certain thinking errors, such as a sense of entitlement, self-justification, blaming others, and taking on a 'victim stance' (e.g., "the police is out to get me"). They often misinterpret neutral remarks as threats (e.g., "he shows me no respect, so I hammered him" [sic]);

- *Anti-social friends, peers, and associates:* This is the idea that social learning occurs by mixing with the 'wrong company'. Gang connections are particularly a problem. In a local study of 300 youth rioters (aged 21 years and below) by the Subordinate Courts of Singapore, 87.6% were reportedly involved with gangs (The Subordinate Courts of Singapore, 1998). In another study in 2005 by Dr. Chu Chi Meng and colleagues at the Ministry of Community, Youth and Sports in Singapore (now Ministry of Social and Family Development), they explored the sociodemographic characteristics, risk, and rate of criminal recidivism in a cohort of 165 male youth offenders in Singapore (Chu *et al.*, 2012). Of this group, 58 were gang-affiliated. They found that gang-affiliated youth offenders were more likely to have histories of substance use, weapon-use, and violence than non-gang-affiliated youth offenders. Gang-affiliated offenders also scored higher on measures of risk for recidivism, and engaged in violent and other criminal behaviors more frequently during the follow-up. In another study, Chu *et al.* (2015) found that gang affiliation in youth was associated with increased criminal recidivism as well and an exaggeration of various criminogenic needs.

A personal account of an ex-gang member is found in a case study below. It demonstrates the emotional and psychological issues the person faces.

CASE STUDY:
How I Got Involved with Gangs

I was indirectly involved because my best childhood friend started his own gang... One thing is that we kept a low profile and definitely led a double life. I am sure you have people who brag about gangs are usually the wannabe who barks louder than they bite. If we want to screw people over, we won't say a thing and then one day magically have people's lives messed upside down. People in school thought we were good kids but we are completely different outside of school...

At first, it was merely a way to showcase our manliness and do whatever the hell we want and give people shit if they rub us the wrong way. In other words, the beginning stages were the "wannabes". Because of our attitude and approach, we actually started to attract a lot of attention and hatred from others. Of course, it also because my friend started the operation of dealing illegal drugs and become quite addicted to the cocaine... over time, a lot of operations becomes more and more on a bigger scale that definitely will put people behind bars for a long long time. I never did drugs not did I helped them in that part of operation. Luckily, I was always someone who always live for the long term and realize that doing shit like that will screw me over completely. I had the forethought and I know jobs run background checks and all these at an early age, so before I got myself to an irreparable situation, I opted out.

Of course, I am also the lucky one because I know the leader since I was a child and that we literally would die for each other and take a bullet for each other.

Several years passed, and one day I just stopped hearing from him. Afterwards, I realized that he was put in prison for myriad of illegal activities. His parents divorced, grandparents went insane. When I went to visit the family, they say they do not have a guy Tony (fictitious name) in the family. It was really sad and upsetting.

I would say based on my experience, people in gang and stay in gang are usually people who had a dysfunctional family without a support system. For many guys, it is a way to mask their insecurity and to feel the "strong" and "powerful" status most people envisioned. It is simply another form of escape from the reality of life. [sic]

Source: Adapted from Wu, 2013 (some details in the text have been amended to anonymise the writer).

The 4 'L's are:

(k) *Lack of happiness and stability in relationships*, such as family and marriage.
(l) *Lack of Education, employment, and achievement*: Studies of prisoners who participated in prison-based education or vocation prison programs show that they are less likely to recidivate upon release than non-participants because they tended to have higher employment rates (see Wilson *et al.*, 2000).
(m) *Lack of prosocial leisure*: 'Idle times make idle hands' is an old but accurate adage. Involvement in pro-social activities reduces delinquency in youth.
(n) *Lifestyle of alcohol, drugs, and substance abuse*: The prevalence of alcohol and drug use is four times higher among offenders than in the general population (Substance Abuse and Mental Health Services Administration, 2011).

Confirming these ideas further was a local study involving interviews with 54 young offenders at Kaki Bukit Center Prisons School, where Tam and Heng looked at factors that 'provoke[d] young people who get into trouble'. The authors found that peer influence, provocation and anger, boredom and thrill, alcohol and drugs, and money were the main reasons why young people committed crimes. The authors explained that there was a need for more training in social competency, minimizing aggressive behaviours, moral reasoning, and helping students find a purposeful direction in life (cited in *Correctional Research Compendium*, Ministry of Home Affairs, 2006).

---

[25] In Singapore, if you join a secret society, you may face the possibility of being jailed without trial under the Criminal Law (Temporary Provisions) Act. The CLTPA was introduced in 1955 when secret societies and gangs were commonplace. In the year (2018), a Bill was introduced in Parliament, which extended the lifespan of the Act for another five years. The Act allows police to dismantle gang memberships and protect witnesses. This Act is usually used as a last resort. In 2017, there were 103 CL detainees; of which 86 were in secret societies, whilst 11 were in unlicensed moneylending and 5 in drug trafficking (Tan, 2018).

> **THINKING POINT**
> **Are Youth Gangs the Same as Secret Societies?**
>
> Dr. Chu Chi Meng and colleagues (Chu *et al.*, 2015) argued that while youth gangs in Singapore tended to adopt the names of secret societies and loosely modelled themselves after triads and secret societies, they were, however, different in some ways:
>
> - Triads and secret societies are considered usually: a) highly organized crime, b) they are interested in economic gains through criminal activities, and c) operate as a whole group, rather than smaller groups.
> - Youth gangs, on the other hand, a) do not typically follow the traditional initiation and rituals; and b) tended to be loosely organized in terms of structure and hierarchy. Also, youth gang[25] membership may primarily satisfy social rather than economic needs.

1.7.5 *Biological and Physiological Factors*

These theories suggest that biology plays a role in criminal behaviour. Cesare Lombroso, an Italian criminologist and physician who lived from 1835 to 1909, argued that criminals were a product of genetic configurations (Hollin, 1992), believing they had huge jaws, high cheekbones, 'handle' shaped ears, insensitivity to pain, and a craving for orgies! Lombroso's work was critiqued on a few grounds, namely for the fact that complex behaviour cannot be explained by physical characteristics alone. 'Family studies' such as the Osborn and West (1979) studies found that 40% of the sons of criminal fathers had criminals record themselves. Other studies have looked at biological correlates such as the following:

- *Genes and Twin studies.* In these studies, researchers compare identical or monozygotic (MZ) and fraternal or dizygotic (DZ) twins. MZ twins shared a higher proportion of the same genes. DZ twins shared about 50% of the genes. In cases where the DZ also shared the same environment, then the differences between them would be due to genetics. Lange (1931) found in his study that there was 77% concordance (i.e., this is the degree to which a pair display the same behavior) for 13 pairs of MZ twins and 12% for 17 sets of DZ twins. Most studies tend to find an average concordance rate of about 55% for MZ twins and 17% for DZ twins. The question is why did this high level of concordance with MZ come about? Could it be due to parents treating MZ/ identical twins in the same way, and therefore giving them the same experience?

- *Adoption studies.* Another way of examining the influence of genetics is to look at children who were adopted. There have been several studies which have looked at this, but a useful one was Mednick *et al.* (1984). Looking at more than 14,000 adoptees, they showed that the percentage of criminal adoptees were higher when both biological and adoptive parents were criminal (Table 1.9).

Table 1.9:   Findings from Mednick *et al.* (1984)

Are biological parents criminal?	Are adoptive parents criminal?	Percentage of criminal sons
Yes	Yes	24.5
Yes	No	20
No	Yes	14.7
No	No	13.5

- *EEG and Neurological factors.* The EEG (Electroencephalogram recordings) is a way of assessing brain functioning. There have been studies that have looked at abnormal EEG and violent behaviour (Gunn and Bonn, 1971). EEG abnormalities was noted to be higher for offenders than for non-delinquent population. Hill and Pond (1952) explored offenders, and noted EEG abnormality in nearly 50% of their cases. Brain damage due to head injuries and tumors have also been linked to crime (Canter, 2008).

- *Serotonin.* Some studies have suggested that violent people may have lower levels of serotonin and are disadvantaged when they have to control their own aggression levels (Virkkunen *et al.*, 1996).
- *Testosterone.* Testosterone plays a role in the arousal of certain brain centres which are connected to aggression. It is involved in the development of the muscular system that is engaged when someone becomes aggressive. There is evidence that testosterone levels may be higher in individuals with aggressive behaviors, such as violent criminals (Batrinos, 2012). However, high testosterone levels have also been found in men with no criminal history. One study has also found that large doses of testosterone increased aggression but only for a small proportion of men (Pope *et al.*, 2000).
- *DNA and Forensic Genetics (FG).* Jobling and Gill (2004) define forensic genetics as 'the application of genetics for the resolution of legal cases'. The main aspect of FG is the use of DNA. Forensic investigators can use DNA to draw conclusions about where we have been and who we have interacted with. DNA is being used to identify, convict, and exonerate suspects. However, it also has its limitations. For instance, it might be undetectable, or is found in such minor traces that makes interpretation difficult. It is true that DNA can be misinterpreted, and their importance exaggerated.[26] For an excellent review of the potential use and limitations of

---

[26] As illustrated by the wrongful arrest of a British man, Adam Scott who was charged with raping a woman in Manchester, the U.K. in 2011. Swabs of the victims's genitals revealed traces of sperm, and one of these swabs at the lab yielded a DNA profile that matched Scott's DNA. The forensic scientist who processed the sample claimed *"strong scientific support for the view that Adam Scott had sexual intercourse with [the victim]."* This was an error. A DNA profile cannot lead to the inference that sexual intercourse took place. Two months after his arrest, Scott's phone records supported his version of events. Finally, Scott was released. An investigation revealed that Mr. Scott had become falsely implicated as a result of accidental contamination of DNA samples within the lab.

forensic genetics, readers should look up *Making sense of forensic genetics* (Sense about Science, 2017).

As a part summary, we need to note that these biological factors are contributing factors and are not causational. This field is broadly known as *'biological positivism'*. Although our biological makeup influences us, it does not determine our behavior and personalities wholly. There is a role for environmental factors as well. Contemporary approaches in biological positivism today do recognise this and use bio-social and bio-psycho-social frameworks. They look at how biological conditions can predispose people to criminality, but examine how environments shape behaviour (Coomber *et al.*, 2015).

1.7.5.1 *Physiology, drugs, and alcohol*

Drug Abuse

A Joint Report by the United Nations Office on Drugs and Crime and the Latin America and the Caribbean Region of the World Bank titled *Crime, Violence, and Development: Trends, Costs, and Policy Options in the Caribbean* (March 2007) reported the following:

> "While levels of crime and associated circumstances vary by country, the strongest explanation for the relatively high rates of crime and violence rates in the region — and their apparent rise in recent years — is narcotics trafficking. The drug trade drives crime in a number of ways: through violence tied to trafficking, by normalizing illegal behaviour, by diverting criminal justice resources from other activities, by provoking property crime related to addiction, by contributing to the widespread availability of firearms, and by undermining and corrupting societal institutions"

(UNODC, 2007)

Durrant (2013) explained that drugs use and alcohol use concern criminologists and psychologists; particularly drugs that can alter mood, perception, thinking, and behaviour. Table 1.10 illustrates the concern with psychoactive drugs:

Table 1.10: Drugs and Their Effects

Drug	Examples	Method	Typical effects
Opiates	Opium, Heroin (local name: White, Ubat)	Ingested, smoked, injected	Euphoria, pain relief, relaxation, nausea, respiration problems,
Stimulants	Cocaine, amphetamine, Methamphetamine (local name: Ice, Ya Ba)	Ingested, snorted, injected	Elation, excitement, reduced fatigue, increased heart rate, paranoia, repetitive behaviors
Hallucinogen	Lsd, mescalin	Ingested	Perceptual distortion, enhanced sensory awareness, disturbed cognition, anxiety and panic
Cannabis	Marijuana (local name: Ganga, Weed)	Oral, smoked	Euphoria, altered perception, impaired memory, bloodshot eyes, increased heart rates
Depressants	Alcohol, barbiturates	Ingested	Euphoria, disinhibiting impaired perception

Source: Adapted from Durrant, (2013) and Central Narcotics Bureau (n.d) ('Growing up drug free').

There appears to be a strong relationship between drug use and crime. While the exact number of drug-related crimes varies in some estimates, it appears to be about 60%, at least in the U.S. (Mumola, 1997).

Durrant (2013) discussed four models of relationships between drug use and crime as follows: 1) drug use leads to crime (e.g., drug users engage in crime, sell stolen goods, and then buy drugs); 2) crime leads to drug use (e.g., drug users celebrate their offending by further drug use); 3) there is another cause (e.g., unemployment) which could lead to both drug use and crime and finally, 4) drug use leads to crimes and crimes in turn also lead to drug use (reciprocal model).

Not all offenders who use drugs are addicted but there is strong evidence of negative effects on performance. For example, research has shown that heroin users display cognitive impairment on verbal fluency, pattern recognition, planning, and the ability to shift attention from one frame of reference to another (Ornstein *et al.*, 2000). Reports that methamphetamine affects cognitive function were supported in a meta-analysis undertaken by Scott *et al.* (2007). Investigating differences in cognitive functioning between methamphetamine-abusing and comparison participants, the analysis revealed deficits in several areas for methamphetamine abusers, including learning and memory, executive functioning, information processing, motor functioning, working memory, and language.

Singapore has a strict zero-tolerance approach towards drug abuse. This approach is multi-pronged and comprises tough legislation, enforcement, intensive preventive drug education, rehabilitation and aftercare regime. Drug abuse is viewed as a social and behavioural problem, and not a public health issue alone. The consequences of drug use can, in fact, be horrendous. In 2006, we saw a case of two-year-old Nurasyura (also known as Nonoi) who was cruelly killed by her stepfather, a drug user. He dunked her into a pail because he could not stand her constant crying. In 2009, there was another case involving six-year-old Edy who was dumped into the Kallang river by a drug user who was caring for him while his parents were in jail for drugs (Alkhatib, 2017).

According to statistics, CNB arrested a total of 3,265 drug abusers in 2016 (this was 3,089 in 2017), and while the number of repeat drug abusers arrested decreased by 7%, the number of new drug abusers arrested was 1,348 in 2016 and 1,249 in 2017.

In 2017, close to two-thirds of new abusers arrested were under 30 years old.

Of those arrested in 2017, the largest numbers were in the ages of 20 to 29 years of age (954 pesons), 30 to 39 years (779), 40 to 49 years (538), 50 to 59 years (402), and 60 years and above (140).

Most of the commonly used drugs in 2017 were Methamphetamine (64%), Heroin (27%), Cannabis (7%), and 'Others' (2%) (Tan, 2018).

CNB remains concerned about the changing attitudes of young people. In a recent survey by the National Council Against Drug Abuse (NCADA),[27] which polled 2,748 people aged 13 to 30, survey findings

---

[27] See https://www.ncada.org.sg/.

revealed that there is a growing number of young people who have a liberal attitude towards drug abuse (from 16% in 2016 compared to 13% in 2013). The Youth Perception Survey revealed that 58% of young people said they learnt about drug-related content via social media. About one-third did not perceive cannabis as addictive. There was a significant increase in the proportion of young people who perceived cannabis as a popular drug of abuse, with numbers standing at 35%, up from 17% in 2013. Overall, respondents for the Public Perception Survey had strong support for Singapore's drug-free approach and laws, with 81% showing negative views towards drugs (Tan, 2017).

A useful study of drug abusers by a team of psychologists from the Home Team was conducted from December 2014 to April 2015. The research involved 700 participants aged 12 to 29 years, comprising 237 abusers and 463 non-abusers. Participants completed a questionnaire that measured the risk and protective factors of drug abuse and their perceptions towards preventive education. The team conducted individual case history interviews and group discussions for an in-depth understanding. They found that some of the reasons why youths experimented with drugs was because: a) their friends told them to try it out; b) they wanted to know the feeling of being high; c) they wanted to forget their problems; d) they wanted to relieve stress; e) they wanted to lose weight; f) they were bored; g) just for fun; and h) they wanted to fit in with the "cool" group.

The study found that the risk factors that contributed to drug abuse were: a) peer influence ("youths may take drugs to bond and remain with their group of friends who take drugs"), b) boredom, c) poor coping skills, d) lack of parental guidance, e) family drug history ("parents or caregivers with drug history can negatively impact the way children feel about drugs"), f) curiosity ("natural curiosity often entice them to experiment with new things"), and g) availability of substances.[28]

There are worrying trends in Singapore about cannabis use as shown in Table 1.11.

---

[28] See "Growing up drug free: a preventive drug education information handbook for parents. From https://www.cnb.gov.sg".

Table 1.11:   Cannabis and Health Effects

The concern with cannabis use today	Adverse health effects of cannabis	Cannabis users today have...
More cannabis users are coming from middle class families.	It is addictive. Users who try to quit report experiencing irritation, sleeplessness, low appetite, anxiety and drug cravings.	No drug background and come from families with no drug background.
More youths are experimenting with cannabis because of social media and drug legislation overseas.	There may be an early onset of psychotic disorders, increased suicide risk and detrimental effects on adolescent brain development.	They perform well in school and have no discipline issues. Peer pressure and wrong information from peers, leads them to have erroneous information about cannabis.
Some users think that cannabis is less harmful than tobacco, which is not correct. Cannabis contains more cancer-causing agents.	Loss of concentration and decline in intelligence.	Youths develop liberal attitudes towards drug use.
Some businesses are marketing cannabis for recreational use.		Youths become open to cannabis use and run the risk of being exposed to other drugs.

Source: Adapted from CNB's "Growing up Drug Free", Central Narcotic Bureau (n.d.).

If you suspect that your friend or family member might be addicted to drug or involved with drugs, call the CNB hotline for advice and CNB will work with you to decide how to manage the situation. Call 1800-325-6666 (24 hours) or contact the National Addictions Management Service (NAMS) at 6-RECOVER (6732-6837). You must remember that there is a rehabilitation framework for youths, which means someone involved with drugs will be placed under various possible management schemes and will not necessarily be jailed. There are several schemes depending on the extent of one's drug use if they are tested positive, and they may be placed under any of the following: a Youth Enhancement Supervision (YES) Scheme; a Community Rehabilitation Centre (CRC) or the Drug Rehabilitation Centre (DRC). Those who have taken drugs but are tested negative may be placed under the ACE program or the Anti-Drug Counselling and Engagement Program (Central Narcotics Bureau, n.d.).

Alcohol Abuse

Scientifically speaking, alcohol may also be viewed as a drug (Foundation for a Drug Free World, n.d.). It is a depressant, meaning that it results in slurred speech, unsteady body movement, disturbed perceptions, and an inability to react quickly. As for how it affects the mind, it is best understood as a drug that reduces a person's ability to think rationally and distorts his or her judgment. Most people drink for the *stimulant* effect, such as a beer or glass of wine taken to "loosen up". However, if a person consumes more than the body can handle, they then experience alcohol's depressant effect (see Table 1.12 for the various drink types and the alcohol content in these drinks). They start to feel "stupid" or lose control (Foundation for a Drug Free World, n.d.).

Alcohol abuse is a significant risk factor for crime. In cross-sectional studies in Canada, Wells *et al.* (2000) reported that heavy alcohol use was associated with experiences of threats and aggression. In New Zealand, alcohol abuse has been associated with violent and

Table 1.12: Drink Type and Alcohol Content

Drink type	Alcohol content in drink
Beer	2–6% alcohol
Cider	4–8% alcohol
Wine	8–20% alcohol
Tequila, Rum, Brandy	40% alcohol
Gin, Whiskey, Vodka	40–50% alcohol
Liqueurs	15–60% alcohol

Source: Adapted from Foundation for a Drug Free World (n.d.).

property offending (Fergusson and Horwood, 2000). It is also estimated that the use of alcohol and drugs in sexual offending is almost 50%, affecting both perpetrators and victims. This is because of 'drink spiking' and the drugs involved in these incidents. GHB and Rohypnol facilitate sexual crimes such as molestation and rape by rendering a victim vulnerable and incapacitated.

Alcohol impairs the decision-making faculties of offenders. Alcohol makes an offender a poor judge of risks and benefits of his or her courses of action. *Alcohol Myopia* refers to the narrowing of attention such that one focuses on the most salient easy-to-process immediate cues in the environment (Giancola *et al.*, 2010). What makes this more problematic is that people's beliefs about their own behaviour can aggravate the situation. For example, if you believe that you will become more aggressive when you consume alcohol, you will be more likely to behave as such. On the other hand, if you believe that you will become quiet and pensive after alcohol use, you will behave that way.

Alcohol does not directly result in aggression, and there are some mediating factors that operate in between and these factors that have been identified are dispositional hostility, irritability, impulsiveness, risk taking, and low empathy (Giancola, 2002). Contextual factors include provocation by others and the drinking environment. Discussed below is a case study which was a significant case in Singapore, involving drug spiking of drinks.

CASE STUDY:
Vicious Date Rapist's Exploits

Serial rapist Tamrin (age 44) raped many women as a date/drug use rapist. He would chat with them via dating applications online or on Facebook, and then proceed to meet them at his preferred bars. He often posed as a professional person, sometimes as a dentist, a soon-to-be graduate student pursuing a Master of Business in the U.S., or a Catholic, and even lied about his father's nationality. In doing so, he psychological groomed his victims — he broke their defences, got them to trust him, and eventually manipulated victims until he got what he wanted.

(*Continued*)

(*Continued*)

Handsome and groomed, Tamrin could convince the ladies to meet him after chatting over a few drinks. He spiked their drinks with Dormicum, a type of sedative and sleeping pill he obtained by telling medical practitioners various false accounts of his wife and child's deaths. Upon the consumption of Dormicum, his victims blacked out. With his victim under the influence of Dormicum, Tamrin then proceeded to check into a cheap hotel rooms where he would rape his victim and video record the process. Before or after the effects wore off, Tamrin would send the victim home on the pretext that they were so drunk that they had made a mess of themselves, which he helped to clean up. Several victims had anterograde amnesia and could not recall anything. Without memory of the events of the previous night, the victims would not report Tamrin to the police, due to their uncertainty regarding the occurrence of indecent acts.

He was eventually caught when he arranged to meet a victim with the intention of raping her. He spiked her drink but before he could move away with her, her alert boyfriend noticed that she began to stare into space, and handed over her mobile phone and handbag to Tamrin. The boyfriend then quickly confronted Tamrin and then brought his girlfriend to the hospital. Though conscious, the potential victim could never recollect how she got to the hospital.

The court found that Tamrin's offences were clearly pre-meditated and his perverted recording of his unsuspecting victims added to the severity of the crime. The court meted down a sentence of 37 years and six months' imprisonment, and 24 strokes of the cane.

1.8 Summary

- Crime and crime management will always be a human-centric enterprise, as long as there are humans committing crime or humans enabling crime using technological or cyber means. Therefore, there will always be a role for psychology and the human sciences. On the other hand, the human sciences are not the only discipline relevant.
- Crime happens in a specific place and time, and is therefore contextual. Given that Singapore has been rated one of the safest places in the world, it is worth analyzing the Singaporean model of crime and criminal behavior.

- Crime is generally very low in Singapore. 'Low crime however does not mean no crime'. Commercial and Internet-related crimes such as scams are on the rise, as Singapore becomes increasingly technologically advanced.
- The major agencies dealing with crime, safety, and disorder are the Singapore Police Force, the Central Narcotics Bureau, the Singapore Prisons Service, the Immigrations and Checkpoints Authority, the Singapore Civil Defence Force, the Casino Regulatory Authority, The Internal Security Department, and the Corrupt Practices Investigation Bureau. The Attorney General's Chamber and the Courts are also major organisations within the criminal justice system. Supporting them are other agencies such as the Health Sciences Authority, the Institute of Mental Health, and the Ministry of Social and Family Development.
- There are several stages in crime processing — the crime is reported, then recorded, investigated, and prosecuted, before the offender is sentenced.
- There are several major theoretical angles to studying crimes. These can be categorized into *S*ituational, *M*acro-Sociological, *F*amily, *P*sychological and *B*iological approaches. They make up the mnemonic "SMFPB" ("Some men find psychology boring!").

Relevant Journals, Books and Resources

American Journal of Policing
Behavioural Sciences and the Law
British Journal of Criminology
Criminal Behaviour and Mental Health
Journal of Police And Criminal Psychology
Journal of Criminal Psychology
Journal of Forensic Sciences
Journal of Forensic Psychiatry
Journal of Forensic Psychiatry And Psychology
Journal of Interpersonal Violence
Journal of Law and Society
Law and Human Behaviour

Legal and Criminological Psychology
Journal of Police Crisis Negotiations
International Journal of Prisoner Health
International Journal of Forensic Mental Health
Probation Journal
Policing
Psychology, Crime And Law
Police Practice And Research
Policing: An International Journal Of Police Strategies And Management.
Sexual Abuse: A journal of sexual aggression
The Prison Journal
The Probation Journal
Stanley Yeo, Neil Morgan and Chan Wing Cheong. 'Criminal Law in Malaysia and Singapore', LexisNexis, 2nd ed., 2012.
S. Chandra Mohan. 'Understanding Criminal Law' (Cases, Comments and Materials. LexisNexis, 2014.
Chan, Yeo and Hor, 'Criminal Law for the 21st Century: A Model Code for Singapore'. Academy Publishing, 2013.

http://statutes.agc.gov.sg
http://www.singaporelawwatch.sg
http://www.singaporeblog.sg
Singapore Academy of Law Journal
Singapore Law Review
Singapore Journal of Legal Studies
Singapore Journal of International and Comparative Law
Singapore Law Blog http://www.singaporelawblog.sg/

Some Relevant Legislation

Penal Code (Cap. 224, Rev. Ed. 2008)
Criminal Procedure Code (Cap. 68, Rev. Ed. 2012)
Evidence Act (Cap. 97, Rev. Ed. 1997)
Misuse of Drugs Act
Prevention of Corruption Act

E-resources

Australasian Centre for Policing Research — http://www.acpr.gov.au/
American Board of Forensic Psychology. http://www.abfp.com/
American Society of Crime Laboratories Directors. http://www.ascld.org
Asian Forensic Sciences Network — http://asianforensic.net/board-member.html
Canadian Police College — http://www.cpc.gc.ca/home_e.htm
FBI Law Enforcement Bulletin
Law Net — http://www.lawnet.com.sg
National Institute of Justice (USA) http://www.ojp.usdoj.gov/nij/
Research Development and Statistics (UK) — http://www.homeoffice.gov.uk/rds/
Singapore Police Force Website http://www.spf.gov.sg/
Singapore Prisons Service Website http://www.sps.gov.sg/
Singapore Courts https://app.statecourts.gov.sg/subcourts/index.aspx

Some Relevant Legal Cases of Interest

Ngiam Chin Boon v PP [1999] 2 SLR[29] 119 (Actus Reus and Illegal omissions)
Abdul Razak bin Dalek v PP [2011] 2 MLJ[30] 237 (Actus Reus and Automatism)
PP v HlaWin [1995] 2 SLR 424, SGCA[31] (Mens Rea and Knowledge)
Madhavan Peter v PP [2012] 4 SLR 613 (Mens Rea and Recklessness)
Mohmad Iskandar in Basri v PP [2006] 4 SLR 440 (Mens Rea and Rashness)
Ng Keng Yong v PP [2004] SGHC[32] 171 (Mens Rea and Negligence)

Sample Research Paper Titles

- What are the sources of data for crime? What are the advantages and disadvantages of each?

---

[29] Singapore Law Reports.
[30] Malaysian Law Journal.
[31] Singapore Court of Appeal.
[32] Sinapore High Court.

- Is crime caused by nature or nurture?
- Design a research project to study the crime of housebreaking/car theft/molestation.

References

Adshead, G. (2016). *The Criminal Mind: The relationships between criminology and psychology.* Lecture at Museum of London, 7 June 2016.

Alkhatib, S. (2016, April 7). Death Penalty a powerful deterrent. *The Straits Times.*

Agnew, R. and Brezina, T. (2010). Strain theories. In *Sage Handbook of Criminological Theory.* Edited by Eugene McLaughlin and Tim Newburn. London: SAGE.

Andrews, D.A. and Bonta, J. (2010). *The Psychology of Criminal Conduct.* Albany, NY: Lexis Nexis. Anderson Publishing.

Ang, J., Diong, S.M., Misir, C., and Cheong, J. (2011). Operations psychology: The Singapore police experience. *Journal of Police and Criminal Psychology, 26*(2), 69–76.

Arseneault, L., Moffitt, T.E., Caspi, A., Taylor, P.J., and Silva, P.A. (2000). Mental disorders and violence in a total birth cohort. *Archives of General Psychiatry, 57*(10), 979.

Arboleda-Flórez, J. (2006). Forensic psychiatry: Contemporary scope, challenges and controversies. *World Psychiatry, 5*(2), 87–91.

Attorney General's Chamber (n.d.). *'Our roles'.* Retrieved from https://www.agc.gov.sg/our-roles/government-legal-advisor/overview-of-functions on 15 September 2017.

Aw, C.W. (2018, March 27). 'Police task force helps reduce online love scams'. *The Straits Times.*

Bank, L., Forgatch, M.S., Patterson, G.R., and Fetrow, R.A. (1993). Parenting practices of single mothers: Mediators of negative contextual factors. *Journal of Marriage and the Family, 55*(2), p. 371.

Batrinos, M.L. (2012). Testosterone and aggressive behavior in man. *International Journal of Endocrinology and Metabolism, 10*(3), 563–568.

Blackburn, R. (1994). *The Psychology of Criminal Conduct: Theory, Research and Practice.*

Brookman, F., Bennett, T., Hochstetler, A., and Copes, H. (2011). 'The Code of the Street' and the generation of street violence in the U.K. *European Journal of Criminology, 8*(1), 17–31.

Brookman, F. (2015). The shifting narratives of violent offenders. In L. Presser and S. Sandberg (Eds.), *Narrative Criminology: Understanding Stories of Crime.* (pp. 207–234). New York: New York University Press.

Campbell, M.A., French, S., and Gendreau, P. (2009). The prediction of violence in adult offenders: A meta-analytic comparison of instruments and methods of assessment. *Criminal Justice and Behavior, 36*, 567–590.

Canadian Superior Courts Judges Associations (CSCJA) (2006). *'About CSCJA'*. Retrieved from http://www.cscja-acjcs.ca on 14 June 2017.

Canter, D. (2008). *Criminal Psychology*. Hodder Education: London.

Casino Regulatory Authority (2015). *Annual Report 2015–2016*. Retrieved from http://www.cra.gov.sg/upload_files/cuteeditor/1/document/CRA%20 Annual%20Report%202015-2016.pdf on 22 Septermber 2017.

Central Narcotics Bureau (2017). *Drug Situation Report 2016*. Retrieved from https://www.cnb.gov.sg/drugsituationreport/drugsituationreport2016.aspx.

Central Narcotics Bureau (n.d.). 'Growing up drug free: guide your child away from harm'. Retrieved https://www.cnb.gov.sg/cnbpde/kids/downloads/default. aspx on 22 September 2017.

Chan, L.G. and Tomita, T. (2013). Forensic psychiatry in Singapore. *Asia-Pacific Psychiatry, 5*(4), 344–351.

Chu, C.M., Daffern, M., Thomas, S., and Lim, J.Y. (2012). Violence risk and gang affiliation in youth offenders: A recidivism study. *Psychology, Crime and Law, 18*(3), 299–315.

Chu, C.M., Daffern, M., Thomas, S., Ang. Y., Long, M., and O'Brien, K. (2015) Determinants of gang affiliation in Singaporean youth offenders: Social and familial factors, *Journal of Aggression, Conflict and Peace Research, 7*(1), 19–32.

Coomber, R., Donnermeyer, J.F., McElrath, K., and Scott, J. (2015). *Key Concepts in Crime And Society*. Los Angeles, CA: SAGE.

Copes, H., Hochstetler, A., and Williams, J.P. (2008). 'We weren't like no regular dope fiends': Negotiating hustler and crackhead identities. *Social Problems, 55*, 254–270.

Corey, D., Allen, S., Aumiller, G., Brewster, J., Cuttler, M., and Gupton, H. (2007). *Police Psychology Core Domains and Proficiencies: Definitions*. Prepared by the Joint Committee on Police Psychology Competencies; International Association of Chiefs of Police, Police Psychological Services Division, Society of Police and Criminal Psychology; American Psychological Association, Division 18, Police and Public Safety Section.

Correctional Research Compendium (2006). *Singapore Prisons Service*. Ministry of Home Affairs.

Cleckley, H.M. (1955). *The Mask of Sanity*. St. Louis: Mosby.

Davies, G.M. and Beech, A.R. (2012). *Forensic Psychology: Crime, Justice, Law, Interventions* (2nd ed.). Chichester, West Sussex: British Psychological Society. BPS Blackwell.

Driver, E.D. (1957). Pioneers in criminology XIV — Charles Buckman Goring (1870–1919). *Journal of Criminal Law, Criminology, and Police Science, 47*(5), 515–525.

Durrant, R. (2013). *An Introduction to Criminal Psychology*. New York, NY: Routledge.

Eysenck, H.J. and Gudjonsson H.G. (1989). *The Causes and Cures of Criminality*. New York, NY: Plenum Press.

Family Justice Courts, Singapore (n.d.). Retrieved from https://www.familyjustice courts.gov.sg/AboutFamilyJusticeCourts/Pages/Overview.aspx on 1 May 2018.

Farrington, D.P., Loeber, R., and Welsh, B.C. (2010). Longitudinal-experimental studies. In Piquero, A.R. and Weisburd, D. (Eds.). *Handbook of Quantitative Criminology* (pp. 503–518). New York: Springer.

Fergusson, D.M. and Horwood, L.J. (2000). Alcohol abuse and crime: A fixed-effects regression analysis. *Addiction, 95*(10), 1525–1536.

Feshbach, N.D. (1982). 'Empathy, empathy training and the regulation of aggression in elementary school children'. In R.M. Kaplan, VJ. Konecni and R. Novaco (Eds.), *Aggression in Children And Youth*. Alphen den Rijn. The Netherlands: Sythoffl Noordhoff International Publishers.

Foundation for a Drug Free World (n.d). 'What is Alcohol?' Retrieved from http://www.drugfreeworld.org/drugfacts/alcohol.html on 18 September 2017.

Glueck, S. and Glueck, E. (1959). *Predicting Delinquency and Crime*. Harvard University Press.

Goring, C. (1913). *The English Convict: A Statistical Study*. London: HMSO.

Groth, A.N., Hobson, W.F., and Gry, T.S. (1982). The child molester, clinical observations. In Conte, J. and Shore, D. (Eds.). *Social Work and Child Sexual Abuse*. New York, NY: Harworth

Giancola P.R., Helton, E.L, Osborne, A.B., Terry, M.K, Fuss, A.M., and Westerfield (2002). The effects of alcohol and provocation on aggressive behavior in men and women. *Journal of Studies on Alcohol, 63*(1): 64–73.

Giancola, P.R., Josephs, R.A., Parrott, D.J., and Duke, A.A. (2010). Alcohol myopia revisited: Clarifying aggression and other acts of disinhibition through a distorted lens. *Perspectives on Psychological Science, 5*(3), 265–278.

Gunn, J. and Bonn, J. (1971). Criminality and violence in epileptic prisoners. *The British Journal of Psychiatry, 118*(544), 337–343.

Gwee, K. (2017). Psychology and psychiatry in Singapore courts: A baseline survey of the mental health landscape in the legal arena. *International Journal of Law and Psychiatry, 52,* 44–54.

Hare, R.D. (1980). A research scale for the assessment of psychopathy in criminal populations. *Personality and Individual Differences, 1*(2), 111–119.

Hare, R.D. (2003). *The Hare Psychopathy Checklist-Revised*. North Tonawanda, NY: Multi-Health Systems.

Hare, R.D. and Neumaan, C.S. (2010). Psychopathy and Forensic implications. In Malatesti, L. and McMillan, J. (Eds.) (2010). *Responsibility and Psychopathy: Interfacing Law, Psychiatry And Philosophy* (pp. 93–123). New York, NY: Oxford University Press.

Harty, S.D., Shaw, J., and Thomas, S., (2004). The security, clinical and social needs in high security psychiatric hospitals in England. *Journal of Forensic Psychiatry and Psychology, 15*, 208–221.

Health Sciences Authority (n.d.). *Applied Sciences: Overview*. Retrieved from http:// www.hsa.gov.sg/content/hsa/en/Applied_Sciences/Toxicology/ Overview. html on 23 January 2018.

Herrnstein, R.J. and Murray, C.A. (1994). *The Bell Curve: Intelligence and Class Structure in American Life*. New York: Free Press.

Hill, D. and Pond, D.A. (1952). Reflections on 100 capital CASE submitted for electroencephalography. *Journal of Mental Science, 98*, pp. 23–43.

Hirschi, T. (1969). *Causes of Delinquency*. Berkeley: University of California Press.

Hollin, C.R. (1992). *Criminal Behaviour: A Psychological Approach to Explanation and Prevention*. London, The Falmer Press.

Hollin, C.R. (2013). *Psychology and Crime: An Introduction to Criminological Psychology*. (2nd ed.). London: Routledge.

Jobling, M.A and Gill, P. (2004) Encoded evidence: DNA in forensic analysis. *National Review of Genetics, 5*(10): 739–751.

Joint Report by the United Nations Office on Drugs and Crime and the Latin America and the Caribbean Region of the World Bank (2007). *Crime, Violence, and Development: Trends, Costs, and Policy Options in the Caribbean*. Report No. 37820. March 2007.

Joyce, P. (2012). *Criminology: A Complete Introduction*. London: Hodder and Strouhgton.

Khader, M., Ang, J., Maan, D.S., Li, P.L., Min, T.S., A., J., and Fen, H.H. (2011). Police Psychology in Singapore: The Red Dot Experience. *Journal of Police and Criminal Psychology, 27*(1), 24–32.

Khader, M., Ang, J., Koh, C.W., Diong S.M., Koh, M., Poh, L.L., and Tan, C. (2007). 'Organisational health in the police: A 3-R approach'. Chapter 6. *Work Stress and Coping Among Professionals,* 85–100. Social Sciences in Asia Series. Brill Publications.

Klenowski, P.M., Copes, H., and Mullins, C.W. (2011). Gender, identity, and accounts: How white collar offenders do gender when making sense of their crimes. *Justice Quarterly, 28*, 46–69.

Kok, L.P., Cheng, M., and Chee, K., T. (1990). *Diminished Responsibility: With Special Reference to Singapore.* Singapore University Press.

Kok, L.P., Cheng, M., and Chee, K., T. (1994). *Mental Disorders and the Law.* Singapore University Press.

Lange, J.S. (1931). *Crime as Destiny.* London: Allen and Unwin.

Lee, H.L. (2017, April 3rd). 'A passion for fairness and justice'. *The Straits Times.*

Leo, T.H.S. (n.d.). Current evidence-based practices in the Singapore prison service. Retrieved http://www.unafei.or.jp/english/pdf/RS_No88/No88 on 14 March 2017.

Lersch, K.M. (2007). *Space, Time, And Crime.* Durham, NC: Carolina Academic Press.

Mednick, S.A., Gabrielli, W.F., and Hutchings, B. (1984). Genetic influences in criminal convictions: evidence from an adoption cohort. *Science, 224,* 891–894.

Mumola, C.J. (n.d.). *Substance Abuse and Treatment, State And Federal Prisoners,* 1997. PsycEXTRA Dataset.

Muncie, J. and McLaughlin, E. (Eds.). (2001). *The Problem of Crime.* SAGE Publications.

Moffitt, T.E. (1993). Adolescence-Limited and Life-Course Persistent Antisocial Behavior: A Developmental Taxonomy. *Psychological Review,* 100: 674–701.

Ng, K. (2017, October 2017). 'Penalties for crime must reflect public opinion: Shanmugam.' *Today.* Retrieved from http://www.todayonline.com/singapore/penalties-crime-must-reflect-public-opinion-shanmugam.

Office of the Surgeon General (2001). *Youth Violence: A Report of the Surgeon General.* Washington, DC: U.S. Department of Health and Human Services, Office of the Secretary, Office of Public Health and Science, Office of the Surgeon General. Retrieved from www.surgeongeneral.gov/library/youthviolence.

Ornstein, T.J., Iddon, J.L., Baldacchino, A.M., Sahakian, B.J., London, M., Everitt, B.J., and Robbins, T.W. (2000). Profiles of cognitive dysfunction in chronic amphetamine and heroin abusers. *Neuropsychopharmacology, 23*(2), 113–126.

Osborn, S.G. and West, D.J. (1979). Conviction records of fathers and sons compared. *British Journal of Criminology, 19,* 120–133.

Koh, B.S. (2016). *Our Guardians.* Straits Times Press.

Pope, H.G., Kouri, E.M., and Hudson, J.I. (2000). Effects of supraphysiologic doses of testosterone on mood and aggression in normal Men: A randomized controlled trial. *Archives of General Psychiatry, 57*(2), 133–140.

Resick, P.A. and Markaway, B.E.G. (1991). 'Clinical treatment of adult female victims of sexual assault'. In Hollin, C.R. (2013). *Psychology and Crime: An Introduction to Criminological Psychology.* (2nd ed.). London: Routledge.

Rutter, M. (1971). Parent-Child Separation: Psychological Effects on The Children. *Journal of Child Psychology and Psychiatry*, *12*(4), 233–260.

Rutter, M. (1987). Psychosocial resilience and protective mechanisms. *American Journal of Orthopsychiatry*, *57*(3), 316–331.

Rowe, D.C. and Osgood, D.W. (1984). Heredity and sociological theories of delinquency: A reconsideration. *American Sociological Review*, *49*(4), 526.

Sandberg, S. (2009). Gangster victim or both? The inter-discursive construction of sameness and difference in self-presentations. *British Journal of Sociology*, *60*, 523–542.

Sandberg, S. (2013). Are self-narratives strategic or determined, unified or fragmented? Reading Breivik's Manifesto in light of narrative criminology. *Acta Sociologica*, *56*, 69–83.

Sarason, J.G. (1968) Verbal learning, modeling, and juvenile delinquency. *American Psychologist*, *23*, 254–266.

Sense about Science (2017). '*Making Sense of Forensic Genetics*'. EuroForGen. Retrieved from http://senseaboutscience.org/wp-content/uploads/2017/01/making-sense-of-forensic-genetics.pdf on 12 December 2017.

Scott, J.C., Woods, S.P., Matt, G.E., Meyer, R.A., Heaton, R.K., Atkinson, J.H., and Grant, I. (2007). Neurocognitive effects of methamphetamine: A critical review and meta-analysis. *Neuropsychology Review*, *17*(3), 275–297.

Singapore Association of Women's Lawyers (2014). *Teens and the Law*.

Singapore Statues Online (2000). *Prisons Act*. Retrieved from http://statutes.agc. gov.sg.

Singapore Statutes Online (2001). Children and young persons Act. Retrieved from http://statutes.agc.gov.sg.

Subordinate Courts of Singapore (1998). 'Typology of youth rioters'. *Research Bulletin*, 10. Retrieved 5 April 2009, from http://app2.subcourts.gov.sg/Data/ Files/File/Research/RB10 Pg1-8.pdf and http://app2.subcourts.gov. sg/ Data/Files/File/Research/RB10Pg9-16.pdf.

Substance Abuse and Mental Health Services Administration (2011). Substances. Retrieved from https://store.samhsa.gov/substances.

Sutherland, E.H. and Cressey, D.R. (1974). *Principles of Criminology*. Chicago: Lippincott.

Siegel, L.J. (2010). *Criminology: Theories, Patterns, Typologies*. Singapore, SG: Wadsworth.

Tam, K.Y.B. and Heng, M. (2006). 'What provokes young people to get into trouble'. *Correctional Research Compendium*, Singapore Prisons Service. Ministry of Home Affairs.

Tan, T.M. (2017, April 27). More young people have liberal attitude towards drugs: Survey. *The Straits Times.* Retrieved http://www.straitstimes.com/singapore/courtscrime/more-young-people-have-liberal-attitude-towards-drugs-survey.

Tan, T.M. (2018, February 6). 'Nearly two thirds of new drug abusers under 30'. *The Straits Times.*

Tan, T.M. (2018, February 7). Criminal detention without trial still a potent weapon'. *The Straits Times.*

Tan, T.M. (2018, February 9). Fewer illegals caught but smuggling on the rise: ICA. *The Straits Times.*

The Corrupt Practices Investigation Bureau (2016). *Annual Report.* Retrieved from https://www.cpib.gov.sg/sites/cpibv2/files/CPIB_Annual%20Report_2016.pdf on 22th September 2017.

The Economist (2017). *Safe City Index.* Retrieved from http://safecities.economist.com/safe-cities-index-2017-interactive-tool on 26th October 2017.

The Subordinate Courts of Singapore (2010). 'Philosophy of Restorative Justice Model'. Retrieved from http://app.subcourts.gov.sg/juvenile/page.aspx?pageid=3854

Tok, L. and Turnbull, H. (2015). *Know the Law.* The Law Society of Singapore.

Virkkunen, M., Goldman, D., and Linnoila, M. (1996). Serotonin in alcoholic violent offenders. In Bock, G.R., and Goode, J.A. (Eds.), *Genetics Of Criminal And Antisocial Behaviour* (pp. 168–177). Chichester, UK: Wiley.

Wilson, D.B., Catherine A.G, and Doris L.M. (2000). A meta-analysis of corrections based education, vocation, and work programs for adult offenders. *Journal of Research in Crime and Delinquency, 37*(4), 347–368.

Weigend, T. (1988). The legal and practical problems posed by the difference between criminal law and administrative penal law. *Revue Internationale de Droit Pénal, 59,* 67–86.

Wells, S., Graham, K., and West, P. (2000). Alcohol-related aggression in the general population. *Journal of Studies on Alcohol, 61*(4), 626–632. doi:10.15288/jsa.2000.61.626.

Winfree, L.T. and Abadinsky, H. (2003). *Understanding Crime: Theory and Practice.* Belmont, CA: Wadsworth/Thomson Learning.

Woon, W. (2017). The public prosecutor, politics and the rule of law. *The Straits Times.* September 29, 2017.

UNODC (2007). *Crime, Violence and Development: Trends, Costs and Policy Options in the Carribean.* Report by United Nations Office on Drugs and Crime and the Latin America and Carribean Region of the World Bank.

Wu, G. (2013). 'What does it feel like to be part of a criminal gang?' *Quora*. Retrieved from https://www.quora.com/What-does-it-feel-like-to-be-part-of a- criminal-gang.

Yeo, S.M., Morgan, N.A., and Chan, W.C. (2015). *Criminal law in Malaysia and Singapore*. Singapore: LexisNexis.

Young, J. (2011). *The Criminological Imagination*. Cambridge: Polity Press.

CHAPTER 2

DECEPTION AND THE DETECTION OF DECEPTION

"Deception can cost billions. Think Enron, Madoff, the mortgage crisis. Or in the case of double agents and traitors, like Robert Hanssen or Aldrich Ames, lies can betray our country. They can compromise our security."

Pamela Meyer
Author of *Liespotting: Proven Techniques to Detect Deception*

2.1 Introduction

Deception surrounds our lives. Most of us have been fooled at some point in our lives. Some of us have been good deceivers. Much of this deception is part of fun and do not cause serious damage to our lives or to society. Think about deception in the games we play, during parties or in sports matches. These small lies or deceptions are not seriously destructive. It is the harmful and damaging falsehoods such as infidelity, cheating, stealing, fraud, sports fraud, impersonation, criminal acts, and terrorism, that cause us worry.

This chapter is about deception and how to become a better lie detector. Read the following case study to get started.

CASE STUDY:
The Charming Wife Killer

Tony Yap attended the wake of his estranged wife, Tannie Lim Shu Min. She had died in Tan Tock Seng Hospital of knife wounds she suffered a few hours before. She had been stabbed multiple times outside the lift by a teenager. This happened on the fourth-floor of the block of flats where she was living with her mother and her four-year-old daughter.

The newspapers carried a photo of Tony kneeling beside his wife's coffin at the wake crying, a regretful husband who had lost his wife. Tony admitted being a bad husband. Yes, he had several affairs, "fouled up" their marriage, gambled at the races, was arrogant and an "unlikeable" person. "She was everything I was not," he said. "She's the angel; I am the devil." He insisted that despite their issues, they still shared a beautiful relationship. He said he did not care that he was a possible suspect in his wife's death. Just before she was stabbed, he had met her at the void deck of Block 923 at Hougang Avenue 9. She had gone up to get a pen to sign

(*Continued*)

(Continued)

certain documents he had brought, he said. He was, he insisted, innocent and was not involved with her death. He did not know who killed her right after she left him. He was being framed, he pleaded. He wondered, if he had done things differently, would she have lived? "What if I did not ask her down? What if I had brought a pen? What if I had gone up with her? A thousand 'what-ifs', but one reality, she's gone."

It was all a big deception act.

Tony, a 30-year-old insurance agent, dangled a reward of $100,000 for someone to kill his wife. The couple were in the midst of divorce proceedings. A 15-year-old boy whom Yap had known for five years took up the offer to kill Tannie. Tony coached his accomplice on how to execute the deed, taunted him when he tried to back out of it, and finally forced him to go through with it, threatening to kill him if he backed out.

He advised the boy on using a red handkerchief to hide the blood-stained knife, so that the bloodstains wouldn't be noticeable. Use a knife that is easily hidden in your clothes, he said. Not too large that it couldn't be hidden and not too small because it wouldn't reach the heart. He also told the boy not to run but to walk calmly when he saw the police, as running would arouse suspicion. Don't leave any cigarette butts on the floor, he reminded, since the police might be able to use forensics to trace the person involved. All in all, Tony was a master deceiver.

With Tannie's death, Tony stood to gain sole possession of their $480,000 Pasir Ris matrimonial flat and custody of their four-year-old daughter from her death. When he was caught and charged for the murder of his wife, and when he took the stand in court to give evidence, he smiled. As he walked out of court he was beaming and looked charming. He seemed to enjoy this new fame.

THINKING POINT
What methods of deception did Tony use? How did he hide his deception?

2.1.1 *Defining Deception*

What is deception? Lying? Withholding the truth?

Professor Aldert Vrij at the University of Portsmouth, U.K., described deception as a "situation when someone intentionally does or says something in order to induce a false belief in someone else" (Vrij, 2000). A similar definition by Zukerman and colleagues is that deception is seen as "as an act that is intended to foster in another person a belief or understanding, which the deliverer considers to be false" (Zuckerman *et al.*, 1981). Professor Elizabeth B. Ford from the Ellevue Hospital Center, Department of Forensic Psychiatry, New York, details four levels of deception (Mitchell, 1986):

- *Level 1 deception* is the most basic form, and appearance. She explains that an organism may be deceptive in its colouring or shape; however, it cannot manipulate when, where, how, or even what deceptive measures it uses. An example would be the sexually deceptive flowers which use their appearance to attract bees and wasps for pollination.
- *Level 2 deception* involves more coordination since the organism or animal can deceive when certain situations arise and can trigger the deceptive manoeuvre. An example of this would be the anglerfish which has a worm-like structure projecting from its head simulating a worm and attracts the anglerfish's prey.
- *Level 3 deception* is where an organism deceives in a certain situation, if they have learned in the past that a manoeuvre yields a particular response in the 'deceived'. Professor Ford mentions the dog that fakes a broken leg in order to get more food or attention. However, she asks if this is an equivalent of lying or representative of conditioned learning. Perhaps the dog does not consider what the owner is thinking to manipulate him or her.
- *Level 4 deception,* or 'intentional deception', is referred to as 'lying'. It involves an organism's ability to perceive or think about the other's reactions or beliefs, and then manipulate those beliefs with one's behavior or speech.

There are several features involved in deception. First, there must be a deliberate attempt to lie either by withholding information or fabricating it. If you *unconsciously* deceived someone (because you did not know something or believed it yourself), that is not deception in a true sense. Intention to deceive and *mens reas* may not have been there (see Chapter 1 for more information on *mens reas*). Second, this is done to others, knowing that they are not aware that they are being deceived. Third, there is no forewarning of the deception that is taking place (when magicians lie/deceive us, for example, we expect it). Fourth, lying does not have to be verbal, and it may be non-verbal (e.g., a fake injury during a football game) or even symbolic (using an item or image to mislead someone, for example, pretending to be a police officer by wearing a police cap). Fifth, deception does not always result in a bad outcome. People sometimes lie to others to make others feel better or to keep harmony. Much of the small everyday lies fall into this category. When someone compliments another, for example, on their dress or hairdo when they do not mean it.

Taking all of these factors into consideration, Professor Aldert Vrij redefined his original definition into another one: deception is "a successful or unsuccessful deliberate attempt, without forewarning, to create in another a belief, which the communicator considers to be untrue" (Vrij, 2008, p. 15).

2.1.2 *How Frequently Does Deception Occur?*

Deception is measured by several methods: (a) asking people to report how many lies they have told, (b) giving participants scenarios and asking them if they would lie or not, and (c) arranging a 10-minute 'get-acquainted' role-play situation where people meet for the first time and noting down how many times they lie. Each of these methods has its limitations (refer to the mantras on 'bad data' and 'no data' in Chapter 1), but would nonetheless yield useful results. The collective findings of this research have been fascinating. People seem to lie more frequently and prevalently than we would expect! It is not a rare form of behaviour at all. Tyler *et al.* (2006), for example, found that in 10-minute 'get-acquainted' conversations, people lied 2.18 times! Most respondents (78%) lied during these 10-minute conversations. People lied mostly about their achievements, personal skills, and finances, and put on a show for others to present their best self. Other informal surveys showed that people often lied about their partner's sexual ability and the Christmas present they received as well (Vrij, 2008). In what is called 'diary studies' where people are asked to diary down their lies, it is found that undergraduates lied two times a day, while community members did it once a day (DePaulo *et al.*, 1996). Participants lied to 34% of all persons they met over the week, and people typically lied more about their feelings, attitudes, and opinions, and less about their plans and actions. More self-serving lies were told (50%) when compared to other-oriented lies (25%).

Is this surprising to you? It should not be, since we may not want to spill our feelings to the people we meet at work or in other settings. Participants who were involved in this study felt that the lies they told were not dangerous, nor did they cause personal distress or resulted in significant life consequences. These everyday lies are quite different from lying to the police about a criminal act or lying about smuggling drugs across the border checkpoints! Will we see different lying rates in the latter situation?

2.1.3 *Types of Lies*

There are lies and there are lies. 'White lies' are lies in everyday social situations that are said to reduce interpersonal conflicts between people (i.e., saying to someone that they look nice in the new dress, when you do not really think so). 'Intentionally self-serving lies' are lies told to evade personal responsibility and serve one's own benefit (contrast this with white lies, which are said to make others feel good). 'Lying by commission' is the fabricating of information. This is active deceit. 'Lying by omission', on the other hand, means lying by leaving out information or giving half-truths. You probably remember situations where people have lied to you but when you asked about it, they said, "Well you didn't ask about that, and so I didn't tell you". Lies have also been classified into *self-oriented* and *other-oriented lies* (DePaulo *et al.*, 1996). *Self-oriented lies* are those told for the deceiver's benefit, and *other-oriented lie*s are those told with the aim of benefiting someone else. False flattery is an example of an altruistic, other-oriented lie (for example, "Oh, you look so nice in that pretty dress, Whistine!") Some would argue that all lies (self or other-oriented) are self-oriented because even flattery (which appears other-oriented) is designed to gain benefit for oneself. Test your skills in Table 2.1.

Table 2.1: Examples of Self and Other-Oriented Lies (Instructions: Place a Tick on the Column You Think is the Right Answer)

Statement	Self-oriented	Other-oriented
1 I lied because I did not want him to know (I wanted some privacy)		
2 After sex, I told my husband that I enjoyed it (did not want to hurt his feelings)		
3 I told her that she was fun-looking even though she was not. (To make her feel positive about herself)		
4 I told Mom I had been studying hard (my mum will kill me if she knew the truth!)		
5 Told my son to clean up the room and get ready for the weekend because we may have visitors (just wanted him to clean up the room!)		

Source: Adapted from DePaulo *et al.*, (1998). Everyday lies in close and casual relationships. *Journal of Personality and Social Psychology*, 74(1), 63–79.

2.1.4 *Deception and Demographic Differences*

Men versus women

Who tells more lies: men or women? Well, they tell different *kinds* of lies. Men, for example, use *self-oriented lies*, such as "I work out often", or 'I just came back from working out at the gym", while women, on the other hand, use *other-oriented lies*, and usually to other women ("nice dress!" and "nice hairstyle"). It has been found that men lie more frequently than women, about their earnings and earning potential. Women, on the other hand, engage in deceptive acts to improve their physical appearance, such as sucking in their stomach (DePaulo *et al.*, 1993).

Group level versus individual level deception

Dr Zarah Vernham and colleagues at the University of Portsmouth, U.K., (Vernham *et al.*, 2016) argued that group offenders differed from individual ones. First, group co-offenders were younger (Van Mastrigt and Farrington, 2009), practised more strategic lying (Cohen *et al.*, 2009), reported more self-interest, and had fewer concerns about using deception in comparison to individual offenders. Dr. Zarah and her team mentioned that there are specific crimes (such as organized crime, terrorism, drug trafficking, burglary, and arson) that involve group level deception, and these are often organized and syndicated crimes. There are also multiple investigative settings (e.g., immigration, airport security, border control, and police stop and search) that are more likely to involve groups of offenders as opposed to lone offenders (Carrington, 2002), and this needs to be examined further in future research. Furthermore, the interviewing of groups brings a different dynamic to the interview process and police will need to decide whether to talk to group members individually or collectively. Collective interviewing allows for interaction cues to be examined, and these cues cannot emerge when interviewing a lone individual or when individually interviewing group members about a joint crime. The researchers also argued that one can determine deception at a social level as well as at an individual level. Finally, she explained that when multiple people need to be questioned, each member loses some control over how the other members behave. Therefore, they have to 'impression manage' others (i.e., attempt to regulate, predict, and control what others might say). This suggests that the strategies employed with groups will differ from those used with individuals.

2.1.5 *Deception by Crime Type*

While there is little research on 'Detection of Deception or DOD by crime types', most investigators who work long enough in any field of crime appreciate that deception may differ by crime-type. For example, housebreakers might walk around houses and have a method of scanning houses to see if anyone is at home. During this scan, they may also assess which room has the most valuables kept. They might also assess the fastest method of entry and the quickest way of escape after they have stolen their goods. When they sell the goods they have stolen, they also probably use a script to explain how they obtained the goods or why they are selling these goods away, if asked. In the U.K., for example, some housebreakers have developed what the police have called the 'Da Pinchi Code'. These look like meaningless symbols daubed on walls or pavements. They are, however, a 'code' for crooks, giving potential housebreakers details about the building, such as whether it is a good target or has an alarm, or has been targeted before successfully. 'X' is a sign of a good target, while five small circles is a sign of a wealthy target (Paterson, 2015). In the same way, deception patterns may differ by other crimes. As a thought exercise, attempt to decipher some of the DOD techniques used for the crimes shown below in Table 2.2.

Table 2.2: Do Different Types of Criminals Differ in the Types of Deception?

Crime type	Pre-offence deception	During offence	Post offence
House breakers	E.g., Looking through house	E.g., Pretending to look for someone who lives there	E.g., Selling the stolen goods at pawn shops
Child sex molesters			
'Sex for Credit' perpetrators			
Loan Sharks			
Love Scam perpetrators			
Shop theft at a 24-hour store			

2.1.6 *Deception in Psychiatric Patients*

Most patients with mental illness do not feign their illness. Some, however, do. 'Malingering' is the intentional production of false or exaggerated physical or psychological symptoms, motivated by external incentives (Ford, 2006). These could include avoiding military duty, full time national-service duty, or just avoiding work. Ford estimates the prevalence of malingering among U.S. mental health patients to be around 1% in civilian clinical practice, and 5% is the military context. Malingering could be seen in inconsistencies in a patient's story in reporting symptoms, inconsistencies in psychological testing results as compared to actual or observed performance, and inconsistencies in reporting how actual symptoms present. Professor Ford (2006) explained that, from her experience working in an emergency medical setting, malingerers will often talk about auditory command hallucinations,[1] hallucinations suggesting that they hurt themselves as a presenting symptom. She explained that this seems excessive, since in a retrospective chart review of 789 psychiatric inpatients in New York City from 1979 to 1980, (from the research of Hellerstein *et al.*, 1987), only 38.4% of those who experienced auditory hallucinations actually reported commands! She stated that the somatic features of real major depression such as a wrinkled brow, psychomotor slowing, constipation, and a stooped, forward posture, are more difficult to fake and less frequently chosen as malingered symptoms. It is generally assumed that malingerers overact their faked illnesses and are more eager to talk about their symptoms than patients with actual mental illness. They show more '*positive*'[2] than '*negative*' psychotic symptoms, and have trouble imitating a psychotic thought process. The most frequently malingered symptoms appear to be auditory hallucinations, amnesia, conversion symptoms, and delusions.

---

[1] '*Command hallucinations*' are auditory hallucinations that instruct the patient to act in a certain manner. They order the patient to perform various actions such as making facial expressions, to those as serious as suicidal or homicidal acts.

[2] Examples of '*positive psychiatric symptoms*' are hallucinations (seeing, hearing, or smelling things that are not really there), delusions (belief in ideas not based on reality), disorganized speech (loose association between ideas, saying odd sentences, incoherence, illogical statements, excessive detail), and or bizarre behaviour. Examples of '*negative psychiatric symptoms*' are social withdrawal, decreased motivation, poor speech (brief replies), inability to experience pleasure (anhedonia), limited emotional expression, and poor attention control.

2.2 Why Do People Lie?

There are many reasons why people lie. In older published research, Turner *et al.* (1975) mentioned five motivations including: (a) to save face, (b) to manage relationships, (c) to exploit, (d) to avoid tension/conflict, and (e) to control situations. However, it seems the main motivations are to serve their self-interest and self-promotion. To tell the truth may mean that they may lose their jobs or marriages! Another reason for lying is 'social', and social lies are told to avoid awkward situations. If someone asked, for example, if you liked their Chinese New Year 'red packet' they gave you (consisting of two dollars), you might tell a lie (and say "yes, thank you"), to avoid an awkward situation. Then, there are there lies that are told to keep things private. People sometimes lie to protect others. In the Bill Clinton scandal, where he had a sexual relationship with a White House intern, he told a lie about this relationship on national television. He was, however, sincere in his disclosure, saying that he had lied to protect his family, wife, and children from embarrassment. Another reason for lying is for secondary gain, such as avoiding full-time national service duty or military duty,[3] or gaining the attention of a loved one. In an interesting cross-cultural study of deception motives, Levine *et al.* (2016) asked participants from Egypt, Guatemala, Pakistan, Saudi Arabia, and the U.S. open-ended questions describing an instance of deception. They found that across cultures, personal transgressions motivated the largest number of reported lies (21.5%), and this was followed by economic advantage (15%), non-economic advantage for self (14.7%), and avoidance (14.4). Interesting, they found that the level of social lies/white lies were remarkably small (they were higher in other American studies), but the authors mentioned that this is probably because these lies were likely go undetected, and some respondents may not consider them deceptive at all.

---

[3] Novelist Joseph Heller coined the term in his novel Catch-22, which described absurd constraints on World War II soldiers. The army psychiatrist invoked 'Catch 22' to explain why a pilot requesting mental fitness evaluation for insanity — (hoping to be found insane and hence cannot fly and will thereby escape dangerous war missions), and this demonstrates his own sanity/mental fitness.

2.3 Why Are People Poor Lie Detectors?

One of the most surprising findings has been that people are poor lie detectors! This includes professional "lie catchers" such as police officers. In my own studies in Singapore testing people to see how good they are in detecting lies, I have tested students, police officers, and other professionals, showing videos of people lying or telling the truth. I found that most people got it right about 50% to 55% of the time, and this is almost like a flip of a coin! (i.e., if you flipped a coin, sometimes you would get it right and sometimes you did not!). This is not surprising as other studies in the world have found the same result. Professor Mike Aamodt and Heather Mitchell published meta-analysis[4] findings of many studies looking at lie detecting accuracy rates in a journal called *Forensic Examiner* in 2005. They demonstrated that most groups were 50% to 60% accurate (see Table 2.3). The results indicated that confidence of the rater (i.e., how confident they felt in their lie detection skills) ($r = .05$, $K = 58$, $N = 6,315$), age ($r = -.03$, $K = 72$, $N = 2,025$), experience ($r = -.08$, $K = 13$, $N = 1,163$), education ($r = .03$, $K = 4$, $N = 522$), and sex ($d = -.03$, $K = 53$, $N = 6,023$) were not related to accuracy in detecting deception. Their study also found that 'professional lie catchers' as a group (such as police officers, detectives, judges, and psychologists) were not more accurate ($M = 55.51\%$, $N = 2,685$) at detecting deception than students and other citizens ($M = 54.22\%$, $N = 11,647$). Why might this be the case? Read on to find out more.

Why *are* people such poor lie detectors? Professor Aldert Vrij explained that there are several main reasons for our poor lie detection skills. This was published in an interesting paper titled *Pitfalls and Opportunities in Nonverbal and Verbal Lie Detection*. First, people are not motivated to detect lies in the first place. The truth can be difficult to handle. Some couples in difficult marriages, for example, do not want to know if their partners are cheating,[5] perhaps because the truth

---

[4] A meta-analysis is a statistical analysis that combines the results of multiple scientific studies, looking for effects of a particular treatment or program.

[5] Someone once told me that she always suspected that her husband was cheating on her but felt there was nothing she could do. They had been married for 20 over the

Table 2.3: Are Professionals Better at Detecting Deception than Students?

Group	Studies/Groups	N	Accuracy %
Teachers	1	20	70
Social workers	1	20	66.25
Criminals	1	52	65.40
Secret Service Agents	1	34	64.12
Psychologists	4	508	61.56
Judges	2	194	59.01
Police Officers	12	655	55.30
Customs Officers	3	123	55.30
Federal Officers	4	341	54.40
Students	156	11,647	54.22
Detectives	7	758	50.80
Parole Officer	1	32	40.2
TOTAL	193	14,379	54.50

Source: Adapted from Who Can Best Catch a Liar? Aamodt, Michael G; Custer, Heather; *Forensic Examiner*, Spring 2006; 15, 1; SciTech Premium Collection.

is hard to handle, or perhaps there are practical issues (i.e., a separation may be bad for the children). Second, some people are exquisite liars and so, it is hard to detect their lies! And these include those whose natural behaviours (natural performers) create honest impressions, those who do not find it difficult to tell a lie, those who do not exhibit emotions such as fear, guilt, or delight when they are lying, and those who take delight in duping others! Third, our ideas about lying behaviors are wrong. Most of us think that liars turn their eyes away, which is really not true. In an interesting paper about global beliefs about lying, the Global Deception Research Team in 2007 found the following: "we uncovered a pan-cultural stereotype: that liars avoid eye contact (with other people). This view was expressed in every one

---

years and had two children. Confronting him might mean that he may walk away from the marriage and the kids. So she never did confront him.

of the 75 countries we studied." The authors argued that most people across the world believed erroneously that because liars should feel ashamed, they should show signs of hiding, withdrawal, and submission. This was, of course, not true all of the time. Gaze aversion is not a reliable indicator of deception. Some liars show this, and some truth tellers show it as well; so, in terms of being a *reliable* indicator (like a thermometer that always reads the same temperature consistently when someone has a fever), it fails to be a reliable indicator. We want a thermometer which always reliably reads the temperature right. Sometimes we do not detect lies because we confuse it with nervous behaviour. Nervousness, on the other hand, is not guilt. This is called the '*Othello error*'.[6] Nervousness upon accusation however is common, and not a sign of guilt or deceit!

2.4 Approaches to Understanding Deception

There are three main approaches in explaining deception according to Vrij (2000). For easy remembering, we can refer to them as the 'A-C-E' approaches: Attempted behaviour control, Cognitive complexity approach), and Emotion approach theory (Vrij, 2000).

- *Attempted Behavioural Control Hypothesis*: The explanation here is that liars realize that observers pay attention to their behaviors and thus over-control their behavior. That is, they try not to look like they are lying (Buller and Burgoon, 1996). However, this is not easy, as some behaviour is beyond our own self-control (e.g., angry feelings results in narrowing of lips involuntarily).
- *Cognitive Complexity Hypothesis*: The idea here is that lying takes mental effort, increases mental load, and makes cognitive processes complex. Lying can result in complex thinking because it is hard to

---

[6] Othello was the Shakespearean hero who married a woman of beauty and nobility. His lack of self-esteem was exploited by a villain, who insinuates that his wife Desdemona is unfaithful because she shows nervous behaviour. When she is unfairly accused, she panics and shows more anxious and nervous behaviour, and Othello feels he is right! Othello finally murders his beloved wife.

lie consistently, since you have to remember all the small details (i.e., the lies you told about time, place, people, actions, etc.) You will get caught if you are inconsistent. People who engage in cognitively complex tasks tend to blink less, have more speech hesitations and errors, speak slower, pause more, and wait longer. This 'thinking on the spot' results in rigidness. Do you remember the time when you were a student, and the teacher picked on you to answer a question? Unless you knew the material really well, you probably panicked and stiffened up. You had to think and there was a 'load' on your cognition. In this instance, you were not lying but if you had to think, you pause, hesitate, and stiffen up. The logic is the same since with a made-up situation such as a lie, you have to think on your feet. That is exactly how this works.

- *Emotional Approach*: The idea here is that lying is linked to guilt, fear, or delight. Guilt then results in gaze-aversion, fear results in physiological arousal and eye-blinks, self-adaptors (touching clothes, hair, face), speech hesitation, errors, and omissions. The delight is a *'duping delight'*, which is a quick thin flash of a smile because of a delight that you are getting away with a lie.

2.5 Techniques for Detecting of Deception (DOD)

We often want to detect the lies (especially the ones that impact our lives) because we need to know who to trust in our lives. It is a survival instinct. For the professional lie catcher, it is a part of their jobs. So, over the years, many techniques have developed. Some are reliable and others not so. Most of these techniques work by establishing a behavior baseline pattern (e.g., a baseline for bodily movement and a baseline for heart rates or baseline for voice patterns), and then a comparison is made between the behavior pattern (during the lying segment or episode) and the baseline. Differences in these comparisons may suggest that *something* is going on (maybe it is a sensitive topic, maybe something that he/she is concerned about and wants to hide, or maybe perhaps just familiarity with the issue?) A difference does not have to mean deception. With these mind, here are some examples of DOD, which exist in the world today.

Handwriting analysis or graphology

Graphologists look at the pressure, rhythm, size, slant, shape, and distribution of the writing on the page (McNichol, 1994). It was the view that indicators of dishonesty may be "wedged writing that looks like a saw tooth, inconsistent form in the writing style, oval-shaped letters that are written upside down, and segmented letters" (Ford, 2006). This sounds exotic but there is no strong research to support the claims of graphologists. Newer scientific based techniques relying on Forensic Linguistics have emerged in recent times. Interested readers should read up on this area. In the U.K., for example, Cardif University offers a MA Course in Forensic Linguistics.

Verbal techniques

A related area is verbal techniques, which refers to the words, phrases, and sentences, and the spoken language people use when they speak or write. Experts have found that there is a difference in verbal language between liars and truth tellers. Liars as a group (compared to truth-tellers) tended to use more pauses, a slightly higher pitched voice, less plausible answers, lowered response length of replies (length of answer and number of spoken words is less), and more negative statements (i.e., statements indicating aversion towards an object, person, or opinion, such as denials, disparaging comments, and negative mood) (Vrij, 2008).

Polygraph

Polygraphs measure physiological reaction.[7] The modern polygraph measures: (a) palm sweating (galvanic skin response), (b) cardiovascular activity (systolic and diastolic blood pressure, measured using cuff on arm, much like the usual blood pressure machines), and (c) breathing (measured by sensors around the chest). The assumption is that liars will experience an autonomic response,[8] which is then measured by a

---

[7] Calling it a 'lie detector' is technically misleading, since it does not do that. It detects physiological responses.

[8] The autonomic nervous system controls internal body processes such as blood pressure, heart and breathing rates, body temperature, digestion, metabolism (thus

polygraph machine. The American Polygraph Association quotes an accuracy rate of 85% to 95% when done by a trained examiner (Steinbrook, 1992). The most widely used polygraph techniques include the 'Control Question Test/comparison Test' (CQT), and the 'Guilty Knowledge Test' (GKT). A discussion of these are beyond the scope of this book, and interested readers should look this up.

Critics have argued that since the polygraph measures physiological response, factors such as interview fatigue, drunkenness, drug use, blood pressure rates (high and low), feeble-mindedness, mental health conditions, lack of fear or concern at being caught in a lie, and the use of antiperspirants can affect the results of the instrument. Interpretation can be challenging, although not impossible (Vrij, 2000). Its effectiveness also relies heavily on good questions and good interviewing techniques (because the questions are the triggering stimulus which is used to provoke a response).

This issue of polygraph use is controversial, but a good investigator knows the limitations of the polygraph in the same way that a good medical physician will know the limitations of his/her thermometer or a stethoscope. Even if the instrument were to be inaccurate for some patients some time, this does not render it totally useless. There is a need to know what the readings mean, when they are not accurate, and what medical conditions affect their accuracy. It is not about the tool but *how* it is used by the toolmaster. The polygraph does have its utility as an investigative aid, even though the results may not be accepted as legal evidence in most courts (Vrij, 2000).

Voice stress analysis (VSA)

VSA is a technique that has been used to measure the stress in one's voice and then by comparing the stress points of the voice with

---

affecting body weight), production of body fluids (saliva, sweat, and tears), urination and defecation, and sexual response. These are controlled by either the sympathetic or the parasympathetic division. The sympathetic division prepares the body for stressful or emergency situations — fight or flight and it increases heart rate and widens (dilates) the airways to make breathing easier. This division also causes palms to sweat, pupils to dilate, and hair to stand on end (Merck Manual, n.d.).

baseline voice measures. The proponents argue that the recorder can pick up differences, which may suggest stress. This is based on detection of laryngeal microtremors movements that indicate deception (Horvath, 1982). However, tremors may not imply deception (Ford, 2006).

Nacro-analysis

Although rarely used today, nacro-analysis has been called the "truth serum". The techniques involve the injection of sodium pentothal into the subject. The person then becomes drowsy and disinhibited, and then discloses the details of the crime/s he committed. Experts describe how military organisations in the West have tried cannabis, mescaline ("Project Chatter"), stimulants and barbiturates ("Twilight Zone"), and lysergic acid diethylamide (LSD) ("Operation Artichoke") (see Bowden, 2003; Lee, 2002). These techniques, however, induce mental suggestibility, which results in inaccuracies, and participants being misled to saying things that they do not mean, and can be coerced to say things that they did not do.

Psychological testing of malingering and deception

A commonly used test is the Structured Interview of Reported Symptoms (SIRS/SIRS2) (Lewis *et al.*, 2002). The SIRS is an interview designed to detect malingering and other forms of feigning of psychiatric symptoms. The SIRS has well-documented accuracy rates (Gothard *et al.*, 1995; Linblad, 1994; Norris & May, 1998; Rogers *et al.*, 1991).

Brain fingerprinting (BF) and the P300 Brain wave technique

The P300 is a brain wave, which some researchers have argued, may be indicative of deception. According to Dr. Farewell, the main proponent of brain fingerprinting (BF), BF "detects concealed information stored in the brain by measuring brainwaves" (Farwell, 2001: 32). The idea is that BF could detect a specific electroencephalogram (EEG) event-related potential called the P300-MERMER, as a response to words/pictures relevant to a crime scene, terrorist training, or bomb-making knowledge. Farewell argued that laboratory and field tests at the Federal Bureau of Investigation (FBI), Central Intelligence Agency (CIA), and the U.S. Navy have resulted in 0% errors and that 100% of correct determinations. This technique, however, has not been independently validated. There has been no independent evaluation. Ford (2006) argued that despite its promise, it is impossible to gauge whether this technique has reached the level of 'general acceptance' in the scientific community because the technique is patented, and therefore not available for analysis. Meijer *et al.* (2012) strongly argued that Farewell's conclusions on the findings of his studies were misleading and misrepresented the scientific status of brain fingerprinting technology.

Thermal imaging (TI)

A promising new development, thermography, involves using an infrared thermal imaging camera to measure facial skin temperature as a cue to deception. The idea is that a liar experiences stress which activates the autonomic nervous system, which then activates the sympathetic nervous system responsible for increased blood flow to the eyes to facilitate rapid eye movement, in preparing the body for the fight-or-flight response. This increased blood flow is detectable in the periorbital region of the face through thermal imaging. An advantage of using thermal imaging is that it is non-invasive. In a 2013 Korean study by Professor Kevin Park and colleagues from the Clinical Neuro-psychology Lab, Chung-Ang University, South Korea, results from a mocked-up laboratory-based study showed that measuring facial temperatures in the periorbital region using thermal imaging was able to differentiate the guilty participants from the non-guilty ones (Park *et al.*, 2013).

Functional magnetic imaging or fMRI

This technique involves the measurement of neutral patterns during cognitive activities. The argument here is that neural activity is different when someone is lying. fMRI studies show an increase in prefrontal cortex activity during lying. The prefrontal cortex has been implicated in planning, complex cognitive behaviour, personality expression, decision-making, and moderating social behavior (Miller *et al.*, 2002). This seems to be consistent with the earlier idea discussed that lying increases cognitive load. The big challenge with these kinds of studies is that the fMRI machine costs a lot of money, and is large and difficult to manevoure. While promising, Porter and Brinke (2010) explained that there are still insufficient published studies which have examined brain function during deception. Therefore, there is a need to be cautious when using this technology in legal settings to prosecute individuals, as there are large individual differences in brain function and no clear brain regions associated with lying.

Using micro-facial expressions

Professor Paul Ekman described 'microexpressions', or facial expressions that last for only a fraction of a second (Ekman & Friesen, 1971) can be used in detecting deception. The problem with this approach is that it requires intensive training to master this skill, since these expressions occur within micro-seconds. People can also control their gaze or look, and smiling skills. They can alter their expressions by 'masking' (replacing a felt emotion with a false one), 'neutralising' (inhibiting a true emotion by appearing neutral), or 'simulating' (expressing an unfelt emotion) (Vrij, 2008). With the advent of newer vision technology which can auto-detect emotions, there may be future promise. There is already available software, but they appear to be in the early stages of development, and are unable to differentiate between the many different types of emotions, which can be expressed facially.

Using bodily cues or body language

There is suggestion that bodily cues can be useful mainly because it is easily trained and cheaper than other techniques of DOD. However, bodily cues may be more detectable in *low-stakes liars*, rather than high-stakes ones. Results show that low-stakes liars show a *decrease*, rather than an increase, in movement during deception. Vrij (2000) argued that liars as a group show less hand/finger movements and leg movement than truth-tellers do. This seems counter-intuitive. We tend to expect more gaze aversion and more fidgety behaviours in liars. The opposite, however, is seen in studies. As a whole, however, liars may appear more rigid, stiff, or over-controlled than usual (when compared with their own baselines of behaviour) for the reasons earlier explained.[9]

In Singapore, a research conducted by the Home Team Behavioural Sciences Centre, and published by Stephanie Chan and colleagues in 2015, showed that liars (as compared to truth tellers) had less hand/finger movement and more head movement. The main caveat to these kinds of studies is that many of these studies have been done with low-stakes liars, and these findings may not be true for high-stakes liars (see Porter and Brinke, 2010). Porter and Brinke argued that for high-stake liars there could be an increase in self-manipulators (e.g., touching their heads).

RESEARCH OF INTEREST
Can We Be Trained to Detect Deception?

It may be possible to enhance detection skills with training. According to Dr. Koller and her colleagues, criminals display non-verbal behaviour that observers can use to recognize hidden hostile criminal intentions (i.e., acting naturally, inconspicuously).

In their article, the team showed that university students, police recruits, inexperienced police officers (POs) and experienced POs, as well as criminal investigators were all able to detect thieves based on their behaviour *before* they committed the crime.

They found that these groups could correctly identify thieves at 'above chance' level from CCTV footages from 50 seconds, before the real theft cases occurred. Furthermore, the higher detection rate and earlier detection by both groups of experienced and inexperienced

(Continued)

---

[9] Remember that these are averaged/group-based findings of liars (versus truth tellers), so there may be *individual differences* within each group. That is, some individual liars *will* use gaze-aversion and some will fidget.

(Continued)

police officers, as compared to students and recruits, suggest theoretical training improves detection performance, regardless of experience. Only investigators outperformed inexperienced POs, despite having been on the job for approximately as long as experienced POs, possibly due to more specialized training and experience in this area of interpreting behaviour during the build-up phase before the criminal act. These findings were also attributed to investigators having greater knowledge of the thieves' *modus operandi* (MO) than the inexperienced POs, and inexperienced POs compared to students and recruits. Understanding the MO, and thus how criminals usually behave while preparing for their crime, allowed them to recognize behaviour patterns that differed from normal behaviours in the given scene.

Source: Koller, C. I., Wetter, O. E., & Hofer, F. (2015). 'Who's the Thief?' The Influence of Knowledge and Experience on Early Detection of Criminal Intentions. *Applied Cognitive Psychology*, 30(2), 178–187.

2.6 Practical Recommendations to Improve the Detecting of Deception (TOOLKIT)

2.6.1 *Systems Solutions to Better Detect Deception*

1. *Ensure organizational processes are designed to detect deception.*
It is easy to forget that people work for organizations. If you want people in an organization to detect deception, ensure that their organizational human resources and performance systems are designed to encourage detection. No matter how well you train enforcement officers, if systems and processes do not encourage lie-detection, accuracy rates will be lower. In one episode (at an international law enforcement agency), a ground operator informed that his immediate supervisor had hinted to him not to detect more cases for the day, because he had to leave early for Thanksgiving Dinner. Needless to say, cases were lower for that day, and there were fewer hits that evening. Organizations should therefore think carefully about the key performance indicators (KPIs) they set for their staff. Once detection

'quotas' were met, frontline operators did not bother staying alert. The point being made here is that supervisors need to think carefully about how to motivate behaviors. In another case, when the organization rewarded detection skills through rewards and recognition schemes, several officers were motivated to be very accurate in their lie-detection skills. Officers felt proud of their performance and personal records. Another common practice is to deploy more officers during peak periods and allow more officers to take a break during non-peak hours. Good liars, however, know this and take advantage of this predictability, often smuggling or carrying dangerous weapons during non-peak times. One good practice, therefore, is for organizations to be unpredictable in their deployment, with a view to detect more. For example, there are 'schedule randomizers' available today, which can create random schedules to reduce predictability, and hopefully enhance detection.

2. *Look at how technological and automated systems can complement human systems to detect deception.*

Detecting deception is not any different from other forms of signal detection. There is, however, a limit to what humans can detect. Humans face fatigue, have poor situational awareness, and deal with information overload. One idea around this is to consider the use of automated computer systems to detect deception. For example, humans may find micro-expressions occurring at 1/25th of a second difficult to pick up. An automated machine, however, might be able to decode these expressions quickly. With today's technology, where even basic digital cameras are able to detect faces and decode emotions, the use of cameras to detect micro-expressions may be possible. It may also be possible in the future to detect rigidities in bodily movements and changes that an individual shows in bodily cues (compared to behaviour baselines) using cameras. These systems may also be used for detecting unusual body movements at particular places of interest (e.g., at train stations, bus stops, venues). Investing in DOD technologies (both hard and 'soft'/behavioral technology) makes sense. However, validating the accuracy and viability of these technologies is equally important.

3. *Culturally informed DOD techniques needed.*

Investigators believe that there are cultural differences in deceptive cues between Western suspects and Asian suspects as well. They contend that there are differences within Asian cultures (e.g., Singaporeans, Chinese, Indians, Thais, Filipinos, Japanese, etc). If this is true, it means that culturally nuanced DOD techniques are needed. More studies are needed in this area. Culture certainly plays a role in other fields of study. For example, negotiation experts approach business negotiation differently with different cultures (Adair & Brett, 2004). While there are individual differences, studies have suggested that people from Western cultures in general tend to have independent, individualistic perspectives, and they understand themselves as being independent from their social groups to which they belong. They may prioritize personal goals over social obligations. People from Eastern cultures tend to have interdependent and collectivist approaches. They tend to understand themselves within the context of the social groups to which they belong, and view themselves as agents constrained by social obligations to maintain harmony and preserve 'face' (Marcus & Kitayama, 1991). This affects the way they negotiate. We also know that counselling, as a discipline, has benefited from multicultural perspectives. Hence, the field of DOD can benefit from culturally-informed perspectives. Investigators must, however, assess how much a person is influenced by his or her cultural values and beliefs in order to determine if a culture-based approach can be used.

4. *Conduct studies on the differences of deception patterns crime types.*

While there are generalities in deception cues, there are likely to be subtle differences by crime type. In murder cases, for instance, we see deception in 'staging', disposable of bodies, and disposal of murder weapons. In terrorism crimes, we see deception in the use of false identities, safe houses, and encryption in emails. In white collar crimes, we see deception in the accounts and books. In scams, we see deception in the form of love scam grooming, and in child sexual crimes, we see the grooming of children. All of these suggest that the nature, type, and scale of deception vary according to the type of crime, although there can be similarities. It is useful to conduct research on the types and variations of deceptive patterns within each crime type.

5. *Conduct more research into the 'cognitive lie detection' technique.*

Recent findings converge towards the notion that a 'cognitive approach' to lie detection works best. The cognitive approach consists of three techniques: (1) imposing cognitive load, (2) encouraging interviewees to speak more, and (3) asking unexpected questions (Vrij *et al.*, 2017). Imposing cognitive load is done by many ways, including asking interviewees to tell their stories in a reverse manner, by instructing interviewees to maintain eye contact, or forced turn-taking when two or more interviewees are being questioned (the interviewer determines who answers). Encouraging interviewees to provide more information is done in several ways. For instance, a supportive interviewer helps the interviewee to speak more through head-nodding and acknowledgement during the interview. Another way is for the interviewer to provide an example of a very detailed 'model answer' to the question and then asking the interviewee to provide a similar detailed answer. Also, interviewees can be asked to provide detailed drawings and finally, using the cognitive interview helps to encourage more information. Asking unexpected questions is clever way of using the cognitive lie detection method. The idea here is that since interviewees anticipate certain questions and prepare for them, the interviewer should ask unanticipated questions. Some examples of unanticipated questions could be questions around how he/she planned the event, temporal questions, or spatial questions (for example, being asked to sketch the place he visited).

Vrij *et al.* (2017) compared the cognitive approach with the standard approach of lie detection, and they found that the cognitive lie detection approach produced far better results. Results showed that there were better results in truth detection (67%), lie detection (67%), and total detection (71%) for both truth and lie detection. This was compared with the standard approach, which was 57% for truth detection, 47% lie detection, and 56% total detection. Vrij *et al.* (2017) qualifies that the cognitive lie detection works using verbal cues. That is, the interviewee must talk. Therefore, an information-gathering approach (as opposed to an accusatory approach) is definitely preferred, since it encourages talking. The stereotypical view sometimes seen in interviewing manuals, which assumes that suspects do not talk (see approach by Inbau *et al.*, 2013) and therefore require an accusatory approach, is erroneous. A better approach would be a rapport-building approach. For example, FBI interviewer Ali Soufan (Soufan, 2011) used an information-gathering approach to obtain rich information about Al-Qaeda. Instead of accusing, he obtained this information by building rapport, truth-seeking, and listening.

2.6.2 *Enhancing Personal Lie-Detection Skills During Interview*

The earlier section was about broader methods of enhancing lie detection. This section is now about how you can become a better lie detector. One method of remembering the tips listed below is the acronym "BAD-QUE"; imagine yourself being in bad queue line! BAD-QUE stands for:

B: Get a *B*aseline;
A: *A*nalyze verbal and non-verbal cues of deception together;
D: *D*etails — ask for more details;
Q: *Q*uestioning style — change and vary it;
U: *U*nanticipated questions; and
E: Use of *E*vidence strategically.

1. *Read the Baseline behaviour and compare behavior of interest against baseline.*
To detect deception, you must have a baseline of behavior, (verbal or non-verbal/body language or physiological cues). This baseline behavior could vary person to person and can be anything idiosyncratic to the person (e.g., foot movement, pen twirling, hand gestures, eye blinking, and so on). Find a way to capture the baseline of an individual, when he or she is relaxed. The best lie detectors use small talk before talking about something relevant to the crime itself (ask about previous school, favourite drink, work, family, etc.). Then ask

about the crime or act and observe the same behaviour again. Is there a difference? Then watch if he shows mental load or a reduction in body movements.

2. *Analyze a combination of non-verbal cues and verbal cues rather than individual cues.*

Verbal and non-verbal cues provide more data than relying on just one set of cues (Vrij, 2008). Relevant verbal cues elicited may support and be consistent or inconsistent with the non-verbal cues. When these cues are not consistent with each other, it may suggest that there is a need to relook your hypothesis that he or she may be lying. If they are consistent, you may be on to something. This "something" may not be deceit or lying *per se*. Treat it as a 'hot' issue, which is provoking a response, and explore it further with more questioning. You should be careful not to be oppressive in your questioning as from a legal angle, evidence obtained by oppressive questioning will be challenged in court.

3. *Ask for more Details and probe for more.*

Adopt an information gathering interviewing style when asking for details. Asking for details on what happened allows you to detect inconsistencies, when information is relayed to you. Remember that to tell lies is not exactly an easy task for the lie-teller, because when you ask for more details, the liar will need to provide more information and each piece of information can be cross-checked later and verified to see if it is true or not. If he says, for example, that he was at the fast food restaurant at Junction '6' Mall, then you could ask more details. Which entrance? Which table at the restaurant? How many people were there when you were there? What food did you eat, and so on? Liars may need to stay consistent on their replies. Furthermore, asking the person to draw out a map or sketch of where they were might also be useful, as research has found that liars would find it difficult to sketch a place they have never been to.

4. *Change the Questioning sequence.*

Ask the person to repeat the information. Liars will have to ensure that they repeat the same information accurately and with great detail. Ask another person to ask the suspect to tell the story to see if the same story, in the same order with the same details being repeated. Ask the suspect to tell the story in reverse order to see if the details are rightly captured. Remember that a truthful person will be able to tell the story in reverse order because he/she recalls a true incident in a reversed manner. A liar, however, will experience cognitive load and find this task difficult to do.

5. *Ask Unanticipated questions and methods.*
Liars often prepare themselves before interviews. They anticipate questions. So, to pick up their deception, it is useful to ask them unanticipated questions (e.g., asking them to draw, role play, etc.) The idea behind this is that truth-tellers will draw on their memory, while liars will not be able to.

6. *Consider strategic use of Evidence (SUE).*
SUE is a technique of withholding and not sharing the evidence you have on the suspect until later (when it is required legally) and asking specific questions about them (Granhag & Hartwig, 2008). This provides a better basis for assessing veracity in early interview situations. When suspects are unaware of the evidence against them, guilty and innocent suspects may act differently. Innocent suspects, for example, would provide details, say that they were at the crime scene (although they did not do the crime) and may not hold back information. They feel no reason to hold back information. Liars (as a group) may avoid providing details relating to the crime event, and even contradict the evidence. They do not want to incriminate themselves. Thus, liars usually provide fewer details than truth-tellers.

2.7 Summary

To conclude this chapter, several points are worth repeating:

- Lying is commonplace and we all do it. We are concerned, however, with the lies that affect our lives. Despite this, we are not good at lie detection for various reasons.
- There are many tools that are being developed for deception detection, and most rely on comparisons made between 'baseline

measurements' and measurements that are triggered by good questioning or some kind of stimuli presented. These differences may indicate that something is going on, not necessarily a lie. Investigators could follow up on these "hot topics", or issues, to find out more.

- Even if a DOD technique shows promise, it may or may not be used for legal purposes. There are several issues here. First, there is the question of whether there is a strong evidence base backing the technique. Second, even if there is a solid scientific evidence base, does the community of scientists agree and is there 'general acceptance' that it is a valid technique? Third, even if there were scientific agreement among prominent scientists, would the criminal justice system accept the technique as suitable for legal purposes? There are serious life and death implications for techniques used for legal purposes, since an individual's life and freedom are at stake.

- There is much room for more research on deception by culture and crime types.

  One method of remembering the tips listed below is the acronym "BAD-QUE". Imagine yourself being in bad queue line queuing for food! BAD-QUE stands for:

  B: Get a *B*aseline;

  A: *A*nalyze verbal and non-verbal cues of deception together;

  D: *D*etails — ask for more details;

  Q: *Q*uestioning style — change and vary it;

  U: *U*nanticipated questions; and

  E: Use of *E*vidence strategically.

Relevant Journals

Journal of Investigative Psychology and Offender Profiling

Journal of Applied Research in Memory and Cognition

Legal and Criminological Psychology

Law and Human Behaviour

Psychology, Crime and Law

Crime Psychology Review

Psychology, Public Policy, and Law

Journal of Police and Criminal Psychology

Journal of Credibility Assessment and Witness Psychology

Useful E-resources

Portsmouth Research Portal: Professor Aldert Vrij. https://researchportal.port.ac.uk/portal/en/persons/aldert-vrij(59be97be-c7bd-4f9b-a07d-c1c40e0eef88)/projects.html
Professor Bella DePaulo Blog. http://www.belladepaulo.com/deceptionpubs.htm
Professor Paul Ekman. https://www.paulekman.com
Pamela Meyer TED Talk. https://www.ted.com/talks/pamela_meyer_how_to_spot_a_liar

Sample Research Paper Titles

1. What are the main processes involved in lying?
2. How can we design a lie detection training program for police officers?
3. If you are asked to detect deception in young offenders involved in drug abuse, how would you go about doing it?
4. The Commissioner of Immigrations has asked you to develop a detection of deception system for fradulent travellers. How would you go about developing a training program for these border control officers?

References

Adair, W.L. and Brett, J.M. (2004). Culture and negotiation processes. In M. J. Gelfand and J.M. Brett (Eds.), *The Handbook of Negotiation and Culture* (pp. 158–176). California: Stanford.

Bowden, M. (2003, October). The dark art of interrogation. *The Atlantic Monthly*, 51–76.

Carroll, M.F. (2003). Malingering in the military. *Psychiatric Annals, 33*(11), 732–736.

Chan, S., Khader, M., Ang, J., Chin, J., and Chai, W. (2015). To behave like a liar: Nonverbal cues to deception in an Asian sample. *Journal of Police and Criminal Psychology, 31*(3), 165–172.

Cohen T.R., Gunia B.C., Kim-Jun S.Y., and Murnighan J.K. (2009). Do groups lie more than individuals? Honesty and deception as a function of strategic self-interest. *Journal of Experimental Social Psychology, 45*(6), 1321–1324.

Depaulo, B.M., Epstein, J.A., and Wyer, M.M. (1993). Sex differences in lying: How women and men deal with the dilemma of deceit (126–147). In M. Lewis and C. Saarni (Eds.), *Lying and Deception in Everyday Life*. New York: Guilford Press.

DePaulo, B.M., Kashy, D.A., Kirkendol, S., Wyer, M.M., and Epstein, J.A. (1996). Lying in everyday life. *Journal of Personality and Social Psychology*, 70(5), 979–995.

Ekman, P. and Friesen, W.V. (1971). "Constants across cultures in the face and emotion." (PDF). *Journal of Personality and Social Psychology*, 17, 124–129.

Farwell, L.A. and Smith, S.S. (2001). Using brain MERMER testing to detect knowledge despite efforts to conceal. *Journal of Forensic Science*, 46(1), 135–143.

Ford, E.B. (2006). Lie detection: Historical, neuropsychiatric and legal dimensions. *International Journal of Law and Psychiatry*, 29, 159–177.

Gothard, S., Viglione, D.J., Jr., Meloy, J.R., and Sherman, M. (1995). Detection of malingering in competency to stand trial evaluations. *Law and Human Behaviour*, 19(5), 493–505.

Granhag, P.A. and Hartwig, M. (2008). A new theoretical perspective on deception detection: On the psychology of instrumental mind-reading. *Psychology, Crime and Law*, 14(3), 189–200.

Grubin, D. and Madsen, L. (2005). Lie detection and the polygraph: A historical review. *British Journal of Forensic Psychiatry and Psychology*, 16, 357–369.

Hellerstein, D., Frosch,W., and Koenigsberg, H.W. (1987). The clinical significance of command hallucinations. *The American Journal of Psychiatry*, 144(2), 219–225.

Horvath, F. (1982). Detecting deception: The promise and the reality of voice stress analysis. *Journal of Forensic Sciences*, 27(2), 340–351.

Inbau, F.E., Reid, J.E., Buckley, J.P., and Jayne, B.C. (2013). *Criminal Interrogations and Confessions*. (5th Ed). Burington, MA: Jones and Bartlett Learning.

Junginger, J. (1990). Predicting compliance with command hallucinations. *American Journal of Psychiatry*, 147, 245–247.

Koller, C.I., Wetter, O.E., and Hofer, F. (2015). Who's the thief? The influence of knowledge and experience on early detection of criminal intentions. *Applied Cognitive Psychology*, 30(2), 178–187.

Lee, T.M.C., Liu, H., Tan, L., Chan, C.C.H., Mahankali, S., Feng, C., *et al.* (2002). Lie detection by functional magnetic resonance imaging. *Human Brain Mapping*, 15, 157–164.

Levine, T., Vaqas A., Mohamed, D., Marleah, A.A., Rasha, G., and Karina. (2016). Toward a pan-cultural typology of deception motives. *Journal of Intercultural Communication Research*, 45, 1–12.

Lewis, J.L., Simcox, A.M., and Berry, D.T. (2002). Screening for feigned psychiatric symptoms in a forensic sample by using the MMPI-2 and the structured inventory of malingered symptomatology. *Psychological Assessment*, *14*(2), 170–176.

Marcus, H.R. and Kitayama, S. (1991). Culture and the self: Implications for cognition, emotion and motivation. *Psychological Review*, *98*(2), 224–253.

Meijer E.H., Ben-Shakhar G., Verschuere B., and Donchin E. (2012). A comment on farwell (2012): Brain fingerprinting: A comprehensive tutorial review of detection of concealed information with event-related brain potentials. *Cognitive Neurodynamics*, *7*(2), 115–154.

Merck Manual (n.d). *Overview of the autonomic nervous system*. Retrived http://www.merckmanuals.com/en-pr/home/brain,-spinal-cord,-and-nervedisorders/autonomic-nervous-system-disorders/overview-of-the-autonomicnervous-system on 4 October 2017.

Miller, E.K., Freedman, D.J., and Wallis, J.D. (2002). The prefrontal cortex: Categories, concepts and cognition. *Philosophical Transactions of the Royal Society of London. Series B, Biological Sciences*, *357*(1424), 1123–1136.

Mitchell, R.W. (1986). A framework for discussing deception. In R. W. Mitchell and N.S. Thompson (Eds.), *Deception, Perspectives on Human and Nonhuman Deceit* (pp. 3–31). New York, NY: SUNY Press.

Mitchell, R.W. and Thompson, N.S. (1993). Familiarity and the rarity of deception: Two theories and their relevance to play between dogs (*Canis familiaris*) and humans (*Homo sapiens*). *Journal of Comparative Psychology*, *107*(3), 291–300.

Park, K.K., Suk, H., Hwang, H., and Lee, J.H. (2013). A functional analysis of deception detection of a mock crime using infrared thermal imaging and the Concealed Information Test. *Frontiers in Human Neuroscience*, *7*(7), 1–11.

Paterson, P. (2015, 16 April). 'X marks the spot... for Da Pinchi Code thieves: Police release list of symbols burglars daub on walls to help identify easy targets'. *Scottish Daily Mail*.

Porter, S. and Brinke, L. (2010). The truth about lies: What works in detecting high-stakes deception? *Legal and Criminological Psychology*, *15*(1), 57–75.

Resnick, P.J. (1999). The detection of malingered psychosis. *Psychiatric Clinics of North America*, *22*(1), 159–172.

Rogers, R., Gillis, J.R., Bagby, R.M., and Monteiro, E. (1991). Detection of malingering on the Structured Interview of Reported Symptoms (SIRS): A study of coached and uncoached simulators. *Psychological Assessment*, *3*, 673–677.

Soufan, A.H. (2011). *The Black Banners: The Inside Story On 911 And the War Against Al-Qaeda*. New York: NY: W.W. Norton.

Steinbrook, R. (1992). The polygraph test — A flawed diagnostic method. *New England Journal of Medicine*, *327*(2), 122–123.

The Global Deception Research Team: A world of lies (2006). *Journal of Cross Cultural Psychology, 37*(1): 60–74.

Turner, R.E., Edgley, C., and Olmstead, G. (1975). Information control in conversations: Honesty is not always the best policy. *Kansas Journal of Sociology, 11*, 69–89.

Tyler, J.M., Feldman, R.S., and Reichert, A. (2006). The price of deceptive behavior: Disliking and lying to people who lie to us. *Journal of Experimental Social Psychology, 42*(1), 69–77.

Van Mastrigt, S.B. and Farrington, D.P. (2009). Co-offending, age, gender and crime type: Implications for criminal justice policy. *The British Journal of Criminology, 49*(4), 552–573.

Vernham, Z., Granhag. P.A., and Mac Giolla, E. (2016). Detecting deception within small groups: A literature review. *Frontiers in Psychology, 7*, 1, 1–14.

Vrij, A. (2000). *Detecting Lies and Deceit: The Psychology of Lying and the Implications for Professional Practice*. Wiley: Chichester.

Vrij, A. (2008). *Detecting Lies and Deceit: Pitfalls and Opportunities* (2nd ed.). Chichester: John Wiley and Sons.

Vrij, A., Fisher, R.P., and Blank, H. (2017). A cognitive approach o lie detection: A meta-analysis. *Legal and Criminological Psychology, 22*, 1–21.

Vrij A., Granhag, P.A., and Porter, S. (2010). Pitfalls and opportunities in nonverbal and verbal lie detection. *Psychological Science in the Public Interest, 11*(3), 89–121.

Zuckerman, M., DePaulo, B.M., and Rosenthal, R. (1986). Humans as deceivers and lie detectors. In P.D. Blanck, R. Buck, and R. Rosenthal (Eds.), *Nonverbal Communication in The Clinical Context* (pp. 13–35). University Park: Pennsylvania State University Press.

CHAPTER 3
CRIMINAL PROFILING

"All persons are puzzles, until at last we find in some work or act the key to the man, to the woman: straightaway all their past works and actions lie in light before us."

Ralph Waldo Emerson

3.1 Introduction

'Criminal profiling' has drawn some flak in recent years. There have been many negative comments in scientific papers about it, saying that it does not work. Many law enforcement organizations in the world today therefore use alternative terms, such as 'behavior analysis', to describe what is essentially still criminal profiling. Whether scientists are comfortable with it or not, criminal profiling is conducted by many law enforcement agencies today, mainly because it is a useful heuristic tool. The bad press of profiling today, however, is the result of the problem of racial profiling, and because some of the profiles generated have turned out to be inaccurate. We should not, however, completely reject profiling because of some bad cases. That is like throwing away the 'baby with the bathwater'. Just because it did not work some of the time does not mean that it will not work all the time. So, we have to understand the potential and the limitations of profiling when we use it.

Is profiling something esoteric in any way? We *all* actually profile others to some degree. It is a survival instinct. We try to figure out our potential life partners, our bosses, our colleagues, our business clients, our future employees, our politicians, and our neighbors. We want to know who they are, what they value, and if they can be trusted. We also want to know whom we cannot trust, and who might be threatening to our families and our loved ones. We cannot achieve perfection in our profiling, but the process is still useful. Likewise, for a law enforcer, profiling the offender just makes good sense. It makes detection, rapport building, interviewing, and cooperation easier. The important thing is to learn to do it right and work towards establishing its effectiveness. Look at the scenarios in Table 3.1 and draft your 'profiles'.

Table 3.1: Profiling in Everyday Life (Activity)

Scenario	Draft a brief profile (what characteristics?)
1. How would you recognise whether your neighbour is a potential extremist? What would you be concerned about?	
2. You attend a recruitment interview for a job you are interested in. How would you profile the culture and climate of the organisation?	
3. You suspect your partner is a potential abuser (physical abuser). What telltale signs are you looking for?	

As you draft this profile, think about the pros and cons of profiling. What are the limitations? When can profiling become problematic? When can you get it wrong?

3.2 Who Are Profilers?

Profilers come from varying backgrounds and have had various kinds of training. Some have been psychologists, criminologists, forensic psychiatrists, academics, and police officers (Copson, 1995). However, the problem today is that there is no accredited professional certification to become a profiler, and this means that there are very varying standards in the way profiling is done. This is one of the reasons why profiling has drawn criticisms.

How can one learn to profile better? If you are a police officer looking to develop profiling skills, you could learn profiling from senior investigative profilers, sign up for profiling courses at police academies (e.g., the FBI Academy), or take specialized courses in investigative or forensic psychology. You could also take courses in criminology. It is worth noting that leaders of profiling units have noted that the best police profilers are those who have learnt to avoid common stereotypes seen in police investigations and learnt to think broadly about the human and behavioural sciences (e.g., rapport building, motivation, stress, mental disorders, etc.). That is, the best police profilers do not think about the crimes using police instincts alone; they are good critical thinkers and 'para-scientists'. Psychologists who wish to conduct criminal profiling could also take advanced courses in criminology or the police sciences, or Master's level courses on forensic or investigative psychology and then collaborate with police officers, such that knowledge from both fields could be combined to generate better profiling practices.

3.3 What Is Criminal Profiling?

In its early days, criminal profiling was defined as a wide variety of techniques whereby information gathered at a *crime scene* was used to infer *motivation* for an offence, and to produce a description of the *type of person* likely to be responsible (Davies, 1992). The Federal Bureau of Investigation (or FBI) defined it as a technique for identifying the major personality, behavioral, and demographic characteristics of an offender based on an analysis of the crimes committed (Douglas *et al.*, 1986). In other words, it involved looking at the crime scene and thinking about who the offender was. Fortunately, things have changed a lot these days, and profiling is no longer just a game of 'whodunit', but also about understanding the crime.

In this book, profiling is defined as an investigative and operational support technique, where information is analyzed using a multidisciplinary approach to infer the behavioral and mental characteristics of offenders and the 'behavioral correlates' involved in a crime type with the purpose of providing recommendations for crime prevention, detection, investigation, and rehabilitation.

There are several differences between this and the earlier definition. First, unlike how criminal profiling is portrayed in Hollywood films, the profiler does not 'catch' the perpetrator. It is the investigator or the detective who is responsible for arresting and bringing in the criminal. The profiler plays an *investigative supportive role*, providing scientifically defensible advice to aid in the investigation. Second, we may use profiles beyond an investigative context, such as in operational contexts, e.g., in immigration settings. Third, profiles are interpreted using knowledge from multiple fields of study, and not just from a single field such as psychology. Criminology, the forensic sciences, the law, and other disciplines are involved. It is multidisciplinary and inter-disciplinary. Fourth, profiles are correlates between variables. These variables are associated. This means that there could be a close relationship between some variables in crime, e.g., paedophiles tend to work at places with access to children. However, this does not mean that one variable is necessarily the cause of the other, and neither is the relationship perfect. So, not all paedophiles work at places where there is access to children. Fifth, the profiles developed are not only useful for policing purposes such as detecting offenders, but also in crime prevention and correctional rehabilitation. One could, for example, develop a profile of sex offenders, which could be useful in designing prison rehabilitation programs for sex offenders. In this application, it would serve the rehabilitation specialists to appreciate both the general profile of the offender type (e.g., housebreakers) and the unique individual profile of an individual housebreaker.

3.3.1 *Nomothetic Profiling (Crime Category Profiling) and Idiographic Profiling (Criminal and Crime Scene Profiling)*

For most us, our identities are at least dual. We are individuals and yet, we are a part of larger groups. We could, for instance, belong to an ethnic group, be a part of a chess hobby group, or a member of a religious group. Criminals can likewise be categorised into groups. They can be classified based on their crimes such as robbers, hackers, or gang members. Or, a robber can also be seen as a unique perpetrator with his or her own individual style. Therefore, there are two ways of thinking about profiling. The first, *nomothetic profiling*, or crime group profiling, describes the study of groups of individuals. Robbers, for example, may be categorized as a group. The second, *idiographic profiling*, or individual criminal/crime scene profiling, is concerned with the individual.

Idiographic profiling: 'Idiography' describes the study of the individual or anything that pertains to the individual (e.g., individual crime scene or individual item). When the term 'idiographic' is used to refer to the individual, the individual is seen as a unique person with a unique life history with properties setting him/her apart from others. In idiographic profiling, we are interested in a particular person. For example, Ahmad's house along Katong Road has been broken into. The question is *who* broke into Ahmad's house? During the investigation, investigators noted that the suspect had U.S. size 11 shoes from a brand called Mikey, based on a shoe print found at the crime scene. The investigators then noted that these resembled construction boots made in China (popular with a certain group of construction workers from a certain country). They also found that the soil type at the crime scene was similar to that in a place called Tanah Merah. Could it have been brought in by someone who lived or worked there? A cigarette butt of a certain brand popular with groups of foreign workers was also found at the scene. These are the areas that investigators would focus on when conducting idiographic profiling. Idiographic crime profiling is useful for individual level interventions, such as the narrowing down of suspects or risk assessments of an individual.

Nomothetic profiling: Nomothetic profiling would be useful in examining and studying the general qualities of a particular group of offenders. We could, for example, investigate the general characteristics of murderers, rapists, or young gang offenders. This is useful for crime prevention messaging or group-level interventions, such as designing school-based crime-prevention training programs or correctional rehabilitation programs.

It is important to differentiate between the nomothetic and idiographic approaches and we should not confuse one for the other. Group-level profiles are useful for group-level interventions and individual-level profiles are useful for individual-level interventions. It is risky to directly apply nomothetic profiles for individual-level interventions. Things can go wrong. For example, the 'group typical or average' profile of rapists across the world shows that most rapists are between the ages of 20 to 35. Drawing from this data, the profiler advises the investigator to look for a 20- to 30-year-old suspect. The offender, however, turns out to be a man in his 50s! The police had gone on a wild goose chase looking for such a person because of these recommendations. Due to this, investigators may lose confidence in the profiler and profiling as a process. This is unfortunate because the data was accurate to begin with (since most rapists tend to be of young age). However, the profile was not applied critically, and the profiler did not take into account the uniqueness of the case details (e.g., the victim's description of an older man).

The opposite is true. For instance, a rape case (idiographic/ individual level) is presented in which the perpetrator is an angry retaliatory rapist. He commits rape to get back at the failure of his romantic relationships. Drawing from this case, the profiler decides to conduct courses across the country, saying that all rapists are angry retaliatory people. Once again, an error is made in application, as this offender's motives may not coincide with those of others. When we confuse individual level and group level issues, this is known as the *levels of analysis confusion*, when a group-level idea or construct is applied directly to an individual-level issue, and vice-versa.

To be an effective profiler, it is important to have *both* nomothetic and idiographic understanding of the crime and/or criminal. Hence, the general rule is to use individual profiles for individual interventions and group profiles for group interventions. It is, however, possible to appreciate the big picture first and then the smaller picture and hence, it is reasonable to understand the nomothetic profile before looking into the idiographic profile. However, the converse is less applicable. That is, one should not look at an individual case and attempt to make inferences about all the general/broader cases. An analogy would be drawn from the world of flowers. We could start from flowers as a genre and then narrow down to particular flower types; for example, roses or orchids. However, we could not start from a rose or orchid to generalise its characteristics to all flowers.

3.4 Profiling as a Sub-Area of Investigative Psychology

Profiling is a sub-field of 'investigative psychology'. 'Investigative psychology' covers the broad area of work that includes detection of deception, management of the trauma of crime victims, investigative interviewing, and the psychology of criminal behaviour, amongst other things. This allows the profiler to draw on different aspects of investigative psychology to inform on the practice of profiling.

Practical uses of profiling

Profiles and profiling have many uses in practice, apart from the well-known one, which is to help identify offenders. First, crime and criminal profiling research may be used to understand the behavioral correlates of crime types and help build up a scientific knowledge base of the study of criminal behavior. For example, what are the behavioral correlates of housebreakers as a criminal group? Second, profiles may be used for criminal detection purposes and to reduce the number of potential suspects. For example, by understanding the characteristics of particular groups of criminals or the crime scene, police investigators may be able to narrow their search strategies. Third, they may be used for crime-prevention. Most perpetrators of child abuse, for instance, tend to be people that the victims may know, rather than strangers;

and knowing this, the police may be able to tailor their crime-prevention programs accordingly. For example, there is little point in reminding children to only beware of strangers, since it is likely that the child molester may be someone that the child already knows. This is true in many intra-familial cases. Fourth, profiling criminals may provide insight into the narratives that criminals may use, equip interviewers with ideas to develop interviewing strategies, enable rapport building, and give an insight to the types of deception to be expected. Fifth, a profile of a person may be used successfully as a courtroom trial strategy. Sixth, profiles may be useful for the design of rehabilitation programs. A profiling program, for instance, which studies the cognitive distortion patterns of sex offenders will be useful in designing a rehabilitation program and in reframing these patterns of distortion. Finally, profiles may also be useful for policymaking. For example, knowing the profiles of those who take loans from loan sharks may allow policymakers to work with banks to design micro-loans schemes, which are more affordable and less damaging to borrowers.

Types of profiling reports

According to behavioral investigative analysts in the U.K., there are many ways in which a profiling report might be used (Rainbow, 2008):

- To provide a *behavioral assessment of the crime scene assessment*;
- To provide a *briefing*: This involves initial thoughts given to investigators, before a fuller, more detailed product is provided;
- To provide a *linking report*: Where an opinion is given by the profiler regarding the likelihood of two or more offences being committed by the same person; and
- Finally, as a *full report* with details provided.

3.4.1 *Assumptions in Offender Profiling*

There are some assumptions made in profiling. First, *behavioral consistency* is assumed (Canter, 1995). Here, we assume that offender's 'characteristics' (C) will influence the way they behave or exhibit 'actions' (A) during a crime ("if C then A"). In other words, we expect offenders to be behaviorally consistent because of stable personal and personality characteristics. Experts believe that this was due to personality characteristic of individuals being consistent. So, crimes that have personal needs and involve just one person show more consistency, but interpersonal crimes (involving others) show less. This research comes from case linkage (Bennell & Jones, 2005), comparative case analysis (Bennell & Canter, 2002), or linkage analysis (Hazelwood & Warren, 2003). Past research supports the assumption that offenders behave consistently within crime types, including sexual assault (Grubin, Kelly, & Brunsdon, 2001; homicide (Salfati & Bateman, 2005; Santtila *et al.*, 2008), burglary (Bennell & Canter, 2002; Bennell & Jones, 2005; Green *et al.*, 1976), robbery (e.g., Woodhams & Toye, 2007), and arson (Fritzon *et al.*, 2001; Santtila *et al.*, 2005).

Second, there is the *homology assumption*. It is believed that certain crime scene behaviours are related to certain offender characteristics. This means that if two perpetrators exhibit similar crime scene behaviour they could also possess similar characteristics (Alison *et al.*, 2002). The evidence for this hypothesis however is not as strong. In Mokros and Alison's study (2002), the authors looked at crime scene behavior, sociodemographic characteristics, and criminal histories of a sample of 100 British male stranger rapists. They tested for similarity between offenders' behaviour at scene and characteristics. They found no evidence to support the homology assumption. This indicated that the process of drawing inferences about background characteristics from crime scene actions is not a simple 'if A then C' equation. Mokros and Alison then explained that the homology assumption failed because it is too simple. It neglected the influence of situational variables, and gave too much importance to personal variables. In response, Goodwill and Alison (2007) showed that when incorporating the situational variables into studies (such as the level of planning or aggression used), it is possible to predict the rapists' characteristics from their crime scene actions.

3.5 The Main Approaches in Criminal Profiling

3.5.1 *Profiling: The Federal Bureau of Investigation (FBI) Approach*

The investigative approach to profiling has been adopted by police investigators. First to develop criminal profiling in Quantico, Virginia, the FBI's Behavioural Sciences Unit had examined profiles in relation to the investigation of murders and serious sexual crimes. Ressler *et al.* (1986) claimed that "facets of the criminal's personality are evident in the offense. Like a fingerprint, the crime scene can be used to aid in identifying the murderer". One of the earliest ways they had classified crimes was into the *organized* and *disorganized* framework (Ressler *et al.*, 1986). This framework was easy to understand, since it was highly intuitive and dependent on whether the crime scene looked messy or neat. As far as the FBI investigators were concerned, some crime scenes were organized (e.g., no evidence was left behind by the perpetrator) whilst others were not (e.g., things such as knives were left behind at the crime scene). According to the FBI, the *organized offender* would lead an orderly life that is also reflected in the way he committed his crimes. He would be of average to high in intelligence, socially competent, and more likely than the disorganized offender to have skilled employment. He would plan his offenses, use restraints on victims, and would bring a weapon with him to commit murder, and bring the weapon away with him from the crime scene.

The *disorganized offender* would be described as reflecting an overall sense of disorder. The disorganization at the crime scene may include leaving evidence such as blood, semen, fingerprints, and sometimes, the murder weapon. There would be minimal use of restraints, and the body would often be displayed in open view, with no attempts at hiding the body or disposal of the body. The disorganized offender was thought to be socially incompetent and to have below-average intelligence. See Table 3.2 for further details.

Table 3.2:　Organized and Disorganized Crime Typology (Murderers)

Organized	Disorganized
Offense planned	Spontaneous offense
Victim is a targeted stranger	Victim or location known
Personalizes victim	Depersonalizes victim
Controlled conversation	Minimal conversation
Crime scene reflects overall control	Crime scene is chaotic
Requires submissive victim	Sudden violence to victim
Uses restraints	Minimal use of restraints
Aggressive acts before death	Sexual acts after death
Body hidden	Body left in view
Weapon usually absent	Weapon often present
Transports victim or body	Body left at death scene
Organized	**Disorganized**
Good intelligence	Average intelligence
Socially competent	Socially immature
Prefers skilled work	Poor work history
Sexually competent	Sexually incompetent
High birth order status	Lower birth order status
Father's work stable	Father's work record poor
Inconsistent childhood discipline	Childhood discipline harsh
Controlled mood during crime	Anxious mood during crime
Use of alcohol with crime	Little use of alcohol
Precipitating situational stress	Minimal situational stress
Living with partner	Living alone
Mobile with car	Lives/eats near crime scene
Follows crime in news media	Minimal interest in media
May change job or leave town	Minimal change in lifestyle

3.5.1.1　*FBI's profiling process*

FBI Agent Robert Ressler and colleagues, who were pioneering profilers at the FBI's Behavioral Sciences Unit (BSU), argued that there were six stages in the process (Ressler *et al.*, 1988). These were[1]:

---

[1] These have been adapted from p. 137 of *Sexual homicide: patterns and motives* by Ressler, Burgess, & Douglas (1988), NY, NY: Free Press.

(1) Profiling inputs

- o Crime Scene (physical evidence, pattern of evidence, body positions, weapons);
- o Victimology (background, habits, family structure, last seen, occupation);
- o Forensic Information (cause of death, wounds, pre/post mortem sexual acts, autopsy reports, laboratory reports);
- o Police Report (background information, police observation, time of crime, who reported the crime, neighbourhood, crime rate);
- o Photos (aerial, crime scene, victim).

(2) Decision Process models

- o Homicide type and style, primary intent, victim risk, offender risk, escalation, time for crime, location.

(3) Crime Assessment (reconstruction of crime, crime classification, organized or disorganized, victim selection, control of victim, sequence of crime, staging, motivation, crime scene dynamics)
(4) Criminal Profile (demographics, physical characteristics, habits, pre-offence behaviour, post-offence behaviour, recommendations to investigation)
(5) Investigation
(6) Apprehension

The information included in a profile may include ethnicity, gender, age-range, employment status, place of residence, forensic and criminal history, educational history, relationship history, personality, and mental state. These profiles may include investigative and questioning suggestions to build rapport.

There have been many criticisms of profiling. Mainly, the FBI's 'organized and disorganized' approach was heavily criticized by the scientific community (see the research article and critique below by Professor David Canter). It was an oversimplification of complex variables into dichotomous categories. Next, it lacked scientific methodological vigour and theoretical underpinnings (Wilson *et al.*, 1997). Third, profiling as a technique was criticized for its claims for effectiveness that were based on the longevity of practice of the FBI profilers, rather than on scientific data. Fourth, much of the profiling that was done was subjective and over-relied on police officer intuition and experience. Fifth, profiles were developed in American settings and could not easily be applied in other non-American settings, especially Asian settings. Crime profiles should be localized to time, place, and culture. In this book, one argument made is that the local environmental and legal considerations should be considered, when conducting profiling. Fifth, conclusions in profiles are ambiguous and unverifiable, so interpretation of profiles can be highly subjective. This results in *confirmation biases* (Alison *et al.*, 2003). Finally, in a more recent critique, Fox and Farrington (2012) argued that more than half of these published studies on profiling (n = 75) did not include any form of statistical analyses. Also, not even one study had attempted to assess the true usefulness of profiling for law enforcement by experimentally evaluating the profiles in the field (Homant & Kennedy, 1998; Snook *et al.*, 2009).

In response to these criticisms, FBI introduced a third category to the taxonomy, the *mixed-type* offender (Douglas *et al.*, 1992). They suggested that the dichotomous categories did not work well for a few reasons. First, the attack may involve more than one offender. Second, there may be unanticipated events that the offender had not factored into his or her planning. Third, the victim may put up resistance during the crime, or the offender may escalate into a different pattern in the course of an offence.[2] For example, although there may be initial planning (suggesting organized thinking) in a certain case of murder, there may be poor concealment of the body (suggesting disorganized scene). Fourth, the offender may be young or under the influence of drugs or alcohol. Hence, his criminal habits may not have developed into a pattern, which may result in a lack of consistency in the style of offense.

---

[2] This point paves the way for how profiling is presently done. Rather than present the behavioural possibility in a certain way, profiling advice is presented as several 'if-then' decision trees of possibilities. For instance, if the victim is compliant, then the offender may not be violent; if she is not, then he may become violent and hurt her.

RESEARCH ARTICLE OF INTEREST
The Organized/Disorganized Typology of Serial Murder: Myth or Model

In their study, Professor David Canter and colleagues found that the sub-features listed under the 'organized and disorganized' typology do not allow for accurate predictions to be made about the offender. They demonstrated this by conducting a study, selecting 100 serial sexual homicide cases, then coding these cases for crime scene and offender characteristics, according to the 'organized/disorganized' type.

Their analysis identified 39 such characteristics. They further examined the co-occurrence of the presence of these characteristics across the 100 cases using Smallest Space Analysis (SSA). Results showed that no particular division was found between the 'organized' and 'disorganized' variables, and most 'organized' variables were in the central region indicating that 'organized' features are common to the majority of offenses, and unlikely to discriminate between the two categories. In sum, 'organized' features tended to be typical of serial killers as a whole. The researchers found that while more 'disorganized' type actions could be identified, these co-occurred in less than half of the crimes and do not form a distinctive type. In short, the scientific basis for the organized–disorganized framework does not appear to be rigorous.

Source: Canter, D.V., Alison, L.J., Alison, E., & Wentink, N. (2004). The Organized/Disorganized Typology of Serial Murder: Myth or Model? *Psychology, Public Policy, and Law*, 10(3), 293–320.

Over time, the FBI profilers adopted more scientific approaches and more studies were published in peer-reviewed journals, collaborating with members of academia (see articles by Hazelwood & Warren, 1999, 2003; Safarik & Jarvis, 2005; Safarik *et al.*, 2002).

In the opinion of this author, many of the criticisms levelled against the FBI seemed to 'throw the baby out with the bathwater'. In our meetings with FBI profilers at Quantico, it was clear that the FBI had never intended to present these profiles as pure science. They were records of patterns observed. These observations were shared with others in the late 1980s and 1990s, albeit in scientific journals. Any new phenomenon starts with observations, which are recorded, analyzed, and discussed. Early observations will lead to further research, eventually developing into scientific knowledge. It seems unreasonable that the FBI was so heavily criticized for their early work. Such criticism is not conducive to the development of the science. Our sense is that this affected the development of future observations by the FBI as the scientific world became overly critical of profiling. As the profiling work at the FBI slowed down, the development of thinking in criminal psychology was impeded. Some police forces today are guarded and careful about openly saying that they undertake criminal profiling, but continue to do it because they appreciate the value of it. Science however takes time to mature, and trials and errors must be tolerated for this to take place successfully. This is true in any field, including physics, biology, engineering, and the social sciences. The danger we need to be aware of is that profiles should not be used as evidence in the court of law since a poorly developed profile can have implications on individual liberties. Profiles can be used as a valuable aid or second opinion in investigations. Fortunately, not everyone gave up on the need for profiling, and in a recent study, Fox and Farrington (2015) found very promising results through the evaluation of the effect of using statistically derived behavioural profiles for burglary offenses on burglary arrest rates (see the Research Article discussed later in this chapter).

3.5.1.2 *More concepts in the FBI's approach*

Modus Operandi (MO)

This refers to a suspect's *method of operation*. Forensic scientist and profiler, Dr. Brent Turvey, explains that the MO protects the person's identity, ensures successful completion of the crime, and facilitates escape (Turvey, 1999). Examples of MO may include the amount and details of planning, special materials used in the commission (ropes, tools, cameras, computers, spy camera pens, etc.), pre-surveillance of a crime scene or victim, offense location selection, use of attack tools, and precautionary acts (avoidance of police, wearing of caps, wearing of masks, etc.).

Signature

Canter and Young argued that the 'most distinct set of actions in a crime that are unique to that crime or criminal may be graced with the term *signature* (Canter & Youngs, 2009, p. 95). These include acts committed by an offender that are idiosyncratic to him or her, but are not needed to complete the offense. For example, a rapist may cut out a piece of the victim's clothing as a trophy and demand that the victim refer to him as her boyfriend. These actions are not characteristic of rape cases in general, thus they would be considered this offender's signature. They are a reflection of the underlying personality, psyche, lifestyle, and developmental experiences of the perpetrator. In a local case, an offender was so obsessed with his desired victim that he sodomized her and then carved his name on her back. This horrible act of violence could be considered as this offender's signature.

THINKING POINT

Why did the offender do this? What did it signify? Which psychological concept might explain for this behaviour?

Victimology

Victimology is the study of victimization. The academic study of victimology examines the psychological effects of crime on victims, relationships between victims and offenders, and interactions between victims and the criminal justice system (Karmen, 2003). It is useful to ask the question of why did *this* specific person became a victim and not others? Who has access to this victim? How might this victim come across to the perpetrator? Victim selection, it is believed, can be non-random (even when the offender says it was opportunistic). Our own interviews with offenders suggested that some criminals think carefully about their choice of victim. For instance, experienced property crime investigators have explained that some homes are more 'burglar-friendly' than others. Understanding victimology has benefits including:

1. *Prevention*: Anti-crime messages can be targeted at those who might be potential victims,
2. *Operational utility*: By knowing the victims' typical characteristics, operations can be conducted in which potential victims are watched in similar environments, where such crimes have occurred, and
3. *Narrowing down to suspect type*: Based on victims' accounts of the perpetrator's looks and behaviour, it is possible to narrow down suspects.

As a part summary to this segment, the question remains: can profiles developed by law enforcement be useful at all? See the following research article, which suggested that this is possible.

RESEARCH ARTICLE OF INTEREST
The Utility of Profiles

Dr. Bryanna Fox and Dr. David Farrington found that arrest rates for one police agency tripled during the year that they applied profiles, developed using the Statistical Patterns of Offending Typology (SPOT) for burglary. Dr. Fox and Dr. Farrington developed SPOT using a Latent Class Analysis (LCA). The LCA allowed for the classification of different styles of burglaries, based on the statistical patterns of offending behaviours and offender traits. The investigators were later on trained to use SPOT to identify the style of offense, and the most probable type of suspects.

Results showed that the profiling trained agency was 3.5 times more likely to close an unsolved burglary, as compared to three matched control agencies. This finding held up even after controlling for pre-existing differences between agencies. The point here is that profiling, when done well with a scientific basis can yield positive results.

Source: Fox, B.H. & Farrington, D.P. (2015). An Experimental Evaluation on the Utility of Burglary Profiles Applied in Active Police Investigations. *Criminal Justice and Behaviour*, 42(2), 156–175.

3.5.2 *Profiling Using Databases*

Sometimes, offender profiles are developed using databases comprising a large number of cases of crimes. There crimes are summarized and analyzed and reports are produced. Several international policing or criminal justice agencies such as Japan's National Research Institute of Police Science (NRIPS), the U.S.'s National Institute of Justice (NIJ), and the Australian Institute of Criminology (AIC) have produced reports on crime and criminal behaviour.

Some databases are used for the tracking of violent offenders. For example, the U.S. Federal Agencies use the Violent Criminal Apprehension Program (VICAP) and their Canadian counterparts use the Violent Crime Linkage Analysis System (ViCLAS). These databases are designed to capture, collate and compare crimes through the analysis of victim details, offender description, *modus operandi*, and forensic and behavioural data (Ressler *et al.*, 1988). Databases and reports produced are used to aid the investigator in tackling a current crime. They are useful for recalcitrant offenders who repeat the same MO over time (e.g., those with a history of mental illness coupled with violence or chronic repeat offenders such as arsonists). On the other hand, because these reports capture crime and criminal behaviour at the nomothetic/group level, they concern the typical/average offender. This is useful for broad-based interventions such as crime prevention or criminal justice policymaking; but it is not as effective in specific case profiling or in narrowing down possible suspects, because it does not draw on information from specific crime scenes. The challenge with using typicality, summary measures, and averages is that while they are good summary statistics, it would be hard to provide an accurate gauge of individual behaviours, since they may not fall squarely into database-prescribed expectations. In a nutshell: we are not averages.[3] Another problem is that any database is a 'garbage in, garbage out' process. The variables included

---

[3] I often use a hypothetical example where I tell students to imagine a theft of psychology exam papers in the department. I then ask for the average profile of psychology students. The answer is often that the average psychology student is female, university undergraduate and in the age range of 19–22. This then means that

into the database are critical and need to be carefully considered or the profile developed from the database is limited in its usage. For example, for a good profile on child abuse, it may be useful to consider not just whether the perpetrator holds a blue-collar or white-collar job, but also his or her job categories and whether such work provides easy access to children. Variables included for analysis should be theoretically premised.

3.5.3 *Profiling Using Clinical Psychology*

Clinical psychologists have been involved in profiling. Using knowledge from clinical psychology, and literature on personality and psychopathology, the clinician attempts to recognize the motivation of the offender, generate possible behavioural characteristics, and create a profile. Some early work by clinical psychologists includes those of British profiler, Dr. Paul Britton, who used his clinical expertise to advice the police. However, the use of profiles in police investigation became the subject of a major controversy, triggered in part by the murder of Rachel Nickell.

In July 1992, Rachel Nickell, a 23-year-old model, was sexually assaulted and battered to death while walking her dog with her two-year-old son in Wimbledon Common, London. The police felt much pressure to find the killer. Their main suspect was a man named Colin Stagg, but they had little evidence against him. They turned to Paul Britton to draw up a profile of the killer and asked him for help in designing a covert operation based on what they knew of the killer. Dr. Britton and the police believed the killer was a sexual sadist, who enjoyed cutting himself. The operation saw an undercover policewoman in a meeting with Stagg, during which she drew out his violent fantasies, through flirting and conversation. Stagg was subsequently arrested and charged based on 'his confession'. During the trial, defence lawyers argued that Britton's evidence was speculative and the judge commented that the police had shown 'excessive zeal' and had

---

all the male students and those above 23 are non-existent! This is an example of how an average can be both right and wrong.

tried to incriminate and entrap a suspect, using deceptive conduct. Britton's evidence was thrown out and the prosecution withdrew its case against Stagg. Paul Britton was required to attend a disciplinary inquiry by the British Psychological Society (Morris, 2000).

The lesson to be drawn from this case is that profiling advice about criminal behavior must be research- and evidence-based. The profiling advice given to the police by Britton was opinion-based. Britton also exaggerated his claims about the effectiveness of his methods. Furthermore, the purely clinical approach assumes that maladjustment or mental illness is the main driving force of crime. While this may be true in some cases, such assumptions cannot be applied to all cases.

3.5.4 *Profiling Using Investigative Psychology*

In 2009, British Professor David Canter coined the term 'investigative psychology' and approached profiling from a scientific point of view. He analyzed known data of offenders using a form of multivariate statistical analysis to reveal patterns in crime cases if they exist. Psychologists and police using this approach analysed the relationships between a large number of variables or "facets" within a crime scene. They examined which variables were most closely related and which were the least related. Professor David Canter puts little faith in the investigative methods developed by law enforcement agencies. He explained that psychologists need to work from the ground up to gather data and classify offenders into criminal categories such as arson, burglary, rape, and homicide.

Several studies have been conducted using the investigative psychology approach on profiles of burglary (Bennel & Canter, 2002), robbery (Woodhams & Toye, 2007), homicide (Salfati, 2003), arson (Canter & Fritzon), and sexual offenses (Almond & Canter, 2007). Interesting questions raised include what characteristics of the crime help to identify the offender; how do we differentiate between offenders; what inferences can be made about the characteristics of the offender that can help identify him or her; and, are there crimes that have been likely to be committed by the same offender? These are not new concerns, and the FBI has been taking these questions into account in their approach to solving crime. However, investigative psychology proposes a more scientific approach towards answering these questions.

The main challenge of Canter's approach is that while it is theoretically and scientifically sound, it is often not deemed as operationally relevant to frontline police officers. Police investigators want crime profiles which can help solve their case, rather than theories of offender motivations or themes. Also, some of the statistics used can appear daunting. In our local context, we have had difficulty applying his work to frontline police officers who find them complex and hard to follow. Also, these profiles may appear nomothetic and are therefore not useful for perpetrator detection or narrowing down the motivation of suspects. Nonetheless, Canter's approach helps in building a strong, scientific, and reliable knowledge base on crimes and criminal offending.

3.5.5 *Profiling Using Geographical Profiling*

THINKING POINT (Activity)
Your Geographical Habits?

Think about how you go to school or to work or to your favourite coffee place. Is there a pattern to your daily routine? Does the pattern change every time? What are the signs or markers that suggest that you were there (e.g., taking the train at a certain time, or buying the same drink, or meeting the same barista)?

Do you live your life oriented to spaces and environments that you prefer? Perhaps your laptop is designed with your favourite stickers? Perhaps your phone has your 'signatures' — apps that you like, music you listen to, and wallpapers that are sentimental to you? Does your room or table reflect your persona? Does your garbage reflect your habits?

Geographical profiling[4] is used to identify the area of an offender's residence from the location of the crime. This is used to narrow down the pool of suspects and for police prioritisation of actions. For example, one interesting idea is the idea of *distance decay*, which is the idea that when people are looking for something, they travel as far as they have to. As the distance between them and the target increases, they will choose the one that is geographically closer to them. Another phenomenon describes that offenders usually commit offenses in places they are familiar with, either because they live there, passed by the area previously, worked there, or grew up there. When people go about their daily life, they might notice targets of crime and this becomes an opportunity for crime (Bull *et al.*, 2015). For example, a housebreaker may notice that a house has many newspapers at its doorstep and guess that the family is on holiday; so, he breaks in. Perhaps a more technologically savvy perpetrator might notice on social media postings that the whole family is away on holiday and may decide to target their house. The cyberspace thus affords a new way of looking at environmental hunting.

Dr. Kim Rossomo, a pioneer in this field, originally developed a hunting-pattern typology representing the search and attack processes of offenders, based on spatial patterns of serial predators. He explained that there were four victim-search methods (Rossmo, 1997):

- *Hunters* search for suitable victims within their awareness space;
- *Poachers* commit crimes by travelling outside their local area by operating from an activity node other than their home base;
- *Trollers* are opportunistic offenders who encounter their victims in the course of their daily activities; and
- *Trappers* have an occupation or a position that brings potential victims to them or use subterfuge to entice suitable victims into their own home or to a location they control.

---

[4]This has a history in environmental criminology, where criminologists would examine where criminals where likely to offend. Geographical profiling is the reverse. (Bull *et al.*, 2006).

Three different types of attack methods were identified:

- The *raptor* attacks his victims immediately upon encountering them;
- The *stalker* follows or watches his victims, and waits for an opportune moment to attack; and
- The *ambusher* commits the crime at locations at which the offender has a great deal of control, such as his residence or workplace, thus the crime sites are more dependent on the offender's own activity space.

For those interested in this field, I recommend Kim Rossmo's and David Canter's 1996 work on *marauders* (hunters) and *commuters* (poachers). The idea here is that marauders move away from their residence to offend, but may return back to their home base, while commuters move out from the home base. Canter proposes that there is little or no overlap between the home base and the offending area, and that the offender moves to a place outside his home range to offend. Canter qualifies that this does not mean that the criminal range is unfamiliar to the offender, but that it is at an appreciable distance from the area in which he habitually operates as a non-offender. The marauder model appears to be more common.

One application of geographical profiling is *hot spots policing* or *place-based policing*, and this will be discussed further in Chapter 6. Places may mean neighbourhoods, such as specific addresses, street, or small address clusters, or street blocks. For example, one method of place-based policing would be to increase officers' time spent at certain hot spots. This was the case in the Minneapolis Hot Spots Patrol Experiment. This experiment was proved to be very successful (National Institute of Justice, 2011).

3.5.6 *Profiling Using Criminalistics and Forensic Science*

Criminalistics or forensic science is the study of crimes and crime scenes using scientific approaches to gather and analyze evidence with the purpose of solving crimes. Some profilers with a background in forensic science have successfully used knowledge from this field to inform criminal investigations. These include Dr. Henry Lee, who has handled many famous cases in the United States. Another popular writer has been Dr. Brent Turvey.

Some examples of forensic science work include the use of DNA profiling and fingerprint analysis. In the Singapore context, experts who have been working on this area include Associate Professor Stella Tan from the National University of Singapore (NUS) and professionals from the Health Sciences Authority (HAS). Common forensic science techniques include *computer forensics* (used in the investigation of money-lending syndicates, cybercrimes such as love scams, and identity fraud), *accident reconstruction* (for major traffic investigations), *forensic dentistry* (used to identify victims involved in air crashes), *fingerprint analysis, DNA analysis, bloodstain pattern analysis* and *document examination* (useful in commercial crime investigations). Take a look at Table 3.3 and make educated guesses about the kind of forensic science/criminalistics evidence you could expect to find in these kinds of crimes.

There are useful aspects of the forensic sciences approach which can inform profiling. The first would be the concept of the 'crime scene'. It is important for profilers to appreciate the dynamic implications of the crime scene. One aspect is the concepts of the *primary, secondary* and *tertiary* crime scenes (Gerberth, 2003). For example, a paedophile might kidnap a child from his/her school

Table 3.3: What Kinds of Forensic Science Evidence Would You Expect? (Activity)

Type of crime/crime scene	Examples of forensic evidence you may expect
Murder victim shot with a firearm	
Commercial crime, or money unaccounted for in bank accounts	
'Happy slapping' incident of a young girl who was beaten up by her friends, in which a video clip was recorded and uploaded onto the Internet	
Housebreaking incident	

(*primary* crime scene), transport the victim in a car (*secondary* crime scene), sexually assault the victim at a park ('third' crime scene), and then dispose of the body at a different park ('fourth' crime scene).

The forensics of a crime is useful when examined alongside data from behavioral analysis. First, the forensics at the crime scenes is an idiographic analysis of the crime, which complements the nomothetic aspects of the crime. In general, we may expect typical burglars (nomothetic analysis) to be young males within the age range of 20–32, with previous criminal history in theft, etc. However, in a specific case, the burglar may use a special type of break-in tool only available in certain shops in Sim Lim Square and wear a military cap. Here, we can combine the idiographic analysis with the nomothetic analysis to better understand the criminal. Second, we should expect the forensics to logically match the behaviors seen at the crime scene and any inconsistencies should suggest that something is not adding up. For example, in most cases involving autoerotic fatalities, no suicide notes are found. Hence, the crime scene may look like that of a suicide (for example, a person found hanging), but if the person has no history of mental illness and no suicide notes are found, then it is less likely to be a case of suicide. Therefore, while important, the forensics of a case does not always provide an accurate picture of what has happened, but when coupled with behavioral analysis, a better approximation of reality can be derived.[5]

There are, of course, limitations. We often think that forensic science is infallible because of the 'CSI effect' or 'CSI infect' (Lawson, 2009). The CSI effect refers to the influence of the media's popularization of certain types of evidence on decision-makers in criminal investigation. For example, actors in the legal system might not treat fingerprint or DNA results critically, or may have unrealistic expectations about the need for such evidence or its accuracy and reliability. For example, we have heard cases where a DNA analysis has been called for even when the suspect admits to the crime and when there were other witnesses who saw the act.[6]

---

[5] This is the triangulation principle referred to in Chapter 1.
[6] This is not entirely wrong since people may admit to crimes they didn't commit to save their loves ones from being caught.

There are also limitations to fingerprint analysis. The U.S.-based National Forensic Science Technology Center argued that even though fingerprint analysis can be very useful, it is not completely reliable. First, there must be a known print in the database that the collected print (from the scene) can be compared to. Second, there is no scientific method to determine the time a print was left on a crime scene. It may have been two hours ago, two days ago or even longer. Third, it is not possible to determine sex, age, or race from a print alone (National Forensic Science Technology Center, n.d.). In a case of wronged identification, 37-year-old American lawyer Brandon Mayfield, who had converted to Islam, was accused to have a role in a terror incident in Madrid, because his fingerprints were supposed to have been found at the crime scene. He was later released after the FBI said they had mistakenly matched Mayfield's fingerprints to a print found on a bag containing detonators at the crime scene. FBI officials attributed the mismatch to the poor quality of the original print.

Even with DNA analysis, there is no guarantee of zero errors. First, cross-contamination at the crime scene is possible. Second, cross-contamination may occur in the laboratory. Third, errors of interpretation of the DNA sample are possible. Finally, evidence can be fabricated using DNA sprays. Even in Singapore, such errors have arisen. On 6 January 2012, it was reported that there was a DNA testing mistake involving 412 criminal cases. The Health Sciences Authority (HSA) explained that a lab manager had prepared a year's supply of reagent solution for DNA testing with a higher-than-usual level of concentration (Lim, 2012). The lab manager had "misread the label" and used 1.0 millimolar (mM) of ethylenediaminetetraacetic acid for the reagent solution, instead of the prescribed 0.1mM. This had led to a "marginal reduction in sensitivity" in the testing of several DNA samples at the HSA's DNA Profiling Laboratory between October 2010 and August 2011. As a result, the 412 cases had to be reviewed by the Attorney General's Chambers (AGC). An inquiry into this mistake was conducted, and the authorities concluded that no one was wrongly convicted because of the mistake. International DNA experts were consulted by the HSA to attest that the error had limited scientific impact on the tests. However, this case has shown that DNA analysis is not infallible, and the data derived from such tests must be treated critically.

3.5.7 *The CLIP Profiling Approach (Recommended)*

It is possible to gather the strengths of the previously discussed profiling approaches and avoid the problems associated with them using the CLIP profiling approach. CLIP is an acronym for **C**riminalistics and Forensic Sciences Considerations, **L**egal and **L**ocal considerations, **I**nvestigation and law enforcement considerations, and **P**sychological and behavioural considerations (Figure 3.1). CLIP[7] puts together different disciplines in the analysis of crimes and criminal behavior. The idea is to look for consistencies and inconsistencies across these disciplines and approaches. The idea of 'cross-checking' for consistencies across these approaches was adapted from Dean (2005). See Table 3.4 for details on what to look for in each area.

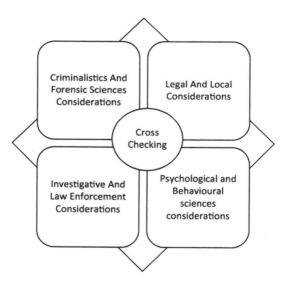

Figure 3.1:   The CLIP Approach and the 4 Domains of C-L-I-P.

---

[7] The CLIP model has been influenced by Dean's Cross+Check model. However, Dean's Cross+Check has four components, 'Database', 'Diagnostic', 'Theoretical' and 'Investigative' which are not similar to the CLIP entirely. Dean does not discuss the importance of forensic sciences, legal, or local factors in crime profiling, although he does discuss investigative issues.

Table 3.4: The CLIP Model of Profiling and Details

Criminalistics and forensic sciences considerations	Legal and local considerations
Criminalistics and forensic sciences considerations	**Legal and local considerations**
For the crime of concern:	For the crime of concern:
1. What does forensic science suggest about the *typical* crime scene for this crime?	1. Are there local laws for this behaviour/crime/deviant act? (Sometimes, no local laws exist for certain transgressions, e.g., marital rape and harassment laws do not exist in all countries in the world)
2. What evidence is usually expected for this crime scene? (e.g., DNA, semen, hair, digital evidence, blood, physical evidence, digital evidence, etc.)	2. How do local laws compare against international laws? In what ways are they similar or different?
3. What do we expect for the crime scene? (e.g., is there a primary, secondary and tertiary crime scene?)	3. Do the laws influence the way things are measured and defined?
4. What specialized reports are required? (e.g. medical autopsies, dental reports, accident reconstruction)	4. Are legal definitions different from psychological ones? Do legal definitions hinder the understanding of behavioural phenomena? What are we not seeing because of the way the laws are defined.
Sources of information:	**Local considerations**
Forensic science and criminalistics literature, forensic reports, autopsy reports, medical reports, crime scene reconstruction reports, etc.	For the crime of concern:
	1. What local cultural, contextual, or environmental issues affect this crime?
Check 'C' with 'L-I-P' to look for consistencies and inconsistencies.	For example, due to the large number of public housing apartments, we have had many incidents of lift-related robberies and molestation cases in the past. We have also had some criminals operating out of China, targeting young local Chinese men with sex-for-credit scams using popular social media sites such as WeChat.

(*Continued*)

Table 3.4:   (*Continued*)

2. Has local research been conducted on this crime?
3. How does the local environment affect crime?
4. How, when, where and for who does this crime occur in the local context?

Sources of information:

Publications from the local police force, crime prevention alert messages and videos (e.g., CRIMEWATCH), and legal publications written by academics.

Cross-check 'L' with 'C-I-P'.

Psychological and behavioural sciences considerations

1. Search and review all relevant psychological and behavioral science material relating to this crime. Read recent publications. What theories are relevant?
2. Review material/research from a) clinical and abnormal psychology; b) forensic psychology; and c) forensic psychiatry.
3. Analyse the typical *behavioral correlates* for this crime
4. What are the *usual motives* for this crime?
5. Think about the behavioral habits or inclinations of the crime type you are looking at (e.g., a paedophile is likely to look for places and spaces to get close to children; a molester is likely to act in crowded places, e.g., at Chinese New Year bazaars, on MRT trains, or at New Year parties)

Investigative and law enforcement considerations

For the crime of concern:
1. What is *typically* expected in terms of

a. Common behavioral patterns/*modus operandi* when committing the crime (single perpetrator vs. group; opportunistic vs. planned, etc.)
b. The deception for this crime
c. The degree of planning, intention, and motivation for this crime (e.g., grooming, blitz/surprise attacks)
d. The common *modus operandi* for this crime
e. Whether there is any indication of 'signature'
f. Incident reports, medico-legal reports (toxicological reports, wound pattern analysis, sexual assault reports, autopsy reports, etc.)

g. Victimology considerations

h. Creating the story and time lines

2. How do investigators *usually* approach this crime? For example, for murder, investigators may first examine the victim's last known contacts or immediate contacts, or the murderer's motives.

3. *Sources* of information:

a. Review 'professional law enforcement' material from major law enforcement agencies such as the FBI Law Enforcement Bulletin; the London Metropolitan Police Home Office Research Series (https://www.gov.uk); the National Institute of Justice (U.S.) database; articles from the Singapore Police Force (SPF), Singapore Civil Defence Force (SCDF), Singapore Prisons Service (SPS), Singapore Sub Courts Publications; the Australian Institute of Criminology; the Royal Canadian Mounted Police; and books by police investigators (e.g., Vernon Gerbeth)

b. Review witness statements relevant to this crime, if available

c. Review victim statements relevant to this crime, if available

d. Review offender statements relevant to this crime.

Cross-check 'I' with 'C', 'L', and 'P'.

Sources of information

Psychology, sociology, psychiatry journals, criminology journals, etc.

Cross-check 'P' with 'C-L-I'

3.5.7.1 *Using CLIP crime profiling in general (nomothetic profile) (for use in crime prevention messaging, policy design and rehabilitation planning)*

Here is an example of using the CLIP approach for profiling date rape as a category of crime.

- *For the 'C' component*, research on the criminalistics of date rape is needed, e.g., on the use of date rape drugs such as GHB or Rohypnol (Date Rape Drugs, 2012). For example, research could unveil that Rohypnol is the trade name for flunitrazepam. Rohypnol has been referred to by street names such as Circles, Forget Pill, Mexican Valium, Mind Erasers, Roach, Roofies, and Roopies. It is a small, round, and white pill that dissolves in liquids. The intoxicating effects of Rohypnol can be felt within 30 minutes and can last for several hours. A drugged person may look and act like a drunk person, and have trouble standing. Rohypnol can cause muscle relaxation, a drunken feeling, problems talking, an inability to remember, and loss of consciousness.
- *From the 'L' perspective*, there is a need to check if date rape laws exist. In Singapore, for instance, there is no specific law on date rape, but they exist in other countries. Again, from the 'L' perspective, there is a need to look at the local environmental and cultural factors. For instance, Singapore may have an active dating scene and dating industry. What are the main clubs and events promoting dating? Could the perpetrator be using one of these?
- *From the 'I' component*, there is a need to look at the dynamics of interviewing and investigation involved in date rape crimes. For example, it would not be surprising that victims may not want to come forward and cooperate with police investigations, since they may blame themselves for agreeing to the date in the first place. Investigators may need to practice much patience and reassure victims that they were not to blame for what happened. Investigating Officers (IOs) would also need to be sensitive about talking to the victims about the rape incident.

- *From the 'P' angle*, there is a need to recognize the different kinds of date rapists and study their sense of entitlement.

3.5.7.2 *TOOLBOX: Using the CLIP approach to narrow down suspects (idiographic applications) — for use in narrowing down suspects, assisting in interviewing and investigation, prosecution, and courtroom work*

When we are using the CLIP approach to narrow down suspects for profiling, there are five steps in applying the CLIP (idiographic profile):

(1) *Develop CLIP nomothetic research analysis of the crime.* Going by the example explored in the previous section, what is the general profile of date rapists that can be obtained from scientific literature reviews?

(2) *Find out specific (idiographic) details of this specific crime* (use CLIP to guide)

   (a) Visit the crime scene and review crime scene evidence.

   (b) Review all photographs and video evidence.

   (c) Study the investigators' current analysis and files.

   (d) Study criminalistics, forensic evidence, medical reports, autopsy reports, etc.: Based on the case facts known, what forensic evidence was obtained? What kinds of drugs were obtained and who has access to such drugs?

   (e) Study victim profiles: Based on the case facts known, analyse the victims' statements. Was there anything in common about the victims' profiles? For example, were they working women in the dating scene, or women whose jobs required them to meet clients one-on-one, such as insurance agents, property agents, and financial advisors?

   (f) Link to other reports/crimes: Were there any reports in the police databases of other cases of drugged women? For instance, could the same perpetrator be drugging his victims in other locations apart from the clubs he usually operates in?

(3) *Conduct an analysis of the crime* and how it might have occurred, including attempting to understand how the criminal act had taken place and the motivations involved.

(4) *Develop the profile using 'if-then' analysis.* After combining both nomothetic and idiographic analyses, the profiler should then provide at least two or three or more possible 'if-then' hypotheses[8] and claims. The idea is not to be fixated onto one possibility alone. This involves hypothesis generation and 'if-then' decision trees. Each claim made in the profile must be scientifically evaluated. Alison *et al.* (2003) discussed how Toulmin's (1958) philosophy of argument[9] could be applied as a model to assist individuals in constructing profiling reports and the claims made in the report.

For example, in the earlier mentioned drug-rape case, a possible hypothesis could be that the perpetrator works as a chemist or a pharmacist who, as a health professional, may have access to said date rape drugs. If this were true, there would be a need to screen all personnel working in these fields and match them against descriptions provided by the witnesses or CCTV footages of their faces. A second possible hypothesis could be that the perpetrator is a dating website predator who prowls through these websites for potential victims. Once this possibility has been established, investigators could check with administrators of these websites for complaints against any of their clients, or work with these web administrators to match the descriptions of the potential suspect against profiles in the system.

---

[8] This concept was described by Goodwill and Alison (2007). They argued that behavior is contextually predicated. For example, a sex offender who grooms children may not need to use violence against them. But this presumes the children are compliant and do not fight him off. Therefore, '*if*' the child is compliant, '*then*' the offender may not be violent. On the other hand, '*if*' the child fights back, '*then*' the offender may express violence towards the child.

[9] Toulmin suggested that arguments must contain (1) a claim (e.g., 'the murderer is under 30 years old'); (2) strength ('an 87% chance that...'); (3) the grounds ('because this is the murder of a 23-year-old woman'); (4) the warrant ('the majority of offenders who murder women less than 25 years old are, themselves, under 30 years old'); (5) the backing research (e.g., 'research by Doctor ABC (2017)' or database) and (6) the rebuttal (i.e., unless indications suggest....) (From Almond, Alison, & Porter (2007)).

(5) Finally, *decide on which is the most possible hypothesis/suspect scenario.* This is to ensure falsifiability[10] and to avoid Barnum[11] statements, where there are many possibilities and creative interpretations. Possible behavioral implications might be identified.

When using CLIP, remember the following: first, CLIP should not be used to identify a specific person, but to narrow down possible suspects. Second, use behavioral explanations and avoid jargon. Merely saying that the offender may be a paedophile is not useful to investigators, since the investigator does not have anything practical to work on. It is more useful to say that we should be looking for someone who looks at child pornography on the Internet and has previous sex offences against children. Third, CLIP analyses should be based on scientific literature and research, and the profiling psychologist or police officer must be able to back up statements if they are challenged in court. In other words, if you say those possible suspects are males between the ages of 25 and 35, you must substantiate this claim with research findings. Fourth, advice must be presented in probabilistic terms. Fifth, avoid Barnum statements in your profile report.

3.5.7.3 *Advantages and disadvantages of CLIP*

The CLIP approach has several advantages. First, it is multidisciplinary and draws on forensic science, law, psychology, and police science (investigation). It does not rely on psychology alone. Next, it is locally

---

[10] In scientific endeavour, 'falsifiability' is the idea that a theory/statement can be found to be false when tested empirically (Salkind, 2010). Thus, when you decide on a likely claim in a profile, you can be proven right and more importantly, proven wrong. When the profile is right every single time because of the way it is ambiguously worded, then it is not falsifiable.

[11] The '*Barnum effect*' occurs when people accept generalisations that are true of nearly everybody, to be specifically true of himself or herself. Most people, for example, will agree with statements such as "you have a great need for other people to like and admire you", and "you have a tendency to be critical of yourself". Good profiles should not include Barnum statements, because they will almost always be correct most of the time and cannot be proven wrong.

contextualized. Many American and European profiles cannot be applied in Singapore because of the different laws, criminal justice system, culture, and environment, so a local context is important. CLIP brings together both the advantages of the nomothetic and ideographic approaches since there are two ways of using CLIP, as earlier discussed. Next, CLIP uses multiple data sources on the crime of concern, providing data triangulation (refer to this point made in Chapter One). In addition, CLIP is scientifically accountable because it draws on research. Furthermore, CLIP provides for possible falsification because the profiler is forced to weigh his most likely prediction and hence, can be proven to be wrong.

There are limitations to the CLIP approach of profiling. First, it is difficult to be multidisciplinary. Psychology students are not always familiar with non-psychological sources such as police manuals, law readings, and forensic science readings. Police officers are likewise not familiar with psychological and sociological material. Therefore, developing CLIP analyses could be time-consuming. Second, response time to real cases could be slow because of the research needed to establish a scientific basis for profiles in each criminal case. There are some ways to resolve these issues. Relevant training using multidisciplinary approaches can help. Another way is by ensuring that scientific research of crime and criminal psychology takes place, and in a proactive manner. Strong working relationships with members of the academia, internal research officers, and university interns who can provide assistance in generating quick literature reviews can help in creating nomothetic profiles. The challenge is not the research itself, but the difficult nature of questions useful for police operations, which needs answering. Some examples of such questions would be: if someone were to self-inflict a wound, such as stabbing himself to make it look like someone else did it, which part of his body would he stab? The third limitation is that the 'if-then' analyses require critical thinking, which might prove to be challenging, as this is often not a regular training in most police officers, although this is learned on-the-job. Finally, CLIP is a new approach that requires evaluation and validation over time. In the opinion of this author, while this last point is important, it is not critical, since it is not a predictive tool but a way of thinking and framing inputs into the profiling process.

3.6 Summary

- Whether we like the idea or not, we all profile others. It is part of our survival instincts. The word 'profiling' ought not to be a bad word. It just needs to be done right and done scientifically.
- Police and law enforcement all over the world will profile criminals and crime, and will continue to do so, because profiles can be a useful heuristic. As with all heuristics, mental shortcuts have their limitations and may create thinking biases and tunnel visions. This does not mean the heuristics are useless and ought to be abandoned. It means that we need to be more mindful of the biases that these heuristics come with. We need to be particularly careful with racial profiling, which does not have any basis. Good profiling is also good critical thinking.
- There are *nomothetic* and *idiographic* profiles, and they each have their uses.
- There are several types of profiling approaches such as the FBI approach, the Database approach, the Forensic Sciences and Criminalistics approach, the Investigative Psychology approach, and geographical profiling.
- This chapter recommends the 'CLIP' approach of profiling, which takes into account Criminalistics, Legal and Local issues, Investigative issues, and Psychological considerations. CLIP is a multidisciplinary approach that enables better triangulation of input while also considering the local context and local laws, which are all important aspects of any investigation.
- Profiling practice should be evidence-based, research-based, and science-based.
- Profiles should be presented in terms of 'if-then' decision trees.
- Good offender profiling techniques bring together the science of crime analysis and the science of criminal behaviour with the professional practice of investigation.

- Effective profiling structures a better and informed way of thinking for enforcement and investigations. It is useful to view profiling as a tool in the larger toolbox of 'investigative psychology', rather than see it as a tool in itself.

Relevant Journals

Journal of Investigative Psychology and Offender Profiling.
The British Journal of Forensic Practice
Journal of Contemporary Criminal Justice
Journal of Police and Criminal Psychology
Journal of Forensic Psychology Practice.

E-Resources

Australian Institute of Criminology https://aic.gov.au/
U.K. Home Office. https://www.gov.uk/government/organisations/home-office/about/research
FBI Lae Enforcement Bulletin. https://leb.fbi.gov/
Royal Canadian Mounted Police Research Reports. http://www.rcmp-grc.gc.ca/pubs/index-eng.htm
National Research Institute of Police Science (Japan) http://www.npa.go.jp/nrips/en/
Ministry of Social and Family Development (Singapore). https://www.msf.gov.sg/research-and-data/Research-and-Data-Series/Pages/default.aspx

Sample Research Essay Titles

- What are the disadvantages and disadvantages of the FBI 'organized and disorganized' framework?
- Is the practice of profiling a useful heuristic or a dangerous bias in thinking?
- How do we avoid 'tunnel vision' and the 'Barnum effect' when we undertake criminal profiling?

- How can we ensure that criminal profiling has a better scientific evidence base?
- How would you develop a nomothetic CLIP profile of serial molesters?

Sample Research Paper Titles

- What are the pros and cons of the FBI organized and disorganized framework?
- Compare and contrast two criminal profiling approaches?
- What are the main steps in the CLIP methods of profiling? (Nomothetic approach?)
- The Commissioner of Police has asked you to develop a criminal profiling program for (Crime category) (nomothetic profile). Discuss how you would go about doing it.

References

Alison, L., Smith, M.D., Eastman, O., and Rainbow, L. (2003). Toulmin's philosophy of argument and its relevance to offender profiling. *Psychology, Crime & Law, 9*, 173–183.

Alison, L., Bennell, C., Mokros, A., and Ormerod, D. (2002). The personality paradox in offender profiling: A theoretical review of the processes involved in deriving background characteristics from crime scene actions. *Psychology, Public Policy and Law, 8*, 115–135.

Almond, L. and Canter, D. (2007). Youths who sexually harm: Multivariate model of behaviour. *Journal of Sexual Aggression, 13*, 217–233.

Almond, L., Alison, L., and Porter, L. (2007). An evaluation and comparison of claims made in behavioural investigative advice reports compiled by the National Policing Improvements Agency in the United Kingdom. *Journal of Investigative Psychology and Offender Profiling, 4*(2), 71–83.

Brantingham, P.J. and Brantingham, P.L. (1978). A theoretical model of crime site selection. In M. Krohn, and R. Akers (Eds.), *Crime, Law, And Sanctions* (pp. 105–118). Beverly Hills, CA: Sage.

Bennell, C. and Canter, D.V. (2002). Linking commercial burglaries by modus operandi: Tests using regression and ROC analysis. *Science and Justice, 42*, 153–164.

Bennell, C. and Jones, N. (2005). Between a ROC and a hard place. *International Journal of Investigative Psychology and Offender Profiling, 2*, 23–41.

Bull, R., Cooke, C., Hatcher, R., Woodhams, J., Bilby, C., and Grant, T. (2015). *Criminal Psychology: A Beginner's Guide.* Oxford: Oneworld.

Canter, D. (1994). *Criminal Shadows — Inside the Mind of the Serial Killer.* New York, NY: Harper-Collins.

Canter, D. (1995). Psychology of offender profiling. In R. Bull & D. Carson (Eds.), *Handbook of Psychology in Legal Contexts* (pp. 343–355). Chichester, U.K.: John Wiley and Sons.

Canter, D. (1996). The environmental range of serial rapists. In *Psychology in Action.* Dartmouth Benchmark Series (pp. 217–230). Hantshire, U.K.: Dartmouth Publishing Company.

Canter, D. (2004). *Mapping Murder: The Secrets of Geographical Profiling.* US: Virgin Books.

Canter, D. (2008). *Criminal Psychology.* London: Hodder Education.

Canter, D., Alison, L.J., Alison, E., and Wentink, N. (2004). The organized/disorganized typology of serial murder: Myth or model? *Psychology, Public Policy, and Law, 10*(3), 293–320.

Canter, D. and Fritzon, K. (1998), Differentiating arsonists: A model of fire setting actions and characteristics. *Legal and Criminological Psychology, 3*, 73–96.

Canter, D. and Youngs, D. (2009). *Investigative Psychology: Offender Profiling and the Analysis of Criminal Action.* Chichester, U.K.: John Wiley & Sons.

Chan, W.C., Hor, M.Y.M, and Ramraj, V. (2005). *Fundamental Principles of Criminal Law: Cases and Materials.* Singapore: Authors.

Chan, W.C. and Phang, A. (2001). *The Development of Criminal Law and Criminal Justice in Singapore.* Singapore: Singapore Journal of Legal Studies, Faculty of Law, and National University of Singapore.

Copson, G. (1995). *Coals to Newcastle? Part 1: A Study of Offender Profiling* (Paper 7). London: Police Research Group Special Interest Series, Home Office.

Date Rape Drugs (2012). Office on Women's Health, U. S. Department of Health and Human Services.

Davies, A. (1992). Rapists' behaviour: A three-aspect model as a basis for analysis and the identification of serial crime. *Forensic Science International, 55*, 173–194.

Dean, G. (2005). The 'Cross-check' system: Integrating profiling approaches for police and security investigations. *Journal of Police and Criminal Psychology, 20*(2), 20–43.

Douglas, J.E., Burgess, A.W., Burgess, A.G., and Ressler, R.K. (1992). *Crime Classification Manual: A Standard System for Investigating and Classifying Violent Crime*. New York, NY: Wiley.

Douglas, J.E., Ressler, R.K., Burgess, A.W., and Hartman, C.R. (1986). Criminal profiling from crime scene analysis. *Behavioural Sciences and the Law, 4*, 401–421.

Fox, B.H. and Farrington, D.P. (2015). An experimental evaluation on the utility of burglary profiles applied in active police investigations. *Criminal Justice and Behaviour, 42*(2), 156–175.

Fritzon, K., Canter, D., and Wilton, Z. (2001). The application of an action system model to destructive behaviour: The examples of arson and terrorism. *Behavioural Sciences and the Law, 19*, 657–690.

Geberth, V.J. (2003) The homicide crime scene. *Law and Order, 51*(11).

Goodwill, A.M. and Alison, L.J. (2007). When is profiling possible? Offense planning and aggression as moderators in predicting offender age from victim age in stranger rape. *Behavioural Sciences and the Law, 25*(6), 823–840.

Hazelwood, R.R. and Warren, J.I. (1999). The sexually violent offender: Impulsive or ritualistic. *Aggression and Violent Behaviour, 5*, 267–279.

Hazelwood, R.R. and Warren, J.I. (2003). Linkage analysis: *Modus operandi* (MO), ritual and signature in serial sexual crime. *Aggression and Violent Behaviour, 8*, 587–598.

Homant, R.J. and Kennedy, D.B. (1998). Psychological aspects of crime scene profiling: Validity research. *Criminal Justice and Behaviour, 25*(3), 319–343.

Goodwill, A.M. and Alison, L. (2007). When is profiling possible? Offence planning and aggression as moderators in predicting offender age from victim age in stranger rape. *Behavioural Sciences and the Law, 25*, 823–840.

Grubin, D., Kelly, P., and Brunsdon, C. (2001). *Linking Serious Sexual Assault Through Behaviour*. London: Home Office, Research Development and Statistics Directorate.

Mokros, A. and Alison, L.J. (2002). Is offender profiling possible? Testing the predicted homology of crime scene actions and background characteristics in a sample of rapists. *Legal and Criminological Psychology, 7*, 25–43.

Morris, S. (2000, November 30). The jigsaw man. *The Guardian*. Retrieved from https://www.theguardian.com/g2/story/0,3604,404994,00.html.

National Forensic Science Technology Center (n.d.). *A Simplified Guide to Fingerprint Analysis*. Retrieved from http://www.forensicsciencesimplified.org/prints/Fingerprints.pdf

National Institute of Justice (2011). *Program Profile: Minneapolis (MN) Hot Spots Experiment*. Retrieved from https://www.crimesolutions.gov/ProgramDetails. aspx?ID=58

Karmen, A. (2003). *Crime Victims: An Introduction to Victimology*. US: Wadsworth Publishing.

Keith, I. and Rudin, N. (2000). *Principles and Practice of Criminalistics: The Profession of Forensic Science*. Boca Raton, FL: CRC Press.

Lawson, T.F. (2009). *Before the Verdict and Beyond the Verdict: The CSI Infection Within Modern Criminal Jury Trials*. Loyola University Chicago Law Journal, *41*, 132–142.

Lim, P. (2012, January 6). Health minister apologises for HSA's DNA lab error. *Asiaone*. Retrieved http://www.asiaone.com/News/Latest%2BNews/ Singapore/Story/A1Story 20120106-320291.html

Rainbow, L.J. (2008). Taming the beast: The U.K. Approach to the management of behavioral investigative advice. *Journal of Police and Criminal Psychology*, *23*, 90.

Ressler, R.K., Burgess, A.W., Douglas, J.E., Hartman, C.R., and D'Agostino, R.B. (1986). Sexual killers and their victims: Identifying patterns through crime scene analysis. *Journal of Interpersonal Violence*, *1*, 288–308.

Ressler, R.K., Burgess, A.W., and Douglas, J.E. (1988). *Sexual Homicide: Patterns and Motives*. New York, NY: Free Press.

Rossmo, D.K. (1997). Geographic profiling. In J.L. Jackson & D.A. Bekerian (Eds.), *Offender Profiling: Theory, Research and Practice* (pp. 159–175). Chichester, U.K.: John Wiley & Sons.

Safarik M.E., Jarvis, J.P., and Nussbaum, K.E. (2002). Sexual homicide of elderly females: Linking offender characteristics to victim and crime scene attributes. *Journal of Interpersonal Violence*, *17*, 500–525.

Salfati, C.G. (2003). Offender interaction with victims in homicide: A multidimensional analysis of frequencies in crime scene behaviours. *Journal of Interpersonal Violence*, *18*, 490–512.

Salfati, G.C. and Bateman, A.L. (2005). Serial homicide: An investigation of behavioural consistency. *Journal of Investigative Psychology and Offender Profiling*, *2*, 121–144.

Salkind, N.J. (2010). *Encyclopaedia of research design*. Thousand Oaks, CA: SAGE Publications.

Santtila, P., Fritzon, K., and Tamelander, A.L. (2005). Linking arson incidents on the basis of crime scene behaviour. *Journal of Police and Criminal Psychology*, *19*, 1–16.

Santtila, P., Pakkanen, T., Zappala, A., Bosco, D., Valkama, M., and Mokros, A. (2008). Behavioural crime linking in serial homicide. *Psychology, Crime and Law*, *14*, 245–265.

Snook, B., Cullen, R.M., Bennell, C., Taylor, P.J., and Gendreau, P. (2008). The criminal profiling illusion: What's behind the smoke and mirrors? *Criminal Justice and Behaviour*, *35*(10), 1257–1276.

Toulmin, S. (1958). *The Uses of Argument*. UK: Cambridge University Press.

Turvey, B.E. (1999). *Criminal Profiling: An Introduction to Behavioural Evidence Analysis*. San Deigo, CA: Academic Press.

White, P.C. (1998). *Crime Scene to Court: Essentials of Forensic Science* (Paperback). UK: Royal Society of Chemistry.

Wilson, P., Lincoln, R., and Kocsis, R. (1997). Validity, utility and ethics of profiling for serial violent and sexual offenders. *Humanities & Social Sciences Papers*. Retrieved from https://core.ac.uk/download/pdf/46937477.pdf.

Woodhams, J. and Toye, K. (2007). An empirical test of the assumptions of case linkage and offender profiling with serial commercial robberies. *Psychology, Public Policy, and Law*, *13*(1), 59–85.

CHAPTER 4

SEX OFFENDING

"Once, in a three-day taping that included several sadists, the material was so overwhelming that both the film crew and I got sick...our immune systems had weakened, I believe, from the beating our souls had taken."

Anna Salter
Author of *Predators: Paedophiles, Rapists, And Other Sex Offenders*

4.1　Introduction

Sex offending is a broad category of crime and sex offenders are a varied group of criminals. The term 'sex offender' applies to individuals who have committed offenses such as rape, incest, Internet grooming, child sexual abuse, up-skirt voyeurism, underwear theft, and molestation, amongst others. Regardless of the type, sex crimes are widely condemned because of their invasive and often interpersonal nature.

Why do sex offenders commit these offences? Is it the result of ineffective sex education, poor personal morals, inadequate impulse control, or mental perversion? This chapter will examine some of the motivations behind sex offending, alongside studies of crime prevention strategies and victimology. Since rape is one of the most heinous of all sex crimes, this chapter will focus mostly on rape. However, there will be some discussion on other kinds of sex crimes. The following case study describes one of the most prominent rape cases that we have seen in Singapore, dubbed 'the Hotel Rapist'.

CASE STUDY:
Hotel Rapist

On 8 April 2003, after more than a week of fantasizing about sexual activity with an air stewardess, Kevin (aged 28) found an opportunity. He found out from some hotel staff that some air stewardesses would be checking-in at the Hotel ABC at 3 p.m. As they arrived, he singled out a stewardess whom he thought was attractive, and he resolved to have his way with her. Armed with a kitchen knife and realistic-looking toy pistol, he followed her (and her friend, who was also an air stewardess) to their room. When one of them used her luggage to keep the hotel room door ajar, Kevin quickly rushed in and shut the door. Then, he pointed the pistol at his victim, repeatedly raped the 31-year-old, and forced her to pose for lewd pictures. He took lewd photos of them in various poses. The victim's 30-year-old colleague claimed that he had molested her.

The sexual assault incident caused lasting trauma to the victims, both of whom were married. Although the stewardess who was raped was given drugs to prevent pregnancy and protect her against sexually transmitted diseases (STDs), she later made the shocking discovery that she was pregnant. She decided to abort the five-week-old foetus and described that decision as "painful and agonizing". She developed phobias of lifts, staying in hotels, and being in quiet places. Even with counselling, she felt that she would not be able to continue working as a flight attendant with such debilitating phobias. Her colleague was equally traumatized and blamed herself for not helping her friend who was raped. Though the offender was acquitted of molest charges because inconsistencies were found in her account to the police and that given to the judge in court, the event was so traumatizing that she developed phobias of darker-skinned men and of staying in hotels alone. Furthermore, her husband found that she had a change in temperament, became less tolerant, and more short-tempered towards their child. Sexual intimacy with her husband became difficult.

Kevin was found guilty for one count of rape and four counts of

(*Continued*)

(Continued)

aggravated molestation, as well as for violating the Arms and Offences Act. The judge sentenced him to 26 years jail term and the maximum 24 strokes of the cane. He remained solemn as the sentence was read out.

Source: Chong (2003). Hotel rapist gets 26 years, 24 strokes. *The Straits Times*.

When cases like these take the headlines, there is panic. Fear strikes us, and we do not feel safe. We remind our children, spouses, and partners to be careful. Despite these fears, the number of sex crimes is not large in relation to the total number of crimes in Singapore. Nonetheless, because of the very personal nature of such sex crimes, there is a great psychological impact on society and victims.

4.2 What is Sexual Violence?

According to the World Health Organization's *World Report on Violence and Heath* (2002), sexual violence is defined as including:

"A wide range of acts, including coerced sex in marriage and dating relationships, rape by strangers, systematic rape during armed conflict, sexual harassment (including demands for sexual favours in return for jobs or school grades), sexual abuse of children, forced prostitution and sexual trafficking, child marriage, and violent acts against the sexual integrity of women, including female genital mutilation and obligatory inspections for virginity. Women and men may also be raped when in police custody or in prison".

This internationally accepted definition of sexual violence is quite broad. The challenge for law enforcement, correctional experts, and psychologists working in the field today is that prevention, intervention, enforcement, and rehabilitation strategies will have to be tailored differently to each type of sex offending behavior. Otherwise, policy recommendations and practical interventions would not achieve maximum effectiveness. For instance, the assessment and rehabilitation of a specific sex offender cannot be effectively conducted if his or her *criminogenic needs* are not accurately identified. Readers interested in the detailed treatment of this subject should refer to advanced texts on this subject. Good places to start are *Assessment and Treatment of Sex Offenders* (Beech *et al.*, 2009) and *Sexual Deviance: Theory, Assessment, and Treatment*, second edition (Laws & O'Donohue, 2008). It is hard to do justice to all the sub-topics within sex crimes in this introductory textbook. Therefore, this chapter will instead mainly focus on the crime of rape.

4.3 Definition of Rape

Rape is defined as forced or otherwise coerced penetration of the vulva or anus, using a penis, other body parts, or an object. The attempt to do so is known as 'attempted rape'. (Krug *et al.*, 2012).

4.3.1 *Sub-categories of Rape*

Rape can be classified into several categories:

- *Date or acquaintance rape*: This occurs during dates and may or may not involve drug use. Date rapists have a strong sense of entitlement (for example, "I paid for this romantic dinner and I have been courting her for so long, and I deserve sex");
- *Gang rape*: Where victim(s) are raped by a group of people. This is common in warfare;
- *Marital or spousal rape*: Where rape occurs within a marriage;[1]
- *Statutory rape*: This is consensual sex with a minor. Statutory rape is determined to have occurred if it is assessed that the young person (even if he/she consented) does not have the capacity to give consent;
- *Prison rape*: Where the act occurs in prisons;
- *Payback or revenge rape*: Where a female of a certain tribe is raped as an act of revenge against men from her tribe;

---

[1] This is a difficult type of crime to investigate from the angle of prosecution since spouses do sometimes separate and get together physically. But, the bottom-line is that if a spouse says no, then sexual coercion may constitute the offence of rape. It is important to seek legal advice on matters such as this.

- *War rape*: This is committed by soldiers or civilians in the context of war as a means of psychological warfare, and where women and girls are forced into sexual slavery and prostitution; and
- *Corrective rape*: This refers to forms of hate crime where LGBT victims are raped to 'correct' their sexual orientation and enforce their conformity to heterosexual norms.

4.4 Legislation on Sexual Violence

4.4.1 *Offences in the U.K. and the U.S.*

In the U.K., Professor Clive Hollin and colleagues (Hollin *et al.*, 2010) argued there are several kinds of sexual offences, which can be divided into the following categories:

- *Non-consensual sexual offences*: Includes rape, sexual assault, and causing or inciting sexual acts;
- *Offences involving ostensible consent*: Involves children, vulnerable adults;
- *Preparatory offences*: Sexual grooming, administering a substance with intent to commit sexual assault;
- *Other offences*: Sex with a relative, sexual activity in public lavatory,[2] exposure, voyeurism, intercourse with an animal, sexual penetration of a corpse; and
- *Exploitation offences*: Indecent photographs of children, abuse of children through prostitution and pornography, sex trafficking.

In the U.S., the laws can vary by state, but according to one example, which is the United States Code, Title 18, Part One, Chapter 109A, some of the laws relating to sexual violence may include (West Virginia Foundation for Rape Information and Services, n.d.):

- Aggravated sexual assault by force or threat;
- Sexual abuse;

---

[2] Intriguingly, this is an offence in the UK under 'Sex in a public toilet' (Section 71, Sexual Offences Act, 2003), and especially when this becomes an irritation and distress to passing witnesses.

- Sexual abuse of a minor or ward;
- Abusive sexual conduct;
- Female genital mutilation; and
- Campus sexual violence.

4.4.2 *Sexual Offences in Singapore*[3]

Rape is presented under Section 375 of the Singapore Penal Code. It is a very serious offence, and a man who forces a woman to have sexual intercourse against her consent will be punished with a jail sentence for up to 20 years, and may be caned or fined (AWARE, 2002). A man commits the offence of 'rape' (Penal Code, Section 375(1)) when he penetrates the vagina of a woman with his penis without her consent; or with or without her consent when she is under 14 years of age. There are more details to this piece of legislation, and readers are advised to read the actual sections of the Penal Code, which goes into greater details.

Legal authors Stanley Yeo *et al.* in their book, *Criminal Law in Malaysia and Singapore* explained that, because of the way the law is defined, a man or boy (male) cannot be a victim of rape as rape is defined as the penile penetration of a vagina. The gender-specific nature of the offence means that the law governing rape in Singapore does not cover sexual violations by men against men, by women against women, or by women against men (Yeo *et al.*, 2012). Other forms of vaginal penetration by another part of the body or by an object, e.g., bottle, stick, object, finger, etc., are not covered by the law governing rape, and these could be classified under other offences such as 'Causing Hurt' or 'Outraging of Modesty'. This can be upsetting to victims who are violated in such a manner, because these acts could cause psychological responses similar to that caused by forced penile penetration. Look at Table 4.1 and discuss whether the following constitutes legal rape.

---

[3] The discussion that follows on the laws and exceptions are presented here only for analysis purposes. As there are always amendments to the law over the years and new Bills being passed in Parliament, some of this information may not be up to date. I have not included all the details of these laws. Readers should always seek legal advice and consult a lawyer, on legal matters they are concerned about.

Table 4.1:   Activity: Legal Rape or Not?

Think about the scenarios and discuss whether they constitute the crime of rape in Singapore. Explain why.

A man pretends to be the husband of a woman; he slips into bed with the woman. She gets aroused, encourages him, and they have sex.

A couple, both aged 13, have consensual sex.

A man attacks a woman, and inserts his finger into her vagina.

A female teacher, aged 30, has sex with her students.

A man with mental illness commits sexual acts on a cat.

It is important to understand the difference between *submission* and *consent* in sexual crimes, because they have different meanings in legal contexts. A woman may "submit" to sexual intercourse, but this does not mean that she legally 'consents'. Rape laws require that both *force* and *lack of consent* be proven before an individual can be convicted of rape, in most international legal environments. Lack of victim resistance, for example, not fighting back, not screaming, and not attempting to escape, is sometimes interpreted as a sign of consent, when this is often not the case, as the victim may 'submit' out of fear.

Furthermore, in some crime prevention materials, women are sometimes told not to resist their attacker, since they may be put in harm's way or killed if they resisted. However, a lawyer may then use this "lack of resistance" in court to explain that the victim did not resist the attacker and, hence, may have possibly consented to the sexual activity. The issue of "consent" remains a critical component in most rape trials today. The Association of Women for Action and Research (AWARE) has a good discussion on the issue of consent (http://www.aware.org.sg). AWARE explains that "consent" is the communication of agreement, by which one person allows another person to give and receive sexual acts. Anything that is done without "consent" trespasses on a person's rights to bodily integrity and sexual autonomy. AWARE argues that consent must be "freely and voluntarily given", and that if a person is in doubt about whether their partner is consenting, they should always check verbally.

4.5 Other Sexual Offences

The offence of 'Statutory Rape'

According to the laws of Singapore, a girl under 16 years of age is deemed to be unable to consent to sex, even if she willingly agrees to sex. Also, the sexual penetration of a person under 14 years old is deemed to be 'rape', or unlawful sexual penetration, and the offender could be charged for 'statutory rape'. All of this relates to the 'age of consent' issue.[4] Across the world, the legal charges for violating age of consent laws can vary from light sentences to being charged for 'statutory rape'. In some countries, the "close in age" concept is applied. This means that a sexual act in which one or both partners are under the age of consent would not be considered criminal, if the partners' age difference is within the limits set by the law. In addition, in some other places in the world, the age of consent is lowered or void if the sexual partners are married. On the other hand, the age of consent can be raised in certain scenarios, for instance, if an older party (e.g., a teacher or preacher) has authority over the younger party, but takes sexual advantage of the victim.

Statutory Penetration of Minor under 16

It is illegal to have sex with a person under the age of 16, with or without the minor's consent. Sex with a person below 16 is called "Statutory Penetration of a Minor Under 16" (S376A, Penal Code). It does not matter if the man/boy or the woman/girl initiated the sex. If a woman initiated sex with a boy under 16, she might be the guilty party under the offence (AWARE, n.d.)

Marital Rape

A husband can commit the legal offence of rape if he forces himself onto his wife, especially if he is estranged and has not been seeing or living with his wife, and then proceeds to have sex with her, especially using force. Even if a rape charge is not possible, a man who forces his wife to have sex may still be guilty of other offences, such as: Voluntarily Causing Hurt

---

[4] One cannot claim that one was not aware of the victim's age.

(S321), Voluntarily Causing Grievous Hurt (S322), Wrongful Restraint (S241), and Sexual Assault by Penetration (S376) (AWARE, n.d.).

Outraging of Modesty (OM) and Insult of Modesty

Outraging of Modesty (OM) refers to the assault or use of criminal force on a person with the intent to outrage modesty. The issue here is *the use of force* in doing so. The interesting aspect of this law is that it does not come under Sexual Offences, but instead, comes under the Section 354 Criminal Force, of the Penal Code. A related offence, which is 354A for Outraging of Modesty in Certain Circumstances, is when OM occurs in a lift in a building or with any person under the age of 14. Table 4.2 shows some interesting statistics regarding OM.

Table 4.2:   Showing Outraging of Modesty (OM) Rates in Singapore

	2010	2011	2012	2013	2014	2015	2016
Females	1,437	1,400	1,417	1,349	1,365	1,279	1,267
Males	74	82	89	86	85	90	101
Total	1,511	1,482	1,506	1,450	1,450	1,369	1,368

Sources: Ministry of Social Development and Family. https://www.msf.gov.sg/research-and-data/Research-and-Statistics/Pages/Violence-Outrage-of-Modesty-Victims.aspx. and the Singapore Police Statistics (https://www.police.gov.sg/news-and-publications/ statistics).

Another charge, which appears similar but is not so, is the charge of 'Insult of Modesty'. This is under Section 509 of the Penal Code, which is "word or gesture intended to insult the modesty of a woman". This covers non-physical acts of sexual harassment, e.g., the taking of photos, flashing, or uttering vulgarities to insult women. For this offence, a person may be sentenced to imprisonment for up to one year, or be given a fine, or both. In a recent court ruling, it was pointed out that this law only protects women and cannot be applied to men.[5]

---

[5] This was a case involving 27-year-old perpetrator who had secretly captured videos of men in sexual acts and men defecating at Paragon and Cathay shopping mall toilets. The judge argued that while the prosecution wanted to charge under 'insulting of modesty', this was not possible, as the law didn't apply to men. The judge explained,

Other sexual offences

There are other important Singaporean legislation relevant to sexual offending, and these include the following:

- Section 376: Sexual Assault by Penetration;
- Section 376A: Sexual penetration of minor under 16;
- Section 376B: Commercial Sex with Minor Under 18;
- Section 376C: Commercial Sex with Minor Under 18 Outside Singapore;
- Section 376D: Tour Outside Singapore For Commercial Sex with Minor Under 18;
- Section 376E: Sexual Grooming of Minor Under 16,
- Section 376F: Procurement of Sexual Activity with Person with Mental Disability;
- Section 376G: Incest (covers incestuous acts with granddaughter, daughter, sister, half-sister, mother, or grandmother);
- Section 377: Sexual Penetration of A Corpse;
- Section 377A: Outrages on Decency.
- Section 377B: Sexual Penetration with Living Animal

Readers should note that there are two other relevant pieces of legislation related to sexual offences. These are not under the Penal Code. They are Section 7 of the Children and Young Persons Act (Cap. 38), which discusses "sexual exploitation of child or young person", and also Part XI of the Women's Charter (Cap. 353), which discusses "offences against women and girls", including issues relating to prostitution and trafficking.

The rise of 'upskirt' photography

In recent years, there has been a rise in 'upskirt' photography cases in Singapore, likely the result of the increasing accessibility of

---

"the fact that male urinals are more open concept than female equivalents, would speak volumes of a differentiated approach to modesty" (Yiyayan, 2017).

smartphones. In October 2016, a local secondary school student was expelled, and several others caned, after they were found to possess upskirt images of six female teachers. Seven boys took these photos and videos, and 23 others shared the images. Offenders who take upskirt photographs of women are usually charged under Section 509 of the Penal Code (Insult of Modesty).

Interestingly, in the U.S., there is a specific law addressing this issue under Section 1301 (108th), called the Video Voyeurism Prevention Act of 2004. This law prohibits knowingly videotaping, photographing, filming, recording by any means, or broadcasting an image of a private area of an individual, without that individual's consent, under circumstances in which that individual has a reasonable expectation of privacy.

Why do perpetrators engage in such acts? Men (and boys) who take upskirt photos of women report doing so for various reasons, including thrill-seeking, peer pressure, using the photographs for their personal sexual gratification, and because they are trying to manage their own psychological issues (e.g., stress, underwear fetishes, and voyeurism).

How are victims affected by these incidents? Victims of upskirt photography report feeling quite traumatized, frightened, shocked, and angry. We should not underestimate the impact that this crime has on its victims. Photographs, videos, or images being circulated online affect victims of such incidents. If emotionally affected, they should seek help from professional counsellors, psychologists, therapists, or mental health professionals.

4.6 Differences between Legal and Psychological/ Behavioural Classifications

There are differences between legal and psychological classifications. This has practical implications for research and intervention. An uncle of a 15-year-old girl who grooms and sexually assaults his niece, for instance, can be charged with either the crime of 'incest' or 'rape'. The mental health professional in-charge of the criminal must appreciate these differences. If the therapist assumes the offender is a rapist because he is charged for the offence of rape when, in fact, his behavior pertains more towards incest and contains dynamics of intra-familial sex abuse (e.g., grooming, feelings of betraying a family member, and so on), then the therapist would not be treating these issues appropriately. This issue also has research implications. Total rape computed in a country (as a legal classification) typically includes statutory rape cases. However, statutory rape cases, while an offence in itself, may involve cases of *consensual sexual relationships* between underage individuals. This is quite different from the forced non-consensual sexual activity. Putting all of these cases together and analysing them as a broad cluster would not rightly capture the characteristics of rape as both a psychological and a behavioral phenomenon of sexual violation.

4.7 Prevalence

Table 4.3 shows the total numbers of rape cases in Singapore. Considering these numbers (including 'statutory rape', which constitutes a good number of these cases), the actual number of rape (excluding statutory rape) cases in Singapore is not large, for a population of about 5.4 million. As shown in Table 4.3, the numbers for rape are generally stable, and do not fluctuate greatly.

Table 4.3: Rape Cases

Crime	2009	2010	2011	2012	2013	2014	2015	2016
Rape	202	165	150	133	120	164	162	151*

Source: https://data.gov.sg, '*'-from Ministry of Family and Social Development website.

4.8 Characteristics of Rapists and Other Sex Offenders

Rapists

While each sex offender type is different, some 'group level' (nomothetic) behavioural characteristics can be uncovered. Research suggests that, in general, rapists as a group tend to possess the following characteristics (Durrant, 2013; Gannon *et al.*, 2008):

(a) be male;
(b) from a low socioeconomic background;
(c) were unemployed and uneducated;
(d) were versatile offenders who committed different kinds of offences (both sexual and non-sexual);
(e) might have been sexually abused as a child;
(f) may have had a history of family violence;
(g) have had a greater number of previous violent convictions;
(h) might use greater levels of aggression and force than child sexual abusers;
(i) were more likely to re-offend violently rather than sexually; and
(j) have higher recidivism rates.[6]

Other researchers looked at typologies. The FBI created a typology of four types. The *power-reassurance* rapist is characterized by feelings of inadequacy and poor social skills, and does not inflict injury upon his victims. The *power-assertive* rapist tends to be impulsive, may use aggressive control, and could abuse substances. He is unplanned, and is unlikely to use a weapon. The third is the *anger-retaliation* rapist, who is motivated by power and aggression. This individual sexually assaults for retaliatory reasons, and degrades or humiliates his victim. The fourth type is the *sadistic rapist* who re-enacts sexual fantasies involving torture or pain. The assaults conducted by this type of rapist is characterized by extensive planning, and may result in the murder of the victim (Hazelwood & Burgess, 1987).

Knight and Prentky (1990) developed the Massachusetts Treatment Center Framework (MTC: R3) for treating rapists during rehabilitation. It classifies nine types of rapists:

1. Type 1 (Opportunistic, High Social Competence);
2. Type 2 (Opportunistic, Low Social Competence);

---

[6] Hanson and Bussiere (1998) found that 19% sexually recidivated and 22% violently recidivated over an average follow-up period of five years.

3. Type 3 (Pervasive Anger);
4. Type 4 (Overt Sadism);
5. Type 5 (Muted Sadism);
6. Type 6 (Sexualized, High Social Competence);
7. Type 7 (Sexualized, Low Social Competence);
8. Type 8 (Vindictive, Low Social Competence); and
9. Type 9 (Vindictive, High Social Competence).

At first glance, several themes are apparent — opportunism, anger, sadism, vindictiveness, and sexuality. However, studies found that the MTC had its limitations, since 25% of the distinctions among different types overlapped and the distinctions were not empirically determined. For example, it is unclear whether the sadistic rapist is motivated by anger, power, or sexual factors.

What about other studies in Asia and Singapore? In 1998, Dr. Philip Beh conducted a study of rape and indecent sexual attacks in Hong Kong. He noted that assailants came from all age groups, with the largest number from the 21 to 30-year-old age range, followed closely by those from the 16- to 20-year-old age group. Offenders tended to have a higher incidence of family pathology, history of unemployment, and offending. Rapists had more premeditation in carrying out the offence when compared to indecent assault offenders. Victims were acquainted with the assailant in 53% of cases. Of the rape cases in which the victim was a stranger, 20% involved robbery. Dr. Beh's analysis found that rape by more than one attacker was reported in 23% of cases. More than 78% of the rapes occurred indoors. For the rapes that occurred indoors, 42% of these were in the assailant's premises, 30% were in the victims' homes, 16% in hotel or motel rooms, and 13% in lifts, staircases, on rooftops, or in refuse rooms of high-rise apartment blocks. Only 15% of rapes occurred outdoors, usually in poorly-lit parks, beaches, and trails, or inside parked vehicles. Perhaps this could be explained by the fact that Hong Kong is a country with many high-rise apartments and few large spaces such as parks or individual houses (as we would see in some parts of the U.S. or Europe).

Beh noted that more than half of the assaults were concentrated between 20:00 and 04:00 hours. Weapons were used in 18% of reported rapes, threats in 29% of cases, and physical force used in 44% of cases.[7] Alcohol and drugs use were reported in 19% of the cases.

Vaginal penetration was observed in 84% of the cases he had studied. While vaginal and anal penetrations made up 3% of the cases, vaginal and oral penetrations were in 6% of cases, and penetration of all three orifices occurred in 1% of cases.

Ejaculation by perpetrator was reported in only 51% of the cases. Could this be because of non-ejaculation of the assailant? Dr. Beh suggested that rape may not be committed for male sexual gratification, but for power assertion, or in response to anger. Only 40% of the victims had their clothing totally removed. The use of condoms was reported in only 4% of cases.

Post-rape victim behavior showed that 38% of victims cleaned or washed their genitalia immediately after the rape, which is a concern for police investigations since forensic evidence is lost. Forensic findings wise, 35% of victims showed signs of bodily injuries, and bleeding from genital injuries was noted in 12% of victims. Vulva injuries were found in 8% of victims, which seemed low. He explained that this lack of injuries could be because of sexual inability of the perpetrator or the inability of the victims to resist the attacker for fear of injury or death. This, he argued, was an important point for the courts to note, as some lawyers tend to argue that rape victims should exhibit more injuries, and doubted the veracity of the victim's claims if little or no injury is found.

In Singapore, a group of researchers looked at men who committed rape (Lim *et al.*, 2001). They interviewed 63 rapists[8] and then compared them with 32 other violent-nonsexual offenders (Violent Controls) and 31 non-violent, non-sexual controls (Non-violent Controls). Their results showed that the mean age of rapists was 37 (Standard Deviation or SD = 11 years) compared to non-violent controls (NVCs) at 43 years and violent controls (VCs) at 38 years. Rapists were, on average, closer in age to the violent controls, but were

---

[7] Discussing this, he makes a good point that it is a common myth that victims of rape must show bodily injuries.

[8] It is unclear from this paper, if statutory rape is excluded from the analysis, but we would assume that they would have been so, since in the authors' later papers (Lim, 2002), it is explicitly mentioned that statutory rape cases were excluded from analysis.

younger than the non-violent controls. The rapist group had a lower level of education compared to the non-violent controls, but there was no difference in education levels between rapists and violent controls.

Compared to non-violent controls, rapists were less educated, came from large families, were in more conflicting relationships with their families, were less likely to have been imprisoned in the past, were less likely to have committed a non-sexual offence, were more likely to have committed a previous sexual offence, were less likely to have used illegal drugs, and were more likely to have had recent exposure to pornography. Rapists were also more likely to be single. When rapists were compared with the violent group, the rapists were again more likely to have come from larger families, experienced more conflict in their families, less likely to have been imprisoned, more likely to have committed a sexual offence, less likely to have committed a non-sexual offence, and had more exposure to pornography.

For all three groups, the researchers noted that the offenders had consumed alcohol or drugs at the time of the offence (rapists 54%; violent controls 69%, and non-violent controls 62%, but the differences were not statistically significant). This point is important since it confirms our discussion made in Chapter 1 about how drugs and alcohol can be criminogenic factors. The study found that six months or less before the incident, these offenders reported viewing pornographic material (rapists 30%, violent controls 26%, and non-violent controls 13%). Many of the offences (27%) occurred in the offender's home, and a proportion (25%) occurred in the victim's place or secluded public places such as the beach or park, and 70% of the victims had known their offenders and 27% were strangers. The mean age of the victims for all groups was 18.7 years (SD = 8.9 years).

The authors make several interesting points. First, these findings are consistent with other research that suggests that rape may be perpetrated by poorly educated men, of low socioeconomic status, and come from large families (Dietz, 1978). Second, many appear to have anti-social tendencies. Third, while the rapists were using pornography, the influence of pornography is unclear. They explained that while studies have suggested that hardcore violent pornography increased violent sexual crimes (Court, 1976), other studies demonstrated that after pornography was legalized in some countries, sexual assaults had decreased (Donnerstein *et al.*, 1987; Kutchinsky, 1973). They concluded by saying that sexual arousal may not be a strong factor in rape offending, but anger and fear may play a bigger role. This is similar to Dr. Beh's findings, which propose that sexual arousal may play *some* part in the offender's motivation, but perhaps not a major part.

In another paper, Dr. Leslie Lim and fellow researchers from various medical institutions compared 66 imprisoned sexual molesters and 37 rapists in terms of their characteristics (Lim, 2002). Statutory rapists were excluded from this analysis. They found that:

(a) there were no differences in the age for these two groups;
(b) a higher proportion of rapists were single men compared to molesters (50% vs. 30%);
(c) most rapists and molesters were employed at the time of committing their offence (though rapists were more likely in manual jobs);
(d) rapists had a lower level of education than molesters;
(e) more rapists drank alcohol at the time of committing sexual assault (92% rapists, 64% molesters); and
(f) there were no statistical differences between the rapists and molesters in relation to illicit drug use (30% and 29% respectively).

Rapists tended to commit rape between 00:00 to 05:59 hours, while molesters were more likely to commit molest between the times of 12:00 to 17:59 hours. As expected, rapists also used secluded places, while molesters tended to use crowded places, staircases, or corridors. Molestation occurred more in public transport, while rape tended to occur more in a hotel.[9] Only a minority of rapists (5%) and molesters (11%) admitted to their prior fantasies about their offences. Molesters reported feeling lonelier. The authors hypothesized that molesters may find themselves in a series of failed and unstable relationships, and hence, may experience loneliness.

---

[9] Recall that in Chapter 2, we discussed how deception differed across crime. This finding suggests that there is also intra-crime variation in deceptive patterns.

The mean ages of rape victims were 23 (SD = 8.9) and molestation victims were 19.9 (SD = 7.9). Victim attraction was perceived to be a reason for molestation in 14% of molesters and 5% of rapists, although the authors qualify that this is quite unlikely to be a factor since many previous studies have suggested that attractiveness does not play a role. In fact, studies have found that young females are not typical rape victims; elderly females and pregnant females have also been targeted (Groth & Birnbaum, 1990; Taylor, 1992). In addition, 76% of rapists and 60% of molesters had pre-planned their assaults, and 53% of rape victims and 37% of molested females were strangers to the offenders. Victims of molestation tended to be relatives, whereas rapists were more likely to be boyfriends, ex-spouses, or ex-lovers of their victims. Molesters were more likely to have multiple sexual partners compared to rapists.

Dr. Leslie made several conclusions. First, he suggested that loneliness seems to be a factor with molesters, perhaps because of unstable emotional relationships. This seemed to support the notion of "courtship disorder", which will be discussed later in this chapter. Second, it seems that both groups were opportunistic to some degree. Third, the use of alcohol seemed to be an important "criminogenic" factor (recall the discussion on alcohol in Chapter 1). Fourth, while there was drug use, the rates for drug use for both groups were not high, perhaps because of the strong anti-drug laws in Singapore. Molesters tended to deny their act of violation, attributing it to be an accident or completely denying it. Another common excuse used by both, but more often by rapists, is to attribute their actions to alcoholic intoxication and not being aware of what they were doing.

4.8.1 *Child Sex Offending*

According to the World Health Organisation, child sexual abuse is:

> "The involvement of a child in an activity that he or she does not fully comprehend, is unable to give informed consent to, or for which the child is not developmentally prepared and cannot give consent, or that violates the laws or social taboos of society. Child

sexual abuse is evidenced by this activity between a child and an adult (or another child) who by age or development is in a relationship of responsibility, trust or power, the activity being intended to gratify or satisfy the needs of the other person. This may include but is not limited to: the inducement or coercion of a child to engage in any unlawful sexual activity; The exploitative use of a child in prostitution or other unlawful sexual practices and the exploitative use of children in pornographic performance and materials" — World Health Organisation: Report of The Consultation on Child Abuse Prevention (1999, pp. 13–14).

Child sexual abuse may take several forms including vaginal or anal penetration with the perpetrator's penis, finger, or other object; oral sex involving fellatio whether by a child upon an adult, or by an adult upon a child; cunnilingus; exhibitionism; the perpetrator touching/fondling intimate parts; and the child induced to touch the perpetrator's intimate parts; and frottage (rubbing genitals against the victim's body or clothing). Some of the indirect actions of abuse could include the offender making sexual comments; getting the child to undress; encouraging children to have sex together; and exposing these children to pornographic material. Sometimes, there is voyeurism in which a person receives sexual gratification from seeing the genitalia of children or witnessing children involved in sexual acts with other children or adults (Elliott *et al.*, 2003).

4.8.1.1 *Child abuse*

Groth *et al.* (1982) classified those who abused children based on the degree to which the sexual behaviour was the basis for psychological needs. The *fixated offender* prefers interaction, and identifies with children socially and sexually. These individuals develop and maintain relationships with children to satisfy their sexual needs. The *regressed child sexual abuser*, on the other hand, prefers social and sexual interaction with adults, and their sexual involvement with children is situational and occurs as a result of life stressors. Regressed abusers are often incest offenders or offenders who sexually assault female adolescents. This is important as not all offenders who sexually assault children are paedophiles. Paedophilia involves a sexual preference for children that may or may not lead to child sexual abuse, e.g., paedophiles may view child pornography but may not, in all instances, sexually assault children, whereas child sexual abuse involves sexual contact with a child that may or may not be due to paedophilia (Camilleri & Quinsey, 2008). There are sub-categorizations within child abuse. There are: a) those whose targets are within their own family and those whose targets are complete strangers, b) those who target only boys and those who target only girls, taking into account some crossovers, and c) paedophiles who prefer pre-pubescent children, and hebephiles who prefer pubescent children (Neidigh & Krop, 1992).

4.8.1.2 *Male and female child sex offenders*

Are there differences between the male and female child sex offender? Research suggests that male child sex offenders are more likely to be older, better educated, and less versatile in crime than the rapist group, and are more likely to have experienced sexual abuse in their childhood (Finkelhor, 2008). Female child sex offenders (or FCSOs) tend to be in the average age range of 26 to 36 years, although this older age bracket may be derived due to younger or older offenders going unnoticed (Vandiver & Walker, 2002; Vandiver *et al.*, 2004). These offenders appear to come from a low to middle socioeconomic background, hold few qualifications, earn significantly less than their male counterparts, and come from verbally, physically, or sexually abusive families (Nathan & Ward, 2001; 2002). Lewis and Stanley (2000) reported that 80% of females charged with sexual assault claimed that they had been sexually abused in the past. This may explain their low self-esteem, traits of severe passivity and dependency, and how they become trapped in abusive relationships throughout adulthood and marriage. FCSOs, like male offenders, may undertake jobs that involve children. A notable feature of FCSOs is the fact that they are highly likely to abuse children sexually, in the company of a male co-perpetrator. FCSOs are usually known to their victims and tend to be caregivers, and they are often mothers, relatives, babysitters, nannies, and maids. Faller (1995) reports that more than half of the 72 FCSOs in her sample were the mother of at least one of their victims. As they knew their victims, FCSOs are often less predatory than male offenders (Gannon & Rose, 2008). Although evidence suggests that boys are more likely to be abused by an FCSO (Finkelhor & Russell, 1984), other researchers report that FCSOs may also abuse girls, or a mixture of both girls and boys (Faller, 1995). Victims of FCSOs tend to be young and pre-pubescent (Vandiver & Walker, 2002). Unlike male offenders, FCSOs are less likely to use substances while offending.

Matthews, Mathews, and Speltz (1991) discovered three main FCSO typologies from the women seen at their clinic. The *predisposed* FCSO tends to: a) initiate abuse on a family member, which may include her children, b) come from a family background with high levels of sexual abuse, and c) experience deviant sexual urges and cognitions associated with their former abuse, e.g., thinking that children enjoy sex with adults. The *teacher/lover* FCSO tends to initiate and conduct sexual abuse with an adolescent victim. They view sexual contact with their victim as adult-like in nature, and as 'affairs'. They see the youth as being equally responsible for the sexual contact, and perceive the victim's sexual experience as enjoyable. These offenders did not appear to have been sexually victimised as children, but may have suffered some emotional and verbal abuse. They believed that most adolescents were highly sexed individuals who will grasp at any opportunity for sex with adult women. The *male-coerced* FCSO commits her abuse under the influence of a male partner, or is sometimes forced by a male partner. She tends to be dependent and often non-assertive. She may hold stereotypical views of male–female roles, has low self-esteem, worries about rejection, and experiences powerlessness. Research suggests that she will stay in that relationship, because she believes that no one else will have her as a partner. She initiates the sexual abuse to maintain her relationship with her partner (Mathews *et al.*, 1997).

4.8.1.3 *Child abuse in Singapore*

In Singapore, the Ministry of Social and Family Development (MSF) defines child sexual abuse as "any act where a child or young person is used for sexual pleasure or is taken advantage of sexually. It also includes exposing a child or young person to sexual acts or pornography" ("Protecting Children in Singapore", 2016, p. 7). In Singapore, the Children and Young Persons Act (The Law Revision Commission, 2001) consolidates the law relating to local children (i.e., those below 14 years old) and young persons (i.e., those 14 years and above, but below 16 years old).

In 2016, there were 107 cases of sexual abuse involving children less than 16 years of age in Singapore. Most of these cases involved molestation. These cases are investigated and managed by the Child Protection Service (CPS) at the MSF. The CPS works with families and caregivers to keep the child safe, and undertakes social investigations. The police manage the criminal investigation (Seow, 2017). While sex abuse cases are significant, the numbers are smaller than the numbers involved for child physical abuse and neglect as shown in Table 4.4.

The effects of being a victim of child sexual abuse (CSA) are great. First, there are major psychological effects such as low self-esteem,

Table 4.4:   Cases of Child Abuses in Singapore

Type/Year	2012	2013	2014	2015	2016
Physical	177	148	161	263	444
Sexual	70	60	56	82	107
Neglect	136	135	164	206	322

Source: Ministry of Social and Family Development, Retrieved from https://www.msf.gov.sg/research-and-data/Research-and-Statistics/Pages/Child-Abuse-Investigations.aspx.

anxiety, depression, anger, post-traumatic stress, substance abuse, sexual difficulties, somatic preoccupation and disorder, and self-injurious behaviour. Second, CSA seems linked with sexual re-victimisation. Third, there is a link between CSA and future high-risk sexual behavior (Lalor & McElvaney, 2010).

While these numbers shown in Table 4.4 appear to be on the rise year on year, the MSF has explained that this is due to increased awareness. Nonetheless, in such cases, it is difficult for victims to come forward and make a report because, most of the time, they know the perpetrator. The Sexual Assault Care Centre managed by AWARE handled 338 cases in 2016 and 234 cases in 2014. They reported that 80% of these cases were committed by someone the victims knew (Seow, 2017). In Singapore, there are several agencies that offer help for child protection cases, and these include:

- Heart@Fei Yue: 6819-9170
- Big Love: 6445-0400
- Pave: 6266-0171
- CPS (MSF) Helpline: 1800-777-0000

4.8.2 *Internet Child Sex Offending*

Research suggests that Internet child pornography offenders tend to be male and younger than other sexual offenders (Webb *et al.*, 2007; Seto *et al.*, 2011). Beech *et al.* (2008) grouped the typology into four types:

1. The first category was individuals who used pornography impulsively and out of curiosity.
2. The second category comprised individuals who accessed or traded pornography to sustain their sexual interest in children.
3. The third category used the Internet as part of a pattern of offline offending, using it to acquire victims and disseminate images.

4. The fourth category consisted of individuals who downloaded pornographic images for non-sexual reasons (e.g., financial gain).

Internet child sex offending is a real concern worldwide, and law enforcement is very concerned about cyber sexual grooming (CSG) over the Internet (see the following section for more information on grooming). Predators can draw children into a façade relationship through grooming, inappropriate sexual advances, and manipulation (Hui *et al.*, 2015). Sexual grooming is punishable under Singapore law, under Section 376E of the Penal Code.

4.8.3 *The Psychological Process of Sexual Grooming*

The National Center for Victims of Crime explained that child sexual abusers often try to get the trust of child victims and their caregivers by 'grooming' them (National Center for Victims of Crime, n.d.). They do this by gaining their trust and breaking down their defences. Grooming steps include the following:

(a) *Identifying the victim*: Deciding which child to select.
(b) *Gaining trust*: Here, the perpetrator may assess vulnerabilities to learn how best to interact with the child. Perpetrators may offer the victims attention, understanding, gifts, or a sympathetic ear.
(c) *Playing a role in the child's life*: The perpetrator works to manipulate the relationship, so that that it appears he or she is the only one who really understands the child.
(d) *Isolating the child*: This is done by offering the child car rides or special extra classes, so that the perpetrator may separate the child from others and gain access to the child alone.
(e) *Creating secrecy*: The perpetrator may convince the child that everything that happens is private communication and secret (letters, emails, or text messages). The perpetrator may threaten the victim with disclosure, suicide, and physical harm.

(f) *Initiating sexual contact*: The perpetrator may initiate physical contact with the victim. It may begin with touching that is not overtly sexual (arm around the shoulder, or pat on the knee). Gradually, the perpetrator may introduce more sexualized touching.

(g) *Controlling the relationship*: Children are afraid of disclosing the abuse and are told that they will not be believed. The child may also feel shame or fear that they will be blamed.

CASE STUDY:
Sexual Grooming

Perpetrator (IZ) met a 14-year-old Filipina at a void deck and became interested in her. They chatted for a while, after which IZ asked the girl for her Facebook account name. One evening, IZ began a Facebook conversation with the girl in which he asked her to meet him again. During their conversation, the girl told IZ "I love you", and IZ replied "me (too)". The girl agreed to meet IZ, and they arranged to meet at the void deck, near a playground. The two met as agreed around 8.30 p.m. and chatted at a staircase. The girl's grandmother, who had discovered the Facebook exchange between the two, confronted the girl. The girl then confessed to her father about IZ. Her father, feeling enraged, held on to the phone and pretended to be the girl. During this conversation, IZ made sexually suggestive comments towards the 'girl', including telling her that his genitals were "in pain". He asked her for nude photographs as well. Even after the father texted, "My daddy will get mad" and "I'm still young", IZ asked the "girl" to "make a date". The police arrested IZ, 41, when he showed up at the girl's home.

IZ, married with children, was sentenced to six months' jail on one count of sexually grooming a minor who is under 16 years old. A forensic examination conducted on IZ's phone found that he had deleted the Facebook exchange between him and the girl. While the prosecution sought six to eight months' jail term, IZ's lawyer argued that IZ been reluctant to meet the girl, and may have only relented after the father became more deliberately provocative. For sexual grooming of a minor under 16, IZ could have been jailed up to 10 years.

Source: Koh (2017). 'Man Who Sexually Groomed A 14-Year-Old Girl Jailed Six Months'. *Yahoo News*. Singapore 13 December 2017.

4.9 Psychological Explanations for Sex Offending

1. *Male socialization theory*

Russell and Bolen (2000) explained in *The Epidemic of Rape and Child Sexual Abuse in the United States* that men are socialized to believe that the use of violence is legitimate if their sexual advances are rebuffed (i.e., that a "no" from a woman actually means "yes"). The authors explained that the "virility mystique" is a feeling of sexual insecurity that may lead some men to commit rape to bolster their self-image and masculine identity.

2. *Socio-cognitive and attitude theories*

This theory explains sex offending. Cognitive distortions may be involved in the maintenance of the sexual abuse. Cognitive distortions may be seen in the offender's post-offence justifications (Gannon *et al.*, 2008). See Tables 4.5 and 4.6.

3. *Social Learning*

This is another explanatory factor. Where do males learn about sex and sexuality? Do they learn it from peers, the Internet, or personal 'trial and error'? Learning about sex and sexuality from unreliable sources such as the Internet may also cause misperceptions about sexuality. For example, young men who watch violent rape pornography may believe that women who are beaten up and raped actually enjoy the sexual assault.

4. *Courtship disorder hypothesis*

This is a theory of sex offending developed in 1986 by Dr. Kurt Freund and Dr. Ray Blanchard at the Department of Psychiatry, University of Toronto, and at the Clarke Institute of Psychiatry, Canada. According to their courtship disorder hypothesis, there is a process in humans that consists of four phases. These are: (a) looking for potential sexual partners; (b) pre-tactile interaction with partners, such as smiling and talking to them; (c) tactile interaction, such as embracing or petting; and (d) finally, sexual intercourse.

The authors explain that in real human courtship, these phases may blend into each other. A disturbance of the 'search phase' manifests as 'voyeurism', a disturbance of the pre-tactile interaction

Table 4.5:   Scales Measuring Offense Supportive Beliefs/Cognitions

Rape Myth Acceptance Scale (Burt, 1980, 1991)	A scale exploring rape myths: o 'Women who go around bra-less or wearing short skirts are asking for trouble.' o 'One reason that women falsely report a rape is that they frequently have a need to call attention to themselves.' o 'Many women have an unconscious wish to be raped, and may then unconsciously set up a situation in which they are likely to be attacked.'
Adversarial sexual beliefs scale (Burt, 1980)	This is a scale that focuses on interaction patterns related specifically to sexual behaviour. o 'Most women are sly and manipulative when they are out to attract a man.' o 'A lot of women gain pleasure from putting men down.'
The Attitudes Toward Rape Victims Scale (ARVS) (Ward, 1988).	The 25-item questionnaire consists of eight positive and 17 negative statements about rape victims that deal with areas of credibility, denigration, deservingness, trivialization, and victim blaming. o 'A raped woman is a less desirable woman.' o 'The extent of the woman's resistance should be the major factor in determining if a rape has occurred.' o 'Women often claim rape to protect their reputations.' o 'Good' girls are as likely to be raped as 'bad' girls o 'Women who have had prior sexual relationships should not complain about rape.'
Rape Empathy Scale (RES): (Deitz *et al.*, 1982)	A measure of perceived empathy for rape victims which consists of 19 items measuring empathy levels toward rape survivors o 'I feel that the situation in which a man compels a woman to submit to sexual intercourse against her will is an unjustifiable act under any circumstances.' o 'In deciding the matter of guilt or innocence in a rape case, it is more important to know about the past sexual activity of the alleged rape victim than the past sexual activity of the alleged rapist.'

Source: Durrant (2013). An Introduction to Criminal Psychology.

Table 4.6: Cognitions of Sex Offenders

Cognitions	Theme
Women are mysterious ("When she says 'no', she means 'yes' or she is playing hard to get", or "Women are sly and manipulative.")	Nature of Harm
Women are sex objects ("She wants it when she dresses like that.")	Sex objects
Male sex drive is uncontrollable ("Sex is just like hunger: when you are hungry, you must eat.")	Uncontrollability
Entitlement ("As a man, I am entitled to sex and a woman's body.")	Entitlement
Dangerous world ("Every man for himself, so I can be callous to others in order to get what I want.")	Dangerous world

Source: Adapted from Polascheck and Ward (2002), Ward and Keenan (1999).

phase manifests as 'exhibitionism', a disturbance of the tactile interaction phase manifests as 'toucheurism' or 'frotteurism', and the disturbance in 'courtship behaviour phase' manifests in 'rape'. The authors explained that *voyeurism* is characterized by a desire to spy on a complete stranger, either in some stage of undress, having intercourse, or in an intimate situation. *Exhibitionism* is characterized by an overwhelming desire to expose the penis from a distance to an unknown person. *Toucheurism* is an overwhelming desire to touch the breasts or genital region of an unknown woman, without her consent. A variant of toucheurism is frotteurism, which is a desire for approaching an unsuspecting stranger from the rear and pressing or rubbing the penis against her. Finally, there are males who commit rape (Freund & Blanchard, 1980).

5. *Finkelhor's Precondition Model* (Finkelhor, 1984)
This is a theory of offending that explains that four pre-conditions must be met before offending. First, there is some *motivation* to offend sexually. Second, one *overcomes internal inhibitions*, such as stress through various means, e.g., alcohol, drugs, and pornography.

Third, one *overcomes external inhibitions*, or obstacles, e.g., by investing time to groom children for sexual purposes. Fourth, offenders *overcome resistance* through gift-giving, pornography, using threats, and through force. While it is itself a useful early explanation, this model has problems with overlapping theoretical constructs. Also, there is almost no mention of the role of attitudes and cognitive factors in contributing to the offending (Durrant, 2013).

6. *The Quadripartite Model* (Hall & Hirschman, 1991)
    This is another offending model which explains that there are four primary motivational precursors to sexual offending. These are: (1) physiological sexual arousal, (2) cognitions that justify sexual aggression, (3) negative affective states, and (4) personality problems. Personality problems could be characterized by chronic personality disorders, disregard for social norms and conventions, and a tendency to behave aggressively. Hall and Hirschman noted that environmental factors, such as sanctions and the use of alcohol, play a part in the perpetration of sexual offences. However, they argue that these four factors are nonetheless crucial. While useful, this theory does not provide an account on how the four factors interact to produce a sexual offence.

4.10 Common *Modus Operandi* (MO)

As the CLIP approach raises the importance of looking at investigative considerations (the 'I' aspect of CLIP), this section discusses the *modus operandi*, or MO, of sex offenders. Sex offenders have used many different MOs. It is important to note that most sex offenders know their victims. For example, they could be colleagues, parents, coaches, religious teachers, and even teachers.[10] These cases would

---

[10] In 17 February 2016, an art teacher molested his 13-year-old student. The art teacher started to talk about unconventional topics such as the boy's leg hair and masturbation, before touching the teenager's private parts (Alkhatib, 2017). In another case, a secondary school teacher was charged in court on February 12, 2018,

typically involve subtler deception methods and usually sexual grooming. The perpetrator would very rarely need to use force upon the victim. However, there are cases in which the offender targets strangers and exhibits predatory behaviours. Some of these offenders make use of the following MOs: (a) pretending to be an authority figure, such as a police officer or a law enforcement officer, i.e., he may wear a police cap or carry a fake warrant card; (b) pretending to be a professional photographer for a modelling agency and then assaulting the victim in hotel room; (c) pretending to be an employer who has a job offer, and interviewing and then raping the victim in hotel room; (d) offering money to young girls to act as their 'temporary girlfriends' (see the following case study). Child sex offenders have used threats against children or offered them toys and gifts. In the case of the "Heartbeat Molester" in Singapore, the offender would pretend to be ill and have the victim touch various parts of his chest and body.[11]

CASE STUDY:
The Internet Predator

Pek Khun was an Internet sex predator. In 1998, he posted this message on an Internet chartroom called "Teens' Channel": "Will pay $500 for a temporary girlfriend." This tactic of luring victims worked because most teenagers could relate to his story. He told potential victims that his girlfriend had dumped him, and that as 'revenge', he wanted to show her that he could find a new partner. To many young schoolgirls, being offered $500 was a lot of money, and they felt that this was just pretend play.

Pek claimed to be a teen like them and spent hours coaxing them to meet him, claiming that he only wanted kisses and affection. Instead,

(Continued)

---

with 20 counts of sexual penetration of a minor from his school. The 39-year-old Singaporean was accused of having sex with his 15-year-old student and sexually abusing her, with her consent (*The Straits Times*, 13 February 2018).

[11] MTCG was known as the "Heartbeat Molester" as he had preyed on 28 young girls over a period of 11 years, often asking his victims to feel his heartbeat before molesting them.

(*Continued*)

he took each one to a multi-storey carpark, and molested or raped them. To buy their silence and sexually abuse them further, Pek had threatened to post the girls' nude pictures online, or send it to their friends and family.

In one of the cases, he promised a 14-year-old victim a $50 *hongbao* (red packet with money) if she did what he wanted (which was some cuddling). However, he raped her and switched the $50 in the *hongbao* with a piece of paper. In the weeks later, she contracted chlamydia, a sexually transmitted disease.

Another victim said she had never had a boyfriend before. "I was just too curious for my own good. I wanted to see if this guy was cute and why he had to find a girlfriend on the Net," she said. She described Pek as a sweet-talker who gave the impression that he was a sensitive guy looking for some affection. "He always had a way of countering any arguments I had, for not meeting him." However, when they met, he hardly said a word and did not seem interested in anything about her, "except for my body", the girl recalled. Tears welling in her eyes, she added: "I always had the idea that my first sexual encounter would be with someone I love and who loves me. But that beautiful dream will now always be just a fantasy." She has avoided chatrooms ever since and rarely goes online now except to do research for her schoolwork. The traumatized teenager is now seeing a psychiatrist. Pek was arrested in July after police officers laid a trap and arrested him.

Source: Chong (2003). '23 Years' Jail, 24 Strokes For Internet Sex Fiend'. *Straits Times*, Singapore, 5 February 2003.

4.11 Forensic Evidence and Criminalistics

Following the recommendation of the CLIP approach, an effective criminal psychologist or police officer will need to appreciate the forensic science or criminalistics aspects of sex offences (the 'C' aspects of CLIP). Forensic specimens can be collected (as shown in Table 4.7):

Table 4.7: Forensic Medical Evidence and Specimens in Sex Crimes

Genitalia	To examine for semen and sperm
	Examine injury to the anus and/or genitals (ano-genital injury) or to other parts of the body (extra-genital injury)
Anus	To look for semen, or lubricant, which might have been used during the assault
Blood fluids	For DNA analysis and to examine blood for drugs
Clothing, fibres	To inspect for foreign material and debris, using microscope visualisation and composition analysis — this may link suspect to victim and/ or crime scene
Hair, pubic hair	To compare with hair found at the scene which could belong to offender (using DNA analysis)
Mouth	To check for semen, and for obtaining DNA
Finger nail scraping	To check for skin, blood, and fibre evidence of offender; may indicate resistance
Sanitary pads	To examine for semen, blood, and hair of offender
Skin	To examine for foreign material from offender
Semen, saliva	To identify suspect; link suspect to victim and/or crime scene; indicate sexual activity; indicate penetration
Urine sample	To check for possible drugging by offender
	Toxicology analysis to determine level of substance in urine
Injuries	Examining for tears, ecchymosis[12] (bruise), abrasions and swellings or TEARS
	May indicate use of force; may indicate resistance
Emotional presentation	State of emotion during medical examination

Source: Adapted from Australian Center for the Study of Sexual Assualt (n.d.).

As part of the medical examination, screenings are done for sexually transmitted infections (STIs), and culture tests are ordered for chlamydia, gonorrhoea, bacterial syphilis, and human immunodeficiency virus (HIV).

Another important consideration for assessment is erectile dysfunction (ED). If the offender has ED, penetration could be less likely, which makes the legal prosecution of rape difficult. The degree of ED must be medically established. An offender with ED

---

[12] This refers to the flat area of haemorrhage under the skin that occurs after a blunt force injury that causes bleeding, but does not break the skin.

could still be capable of penetration or partial insertion, which could be used to make the case of rape. One study by Bownes and O'Gorman (1991) reported that sexual dysfunction has been known to occur in a proportion of rapists during the assault (compare this finding with the report by Dr. Beh, discussed earlier in this chapter). The most common dysfunctions reported were ED and absent/retarded ejaculation. In that study, out of 50 victims of rape, 20% of victims reported that their assailant experienced ED at some point during the assault, and a further 12% reported retarded ejaculation or failure to ejaculate.

Should we *always* expect genital injuries in victims of sexual crime? WHO's *Guidelines for Medico-Legal Care for Victims of Sexual Violence* (2003) explained that visible signs of injuries after an attack are rare, and are usually confined to minor abrasions to the posterior fourchette and introitus. To complicate things, injury to the hymen (sufficient to cause bleeding) may occur in some females previously unaccustomed to sexual intercourse. On the other hand, not all women will have injury to their genitals, that will be visible on examination. In many cases, no injury would be found, according to WHO. If a mature, sexually active woman does not resist (because of fear of harm) and penile penetration of her vagina occurs, it is possible for no injury to occur. The manual explained that this does not disprove the victim's claim that she was raped. Studies (e.g., Biggs *et al.*, 1998; Bowyer & Dalton, 1997) indicated that less than 30% of premenopausal women would have genital injuries visible to the naked eye after non-consensual penetration. This figure increased to less than 50% in post-menopausal women.

In child sexual abuse cases, the manual explained that some of the possible signs to look out for included unexplained genital injury, recurrent vulvovaginitis, vaginal or penile discharge, bedwetting, faecal soiling, anal complaints (i.e., pain or bleeding), pain on urination, pregnancy, presence of sperm, and urinary tract infections (UTIs). However, it is useful to examine these indicators in conjunction with psychological and behavioral indicators in the child such as depression, low self-esteem, sexualized behaviours, poor performance in school, eating disorders or body image concerns, and hyper-arousal (WHO, 2003).

4.12 Preventing and Managing Sexual Offending

4.12.1 *Situational Crime Prevention*

Situational crime prevention (SCP) may be a strategy against rape and sexual crimes. The idea is to work on the situational and environmental factors affecting sexual offending rather than only on the offender's motivation. Situational crime prevention (SCP) has two aspects: (1) the idea of *rational choice* (Cornish & Clarke, 1986); and (2) the idea of *routine activities* (Cohen & Felson, 1979) (as discussed in Chapter 1). The assumption is that the sex offender 'rationally' weighs up the criminal opportunity regarding risk and reward. A sex crime is more likely to be committed when it requires little effort; there is a low risk of detection and punishment, and when he/she anticipates a highly desired reward. The second aspect of SCP is that criminal behaviour involves interactions between the characteristics of the 'actor' and the 'situation' in which the act is enacted.

As an example, Wortley and Smallbone (2006) explained how SCP could be applied to the prevention of child sexual abuse. They proposed that sexual abuse prevention efforts can be organized according to four types of settings:

1. Domestic settings (since offences tend to occur here);
2. Organisational workplace settings;
3. Public settings, for example, certain hot spots such as parks or public toilets; and
4. Virtual/internet settings.

Wortley and Smallbone argued that SCP is most suited to very specific problems, and the more specific, the better. Hence, the starting point is to narrow the target of specific prevention measures. They explained that the actions to prevent sexual abuse in schools will be very different from what is required to prevent sexual assaults in and around dance clubs, which will again be very different from what is required to prevent other crimes, such as Internet child pornography. Interventions are usually designed to make the problem behaviour riskier, more difficult to enact, less rewarding, less permissible or excusable, and less tempting.

The idea here is to: (a) change the aspects of physical environments and the ways in which people routinely interact with these environments; (b) control access to the setting; (c) increase natural surveillance; (d) eliminate blind spots; (e) increase capable guardianship; (f) decrease vulnerabilities of potential victims or crime targets; and (g) clarify rules and expectations for expected behaviour. There is a growing number of publications looking at the application of SCP in the area of sex crimes, and interested readers should look up Erooga (2012), Kaufman (2010), Smallbone *et al.* (2008), Terry and Ackerman (2008), and Wurtele (2012).

4.12.2 *TOOLKIT: How to Interview Victims of Sex Crimes*

Each victim is different. So, a 'one size fits all' approach can be ineffective. Different sex crimes result in different reactions as well. For example, while most victims are affected at the emotional and psychological level, the interpersonal dynamics are different for intra-familial sex crimes, as opposed to stranger predatory sex attacks. The National Center for Victims of Crime (NCVC) explains that the 'primary injuries' victims may suffer could include physical, financial, and emotional and psychological injury. However, when victims do not receive sensitive support and intervention from the criminal justice system, they suffer 'secondary psychology injuries' (NCVC, n.d.). In addition, each victim's experience is different, and we should not 'expect' a typical response. For some victims, recovery can take months or years (NCVC, n.d.).

In general, it is useful to consider providing a sense of safety (physical and psychological), providing emotional support, and providing informational support to the victims. Some good practices based on guidelines provided by the NCVC are as follows:

- *Greet the person by his/her name.* Remind the person that they are in a safe place. Introduce yourself and tell her/him your role and what is to happen over time during the investigation, or what to expect at the medical examination or during the court[13] processes. Provide a contact number if you can.

---

[13] In some instances, the court may agree to have the victim use video link to provide testimony.

- *Display a calm and relaxed demeanour.* Listen and support. Do not rush through the meeting as these events may be significant and traumatizing for the victim. Be empathetic and non-judgmental.
- *Be sensitive when speaking to victims.* Treat all victims or survivors with respect and dignity, no matter their social status, sexual orientation, lifestyle, gender, occupation, and previous criminal or sexual history.
- *Do not expect stereotypical emotional responses.* Do not expect all rape victims to appear traumatized or to be crying. Some victims control their emotions and do not want to cry or break down because they do not want the offender to defeat them mentally. Hence, it is important not to interpret this as a possible false report. Not every crying victim is being genuine, and not every calm and collected victim is deceitful. Each person is different.
- *Be careful with your questioning techniques.* For instance, asking "Why were you out alone?", "Why did you follow him home if you did not agree to the sex?", "What were you wearing when you were raped?", "Did you agree to follow him back to his place?" can come across as being very insensitive. Just because someone agreed to follow another back home for a drink does not mean she deserved to be raped.
- *Give a sense of safety, as some victims prefer a familiar person present during the process of investigation* (especially someone young, a teen, an elderly person, a vulnerable person, or a person with disability). If the person can communicate, ask the victim/survivor, rather than assume that they will always want their parent or teacher present. Do appreciate that in some Asian settings, some victims may not feel comfortable for their parents, boyfriends, family, or colleagues to know about the sexual assault because of feelings of embarrassment, shame, or 'losing face'.
- *In some cases, victims of sexual violence may experience trauma.* Some victims may experience post-traumatic stress, which includes sleeping problems, nightmares, flashbacks, intrusion of thoughts, tension, irritability, avoidance and withdrawal, feelings of estrangements, and memory trouble (NCVC, n.d.). Research has argued that there could be a syndrome called rape trauma syndrome (RTS), which is deemed to be trauma unique to rape victims

(Burgess & Holmstrom, 1974). However, the scientific evidence for RTS is not strong. Critics have argued that RTS is not unique and that these symptoms are similar to post-traumatic stress disorder (PTSD) (O'Donohue *et al.*, 2004).

In the year 2018, changes are expected in Singapore to provide support to victims of sexual crimes and victims who may be traumatized. The government is looking into the possibility of making changes to the Criminal Procedure Code and Evidence Act, such that video recorded statements of vulnerable victims may be used in place of oral 'evidence in chief'.[14] The idea here is that this measure will reduce the trauma of the victims having to repeatedly retell their ordeal and account in court (Vijayan, 2017).

Realising the stress and potential trauma these victims might face, the Ministry of Home Affairs (MHA) and Ministry of Law (MinLaw) in Singapore started a One-Stop Abuse Forensic Examination (OneSAFE) Centre.[15] The police, together with Singapore General Hospital (SGH), have set up this centre. It provides medical examinations for adult rape victims whose cases are reported within 72 hours of an assault. Specialists from SGH's Obstetrics and Gynaecology Department will attend to victims at their convenience and privacy. This removes the need to travel to the hospitals. Fifty trained volunteers from the Victim Care Cadre Programme will provide emotional support to victims.[16] During court proceedings, judges have the power to protect victims using gag orders, closed-door hearings, and a witness

---

[14] When a witness is called to give evidence, s/he will be questioned first by the lawyer representing the party calling them. This is the 'examination-in-chief'. The aim of this is to elicit from the witness all the facts supporting that party's case that are within the personal knowledge of that witness (Health and Safety Executive, n.d.).

[15] Malaysia also has a similar centre called the One Stop Crisis Center or OSCC, which is one of the services provided by the Emergency and Trauma Department in all Ministry of Health hospitals in Malaysia established since 1996. It is meant to assist the survivors or victims of crisis with the involvement of multiple agencies under one roof to respond to rape, child abuse, sodomy and domestic violence.

[16] Trained by the Police Psychological Services Division, Singapore Police Force.

support programme. Lawyers are not allowed to vilify or insult a witness (Ong, 2017).

4.12.3 *Sex Offender Registries as Preventative Measure?*

Some countries like Australia, some states in the U.S., Canada, New Zealand, South Korea, Taiwan, and the U.K. use sex offender registries.[17] Do they work? Community registration and notification is a very modern social policy. In America, there is a law called "Megan's Law", which is an informal name for state laws that require law enforcement authorities to make information available to the public regarding registered sex offenders. Such laws were created in response to the murder of Megan Kanka.[18] In the U.K., the child sex offender disclosure scheme is informally known as "Sarah's Law",[19] and it allows anyone to formally ask the police if someone with access to a child has a record for child sexual offences. Police will reveal details confidentially to the person determined to be the most able to protect the child (usually parents, carers, or guardians) if they think it is in the child's interests (Somerset & Avon, n.d.).

However, Levenson (2008) argued that there is little evidence that registration reduces sex crimes. In Iowa in the U.S., there was no differences found in the reconviction rates of registered and unregistered sex offenders. This suggested that registration had little impact. Also, about 3% of registered sex offenders were convicted of a new sex crime after four years, compared with the 3.5% recidivism rate of unregistered sex offenders. In another state, Wisconsin, high-risk sex offenders

---

[17] In some countries, this is more like a criminal history record database rather than a specific sex offender registry.

[18] The seven-year-old was raped and killed by her neighbour Jesse Timmendequas. Jesse had two previous convictions for sexually assaulting young girls. He failed to go to counselling, and participated little in the treatment program. He lured Kanka into his house, raped her, and then killed her from strangulation with a belt. He then placed her body in a nearby park. The next day, he confessed to investigators and led police to the site.

[19] Eight-year-old Sarah Payne was murdered by paedophile Roy Whiting in West Sussex, U.K., in 2000. Investigations revealed that Sarah had been abducted and sexually assaulted by Whiting.

exposed to community notification had higher rates of recidivism (19%), compared to those with no community notification (12%). Also, community notification can result in harassment, vigilantism, and migration for sex offenders. Other research (Rapp, 2012) argued that the public might socially isolate the offender, inhibit the offender's ability to secure housing and employment, and harass the offender. After imprisonment, the person may not be able to move back in with his or her family because of residential restriction laws, and there are other problems when the homes of registered sex offenders are too close to a school or a day care centre (Joyce, 2012).

4.12.4 *Assessing Sex Offenders*

Andrews and Bonta (1998) developed several fundamental principles of offender treatment. These were *risks*, *needs*, and *responsivity*. The idea of the 'risk' principle is to match the level of service to the offender's risk to re-offend. The 'needs' principle means that we should assess criminogenic needs and target them in treatment. The 'responsivity' principle means that we should maximize the offender's ability to learn from a rehabilitative intervention by providing treatment, and tailoring the intervention to the learning style, motivation, abilities, and strengths of the offender. More about this will be discussed in Chapter 6. There are many measures which can be used to assess the risk of sex offending. These risk assessments were developed specifically for sexual offenders, and have been used for sentence enhancement, institutional placement, and community notification. Some of the more common ones are as follows:

The Minnesota Sex Offender Screening Tool (Revised)
(MnSOST-R)

The MnSOST-R (Epperson *et al.*, 1998) involves 16 items concerning the sex offender; 12 of which are historical data and the remaining four are based on aspects of institutional information. The historical items are:

(1) number of sex crime cases/victims;
(2) length of sexual offending history;

(3) whether the offender was under supervision at the time of arrest for sexual offense;

(4) any sexual offense committed in a public place;

(5) force or threat of force involved;

(6) any sexual offense within a single incident involving multiple acts perpetrated on a single victim;

(7) number of different age groups victimized across all sexual offenses;

(8) whether victim was aged 13–15 years, and offender five or more years older;

(9) whether victim was stranger in any sexual offense;

(10) whether offender displayed adolescent antisocial behaviour;

(11) substantial drug or alcohol abuse in the year prior to arrest;

(12) employment history.

The institutional items are:

(13) discipline history while incarcerated;

(14) involvement in substance use treatment;

(15) participation in sex offender treatment; and

(16) age at time of release.

MnSOST-R seems to have a moderately high level of prediction. Epperson *et al.* (1998) reported that for sexual recidivism, the MnSOST-R is a reliable and valid tool to predict recidivism among sex offenders. However, critics have argued that for it to work well, there is a need for good prisons institutional data and records.

The Sex Offender Risk Appraisal Guide (SORAG)

SORAG (Quinsey, 2008) contains 14 items, and is an instrument designed to predict violent recidivism among serious offenders. The items on the scale are as follows:

(1) lived with both biological parents until age 16;

(2) elementary school maladjustment;

(3) history of alcohol problems;
(4) never been married at time of index offense;
(5) criminal history score for non-violent offenses;
(6) criminal history score for violent offenses;
(7) number of convictions for previous sexual offenses;
(8) history of sexual offenses only against girls below 14 years of age (negatively scored);
(9) failure on prior conditional release;
(10) age at index offense (negatively scored);
(11) diagnosis of any personality disorder;
(12) diagnosis of schizophrenia (negatively scored);
(13) phallometric test results indicating deviant sexual interests; and
(14) psychopathy checklist (revised) score.

Studies have found that the SORAG has reasonably good predictive validity (Rice *et al.*, 2013).

The Sexual Violence Risk-20 (SVR-20)

This SVR-20 is divided into three sections: (1) Psychosocial Adjustment, (2) Sexual Offences, and (3) Future Plans. The Psychosocial Adjustment comprises factors that are historical and includes sexual deviation, early childhood victimisation, psychopathy, and mental illness. The Sexual Offenses section includes items that are historical, and current sexual offense details such as types of sex offenses, physical harm to victim(s), and use of weapons or threats of death during sex offenses. The Future Plans section comprises two items looking at realistic plans and negative attitude toward intervention. Hart and Boer (2009) looked at inter-rater-reliability of the SVR-20 from Canada, Spain, Sweden, Austria, the Netherlands, and Germany, and reported fairly good reliabilities for it. Studies looking at the predictive validities, however, report mixed results (Rettenberger *et al.*, 2009).

Rapid Risk Assessment for Sex Offence Recidivism (RRASOR)

The RRASOR (Hanson, 1997) scale was developed to screen offenders into relative risk levels, and includes measures of criminal history, age at release, gender of victim, and victim–offender relationship. The RRASOR has four items. On average, the RRASOR shows a correlation of 0.27 with sexual recidivism, appearing to be better than other measures, which showed a correlation of about 0.10 (Epperson *et al.*, 1998). Hanson (1997) used the tool to assess the likelihood of a new sexual arrest, conviction, or imprisonment of five and 10 years following release from prison. He found that those with a score of '0' on the instrument had a recidivism rate of 4.4% after five years and a 6.5% after 10 years, and those with a score of '5' had a recidivism rate of 50% at five years and 73% after 10 years. This instrument was designed based on ease of use, has a short list of items, and did not include all factors associated with sexual recidivism (Institute of Public Policy, 2006).

The Static-99

The Static 99 (Hanson & Thornton, 2000) is a 10-item actuarial assessment instrument for use with adult male sexual offenders who are at least 18 years of age. It was designed to be used explicitly for adult male offenders who have been convicted of a sex offence where direct contact occurred between them and a victim. Therefore, this is not useful for assessing individuals who have been convicted of prostitution, pimping, public indecent exposure, and illicit pornography (Institute of Public Policy, 2006). The scale looks at items such as:

(1) Age of offending,
(2) Persistence of sexual offending,
(3) Prior sex offences,
(4) Sexual deviance,
(5) Gender of victims, etc.

Despite its success, the predictive accuracy is only moderate, and the scores have no intrinsic meanings. The Static-99 is moderately accurate in predicting sexual and violent recidivism in the U.K. and the U.S. (Beech *et al.*, 2000; Stalans, 2004).

4.12.5 *Sexual Deviance, Paraphilia and Offending*

Paraphilia has been associated with sexual offending. This would especially be so if one had a voyeuristic disorder (spying on others in private activities), exhibitionistic disorder (exposing the genitals), frotteuristic disorder (touching or rubbing against a non-consenting individual), or a paedophilic disorder (sexual focus on children). According to the Diagnostic and Statistical Manual of Mental Disorders (DSM-5) (fifth edition), paraphilia denotes "any intense and persistent sexual interest other than sexual interest in genital stimulation or preparatory fondling with phenotypically normal, physically mature, consenting human partners"[20] (American Psychiatric Association, 2013, p. 685). The manual goes on to explain that some paraphilias concern the individual's erotic *activities* and others are concerned with the erotic *targets*. The manual explains that "examples of the former might include intense and persistent interests in spanking, whipping, cutting, binding, or strangulating another person", while examples of the latter would include "intense or preferential sexual interest in children, corpses, or amputees, as well as intense or preferential interest in nonhuman animals such as horses or dogs or in inanimate objects such as shoes or articles made of rubber", (American Psychiatric Association, 2013).

Another important point of consideration is that the DSM-5 makes the distinction between *paraphilia* and *paraphilic disorders*. An individual may have paraphilia but may not have a disorder. According to the DSM, "a paraphilic disorder is a paraphilia that is currently causing distress or impairment to the individual or a paraphilia whose satisfaction has entailed personal harm or risk or harm to others. A paraphilia is a necessary, but not a sufficient condition, for having a paraphilic disorder and a paraphilia by itself does not necessarily justify or require clinical intervention" (American Psychiatric Association, p. 686).

---

[20] The manual qualifies that for older persons or the medically ill, the criteria for intensity of sexual interest may be hard to fulfil. In such cases, "paraphilia may be defined as any sexual interest greater than or equal to normophilic sexual interests" (DSM-V, p. 685).

In an interesting study looking at types of paraphilia, Rajan and Katharine (2012) reported that the rate of paraphilia in sex offenders is between 25% and 75%. However, they noted that not all sex offenders have paraphilia, and most people with paraphilia do not commit offences. They cited that among child molesters, extra-familial offenders have high rates of paedophilia, but most incest offenders are not clinically paedophilic (that is, following the DSM-V criteria). Most rapists do not have paraphilia, and very few are sexually sadistic. Some sexual offenders may have multiple paraphilia. The authors noted that deviant sexual interests, particularly paedophilia, sexual sadism, and multiple paraphilia are associated with sexual recidivism. Other paraphilia probably increases the risk of re-offending in specific types of offenders (e.g., frotteurism in a man convicted of breach of the peace for rubbing himself against women on buses.)[21]

The DSM-5 states that it is not rare for an individual to have two or more paraphilia. One horrific but nonetheless illustrative case is that of Albert Fish, who was involved in several paraphilic crimes, discussed in the following case study.

CASE STUDY:
Case of Albert Fish

Hamilton Howard "Albert" Fish was also known as the Gray Man, the Werewolf of Wysteria, the Brooklyn Vampire, the Moon Maniac, and the Boogey Man. He was a child rapist and a cannibal. He was a suspect in at least five murders during his lifetime. He was put on trial and convicted for the kidnapping and murder of Grace Budd. Fish derived sexual pleasure from sadistic and masochistic acts, such as infibulation (self-torture of genitals), flagellation (spanking), anthropophagy (consumption of human flesh), paedophilia, and lust murder. Shown below is a letter that Albert had written to the Budd family about his meeting and murder of their daughter (Heimer, 1971).

(Continued)

---

[21] In the 2017 Singapore police annual crime brief, it was reported that in 2017, Outraging of Modesty increased by 22% overall. Of this, 34% occurred in nightspots while 60% occurred in transport settings. Could these have been acts of frotteurism?

(Continued)

My dear Mrs. Budd,
...On Sunday, June the 3, 1928, I called on you at 406 W 15 St. Brought you pot cheese, strawberries. We had lunch. Grace sat in my lap and kissed me. I made up my mind to eat her, on the pretence of taking her to a party. You said yes she could go. I took her to an empty house in Westchester I had already picked out. When we got there, I told her to remain outside. She picked wild flowers. I went upstairs and stripped all my clothes off. I knew if I did not, I would get her blood on them. When all was ready, I went to the window and called her. Then I hid in a closet until she was in the room. When she saw me all naked, she began to cry and tried to run downstairs. I grabbed her, and she said she would tell her mama. First I stripped her naked. How she did kick, bite and scratch. I choked her to death then cut her in small pieces so I could take my meat to my rooms, cook and eat it. How sweet and tender her little ass was roasted in the oven. It took me nine days to eat her entire body. I did not f__k her, though, I could have had I wished. She died a virgin.

Source: "Albert Fish". Crime Library. Retrieved 16 December 2017

When undertaking assessments of sexual offending, it is important to understand some of the paraphilia, which may or may not be related to criminal offending (Laws & O' Donohue, 1997):

- *Sexual masochism and sexual sadism.* With sexual masochism, individuals report intense sexual arousal from the act of being humiliated, battened, bound, and made to suffer as manifested by fantasies or behaviour. The prevalence for masochism is not known according to the DSM but is estimated, using Australian data, to be at about 2.2% of males and 1.3% of females involved in bondage, discipline dominance, or submission in the past 12 months. The mean age onset of this is about 19 years of age. Sometimes, this occurs together with other paraphilic disorders such as transvestic fetishism. Sexual sadism refers to the intense sexual arousal from the physical or psychological suffering of another person as manifested by fantasies and behaviours. The DSM-5 reports that the prevalence of this is unknown, but ranges from 2% to 30%. Furthermore, among individuals who have committed sexually motivated homicides, the rates of sexual sadism disorder can range from 37% to 75%. Some studies have reported that the onset of sexual sadism in males is 19.4 years (American Psychiatric Disorders, 2013).

- *Underwear fetishes and underwear theft*: One of the first cases discussed in Chapter One involved underwear theft. Underwear theft is very common. It is not illegal nor a crime. However, if one steals or does something because of a fetish, then the activity becomes a criminal act. Underwear fetishism refers to the arousal experienced from observing or handling certain types of underwear, including panties, stockings, pantyhose, and bras. Some people experience sexual excitement from wearing certain types of underwear, and some others experience sexual excitement when observing or handling certain types of underwear worn by another, or watching somebody putting on their underwear, or taking it off. Some may steal used and dirtied underwear to get satisfaction.

- *Zoophilia* refers to sexual contact with animals. Beetz (2002) distinguished between *zoophilia* and *bestiality*, saying that zoophilia referred to an emotional attachment to animals that is related to a preference for animals as sexual partners, or that includes a sexual attraction, while bestiality describes any sexual contact of humans with animals or physical contact to animals that results in sexual arousal for the involved human (Kinsey *et al.*, 1948, 1953). In their sample of men, 8% reported having had a sexual experience with an animal. One-third of those involved had had their first experience by the age of nine, with peak active incidence (6%) occurring between 10 and 12 years old. Their study showed that this figure dropped to 1% in the 21- to 25-year age group. Prevalence rates were much higher in rural agrarian populations. Bestiality can be a cause for concern, because Masters and Lea (1963) claimed that the lines between bestiality and sadism were blurred, and that some people practicing bestiality may be latent sadists and lust murderers. Furthermore, FBI profilers Ressler *et al.* (1986) found that 23% of their incarcerated sample of 36 sexual murderers showed an interest in bestiality. They believed that for sadistic offenders and sex murderers, the abuse of animals might serve as a rehearsal for the abuse or killing of a human, including planned tortures, sexual gratification, and murder itself.

- *Urophilia*. Urophiliacs derive sexual pleasure from urinating on (and/or being urinated upon by) another person. Denson (1982) found that the urine fulfilled many different functions for urophiles, including serving as a fetishistic object, being used to humiliate or be humiliated, and capturing the 'spirit' or 'essence' of a sexual partner. Based on the case studies examined, Denson argued that urination may serve masochistic and/or sadistic purposes and therefore, it should be labelled 'uromasochism' or 'urosadism'.

'Fetish' and 'paraphilia' are often confused, but 'fetish' refers to a strong sexual preoccupation with an object, material, or non-genital body parts. Therefore, fetishism is a subcategory of paraphilia. Fetishism involves recurrent and intense sexual arousal from non-living objects or a highly specific focus on non-genital body parts. 'Fetishism disorder' is established when this intense focus is also accompanied by fantasies and behaviours that cause clinically significant distress in social and occupational areas of functioning (American Psychiatric Association, 2013).

Scorolli *et al.* (2007) published an interesting study titled *Relative Prevalence of Different Fetishes*, where they looked at the common fetishes. Using Internet data, their study involved 381 discussion

---

CASE STUDY:
A Fetish for Wallets

LJQ was a 47-year-old executive with an economics degree who went on a stealing spree to satisfy his fetish for the smell of leather wallets. He was convicted of taking wallets from nine women over an eight-month period. However, he was spared a prison sentence and placed on three years' probation instead. Before this, LJQ had also been jailed four times since 1986 for stealing to satisfy his craving. According to a psychiatric report, LJQ began sniffing his sister's wallets and belongings at the age of seven. As he grew older, he began to have recurring sexual urges involving his sister's wallet. LJQ's lawyer said his client's crimes were triggered by his inability to cope with his mental condition.

Source: Chong (2013).

groups involving about 5,000 individuals. They concluded that the 'preferences for body parts/features' and 'objects usually associated with the body' were the most common fetish (33% and 30%, respectively). See Tables 4.8 and 4.9 for the ranking order of sexual references of body parts and objects associated with body.

Table 4.8: Sexual Preferences for Body Parts

Sexual preferences for body parts or features	Members in Internet discussion group	Relative frequency (%)
Feet, toes (paedophilia)	44, 722	47
Body fluids, e.g., blood, urine, as golden/ brown showers, water sport, etc. (urophilia, scatophilia, lactaphilia, menophilia, mucophilia)	8,376	9
Body size, e.g., obesity, tallness, shortness, etc. (chubby chasers, nanophilia)	8,241	9
Hair (trichophilia)	6,707	7
Muscles	5,515	5
Body modifications, e.g., tattooing, piercing, ringing (stigmatophilia)	4,102	4
Genitals (medophilia)	3,336	4
Belly or navel (alvinophilia)	2,861	3
Ethnicity (xenophilia)	2,681	3
Breasts (mammaphilia)	2,602	3
Legs, buttocks (crurofact, pygophilia)	1,830	2
Mouth, lips, teeth (odontophilia)	1,697	2
Body hair, pubic hair (hirsutophilia, and pubephilia)	864	<1
Nails	669	<1
Nose (nasophilia)	316	<1
Ears	91	<1
Neck	88	<1
Body odour (mysophilia, osmophilia)	82	<1

Source: Adapted from Scorolli *et al.* (2007).
Note: Do note that a group could contribute to more than one entry.

Table 4.9:   Sexual Preferences for Objects

Sexual preferences for objects associated with the body	Members in discussion group	Relative frequency (%)
Objects worn on legs and buttocks (stockings, skirts, etc.)	27,490	33
Footwear	26,739	32
Underwear	10,046	12
Whole-body wear (costumes, coats, etc.)	7,424	9
Objects worn on trunk (jacket, waistcoat)	7,226	9
Objects worn on head and neck (hats, necklaces, etc.)	2,357	3
Stethoscopes	933	1
Wristwatches, Bracelets, etc.	716	<1
Diapers	483	<1
Hearing aids	150	<1
Catheters	28	<1
Pace-makers	2	

Source: Adapted from Scorolli *et al.* (2007).
Note: Do note that a group could contribute to more than one entry.

4.12.6 *Treating Sex Offenders*

Psychosocial treatment programs

One example of a Sex Offender Treatment Program is the U.K. Prisons Service program, called the Core Sex Offender Treatment Programme (Core-SOTP). This is a cognitive-behavioural group program for adult men with an IQ level of 80 or above, who have been convicted of a sexual offence (National Offender Management System, 2013). The programme is suitable for those with medium-risk of sexual re-offending. Core-SOTP helps offenders develop an understanding of how and why they came to commit sexual offences, focusing on those factors that have an established relationship with sexual re-offending. The programme encourages offenders to develop meaningful life goals and to practice new ways of thinking and behavioral skills that will lead them away from offending.

The program comprises of about 84 sessions, each lasting 2.5 hours. Treatment is delivered in a closed-group format, up to five times a week, and takes six months to complete on average. The Core-SOTP has 20 blocks:

(1) establishing the group,
(2) understanding offence-related thinking,
(3) coping strategies,
(4) my history,
(5) active accounts,
(6) fantasy,
(7) patterns in my offending,
(8) goal setting,
(9) cost and gains of offending,
(10) old me,
(11) reviewing my treatment needs,
(12–15) understanding victim harm,
(16–19) getting to a new 'me', and
(20) ending.

The program aims to target the key risk factors for sexual offending, which can be broken down into four areas:

(1) *Offence-Related Sexual Interests.* An obsession with sex, a sexual interest in children, a sexual interest in violence, and other offence-related sexual interests,
(2) *Offence-Supportive Attitudes.* The belief that men should dominate women, beliefs that support the abuse of children or the rape of adult women, the belief that men have a right to sex, beliefs that women cannot be trusted,
(3) *Relationships.* Feeling inadequate, feeling angry, suspicious and wanting to get one's own back, lack of emotionally intimate relationships with adults,
(4) *Self-Management.* Impulsivity, poor problem solving, and poor emotional control.

These SOTPs are designed to be delivered by para-professionals staff, such as prison officers, education officers, and assistant psychologists. Suitability for this work is competency-based, and not based on professional qualifications. Staff must first be assessed as suitable to become a facilitator. This will involve completion of various psychometric assessments and interviews with local managers. Candidates have to pass an assessment.

Evaluating the effectiveness of sex offender programs, Lösel and Schmucker (2005) conducted a large meta-analysis assessing the effectiveness of sex offender treatment. Altogether, taking 69 studies and a combined total of 22,181 subjects, researchers found an average sexual recidivism rate of 11.1% for treated sex offenders and 17.5% for untreated sex offenders, based on an average follow-up period of slightly more than five years. Treated offenders showed six-percentage points or 37% less sexual recidivism than controls. Hanson *et al.* (2009) examined 23 studies and found an eight-percentage point difference (10.9% and 19.2%, respectively) between treated offenders and untreated controls in sexual reconviction. Sex offender programs, which follow the 'risk, need, and responsivity' principles, lead to the largest reductions in reconviction. Medium- and high-risk sexual offenders benefited most from treatment. Schmucker and Lösel (2009) also combined 26 high-quality research studies of sex offender treatment, and found that the sexual offending reconviction rate for treated offenders was, on average, 3.4-percentage points lower than that for untreated offenders. The bottom line is: while the treatment does not make a huge difference in terms of impact, it does make some difference to recidivism rates.

RESEARCH OF INTEREST
Navy SOTP: Promoting Community Safety

An example of sex offender treatment programs is the Navy Sex Offender Treatment Program (SOTP), conducted by the Naval Consolidated Brig Miramar in San Diego for military personnel serving prison sentences for sex offenses.

An advisory committee formed by personnel from a range of disciplines from law enforcers to psychiatrists, spiritual leaders, victim advocacy, and

(Continued)

(Continued)

treatment therapists inform the SOTP. This voluntary SOTP was directed at those who were convicted of a sex offense involving a minor, admitted a degree of responsibility for the offense, and were willing to discuss his sexually deviant behaviour in detail.

It is a cognitive–behavioral treatment program that focuses on relapse prevention, and includes psychophysiological assessments, intensive group therapy, educational seminars, and training in cognitive–behavioural management techniques. Themes covered included cognitive restructuring, victim impact, cognitive/behavioural arousal reduction techniques, covert sensitization, relationship skills, and sexuality and relapse prevention.

The offenders go through the group therapy three times a week and are required to complete daily assignments (e.g., writing down 40 things they would lose by re-offending) over 26 months for Phase 1. A therapist led each group. The therapists provided treatment programs and/or personal counselling for issues such as substance abuse, violence, or personal abuse history problems. For Phase 2, they met in maintenance groups once a week, until their release. Upon return to the community, they are highly encouraged to continue treatment with a therapist. They also must agree to a waiver of confidentiality, periodic supervisory polygraph examinations, and physiological assessments of sexual interests, unsupervised use of computer equipment, no purchase, possession, or viewing of pornography, no patronizing of high-risk areas (e.g., adult bookstores, strip clubs), no use of alcohol or other controlled substances, and no (in)direct contact with children unless approved. The therapists also meet with the offenders and their families jointly, and rope in the family members as part of the accountability network to help the offender avoid risky behaviours.

Source: Marin, T.M. and Bell, D.L. (2003). Navy Sex Offender Programme: Promoting Community Safety. *Corrections Today*, pp. 84–87.

Medical approaches

Do medical and biological approaches work? Two biological interventions are *surgical castration* and *hormonal medication*. Lösel and Schmucker (2005) concluded that both these methods did have good effects on recidivism rates. They argued that biological interventions combined with psychological treatments might achieve maximal effect. On the other hand, in a review by Khan *et al.* (2015) titled *Pharmacological Interventions for those who have Sexually Offended or are at Risk of Offending*, the authors noted that medications have in fact been used to treat sex offenders (i.e., 'anti-libidinal' medications) by limiting the sexual drive (libido). There are two types of medications: (1) those that work by suppressing testosterone (e.g., progestogens, antiandrogens, and gonadotropin-releasing hormone (GnRH) analogues); and (2) those that reduce sexual drive by other mechanisms, i.e., antipsychotics and serotonergic antidepressants (SSRIs). The authors examined seven randomised trials involving 138 participants. Controls included placebo (five studies), psychological treatment (one study), and a combination of psychological and pharmacological treatment (one study). Five studies took place in the community and two in a secure hospital. Results showed that no re-offending occurred during one study at a two-year follow-up for the intervention group (n = 10). Another showed a 20% rate of re-offending among those in the combined treatment group (n = 15). Two studies did not report re-offending rates. Three community studies did not formally report re-offending at all, focusing largely on 'abnormal sexual activity'. Considering these results, the authors concluded that,

"These seven trials (published more than 20 years ago), examining only a limited number of drugs, provide an inadequate evidence base to guide practice. Not only were the trials small, but they also were of short duration, included varied participants, and none trailed the newer drugs currently in use, particularly SSRIs or GnRH analogues. The results of this review, therefore, do not allow firm conclusions to be drawn regarding pharmacological interventions as an effective intervention for reducing sexual offending." (p. 3)

4.13 Summary

- There is much heterogeneity in sexual offending, not just across the types of sexual crimes, but within each category. While this chapter in this introductory book focuses mainly on the crime of rape, interested readers should research other types of sex offending.

- It is important to appreciate the differences between the legal and psychological definitions of rape. Confusing these aspects will not enable us to research, understand, and respond well to any particular type of sex crime.
- There are many behavioural characteristics of sex offending. However, an important aspect of sex offending is the psychological process of sexual grooming, which can be subtle and easily missed.
- There are many explanations of sexual offending which have been laid out, and the role of cognitions is a particularly important area to study.
- Psychologists must appreciate the important of forensic evidence when they work in the area of sex crimes as things may not be as straightforward as it may seem (for example, a victim of sex crime may not show genital bruises).
- It is important to ensure that victims of sexual crimes are well managed to prevent secondary victimisation by the criminal justice system.
- From the angle of prevention, there is much more work to be done in the area of situational crime prevention, especially since sex offending occurs in a particular time and place, such as in crowded train stations or clubs, or in the case of child abuse, in places like the school, homes or neighbours. Practitioners, however, will have to appreciate what works, when, for whom, and how.
- Finally, the treatment of sex offenders prevents or mitigates the risk of re-offending.

Relevant Journals

Journal of Sex Research
Journal of Sexual Medicine
Sexual Abuse
Journal of Sexual Aggression
Sexual Offender Treatment
Journal of Forensic Psychology

Criminal Justice and Behaviour
Annals of Sex Research
Sexuality Research and Social Policy

E-Resources

http://www.esextherapy.com/ [American Academy of Clinical Sexologists]
http://www.iasr.org/ [International Academy of Sex Research]
http://www.iatso.org/ [International Association for the Treatment of Sexual Offenders (IATSO)]
http://www.indiana.edu/~kinsey/ [Kinsey Institute for Research in Sex, Gender, and Reproduction]
http://www.siecus.org [Sexuality Information and Education Council of the U.S. (SIECUS)]

Some Relevant Legal Cases

PP vs Heng Swee Weng (2010). 1 SLR 954 (Elements for OM Offence)
PP vs Victor Rajoo (1995) 3 SLR (R) 189 (Absence of Consent)
Siew Yit Beng (2000) 2 SLR (R) 785 (Absence of Consent)

Sample Research Essay Questions

- What role do cultural factors play in sex offending? Do Asians react differently as victims of sex crimes?
- Do a prevalence study on any sexual behaviour of interest/ sex crime (using the Singaporean context). Some examples could be upskirt photography, 'sexting'/child sexual abuse, or voyeurism.
- What is the psychological impact of being a victim of sexual crime?
- How would you teach crime prevention to children? Think of novel ways (e.g., in the form of a children's book).
- The Program Director has asked you to develop a sex offender treatment program for rapists. How would you design such a program and what would you include in it?

References

Alkhathib, S. (2015, October 26). Credit-for-sex scams up 10-fold. *The New Paper*. Retrieved from http://www.tnp.sg/news/singapore/credit-sex-scams-10-fold

Alkhatib, S.I. (2017, November 16). Teacher on trial for allegedly molesting male student in school's art room. *The Straits Times*.

American Psychiatric Association (2013). *Diagnostic and Statistical Manual* (5th ed.). Washington, DC: American Psychiatric Publication.

Andrews, D.A. and Bonta, J. (1998). *The Psychology of Criminal Conduct* (2nd ed.). Cincinnati, OH: Anderson.

Association of Women for Action and Research (AWARE) (n.d.). *Learn more about sexual assault and sexual harassment*. Retrieved from http://www.aware.org.sg/information/sexual-assault/

Australian Center for the Study of Sexual Assault (n.d.). Retrieved from https://aifs.gov.au/sites/default/files/publication-documents/issues15.pdf.

Beech, A., Craig, L., & Browne, K. (2009). *Assessment and Treatment of Sex Offenders: A Handbook*. New York, NY: John Wiley & Sons.

Beech, A.R., Elliot, I.A., Birgden, A., and Findlater, D. (2008). The Internet and child sexual offending: A criminological review. *Aggression and Violent Behaviour*, *13*, 216–228.

Beech, A., Beckett, R., and Fischer, D. (2000). *Outcome data of representative UK sex offender treatment programs: Short-term effectiveness and some preliminary reconviction data*. Manuscript in preparation.

Beetz, A. (2002). *Love, Violence, and Sexuality in Relationships Between Humans and Animals*. Aachen: Shaker Verlag.

Beh, P.S.L. (1998). Rape in Hong Kong: An overview of current knowledge. *Journal of Clinical Forensic Medicine*, *5*(3), 124–128.

Biggs, M., Stermac, L.E., and Divinsky, M. (1998). Genital injuries following sexual assault of women with and without prior sexual experience. *Canadian Medical Association Journal*, *159*, 33–37.

Bonta, J. and Andrews, D.A. (2007). Risk-Need-Responsivity Model for Offender Assessment and Rehabilitation. *Public Safety Canada*. Retrieved from http://www.pbpp. pa.gov/Information/Documents/Research/EBP7.pdf

Bownes, I.T. and O'Gorman, E.C. (1991). Assailants' sexual dysfunction during rape reported by their victims. *Medicine, Science, and the Law*, *31*(4), 322–328.

Burgess A.W. and Holmstrom, L.L. (1974). Rape trauma syndrome. *American Journal of Psychiatry*, *131*, 981–986.

Burt, M.R. (1980). Cultural myths and supports for rape. *Journal of Personality and Social Psychology*, *38*(2), 217–230.

Burt, M.R. (1991). Rape myths and acquaintance rape. In A. Parrot & L. Bechhofer (Eds.), *Acquaintance Rape: The Hidden Crime*. New York, NY: Wiley and Sons.

Camilleri, J.A. and Quinsey, V.L. (2008). Paedophilia: Assessment and treatment. In D.R. Laws & W.T. O'Donohue (Eds.), *Sexual Deviance: Theory, Assessment, and Treatment* (2nd ed., pp. 183–212). New York, NY: Guilford.

Chong, E. (2003, February 2003). 23 Years' Jail, 24 Strokes for Internet Sex Fiend. *The Straits Times*.

Chong, E. (2003, November 29). Hotel rapist gets 26 years, 24 strokes. *The Straits Times*.

Chong, E. (2013, March 22). Man with sexual fetish for wallets jailed 13 months. *The Straits Times*. Retrieved from http://www.straitstimes.com/singapore/man-with-sexual-fetish-for-wallets-jailed-13-months.

Cohen, L.E. and Felson, M. (1979). Social change and crime rate trends: A routine activity approach. *American Sociological Review*, *44*, 588–608.

Cornish, D.B. and Clarke, R.V.G. (1986). *The Reasoning Criminal: Rational Choice Perspectives on Offending*. New York, NY: Springer-Verlag.

Court, J.H. (1976). Pornography and sex crimes: A revaluation in light of recent trends around the world. *International Journal of Criminology Penology*, *5*, 129–157.

Davies, G.M. and Beech, A.R. (Eds.) (2012). *Forensic Psychology: Crime, Justice, Law, and Interventions*. Chichester: John Wiley and Sons.

Davis, P. (1954). *Sex Perversion and the Law* (Vols.1–2). New York, NY: Mental Health Press.

Deitz, S., Blackwell, K.T., Daley, P.C., and Bentley, B.J. (1982). Measurement of empathy toward rape victims and rapists. *Journal of Personality and Social Psychology*, *43*(2), 372–384.

Denson, R. (1982). Undinism: The fetishization of urine. *The Canadian Journal of Psychiatry*, *27*(4), 336–338.

Dietz, P.E. (1978). Social factors in rapist behaviour. In R.J. Rada (Ed.), *Clinical Aspects of The Rapists* (pp. 59–115). New York, NY: Grune and Stratto.

Durrant, R. (2013). *An Introduction to Criminal Psychology*. New York, NY: Routledge.

Elliott, J. M., Thomas, J.I., and Chua, C.Y. (2003). *Research Monograph No. 5. Child Sexual Abuse in Singapore: Professional and Public Perceptions*. Singapore: Singapore Children's Society.

Erooga, M. (2012). *Creating Safer Organisations: Practical Steps to Prevent the Abuse of Children by Those Working with Them*. West Sussex: Wiley.

Faller, K.C. (1995). A clinical sample of women who have sexually abused children. *Journal of Child Sexual Abuse, 4,* 13–30.

Finkelhor, D. (2008). *Childhood Victimization: Violence, Crime, and Abuse in the Lives of Young People.* New York, NY: Oxford University Press.

Finkelhor, D. and Russell, D. (1984). Women as perpetrators: Review of the evidence. In D. Finkelhor (Ed.), *Child Sexual Abuse: New Theory and Research* (pp. 171–187). New York, NY: Free Press.

Gannon, T.A. and Rose, M.R. (2008). Female child sexual offenders: Towards integrating theory and practice. *Aggression and Violent Behaviour, 13*(6), 442–461.

Gannon, T.A. and Ward, T. (2008). Rape: Psychopathology and theory. In D.R. Laws, and W. O'Donohue (Eds.), *Sexual Deviance: Theory, Assessment, and Treatment* (2nd ed., pp. 336–355). New York, NY: Guilford Press.

Groth, A.N., Longo, R.E., and McFadin, J.B. (1982). Undetected recidivism among rapists and child molesters. *Crime and Delinquency, 128,* 450–458.

Groth, A.N. and Birnbaum, H.J. (1990). *Men Who Rape: The Psychology of the Offender.* New York, NY: Plenum Press.

Gannon, T.A., Collie, R.M., Ward, T., and Thakkar, J. (2008). Rape, psychopathology, theory and treatment. *Clinical Psychology Review, 28,* 982–1,008.

Hall, G.C. and Hirschman, R. (1991). Toward a theory of sexual aggression: A quadripartite model. *Journal of Consulting and Clinical Psychology, 59*(5), 662–669.

Hanson, R.K. and Bussiere, M.T. (1998). Predicting relapse: A meta-analysis of sexual offender recidivism studies. *Journal of Consulting and Clinical Psychology, 63,* 348–362.

Hanson, R.K., Bourgon, G., Helmus, L., and Hodgson, S. (2009). The principles of effective correctional treatment also apply to sexual offenders: A Meta-analysis. *Criminal Justice and Behaviour, 36,* 865–891.

Hanson, R.K. and Thornton, D. (2000). Improving risk assessments for sex offenders: A comparison of three actuarial scales. *Law and Human Behaviour, 24*(1), 119–136.

Hart, S.D. and Boer, D.P. (2009). Structured Professional Judgement Guidelines for Sexual Violence Risk Assessment: The Sexual Violence Risk-20 (SVR-20) and Risk for Sexual Violence Protocol (RSVP). In R.K. Otto & K.S. Douglas (Eds.), *Handbook of Violence Risk Assessment.* Oxford: Routledge.

Health and Safety Executive (n.d.). *Witnesses giving evidence in court.* Retrieved from http://www.hse.gov.uk/enforce/enforcementguide/court/oralwitnesses.htm.

Hollin, C.R., Hatcher, R.M., and Palmer, E.P. (2010). Sexual offences against adults. In F. Brookman, T. Bennett, M. Maguire, & H. Pierpoint (Eds.), *Handbook on Crime*. Cullompton: Devon Willan.

Hui, D.T., Xin, C.W., and Khader, M. (2015). Understanding the behavioural aspects of cyber sexual grooming. *International Journal of Police Science and Management*, *17*(1), 40–49.

Institute of Public Policy (2006). *Sex offender risk assessment*. Retrieved from http://www.mosac.mo.gov/file.jsp?id=45355.

Kaufman, K. (Ed.) (2010). *The Prevention of Sexual Violence: A Practitioner's Sourcebook*. Fitchburg, MA: Neari Press.

Knight, R.A., Prentky, R.A., and Cerce, D. (1994). The development, reliability, and validity of an inventory for the Multidimensional Assessment of Sex and Aggression. *Criminal Justice and Behaviour*, *21*, 72–94.

Krug, E.G., Dahlberg, L.L., Mercy, J.A., Zwi, A.B., and Lozano, R. (Eds.) (2002). *World Report on Violence and Health*. Geneva: World Health Organisation.

Khan, O., Ferriter, M., Huband, N., Powney, M.J., Dennis, J.A., and Duggan, C. (2015). Pharmacological interventions for those who have sexually offended or are at risk of offending. *The Cochrane Database of Systematic Reviews*, *2*.

Kinsey, A.C., Pomeroy, W.B., and Martin, C.E. (1948). *Sexual Behaviour in the Human Male*. Philadelphia, PA: W.B. Saunders.

Kinsey, A.C., Pomeroy, W.B., Martin, C.E, and Gebhard, P.H. (1953). *Sexual Behaviour in the Human Female*. Philadelphia, PA: W.B. Saunders.

Knight, R.A. and Prentky, R.A. (1990). Classifying sex offenders: The development and corroboration of taxonomic models. In W.L. Marshall, D.R. Laws, & H.E. Barabaree (Eds.), *Handbook of Sexual Assault: Issues, Theories and Treatment of the Offender* (pp. 27–52). New York, NY: Plenum.

Koh, W.T. (2017, December 13). Man who sexually groomed a 14-year-old girl jailed six months. *Yahoo News*.

Kutchinchy, B. (1973). The effect of easy availability of pornography on the incidence of sex crimes: The Danish experience. *Journal of Social Issues*, *29*, 163–181.

Lalor, K. and McElvaney, R. (2010). Child sexual abuse, links to later sexual exploitation/high risk sexual behaviour and prevention/treatment programmes. *Trauma, Violence and Abuse*, *11*, 159–177.

Laws, D.R. and O' Donohue, W. (Eds.) (1997). *Sexual Deviance: Theory Assessment and Treatment*. New York, NY: Guilford.

Levenson, J. (2008). Sex offender community notification (Megan's laws). In B.L. Cutler (Ed.), *Encyclopaedia of Psychology and Law* (Vol. 2, pp. 722–725). Thousand Oaks, CA: SAGE Publications.

Lewis, C.F. and Stanley, C.R. (2000). Women accused of sexual offences. *Behavioral Sciences and the Law*, *18*, 73–81.

Lim, L.E.C., Gwee, K.P., Woo, M., and Parker, G. (2001). Men who commit rape in Singapore. *Annals of Medicine*, Singapore, *30*, 620–624.

Lim, L. (2002). Sexual Assaults in Singapore: A Comparative Study of Rapists and Molesters. *Medicine, Science and the Law*, *42*(4), 344–350.

Lösel, F. and Schmucker, M. (2005). The effectiveness of treatment for sexual offenders: A comprehensive meta-analysis. *Journal of Experimental Criminology*, *1*(1), 117–146.

Mathews, R., Hunter, J.A., and Vuz, J. (1997). Juvenile female sexual offenders: Clinical characteristics and treatment issues. *Sexual Abuse: A Journal of Research and Treatment*, *9*, 187–199.

Matthews, J.K., Mathews, R., and Speltz, K. (1991). Female sexual offenders: A typology. In M.Q. Patton (Ed.), *Family sexual abuse: Frontline research and evaluation* (pp. 199–219). London: Sage Publications.

Marin, T.M. and Bell, D.L. (2003). Navy sex offender programme: Promoting community safety. *Corrections Today*, *65*, 84–87.

Masters, R.E.L. and Lea, E. (1963). *Sex Crimes in History: Evolving Concepts of Sadism, Lust-murders, and Necrophilia from Ancient to Modern Times*. New York, NY: Julian Press.

Ministry of Social and Family Development (2016). *Protecting Children in Singapore*. Singapore: Author.

Neidigh, L. and Krop, H. (1992). Cognitive distortions among child sexual offenders. *Journal of Sex Education and Therapy*, *18*, 208–215.

Nathan, P. and Ward, T. (2001). Females who sexually abuse children: Assessment and treatment issues. *Psychiatry, Psychology and Law*, *8*, 44–55.

Nathan, P. and Ward, T. (2002). Female sex offenders: Clinical and demographic features. *Journal of Sexual Aggression*, *8*, 5–21.

National Center for Victims of Crime (n.d.). *Grooming Dynamic*. Retrieved from http://victimsofcrime.org/media/reporting-on-child-sexual-abuse/groomingdynamic-of-csa.

National Offender Management Service (2013, November). Retrieved from https://www.gov.uk.

O'Donohue, W., Carlson, G.C., Benuto, L.T., and Bennett, N.M. (2004). Examining the scientific validity of rape trauma syndrome. *Psychiatry, Psychology and Law*, *21*(6), 858–876.

Ong, J. (2017, January 29). New forensic centre, extra training to better protect sexual crime victims. *Channel News Asia*. Retrieved from https://www.

channelnewsasia.com/news/singapore/new-forensic-centre-extra-training-to-better-protect-sexual-crim-7586598.

Polaschek, D. and Ward, T. (2002). The implicit theories of potential rapists: What our questionnaires tell us. *Aggression and Violent Behaviour, 7,* 385–406.

Quinsey, V. (2008). Sex Offender Risk Appraisal Guide (SORAG). In B.L. Cutler (Ed.), *Encyclopaedia of Psychology and Law* (vol. 2, pp. 730–730). Thousand Oaks, CA: SAGE Publications.

Quinsy, V.L., Rice, M.E., and Harris, G.T. (1995). Actuarial Prediction of Sexual Recidivism. *Journal of Interpersonal Violence, 10,* 85–105.

Rajan, D. and Katharine, R. (2012). What clinicians need to know before assessing risk in sexual offenders. *Advances in Psychiatric Treatment, 18,* 467–478.

Rapp, L. (2012). Sex offender registration. In S.M. Barton-Bellessa (Ed.), *Encyclopaedia of Community Corrections* (pp. 413–414). Thousand Oaks, CA: SAGE Publications.

Ressler, R.K., Burgess, A.W., Hartmann, C.R., Douglas, J.E., and McCormack, A. (1986). Murderers who rape and mutilate. *Journal of Interpersonal Violence, 1,* 273–287.

Rettenberger, M., Hucker, S.J., Boer, D.P., and Eher, R. (2009). The Reliability and Validity of the Sexual Violence Risk-20 (SVR-20): *An International Review. Sexual Offender Treatment,* 4(2).

Rice, M.E., Harris, G.T., and Lang, C. (2013). Validation of and revision to the VRAG and SORAG: The Violence Risk Appraisal Guide–Revised (VRAG–R). *Psychological Assessment, 25*(3), 951–965.

Russell, D.E.H. and Bolen, R.M. (2000). *The Epidemic of Rape and Child Sexual Abuse in the United States.* Thousand Oaks, CA: Sage Publications.

Seow, B.Y. (2017a, April 3). More allegations of children sexually abused by family. *The Straits Times.*

Seow, B.Y. (2017b, April 3). Many find it difficult to report sex offences. *The Straits Times.*

Somerset and Avon Rape and Sexual Abuse Support (n.d.). *Sarah's law.* Retrieved from https://www.sarsas.org. uk/sarahs-law/

Seto, M.C., Hanson, K.R., and Babchishin, K.M. (2011). Contact sexual offending by men with online sexual offences. *Sexual Abuse: A Journal of Research and Treatment, 23,* 14–45.

Singapore Statutes Online (2015). *Rape.* Retrieved from http://statutes.agc. gov.sg

Smallbone, S., Marshall, W.L., and Wortley, R. (2008). *Preventing Child Sexual Abuse: Evidence, Policy and Practice.* Cullompton, Devon: Willan Publishing.

Stalans, L.J. (2004). Adult sex offenders on community supervision: A review of recent assessment strategies and treatment. *Criminal Justice and Behaviour, 31,* 564–608.

Scorolli, C., Ghirlanda, S., Enquist, M., Zattoni, S., and Jannini, E. A. (2007). Relative prevalence of different fetishes. *International Journal of Impotence Research, 19*(4), 432–437.

Schmucker, M. and Lösel, F. (2009). *A systematic review of high-quality evaluations of sex offender treatment.* Paper presented at the Annual Conference of the European Society of Criminology, Ljubljana, Slovenia.

Taylor, P.J. (1992). Victims and survivors. In J. Gunn & P.J. Taylor (Eds), *Forensic Psychiatry* (pp. 885–944). London, Butterworth Heinemann.

The Straits Times (2018, February 13). *Teacher charged over sex with student.* Retrieved http://www.straitstimes.com/singapore/courts-crime/teachercharged-over-sex-with-student.

Terry, K.J. and Ackerman, A. (2008). Child sexual abuse in the Catholic Church: How situational crime prevention strategies can help create safe environments. *Criminal Justice and Behaviour, 35,* 643–657.

Vandiver, D.M. and Walker, J.T. (2002). Female sex offenders: An overview and analysis of 40 cases. *Criminal Justice Review, 27,* 284–300.

Vandiver, D.M. and Kercher, G. (2004). Offender and victim characteristics of registered female sexual offenders in Texas: A proposed typology of female sexual offenders. *Sexual Abuse: A Journal of Research and Treatment, 16,* 121–137.

Ward, C. (1988). The Attitudes toward Rape Victims Scale: Construction, validation, and cross-cultural applicability. *Psychology of Women Quarterly, 12,* 127–146.

Ward, T. and Keenan, T. (1999). Child molesters' implicit theories. *Journal of Interpersonal Violence, 14,* 821–838.

Webb, L., Craissati, J., and Keen, S. (2007). Characteristics of Internet child pornography offenders: A comparison with child molesters. *Sexual Abuse: A Journal of Research and Treatment, 19,* 449–465.

West Virginia Executive Branch (n.d.). Video voyeurism prevention act of 2004. Retrieved from http://www.privacy.wv.gov/tips/Pages/VideoVoyeurism PreventionAct.aspx.

West Virginia Foundation for Rape Informational Services (n.d.). Retrieved from http://www.fris.org/home.html

White, J.H. (2007). Evidence of primary, secondary, and collateral paraphilia left at serial murder and sex offender crime scenes. *Journal of Forensic Science, 52*(5), 1194–1201.

Wortley, R. and Smallbone, S. (2006). Applying situational principles to sexual offences against children. In R. Wortley & S. Smallbone (Eds.), *Situational prevention of child sexual abuse*. Monsey, NY: Criminal Justice Press.

World Health Organisation (1999). *Report of the Consultation on Child Abuse Prevention*. Geneva: World Health Organization.

World Health Organization (2002). *World Report on Violence and Health: Summary*. Geneva: World Health Organization.

Wurtele, S.K. (2012). Preventing the sexual exploitation of minors in youth serving organisations. *Children and Youth Services Review, 34,* 2442–2453.

Yeo, S., Morgan, N., and Chan, W.C. (2012). *Criminal Law in Malaysia and Singapore*. Singapore: LexisNexis.

Yijayan, K.C. (2017, December 30). Insulting modesty' law does not apply to men, rules court. *The Straits Times*.

CHAPTER 5
VIOLENT OFFENDING

"It is forbidden to kill; therefore, all murderers are punished unless they kill in large numbers and to the sound of trumpets."

Voltaire
French Enlightenment writer, historian, and philosopher

5.1 Introduction

Just like sexual offending in the previous chapter, violent offending is a rich and heterogeneous category of crime. There are so many ways to kill and hurt someone. Just think of the following: assassination, cannibalism, child murder, consensual homicide, feticide,[1] honor killing, infanticide, domestic-violence related murder, mass murder,

---

[1] Death of a foetus.

murder–suicide, torture murder, and Internet homicide. The list goes on. Why do men (and women) kill? What motivates them?

This chapter is about homicide and the characteristics of violent offending. However, because murder and homicide are the most serious of violent crimes, this chapter will focus on homicide.

What you may discover is that most murderers are not serial killers, most murder cases usually involve one perpetrator and one victim who is usually someone known to the perpetrator (stranger killings happen but are rare). The reasons for homicide tend to be emotional and interpersonal (crimes of passion), although these acts are still rational. That is, people who kill do not lose their rationality even if they are driven by strong emotions. Most know what they are doing. So, the calculated cold-blooded killer is good television. As an introduction to this topic, read the following case study on the psychopathic serial killer.

CASE STUDY:
The Psychopathic Serial Killer

Whether John Martin Scripps (a Briton, aged 35) was indeed a psychopath, we cannot be sure. Scripps seemed to have little regard for others and lacked empathy — the ability to stand in someone else's shoes and understand how they feel. Here is his story.

On March 8, 1995, Scripps befriended brewery engineer Gerrard George Lowe (a South African, aged 32) at Changi Airport. Scripps appeared smiley and charming, easily convincing Lowe to share a room with him. After Lowe agreed, the duo checked into RV Hotel that same day. That night, Scripps hit Lowe several times on the head using his 1.5kg camping hammer, until Lowe collapsed onto the carpeted floor. He alleged that Lowe was a homosexual and that he had touched him inappropriately. In the morning, Scripps proceeded to tell the hotel receptionist that he had kicked Lowe out the previous night and that Lowe's name should be deleted from the registration system. He then went on a shopping spree using Lowe's credit cards, withdrawing more than $8,000 in cash, and buying a $499 videocassette recorder. He even attended a Singapore Symphony Orchestra performance before flying to Bangkok, where he

(Continued)

(Continued)

murdered two more tourists he befriended. Lowe's body parts were found in black plastic bags in the waters of the Singapore River near Clifford Pier days later, and those of the two victims murdered in Thailand were found in a disused tin mine in Phuket's Kathu district. On March 19, Scripps returned to Singapore, carrying his murder tools, the three victims' cheques, passports, credit cards, and belongings, as well as US$40,000 in cash. With the incriminating evidence on him, Scripps was swiftly arrested at the airport.

On September 18, 1995, Scripps was formally charged for Lowe's murder in the Singapore court. It was reported that, at times while in court, Scripps appeared to be like an obstinate schoolboy unwilling to answer questions; at other times, eager to please; and at times, apparently lost in a world of his own. Regardless, finding Scripps to be a calculative killer who set out to murder and rob the unsuspecting Lowe, Justice T.S. Sinnathuray eventually sentenced him to death by hanging.

Source: Tan, Ooi Boon (11 November 1995). "Body parts case — Martin guilty". *Straits Times*. Singapore.

THINKING POINT

1. Based on the facts provided, why did Scripts do what he did?
2. Why did Scripps dismember his victims?

5.2 Defining Violence and Homicide

5.2.1 *Defining Violence*

Violence has been defined as the intentional infliction or threat of physical harm against another person (Eisner, 2012). Violence has often been characterized by the use of physical force exerted for the purpose of inflicting injury, pain, discomfort, or abuse on a person/persons or for the purpose of damaging or destroying property. The intriguing aspect about homicide and violence is that in some instances, violence may be condoned. Society, for example, would be accepting of the police using *reasonable* force against resisting persons, soldiers who kill in war, or victims who protect themselves when they encounter a criminal. When we discuss violence, we are therefore more concerned with *violence committed without justification*, rather than violence in general.

5.2.2 *Defining Homicide*

What is homicide? Taking a global view, the United Nations Office of Drugs and Crime (UNODC) uses the term 'homicide' to refer to 'intentional homicide' and 'unlawful death purposefully inflicted on a person by another person' (UNODC, 2011). They explained that for the sake of simplicity, the terms 'homicide' and 'murder' are used as shorthand for 'intentional homicide'. Furthermore, the definition concerned itself with those acts in which the perpetrator intended to cause death or serious injury by his or her actions, and hence, excludes deaths related to conflicts, deaths caused when the perpetrator was reckless or negligent, as well as killings that are considered justifiable according to law (such as those by law enforcement agents in the line of duty or in self-defence).

The United Nations acknowledges the challenge in developing a comprehensive typology for homicide. This is especially so because types can be identified on the basis of premeditation, motivation, context, instrumentality and perpetrator–victim relationship (UNODC, 2013).

From the angle of crime prevention, however, the UN uses three sub-types of homicide definitions: (1) homicide related to *other criminal activities* (committed by organized criminal groups and those committed while perpetrating acts such as robbery); (2) *interpersonal homicide* in which homicide is not instrumental to the accomplishment of a secondary goal, but is a means of resolving a conflict and/or punishing the victim through violence when relationships come under strain; and (3) *sociopolitical homicide*, which originates in the public sphere and are typically committed as an instrument for advancing social or political agendas. For example, in some countries, people are killed for what they represent and/or for the message that such killings can convey to the general public (UNODC, 2013).

In Australia, the Australian Institute of Criminology uses the term 'homicide' to mean a person killed (unlawfully); that is, a homicide incident is an event in which one or more persons are killed at the same place and time (Bryant & Cussen, 2015). Homicide, according to them, is defined by the criminal law of each Australian state and territory, and that varying definitions exist between states and territories in terms of its degree, culpability, and intent. Their definition of homicide includes all cases resulting in a person/persons being charged with murder or manslaughter. Excluded from this definition are industrial accidents involving criminal negligence (unless a charge of manslaughter is laid). Lawful homicide, including that by police in the course of their duties, is excluded.

Not everyone agrees with these definitions, and a leading expert on homicide, Professor Fiona Brookman, explained that the term 'homicide' refers to the killing of a human being, *whether or not the killing was lawful or unlawful* (Brookman, 2015). She reminds readers, however, that the crime of murder or homicide can be legally and socially constructed. She explained that because different countries have different legal codes on homicide, sometimes, the way 'killings' are defined may change over time, as homicide is a crime that can be socially constructed. She explains further that very rarely do people agree about 'killings by corporations' in a major nuclear incident, or environmental crimes that cause death.[2] This becomes even more complex when one has to think about ascertaining blame and 'culpability' of responsibility for the action. For example, people will view an incident where a child sex offender who kills a child, quite differently from an incident where a young teenage mother kills her unwanted new-born child. So, society may view issues of 'culpability' differently. 'Culpability' refers to the degree to which the perpetrator is seen to be responsible for the act and its consequences (Brookman, 2015).

ACTIVITY

Think about the following types of killings, the victims and the circumstances shown in Table 5.1. Tick off whether you think it is excusable.

---

[2] In Singapore, workplace deaths are taken seriously. It was reported that workplace deaths have dropped to a 13-year low (41 in 2017, 66 in 2016, and 66 in 2015). Reports however have cautioned against reading too much from just one year's figure. To send a strong message, Prime Minister Lee Hsien Loong has set a target of having one workplace fatality per 100,000 workers by 2028. In addition, amendments have been made to the Workplace Safety and Health (WSH) Act (Yuen, 2018).

Table 5.1:   Types of 'Killings'

Incident	Who is responsible?	Excusable Yes or no?	Acceptable or Unacceptable?
Euthanasia			
Abortion			
Teenager who panics and leaves her infant on a HDB rooftop and infant dies.			
Industrial chemical leakage that kills five workers working in chemical plant			
Mentally ill patient who charges with a chopper at a police officer, who is then shot by the police officer			

5.2.3 *Violence Versus Aggression*

Psychologically speaking, violence and aggression are different. Violence is an extreme form of aggression and involves physical force. Aggression, however, may or may not involve violent force. Think of a passive aggressive person who makes snide comments and appears hostile, but never actually hits at anyone. Someone may appear indirectly aggressive without actually being behaviourally violent. For example, stalking an ex-lover for some years (Bartol, 2002).

5.2.4 *Instrumental Versus Reactive Aggression*

There are further sub-types of aggression: *instrumental* and *reactive/ expressive aggression*. Instrumental aggression is goal-directed. Harm to another is not the primary goal of the aggressive act, although it can be a secondary result. For example, robbers may end up attacking people in a household during the course of their robbery. Reactive or expressive aggression has the intention to harm someone as its primary goal. This is usually related to anger, fear, frustration, or stress. Professor Clark McCauley makes an interesting point that aggression may, at times, involve *both* reactive and instrumental aggression, such as when a parent spanks a child for going into the street where there are cars zooming by. The spanking and accompanying nagging may be aimed at keeping the child out of the street in the future (instrumental aggression), but it may express the parent's fear and anger (reactive aggression) in reaction to the child's disobedience at the same time.

Practitioners may want to understand what drives someone's aggression. Someone who smashes the car window to steal a laptop is doing so to sell the product to get some money to buy drugs that he is addicted to (instrumental violence). On the other hand, he may do it because he hates rich people who own fancy cars, and he feels anger and jealously towards them and their cars (expressive aggression). Rehabilitation specialists who misdiagnose these (criminogenic) needs or motivations may not treat the real problem/issue. If the need is misdiagnosed, the therapist may end up teaching anger management, skills, when in fact the client may need drug addiction management programs.

RESEARCH ARTICLE

Offender and Crime Characteristics of Female Serial Arsonists in Japan

Wachi and colleagues did a study of Japanese female serial arsonists (nomothetic profile). The data was a sample from the national police register containing all male and female arson cases in Japan between 1982 and 2005. Serial arsonists were 6% of the arson offenders. Of these, 12% were female arson offenders, resulting in 83 female serial arsonists.

The mean age of female serial offenders seemed older than expected at 37.6 years, and 43% of them were unemployed. Nearly half were married, 28% had a history of mental problems, and 22% had a prior arrest, usually for theft (19%). Most female serial arsonists would go to a place near their home with a lighter and set fire directly to combustible materials.

These arsons could be differentiated in terms of either *expressive* or *instrumental* actions. Expressive arsons were opportunistic and their impulsive acts were motivated by emotional distress. The fires were mostly set close to home. Expressive arsons were characteristic of 66% of the females. Instrumental arsons, on the other hand, were motivated by

(Continued)

(*Continued*)

revenge, and involved planned and goal-directed behaviors. They were committed by 13% of the females. Instrumental arsonists tended to travel further from home.

Source: Wachi, Taeko Watanabe, Kazumi Yokota, Kaeko Suzuki, Mamoru Hoshino, Maki Sato, Atsushi Fujita, Goro. (2007). Offender and crime characteristics of female serial arsonists in Japan. *Journal of Investigative Psychology and Offender Profiling,* 4, 29–52.

5.3 Characteristics of Violent Crimes and Homicides

What does international research suggest about the characteristics of violent offenders? There have been several interesting findings reported in the United Nations Office of Drugs and Crime report on violent crimes (UNDOC, 2011, UNODC 2013), and they are as follows.

Rates of homicide

The UNODC estimates that intentional homicide in 2012 amounted to a total of 437,000 at the global level. The largest share was in the Americas (36%), and Africa and Asia (31% and 28%, respectively). Europe, Australia, and New Zealand accounted for the lowest shares of homicide. The 2012 average global homicide rate was 6.2 per 100,000 population. The highest rates were in the Americas (16.3/100,00) and Africa (12.5/100,000), and Asia had the lowest (2.9/100,000). In 2013, Singapore rate was 0.2/100,000.

Economic development

The largest shares of homicides occurred in countries with lower levels of human development and high levels of income inequality. Economic performance affects homicide rates positively and better economic growth seems to reduce homicide rates in most countries across the world. The UNODC reported that homicide rates in South America, for example, had decreased during periods of economic growth in the last 15 years, and the same pattern has been noted in Russia. There appears to be many reasons for this, including the role that the 'rule of law' principle plays, since it follows economic development. Economic development results in employment and employment itself is a protective factor preventing crime (as discussed in Chapter 1).

Rule of law

Long-term sustainable economic and social development requires the 'rule of law' to be in place. In most countries where there has been a strengthening of the rule of law, there has been a decline in the homicide rate and violent crimes; while most countries where homicide has increased have had a relatively weak rule of law.

Means of homicide

Forty-two percent of global homicides are committed using firearms.[3] Homicides in the Americas are more than 3.5 times as likely to be perpetrated with a firearm than in Europe (74% versus 21% respectively). The use of firearms is prevalent in the Americas, where two-thirds of homicides are committed with guns, whereas sharp objects[4] such as knives are used more in Oceania[5] and Europe. In the U.K., sharp objects accounted for two out of every five homicides in 2011/2012 (Government of U.K., 2012). The consumption of

---

[3] Gun-related incidents appear to be on the rise in the U.S. The February 2018 Florida shooting where a young man shot 17 students was the 18th incident in 2018 (*The Straits Times*, February 18, 2018).

[4] The UNODC 2013 report explains that homicides result from cuts or slashes caused by sharp objects, such as knives, machetes, razors, swords and bayonets, as well as broken glass, but sharp objects, including less conventional examples such as screwdrivers, ice picks or stilettos, can also be used to stab or puncture. Such instruments are relatively easy to obtain and to conceal.

[5] which includes Australia, New Zealand, Micronesia, and Polynesia.

alcohol and drugs increases one's risk of becoming a victim or perpetrator of violence. In Sweden and Finland, for example, more than half of all homicide offenders were intoxicated with alcohol when they committed homicide. In Australia, data suggests that nearly half of all homicide incidents were preceded by alcohol consumption (UNODC, 2013).

Intimate partner homicide victims

In many countries, intimate partner/family-related homicide has been the major cause of female homicides. In 2008, 35% of female homicide victims were murdered by spouses or ex-spouses, and 17% by relatives. Women accounted for 77% of all the victims of intimate partner/family-related homicide. The regions with the highest numbers of women victims reported by UNODC in 2013 were Asia (19,700), followed by Africa (13,400). The lowest was in Oceania (200).

Male as victims

According to international statistics, seventy-nine percent of all homicide victims globally are male, and 95% of homicide perpetrators are also male. The global male homicide rate is about four times more than females (9.7 versus 2.7 per 100,000) and is highest in the Americas (29.3 per 100,000 males), where it is nearly seven times higher than in Asia, Europe, and Oceania (all under 4.5 per 100,000 males). This is due to the higher levels of homicide related to organized crime and gangs in the Americas. About 43% of all homicide victims are aged 15–29, and mostly likely to be living in the Americas.

Location

Across the world, the home is the place where a woman is most likely to be murdered, whereas men are more likely to be murdered in the street.

Demographics

Demographically, across the world, the typical homicide pattern is a man killing another man (about 70%). The global picture shows that young males are most at risk due to their increased likelihood of participating in violence-prone activities such as street crime, gang membership, drug consumption, possession of weapons, and street fighting.

5.4 Causes of Violence: Theories and Explanations

Bartol and Bartol (2008) explained that there are several main causes of violence, as follows:

- *Biological explanations.* These theories explain that there are biological factors interacting with the social environment, which might explain for violence. Some examples are: (a) links between aggression and brain damage resulting from toxins (lead paint); (b) traumatic head injury as a result of fighting or accidents, child abuse, traffic accidents; and (c) alcohol and drug ingestion by mother during pregnancy. Economist Rick Nevin, at the National Center of Healthy Housing, U.S., looking at data across several nations, argued that there is a "very strong association between preschool blood lead and subsequent crime rate trends over several decades in the U.S., Britain, Canada, France, Australia, Finland, Italy, West Germany, and New Zealand (Nevin, 2007, p. 315).
- *Socialization*: These theories explain that violence is learnt and developed through the learning of scripts (Bartol, 2008). Aggressive, anti-social behaviors can be learnt from others (through television, movies, and fictional characters). There are suggestions that children can learn aggressive anti-social behaviors from their peers, family, and the media. An American Psychological Association (APA) Committee on Violence in Video Games and Interactive Media, of the Media Psychology Division, reviewed the research and concluded that exposure to violence in video games increases aggressive thoughts, behavior, and angry feelings among youth. In addition, this exposure reduces helpful behavior and increases

physiological arousal in children and adolescents. They concluded that violence in video games appear to have similar negative effects as viewing violence on television, but may be more harmful because of the interactive nature of the former (APA, 2005).

- *Cognitive influences:* The APA suggests that violent persons have different ways of interpreting information (APA, 1996). Aggressive persons perceive hostility in others, when there is none. This is called *hostility attribution bias.* It appears that violent persons are less efficient in their thinking of non-violent ways to deal with conflicts and are more accepting of violence. For example, in our own work with young males in gangs, one person reported that "it is acceptable to whack him if he showed me disrespect", and "if he scolded my mother, then I must beat him up badly".

- *Situational factors:* Characteristics of an environment may induce stress and frustration leading to aggression. In places where there are large crowds of people with loud noises or unpleasant sights, such conditions can provoke aggression. This is one of the reasons why fights often break out in clubs and streets. The presence of alcohol and drug consumption makes things worse (the role of drugs and alcohol is discussed in Chapter 1). Needless to say, the presence of weapons also increases the chances that conflict will occur. The Little India Riot which occurred in Singapore (after 40 years without riots) is a good example of how violence can erupt when there are a large number of young men who have consumed a lot of alcohol. Interested readers should look up the Committee of Inquiry Report on the Little India Riot.

RESEARCH ARTICLE OF INTEREST

The Role of Cultural Attitudes Condoning Violent Honour Killing Attitudes Among Adolescents in Amman, Jordan

This article discusses honor killings mainly in the Maghreb region, the Middle East, Western and Central Asia. This article explained that females are sometimes killed by their family when they carry out a 'dishonorable act', such as premarital sex, adultery, pregnancy out of wedlock, and contact with a man who is not a relative.

(Continued)

(Continued)

Dr. Manuel Eisner and Dr. Lana Ghuneim studied honor killing attitudes in Amman, Jordan. The researchers found that 40% of boys and 20% of girls of 856 students (aged 14 to 16 years old, 53.2% females) believed that killing a daughter, sister, or wife who has dishonored the family can be justified. Also, adolescents who held traditional political beliefs believed interactions between same-aged girls and boys to be wrong, and those who carried out 'moral neutralization' (i.e., seeing honor killing as a justifiable and respectable cleansing response to the 'shameful act') were more likely to endorse honor killing.

Political traditionalism and moral neutralization were more seen in males, and a gender effect was observed, where they endorsed honor killings more than females. The participant's father's harsh authoritarian and patriarchal style of discipline on beliefs about the acceptability of honor killings had a greater effect on males (than females). Adolescents whose parents were of low education levels were also more likely to endorse conservative expectations about decency and chastity. The article argued that coherent messages about the wrongfulness of honor-related violence and the importance of gender equality must be promoted by political, religious, and economic elites.

Source: Eisner, M. and Ghuneim, L. (2013). The Role of Cultural Attitudes Condoning Violent Honour Killing Attitudes Among Adolescents in Amman, Jordan. *Aggressive Behaviour*, 39(5), 405–417.

5.5 Characteristics of Homicide Offenders

Taking findings by US and international studies on violence and homicide, research evidence confirms that there are several characteristic features (Bartol & Bartol, 2008):

Number of offences. The majority of homicides are single incident offences, and not multiple killings, as we would sometimes see in the movies.

Marginalization: In most societies, people who are socially marginalized seem to commit the majority of homicides.

Employment: Violent perpetrators tend to have irregular or no employment. Large proportions of them suffer from a combination of problems, including substance abuse and mental health problems.

Nature of offending: Typical homicide is committed either during the course of committing another offence, or is often perpetrated against an intimate partner or friend/acquaintance. This is probably the unfortunate aspect about homicides, since people end up killing their friends, loved ones, or acquaintances.

Age: Most people who typically committed homicide are from the ages of 18 to 25, even though there are older perpetrators.

Gender: Most homicide involves single male victims. Female victims were highly likely to be killed by someone they knew (intimate partner homicides).

Nature of relationship: When there is a known relationship between the offender and victim, it is often a domestic relationship or friendship.

5.6 Prevalence Rates of Homicide in Singapore

The prevalence rates of murder and other violent crimes are shown in Table 5.2.

Table 5.2: Singapore Statistics on Murder and Other Violent Crimes

	2009	2010	2011	2012	2013	2014	2015
(i) Murder	19	19	16	11	16	14	14
(ii) Serious Hurt	406	429	406	452	476	513	473
(iii) Rioting	283	262	172	191	162	166	114

Note: Data from serious hurt and rioting are presented for comparison purposes.

THINKING POINT

1. What is the average murder rate in Singapore in the last three years?
2. Why is the murder rate so low? What might account for these rates? (Efficient policing? Strict laws? Small dense living where murders might be noticed?)

Read the article below and test your own responses to the above questions to the findings of the article.

(Continued)

(*Continued*)

RESEARCH ARTICLE

A Study of Homicide Trends in Singapore from 1955 to 2011

This paper discussed a study of homicide trends in Singapore from 1955 to 2011. The data was obtained from the United Nations Surveys of Crime Trends and Operations of Criminal Justice Systems, the World Health Organization Mortality Database, and the Post-Mortem Survey of Homicides in Singapore. The trends observed are described as follows:

1. Changes in homicide rates
There was an uneven decline from 1955 to early 1970s (from 3.5 to two cases per 100,000 people). The rates fluctuated around two cases per 100,000 from early 1970s to 1990. There was also a relatively steady decline from 1990 to a low point of 0.21 cases per 100,000 in 2011.

2. Profile of offenders victims
The peak age of offending was from 16 to 24 years and prevalence rates decline sharply after this. The peak age of victimization was 15 to 25 years in the 1970s, and this increased in range to 15 to 49 years in the 1980s. However, from the 1990s, victimization is well spread out across all ages.

In terms of gender, a large majority of offenders are males, but there is a slight increase in proportion of females over the years. The proportion of female victims rose over the years, to reach almost 50% in the 2000s. The majority of cases are male offenders murdering male victims but rates of homicides involving female offenders and/or victims are rising.

3. Motive and modus operandi
In terms of motives, there was an increasing proportion of homicides committed with 'expressive intent' (for intrinsic gratification, expression of hate, anger, or vengeance) over the years, and a smaller proportion of those with 'instrumental intent' (oriented to a specific goal, e.g., robbery). As homicide rates dropped over the years, the previously high proportion of publicly committed cases dropped, and more cases were taking place privately in the 2000s onwards. Guns accounted for less than 1% of

(*Continued*)

(*Continued*)

homicides over the years; instead, a knife was the most common weapon in Singapore. The proportion of cases that occurred without a weapon rose significantly in the 2000s.

4. Explanations for decline in homicide rate

The authors concluded that the main institutional factor accounting for the decline of homicides is possibly the effectiveness of the Singapore Police Force (SPF) post-independence. The use of community policing rather than a reactive, incident-centred mode of operation by the SPF may have played a part. Another factor could be the use of the death penalty for murder cases. Finally, as far as economic factors were concerned, rates declined as income inequality rose from 1990 to 2011, counter to strain theory.[6] Yet, another factor could be the rise in affluence levels since 1970, which possibly offset frustration effects. In addition, unemployment had been low, showing that individuals had productive opportunities and did not need to resort to illegitimate means to get what they want. Moreover, a high standard of education was available at nominal cost, and high social mobility due to the political ideal of meritocracy were possibly explanatory factors for lowered homicide rates.

In its conclusion, the article argued that cultural factors were at play. First, a 'civilizing process' occurred after Singapore's independence as Singaporeans had better education. There were better industrial relations regulatory frameworks, making open conflict a last resort for the people. Second, government-initiated community engagement programs raised the civility of Singaporeans. Third, anti-social behavior was reduced effectively through government policies (i.e., vandalism, spitting in public, and littering were the subject of criminal sanctions). Fourth, demographic factors such as the decrease in male-on-male violence involving younger offenders and the decrease in male residents in Singapore aged 15 to 29 years from 1957 to 2011 may have accounted for the lowered homicide rates.

Source: Tai, W. S. and Tang, G. H. (2014). *Home Team Journal*, (5), 74–87.

---

[6] This was discussed in Chapter 1.

5.7 Laws Relating to Homicide

5.7.1 *Murder and Culpable Homicide*[7]

Section 299 of the Singapore Penal Code reads that "whoever causes death by doing an act with the intention of causing death, or with the intention of causing such bodily injury as is likely to cause death, or with the knowledge that he is likely by such act to cause death, commits the offence of Culpable Homicide."

Section 300, states that an act may be considered Murder, if:

(a) The act by which the death is caused is an act done with the intention of causing death;
(b) It is done with the intention of causing such bodily injury, as the offender knows it may likely cause the death of the person to whom the harm is caused;
(c) It is done with the intention of causing bodily injury to any person, and the bodily injury is sufficient to cause death; or
(d) The person committing the act knows that it is so imminently dangerous that it must in all probability cause death.

In terms of punishment meted out for Murder, Section 302 of the Penal Code explains that whoever commits murder within the meaning of Section 300(a) shall be punished with death, but whoever commits Murder within the meaning of Sections 300(b), (c), or (d) shall be punished with death or imprisonment for life and be liable to caning.

In Singapore, the Penal Code sets out that there is a mandatory death penalty when a person is convicted of murder. However, in cases where the person did not have the intent to murder, the offence of 'Culpable Homicide Not Amounting to Murder' is

---

[7] This section on the laws and exceptions are presented here only for discussion purposes. As there are always amendments to the law over the years and new Bills being passed in Parliament, some of this information may not be up to date. I have not included all the limbs and details of these laws. Readers should always seek legal advice and consult a lawyer, on legal matters they are concerned about.

sometimes made out. If the defence of 'grave and sudden provocation', 'sudden fight', and 'abnormality of mind' is made out and accepted by the Court, then Murder may be reduced to 'Culpable Homicide Not Amounting to Murder'. This latter offence may carry a sentence of life imprisonment or a prison term of up to 20 years and a fine or caning. However, this will be more of the exception than the rule, in order for the law to have a deterrent effect (AWARE, 2002).

Another important section[8] is Section 307 which is 'Attempted Murder'. The section reads that:

'Whoever does any act with such intention or knowledge and under such circumstances that if he by that act caused death he would be guilty of murder, shall be punished with imprisonment for a term which may extend to 15 years, and shall also be liable to fine; and if hurt is caused to any person by such act, the offender shall be liable either to imprisonment for life, or to imprisonment for a term which may extend to 20 years, and shall also be liable to caning or fine or both'.

In the U.K., a person is liable for Murder through causing a person's death, whether by act or omission, either with intent to kill or with intent to cause grievous bodily harm. That liability may be reduced to 'Manslaughter', if the killing stemmed from provocation, diminished responsibility or a suicide pact. This is usually known as 'Voluntary Manslaughter' in the U.K. Also, where there is no apparent intent to murder, an individual may be liable to conviction

---

[8] In one local case, a man repeatedly stabbed a student nurse and was charged for Attempted Murder. It started when he wooed her. She initially played along but later apologised, telling him "it was a joke all along". She rejected his advances but he refused to accept her rejection. He later asked for her hand in marriage but she didn't agree. He behaved aggressively on being rebuffed but left after the police were called. He went home, hid a knife in his sock and slept at the void deck to wait for her. At about 8.30 a.m. the next day, he demanded that she talk to him. When she refused, he stabbed her in the lower back and abdomen. The woman's parents rushed down upon hearing her screams (Lum, 2018).

for 'Involuntary Manslaughter', if it is shown that they acted in a reckless or negligent manner that resulted in death (Bookman, 2015).

In the U.S., the law relating to murder varies according to jurisdiction (there are 52 jurisdictions in the U.S.). There is a hierarchy of acts relating to homicide. 'First degree murder' and 'felony murder' are the most serious, followed by 'second degree murder', followed by 'voluntary manslaughter' and 'involuntary manslaughter', and finally, 'justifiable homicide'.

5.7.2 Relationship between Homicide Offences and the Law

If murder is a crime requiring intention, a person who is mentally unsound or incapable of entertaining intention or knowledge cannot be entirely responsible for homicide. This is usually dealt with under Section 84 of the Penal Code ('Insanity') or Exception 7 to Section 300 ('Diminished Responsibility').[9]

Section 84 of the Penal Code states that nothing is an offence which is done by a person who is (at the time of committing the offence) of unsoundness of mind, is incapable of knowing the nature of the act, or what he is doing is either wrong or contrary to law. This applies to cases where the individual is so severely psychotic or maladjusted in some manner that he is incapable of being aware of his actions, or that they are wrong. Not all psychotic individuals, however, will qualify for this legal defence, for even while being psychotic, they may be fully *aware* of their wrongful actions. A psychotic individual may or may not qualify for the defence of 'Diminished Responsibility'. Exception 7 to Section 300 of the Penal Code states that:

> "Culpable homicide is not murder if the offender was suffering from
> such abnormality of mind (whether arising from a condition of

---

[9] While not directly homicide relevant, another important piece of legislation is The Singapore Mental Health (Care and Treatment) Act (2008) which allows a designated medical practitioner at the Institute of Mental Health (IMH) to sign a form allowing the involuntary admission of an individual suffering from a mental illness into the IMH for treatment, for up to 72 hours.

arrested or retarded development of mind or any inherent causes or induced by disease or injury) as substantially impaired his mental responsibility for his acts or omissions in causing the death or being a party to causing the death".

In a paper by Koh *et al.* (2005), Singapore researchers from the Institute of Mental Health (IMH), the National University of Singapore (NUS), and the Ministry of Health (MOH) studied individuals with mental illnesses charged with murder or voluntary causing hurt (VCH). They were interested to see if homicide offenders were psychiatrically different from violent 'Voluntarily Causing Hurt' (VCH) offenders. They compared these offenders between 1997 and 2001.[10] They found that:

- The homicide and the control group had very similar demographic backgrounds;
- Mentally ill or abnormal homicide offenders were less likely to have a positive history of violence compared to controls;
- The alcohol use patterns were also different. Half (50%) of homicide offenders used alcohol within 24 hours of the offence, while this was 22.5% for the VCH offenders;
- Schizophrenia was more common with the control group (27 VCH offenders had schizophrenia compared to six homicide offenders);
- Personality disorders and mental retardation issues across the two groups were not significantly different;
- In subjects who were psychotic, the authors reported that symptoms did not differ. The proportions of those with auditory hallucinations, command hallucinations and morbid jealousy did not differ across the two groups. What was different was that homicide offenders tended to have more paranoid delusions compared to the control group;

---

[10] Readers must remember that these results are about offenders with mental illness; 57 of the 110 homicide offenders had mental illness, while the remaining half did not have mental illness.

- There were differences in the methods used for causing harm or death. 'Blunt trauma'[11] was used more by the control group, while 'sharp' and 'blunt trauma' as a combination was used more by the homicide group. No other differences were found for other methods (e.g., biting, burning, strangling, throwing from height); and
- A greater number of homicide victims (compared to VCH victims) were female.

In another paper by Dr. Koh and colleagues at IMH (Singapore)[12] in 2006, they looked at the relationship between mental illness and violent offenders in Singapore (Koh *et al.*, 2006). They looked at individuals charged with murder from 1997 to 2001, all of whom received a psychiatric assessment. They studied 110 individuals charged with murder and the authors examined prison medical records, psychiatric history records, and documentation on these offenders. They found the following profile of perpetrators:

- In 70 of the 110 cases, one offender killed one victim.
- Most (60%) were unmarried males, with 31% married and 2% divorced/widowed.
- Most in the 20- to 39-year age group (66%), had minimum primary/secondary education (81%).
- Fifty-seven out of 110 persons were found not to suffer from any mental illness.
- Most were unskilled workers (47%) or jobless (26%).
- Alcohol abuse and alcohol dependence disorders accounted for the largest diagnostic group (16.4%), while depressive disorders accounted for 9.1% of the accused persons and schizophrenia accounted for 5.5%.

---

[11] Blunt trauma is physical trauma to a body part, either by impact, injury or physical attack. Blunt trauma is contrasted with penetrating trauma, in which an object such as a projectile or knife enters the body. A punch to the face can cause blunt trauma. A car accident where the body hits against the steering wheel can also cause it.

[12] This was a paper titled 'Psychiatric aspects of Homicide in Singapore: a 5-Year Review (1997–2001)'.

- Anti-Social Personality Disorder was about 2%, and Acute Stress Disorders was also about 2%. The authors noted that for most of the psychiatric diagnosis, alcohol-related disorders were a co-morbid disorder.
- Outcomes-wise: Of the 110 accused persons, only three persons (2.7%) were assessed by the psychiatrists to be of 'unsound mind' at the time of the offence.
- Victim profile: About 65% were males and 35% females. Males were almost twice as likely to be killed compared to females (consistent with international findings). Eighty-two (77.4%) of the victims were Singapore citizens/permanent residents, while 24 (22.6%) were foreigners. Most victims were in the 10- to 19-year age range. Most (46%) were victims of sharp instruments (stabbed or slashed), followed by blunt instruments (31.1%). Also, most murder victims were acquaintances or friends (24.8%) or opposing gang member (about 18%), and relatives (16.8%). Strangers constituted about 14% of victims, and 25.9% of the victims were found to have consumed alcohol within the 24 hours preceding the murder.

The authors made several conclusions. First, perpetrators of murder have been shown to have an increased incidence of psychiatric disorders. Next, alcohol and other illicit substance use are frequently found to be associated with homicide, and they argued that authorities are encouraged to enhance campaigns to dissuade alcohol abuse. Third, schizophrenia was over-represented in the study group (6.4%) compared to the general population.

The findings appear to be consistent with others, which suggest that some individuals with mental illness may be at risk for violent crimes. For instance, Fazel and Grann (2004) looked at a study of all 2,005 individuals convicted of homicide or attempted homicide in Sweden from 1988 to 2001 and found that 229 (11%) had schizophrenia or bipolar disorder. Substance abuse and medication non-compliance were significant risk factors. Large and colleagues conducted a systematic review and meta-analysis of population-based studies conducted in developed countries of homicide. They looked specifically at offences committed by persons diagnosed with schizophrenia. Their study found that rates of homicide by people diagnosed with schizophrenia were strongly correlated with total homicide rates (R = 0.86) (Large *et al.*, 2009).

In another study, it was observed that almost half of the homicides committed by people with psychotic illnesses occurred before initial treatment. This suggested an increased risk of homicide, during the first episode of psychosis. Meta-analysis of these studies showed that 38.5% of homicides occurred during the first episode of psychosis, prior to initial treatment. Homicides during first-episode psychosis occurred at a rate of 1.59 homicides per 1,000, equivalent to 1 in 629. The annual rate of homicide after treatment for psychosis was 0.11 homicides per 1,000 patients, equivalent to one homicide in 9,090 patients with schizophrenia per year. Earlier treatment of first-episode psychosis might prevent some homicides (Neilssen & Large, 2010). Another useful meta-analysis looking at risk factors for violence in psychosis was conducted by Witt *et al.* (2013) who completed a systematic review and a meta-regression analysis of 110 studies involving 45,533 individuals. A total of 39,995 (87.8%) were diagnosed with schizophrenia, 209 (0.4%) were diagnosed with bipolar disorder, and 5,329 (11.8%) were diagnosed with other psychoses. Their findings noted that dynamic risk factors included hostile behavior, recent drug misuse, non-adherence with psychological therapies, higher poor impulse control scores, recent substance misuse, recent alcohol misuse, and non-adherence with medication. The strongest static factor was previous criminal history factors.

5.8 Investigating Homicide and Death Scenes

As earlier discussed in the profiling chapter, a CLIP analysis can be useful. For this section, we will discuss investigative and forensic considerations. It is useful for psychologists to appreciate the investigative tools, equipment used by investigators, and forensic evidential issues relating to death investigations. This is useful from two angles. First, they suggest what is being collected and examined. Second, psychologists supporting investigations need to be aware that they should not contaminate the evidence collection processes.

According to the Death Investigation Manual of the National Institute of Justice (NIJ, 2011), common investigative tools needed are as shown in the Table 5.3 (note that the equipment needed are not just for homicide, but death in other circumstances as well, for e.g., suicide, accident, disasters, etc.

Table 5.3:   Common Investigative Tools and Equipment Used

Alternate light source	Barrier sheeting or tent (to shield body/area)	Biohazard plastic trash bags
Blood collection tubes	Body bags with locks	Body identification tags
Camera equipment	Crime scene tape	Bags to safekeep written evidence (e.g., suicide notes)
Disposable protective suit and face and Eye protection, hair cover, masks	Evidence seal/tape	Latent print kit
Latex gloves	Measurement instruments	Packaging material (e.g., clean unused paper bags, envelopes, metal cans, tape, rubber bands).
Scene safety equipment (e.g., biological/chemical/ industrial/disaster/fire, hardhat, reflective vest, steel bottom boots,	Specimen containers	Thermometer (ambient and body temperature).
Trace evidence recovery equipment (e.g., blades, cotton-tipped swabs, syringe, forceps, gunshot residue and magnifying glass, large gauge needles, blood test kit, scalpel handle, tweezers, etc.)	Sharps container	Shoe/boot covers

5.8.1 *Evaluating Success in Homicide Investigations*

Brookman and Innes (2013) argued that police usually look at a successful homicide investigation as involving a suspect being identified, charged, and ultimately convicted preferably for murder. This is mainly because they feel that justice is served when a murderer gets caught. However, homicide has a fairly high 'outcome' success and it may be restricting to merely measure success in terms of outcomes. For example, in the U.K., between 2000 and 2010, suspects were identified and charged in an average of 90% of cases in England and Wales (Smith *et al.*, 2012). In Singapore, solve rates are also quite high. Unlike what we watch on television, most times the police *do* know who did it. Police themselves feel that outcomes are a poor measure of their work, as in most cases, the identity of a prime suspect will be quickly apparent, even though in a minority of cases, identification is complex and may take months or years to complete. Most homicide investigators spend a lot of time preparing the case file for court (Innes, 2003), and sometimes, this can take many months. Brookman and Innes argued there are four alternate definitions of investigative success: (1) outcome success (e.g., you get an arrest and successful prosecution); (2) procedural success (e.g., the investigation was done properly, in the quickest time possible, with integrity, and justice is served); (3) community impact reduction success (e.g., addressing the sense of fear in the community and whether the streets are safe); and (4) preventive success (e.g., predicting, preventing and pre-empting homicide; setting up MARACs),[13] looking at means to prevent homicide by looking at upstream measures, such as domestic violence, violence at home, violence in clubs, and so on.

Why might all this be important to forensic psychologists? First, victim management is critical in obtaining support from affected families. Psychologists can assist in this area. Second, psychologists can assist in the preventive aspects of homicide by researching the upstream issues which contribute to homicide (e.g., domestic violence).

---

[13] These are multi-agency risk assessment conferences (Maracs). They coordinate community responses and bring together representatives from different agencies to address those cases of abuse (e.g., domestic abuse) likely to result in serious harm or homicide.

5.9 Forensic Sciences Considerations in Homicide

Common duties related to death investigation include:

- Scene investigation;
- Notification of the next-of-kin;
- Gathering information leading to identification;
- Handling personal property;
- Follow-up investigation;
- Photography;
- Providing autopsy support; and
- Court testimony.

Usually, upon arrival at the scene and prior to moving the body, the investigator/the pathologist would note the presence of each of the following in his/her report (Parhlow, 2010; National Institute of Justice, 2011):

- Livor (e.g., color, location) consistent/inconsistent with position of the body;
- Rigor (e.g., stage/intensity, location on the body);
- Degree of decomposition (e.g., putrefaction, mummification, skeletonization);
- Insect and animal activity;
- Scene temperature (method used and time estimated); and
- Description of body temperature (e.g., warm, cold, frozen) or measurement of body temperature (method used and time of measurement).

(Parhlow, 2010; National Institute of Justice, 2011)

5.9.1 *Psychology, Behavior, and Crime Scene Evidence*

The forensic pathologist best handles the forensic issues at the crime scene. In trying to appreciate the forensic psychology and criminal behavior issues, we cannot afford not to appreciate the broader issues related to dynamics of the scene of the crime.

It is useful to appreciate at least some of the human dynamics and behaviours relating to the NASH categories often seen in death investigations. NASH stands for *N*atural (death), *A*ccidental, *S*uicide, or *H*omicide. Was the nature of the death, accidental, suicidal, natural, or a homicide? What the accompanying crime scene and psychological characteristics for each type? The criminal/forensic psychologist must have some basic understanding of the differences between these.

See Table 5.4 and make some educated guesses about the kinds of forensic and behavioral evidence that could be involved in these cases.

Table 5.4:   NASH and Types of Evidences

Type of death	What forensic evidence to expect?	What behavioral evidence?
Natural		
Accidental		
Homicide		
Suicide		

As an illustration, there was a case in the U.S. where three teens called the police to say that their buddy Alex had shot himself in the face, and that he had committed suicide because of personal problems. The forensics team later established that Alex could not have done it, as there was no gun shot residue (GSR) on his hand, and the shot was not taken at close range (which would have been if it were a suicide). From the psychology angle, if Alex were suicidal, then he may have left some signs of this (e.g., suicide note, family may have noticed this, classmates would have noted this, and so on). Also, he did not express sadness and instead, showed future planning and hope. The point being made here is that forensics of the scene must *generally* match with the behavioral aspects of it. In this case, it did not. Investigations later showed that the four friends were fooling around with a revolver when it accidentally fired and shot Alex in the face. The friends panicked and cooked up a story of suicide. Fortunately, the truth was revealed. Therefore, there is a need to ensure some consistency between the crime scene, forensic, and the behavioral/psychological evidence.

5.10 Psychological Aspects of Violence Risk

How would you assess the risks or threats that someone might be violent? Here are some possible ways proposed by Michael H. Corcoran and James S. Cawood in *Violence Assessment and Intervention: The Practitioner's Handbook* (2008). Some of the indicators have been adapted for the Singapore context. See Table 5.5 for details on the domains on violence assessment.

Table 5.5: Domains of Violence Assessment

Examine the person's mental health history

- Is the person seeing any psychiatrist, psychologist, counselor, religious person, or marital therapist? What are they seeing them for? Any assessment of violence?
- Does person have any diagnosis, treatment for depression, paranoia,[14] bipolar disorder, schizophrenia, borderline personality disorder (BPD), narcissistic personality disorder (NPD), or antisocial personality disorder (ASPD)?
- Is the person suicidal or homicidal?
- Has the person ever mentioned 'hearing voices' or 'seeing things' (i.e., possible psychotic episodes)?
- Does the person hallucinate, particularly experiencing command-type hallucinations?
- Is the person considered to be 'strange' or 'weird' by anyone? Why?
- Does the person have psychotic/not-of-reality thoughts, particularly with violent content?
- Did the person show lack of compliance with medical treatment/psychiatric treatment(s)?
- Does the person have a hostile or aggressive attitude toward others?
- Does the person have violent thoughts or fantasies?

Examine the person's medical history

- Any previous history of major accidents or traffic injury? Known medical records to be examined? Are there records of recent major head trauma? Brain lesions or tumors, which could have contributed to violent behavior? Traumatic Brain Injury?
- Lack of compliance with medical or psychiatric treatment(s) after injury?

(Continued)

---

[14] In a case I was familiar with, a foreign police officer had paranoid delusions and he had protected him by keeping multiple locks on his door. He suspected his own police officers of spying on him and hence was very difficult in his dealings. When we enquired about how he was protecting himself, he explained that he had a ready loaded gun in his office drawer and would fire at the person who was out to get him. Sometimes people who have paranoid delusions are not violent individuals, but their violent actions are often a self-preservation strategy.

Table 5.5: (*Continued*)

Examine the person's family history

- History of violence or abuse, physical, or sexual?
- Parent(s) ever arrested/used drugs?
- Unstable family relationships?

Examine the person's interpersonal relationship history

- Any known history of domestic or family violence?
- Verbal or physical abuse, either as instigator or victim?
- Any known history of sexual or other harassment? Stalking?
- Promiscuous sexual behavior?
- Many short-term relationships?
- Parasitic lifestyle?

Examine the person's negative employment history

- Cannot hold on to a steady job for long, keeps changing jobs?
- Leaves job and changes job often, and cites negative perception of personal treatment, i.e., has strong feelings of anger, injustice or humiliation, and feeling desperate or trapped?
- Has a pattern of declining savings, income because of job instability?
- Consistently choosing employment lower than his/her intellectual ability?
- Any signs of unhappiness expressed in the social media?

Examine the person's history of violent behavior or conflict

- Parasitic lifestyle (e.g., living off others)?
- Was involved in crime/delinquent behavior at young age?
- Hostile or aggressive attitude to others?
- Bullying and/or victim of bullying?
- Initiating physical violence toward others (e.g., secret society/gang involvement)?
- Has restraining orders (e.g., Personal Protection Order[15] or Domestic Exclusion Order)[16] taken against them?

(*Continued*)

---

[15] In Singapore, the court may insist that the offender cannot use violence against the family member. Under Section 65(1) of the Women's Charter, the Court will grant a personal protection order, if family violence has been committed or is likely to be committed against someone, and that such an order is necessary for protection (AWARE, n.d.).

[16] Domestic Exclusion Order (DEO) excludes or restricts the respondent from entering the applicant's residence or parts of the residence.

Table 5.5: (*Continued*)

- Violated terms or conditions of legal orders, or probation?[17]
- Arrested or convicted of violence toward others?

Examine the person's substance use (abuse) history

- Use of substances causes aggressive or violent behavior?
- Use of alcohol, methamphetamine, or cocaine?
- Use of any substance with resulting job loss, memory loss or loss of consciousness?
- Any criminal records with the police or the Central Narcotics Bureau (CNB)?

Examine the person's relationship with use of weapons

- Does person have any strange habits or interests involving weapons?
- Any unusual interests in special and unusual websites on the Internet relating to interest in weapons?
- Inappropriate display of weapons (e.g., knife, gun, stick, chopper)?
- Use of weapons to intimidate or frighten?
- Gets very worked up when a weapon is thought of or used?
- Intense preoccupation with violent use of weapons?
- Acquisition or modification of a weapon; linked to an emotional event?
- Discussed with others about potential use of dangerous weapon?
- Any information about these obsessions reported on social media?

Examine the person's recent or current events and conditions

- Impulsiveness?
- General relationship problems?
- Lack of personal support from others?
- Stress?
- Primary relationship disruption (i.e., separation, divorce, loss of loved ones, relationship affected)?
- Substance abuse (particularly alcohol, methamphetamine/cocaine)?

(*Continued*)

---

[17] In Singapore, probation is an alternative order option by the Court when dealing with offenders who may otherwise be sent to penal or corrective institutions such as Juvenile Homes, Reformative Training Centre, or the Prisons. Probationers can continue with most of his/her day-to-day activities such as school, work or National Service. The Probation Officer will discuss the probationer's progress with the parents, school or employer before updating the Court (Ministry of Social and Family Development, n.d.).

Table 5.5:   (*Continued*)

- Employment problems?
- Legal problems, being investigated for something, including commission of crimes?
- Health problems (diagnosed with a chronic or acute health problems, e.g., HIV, cancer, tumor)?
- Any information available on social media?

Obviously, the presence of any of these historical facts or behaviors does not mean that the person will act violently. However, the more destabilizing the factors, coupled with a history of instability and inappropriate thoughts and actions, the higher the risk might possibly be.

5.10.1 *Concept of "Duty to Warn"*

If someone talks about harming another, do you have the duty to warn potential targets? If there is a serious potential for violence, which might harm others, you may have a duty to warn the potential victims, even if it compromises client confidentiality. Not doing so may possibly open the clinician or practitioner to litigation.[18] This idea came about because of a case in 1969 when a graduate student at the University of California in Berkeley disclosed to his psychotherapist that he wanted to kill a young woman named Tatiana Tarasoff because she rebuffed him. The therapist believed that this man would carry out his threat and reported him to the university campus police. However, the campus police did not think it was serious enough and, months later, Ms. Tarasoff was stabbed to death by the man. Her parents sued the University, and the Supreme Court of California, ruled that:

> "When a doctor...determines or should determine, that a warning is essential to avert danger arising from the medical or psychological condition of his patient, he incurs a legal obligation to give that warning... Thus, it may call for him to warn the intended victim, to

---

[18] Many countries do not mandate this by legal requirement. In Singapore, there is no legal requirement for a 'duty to warn'. However, a professional may do so on moral grounds and a duty of care.

notify the police, or to take whatever steps are reasonably necessary under the circumstances." (Chong, 2015).

Professor Chong Siow Ann from the Institute of Mental Health (Singapore), who discussed this issue, explained it even further:

"The corollary of this case, which has established its place in the annals of psychiatry, is that doctors and psychotherapists have a duty to protect identifiable individuals from any danger if they have information that could prevent harm. In this sort of situation, the duty to protect the community trumps the duty to protect patient confidentiality." (Chong, 2015)

Of course, the question is really whether the risk is severe enough to breach confidentiality, who needs to be informed under the duty-to-warn concept, and how much they need to be told. Experts argue that the 'interrelated concentric circles' concept is useful in determining notification. The potential target could be notified first, and then those closest to victim like family and friends (closest relatedness) and then workplace colleagues (next outer relatedness), assuming there are risks to these parties.

In making this assessment and these interventions, we have to remember that any risk assessment you make on someone may potentially be used against you as a professional in court (by the defendant). Thus, you have to ensure that your risk and threat assessments are scientifically defensible; use an assessment protocol that includes a review of all legally available public and private records, if available. Next, corroborate your assessment with other interviews with collateral witnesses. Also, consider the use of organized information analyses and structured risk assessment protocols and, finally, try to interview the subject of the assessment to get a better understanding of the individual, if that is possible.

5.10.2 *The Possible Link between Domestic Violence and Homicide*

Even though the focus on this chapter is on homicide, there is good reason to include a smaller section here on domestic violence, mainly because there is a risk that domestic violence could lead to homicide. Domestic violence is defined as threatening behavior, violence, or abuse (psychological, emotional, financial, sexual, or physical) between adults who have been intimate partners or are family members, regardless of gender or sexuality (Home Office, 2005). In the literature, the term 'intimate partner violence' has been used synonymously with other terms such as domestic abuse, wife abuse, spousal abuse, spouse battering, and family violence (Canter, 2008). While both men and women can commit abuse, men tend to commit violence against women more frequently.

The U.S. Centers for Disease Control and Prevention analyzed the murders of women in 18 U.S. states from 2003 to 2014, finding a total of 10,018 deaths. Of those, 55% were intimate partner violence-related, meaning that they occurred at the hands of a former or current partner, or the partner's family or friends. Of this, in 93% of those cases, the perpetrator was a current or former romantic partner. Contrary to popular views, strangers committed 16% of all female homicides. The report explained that about one-third of the time, couples had argued right before the homicide took place, and about 12% of the deaths were associated with jealousy. The majority of the victims were under the age of 40, and 15% were pregnant. About 54% were gun deaths (Centers for Disease Control and Prevention, n.d.). All these suggest that domestic violence cases should not be underestimated or ignored.

Several useful risk assessment instruments have been developed specifically for domestic violence, which are worth mentioning. They are the Conflict Tactics Scale (Straus, 1979); The Danger Assessment Instrument (Campbell, 1995), the DV-MOSAIC (de Becker, 2000) and more recently, the SARA (Spousal Assault Risk Assessment Guide) and the B-Safer (Brief-Spousal Assault Form for the Evaluation of Risk) (Department of Justice, Canada, 2004).

5.11 Violence Risk Assessment Using Structured Risk Assessment Tools

There are tools, which may be used for violence risk assessment. Assessment tools of the previous generations of risk tools were divided into the 'actuarial group' and the 'clinical judgment' group. The recent generation of tools takes the blended approach called Structured Professional Judgment (SPJ). According to Douglas *et al.* (2014), the SPJ measures adopt non-algorithmic, non-numeric decision processes, and risk estimates. They do so to avoid the pitfalls inherent in actuarial approaches. The SPJ model uses a simple, narrative approach to risk estimation, requiring evaluators to come to a decision of 'low', 'moderate', or 'high' risk. Although specific cut-points are not provided, generally speaking, the more risk factors that are present, the higher the risk will be. The greater the risk, the more intervention efforts are needed. The SPJ approach, however, also allows for exceptions to this general rule. If, for instance, a person has a small number of highly compelling risk factors (that is, you do not need many high-risk factors) that may mean he/she has a high risk for violence (i.e., threats of homicide, or a history of acting on said threats), and then a decision of 'high risk' could be justifiable. This SPJ approach was incorporated into the newer generation of tools of violence assessment.

There are presently several well-known violence risk assessments, such as the following:

- Historical/Clinical/Risk Management 20-item scale (HCR-20),
- Spousal Assault Risk Assessment Guide (SARA),
- Structured Assessment of Violence Risk in Youth (SAVRY),
- The Risk for Sexual Violence Protocol (RSVP),
- Sexual Violence Risk-20 (SVR-20),
- The Danger Assessment Instrument (Campbell, 1995)
- And the Brief Spousal Assault Form for Evaluation of Risk (B-SAFER)

What follows below are further details on the VRAG and the HCR:

The Violence Risk Appraisal Guide (VRAG)

The VRAG (Qunisey *et al.*, 2006) is an actuarial risk assessment instrument, developed to determine the probability of re-offending. It was developed on a sample of 618 male offenders from a high security hospital, and 12 risk variables that correlated best with re-offending were determined (using multiple regression analyses). In their original study, the predictive accuracy of the VRAG corresponded to an AUC[19] (Area under the curve) of 0.76 (Quinsey, 1998). The items of the VRAG are as follows:

1) Lived with both biological parents to age 16 (except for death of a parent),
2) Elementary school maladjustment,
3) History of alcohol problems,
4) Marital status,
5) Criminal History Score for non-violent offences,
6) Failure on prior conditional release for parole or probation,
7) Failure to comply; bail violation, and any new arrests while on conditional release,
8) Age at index offence,
9) Victim injury,
10) Any female victim,
11) Meets criteria for any personality disorder,
12) Meets criteria for schizophrenia, and
13) Psychopathy checklist score.

Generally speaking, each item is coded and then a total number summated. The general idea was that the higher the score, the higher the risk of violent behaviour.

The HCR-20: A Structured Clinical Rating Scale for Risk of Future Violence

The Historical-Clinical-Risk Management-20 (HCR-20) has been validated with various samples, including people in medium-security hospital services (Gray *et al.*, 2008), intellectual disability forensic services (Gray *et al.*, 2007), and community psychiatric settings (Doyle & Dolan, 2006). HCR-20's predictive validity has been

---

[19] Accuracy is measured by the area under the curve. An area of 1 represents a perfect test; an area of 0.5 represents a worthless test.

reported in Campbell *et al.* (2009) and Fazel *et al.* (2012). The HCR has been updated, and Kevin S. Douglas and colleagues discussed the HCR-20 Version 3 in the *International Journal of Forensic Mental Health* (Douglas, 2014), explaining that there was a need to revise and refine the items in keeping with the changes in the understanding of risk factors and the advanced use of structured judgment protocol over the last few years. The HCR-20 (Version 3) has the following items:

Historical Scale

Historical factors refer to areas of past functioning, behaviors, and experiences:

H1. Violence
    a. As a child (12 and under)
    b. As an adolescent (13–17)
    c. As an adult (18 and over)
H2. Other Antisocial Behavior
    a. As a child (12 and under)
    b. As an adolescent (13–17)
    c. As an adult (18 and over)
H3. Relationships
    a. Intimate
    b. Non-Intimate
H4. Employment
H5. Substance use
H6. Major Mental Disorder
    a. Psychotic disorder
    B. Major mood disorder
    c. Other major mental disorders
H7. Personality Disorder
    a. Antisocial, psychopathic, and sissocial
    b. Other personality disorders
H8. Traumatic Experiences
    a. Victimization/trauma
    b. Adverse childhood experiences

H9. Violent Attitudes
H10. Treatment or Supervision Response

Clinical Scale

Clinical factors focus on recent or current psychosocial, mental health, and behavioral functioning:

C1. Insight
    a. Mental disorder
    b. Violence risk
    c. Need for treatment
C2. Violent Ideation or Intent
C3. Symptoms of Major Mental Disorder
    a. Psychotic disorder
    b. Major mood disorder
    c. Other major mental disorders
C4. Instability
    a. Affective
    b. Behavioral
    c. Cognitive
C5. Treatment or Supervision Response
    a. Compliance
    b. Responsiveness

Risk Management Scale

Risk Management factors refer to areas of future functioning, psychosocial adjustment, living situation, and use of professional plans:

R1. Professional Services and Plans
R2. Living Situation
R3. Personal Support
R4. Treatment or Supervision Response
    a. Compliance
    b. Responsiveness
R5. Stress or Coping

While these tools look intuitive enough to use, they can be complex as multiple sources of data are considered. Information is often not readily available. Typically, practitioners who want to use these tools have to undergo some weeks of training to appreciate these scales, the items involved, and how to apply them to cases.

5.12 Treating Violent Offenders

In the world today, there are many programs which have been developed to treat violent offenders. Readers interested in this subject should look up the review by Professor Devon Polaschek at the University of Wellington, New Zealand, and Rachael M. Collie, in an article titled "Rehabilitating Serious Violent Adult Offenders: An Empirical And Theoretical Stocktake" published in *Psychology, Crime and Law*. While not an exhaustive listing, some examples of Violent Offender Treatment Programs or VOTPs include:

- *Cognitive Skills Training (CST)*. Canada's CST program is based on the cognitive deficit model. Offenders participate in 36 two-hour sessions in closed groups of 10, in both community and prison settings. Before the program, participants were assessed for evidence of targeted deficits, including failure to recognize and solve interpersonal problems, impulsive, concrete, and rigid thinking. The program had a small effect on recidivism.
- *Cognitive Self-Change (CSC)*. CSC has three phases; two while in prison and the third is community-based. The logic of these programs is that: (1) violence is a learnt behavior that is adopted as a way of coping; (2) patterns of criminal behavior include a variety of criminal acts and not just violent actions; and (3) patterns of violent and criminal behavior are connected to one another through thinking/cognitive patterns. Attendance at the program is compulsory for violent offenders. The program is run in open groups, and individualized for each participant. Attendance ranged from two to four sessions a week, and lasted from 18 months to three years, depending on the offender's

release date. Participants are taught to recognize, self-monitor, and control criminogenic thinking. Participants developed relapse prevention plans prior to release, which are then monitored in the community phase.

- *The Self-Change Program for Violent Offenders* has six blocks of training (Howitt, 2009), as follows:

  (1) Skills which allow offenders to observe and report their thoughts, feelings, and attitudes are taught;
  (2) Identification of the thinking pattern which have and will result in their offending and violent behavior;
  (3) Offenders try to identify new ways of thinking and stopping these thought patterns;
  (4) A relapse prevention program is prepared, and strategies are practiced;
  (5) The offenders practice the relapse prevention plan in prisons; and
  (6) The final training block will have the offender back in the community with structured support and supervision.

- *MANALIVE.* In Singapore, Leo (n.d.) discusses how the MANALIVE program has been used in the Singapore Prisons Service, among other violent offender treatment programs. MANALIVE is an open-group Cognitive Behavioural Therapy-based violence treatment program which incorporates narrative therapy for violent men. Leo mentioned that preliminary analyses revealed a good effect size for the treatment program.

RESEARCH ARTICLE

Anger Management and Violence Prevention: Improving Effectiveness

This paper argues that past studies have found that anger management treatment had a moderate to large effect on reducing anger problems. However, most research was conducted with university students rather than offenders. Few studies were conducted with offenders. In two studies

(Continued)

(Continued)

conducted with violent offenders in Australia, participants who underwent the anger management program did not differ from the control group on their anger experience, anger expression, aggressive behavior, and prison misconduct.

This paper discussed that anger management trainings have several common components such as relaxation training, social skills training, and cognitive restructuring. Table 5.6 shows the summary of the anger management programs as presented in Howells *et al.* (2002).

Table 5.6: Outline of the South Australian Anger Management Program and the Western Australian Skills Training for Aggression Control

Session	South Australia	Western Australia
1	Understanding what anger is	Understanding anger
2	Recognizing anger and change	Recognizing our anger/monitoring our anger
3	Staying in control by using timeout and relaxation	Staying in control of our anger/using timeout and relaxation
4	Socialization identifying early patterns	Identifying early patterns/increasing awareness of our thoughts/beliefs: changing negative thoughts to positive thoughts
5	How thoughts and beliefs affect anger	Becoming friends with ourselves/coping with provocation using self- talk
6	Communication	Enhancing the way we communicate
7	Styles of communication	Expressing anger assertively
8	Stopping the violence in relationships	Managing our anger in close relationships/developing positive relationships
9	Managing our anger in close relationships	Conflict resolution
10	Making a commitment to relapse prevention	Review/relapse prevention

Source: Adapted from Howells *et al.* (2001).

(Continued)

(Continued)

The current study assessed 200 male offenders in South and Western Australia before and after they participated in an anger management program. It was found that the overall impact of the anger management intervention was small. However, participants who underwent the anger management program showed an increase in anger knowledge, more than the control group. Despite the initial small difference, this improvement in anger knowledge for the treatment group was maintained and further increased over a six-month follow-up. It was also found that participants who were high in anger and low in anger control at the pre-treatment assessment showed the most drastic change after undergoing the anger management program. In addition, those who were motivated and prepared for change showed greater improvements after the program. Additionally, the anger management treatment with high program integrity (i.e., program is delivered as planned) had a greater positive impact on its participants.

There are several possible explanations for the low impact of these anger management programs. Firstly, in a correctional setting, program participants tend to face problems of low motivation and treatment resistance as they are usually enrolled into the program against their will. Secondly, the anger management programs may lack intensiveness in the correctional setting, with the program content being too complicated with limited opportunity to practice skills learned. Thirdly, offenders may be distrustful and resentful, as they are concerned that their disclosure may affect their release plans. Also, offenders may have multiple psychological and social problems that could have affected these treatment results.

The authors provided recommendations to help develop future anger management programs: anger programs should be maintained as one of the core elements of treatment programs; offenders should be pre-assessed to determine their suitability for the anger management program; programs should increase in intensity by extending the length of the programs and revising the content to make it more treatment-focused; ongoing evaluation should be implemented to monitor treatment effectiveness; and finally, the program integrity needs to be monitored.

Source: Kevin Howells, Andrew Day, Susan Bubner, Susan Jauncey, Paul Williamson, Ann Parker and Karen Heseltine (June 2002). Australian Institute of Criminology.

5.12.1 *Cultural Inclusiveness in Rehabilitation*

What is the role of culture in rehabilitation? In an interesting piece by Dr. Joe Thakker from the University of Waikato, New Zealand, on *The Role of Cultural Factors in Treatment* (Craig *et al.*, 2014, Chap. 21), the author makes an interesting point about an individual's cultural background and how it may impact the process of rehabilitation. This is an important factor usually missed out in treatment, which assumes a "one size fits all" model. Thakker explains that while the RNR program has proven useful, it does have some limitations, namely that it focuses too much on 'needs' which appear to be the main factor. She explains that culture[20] plays a role, in the following ways. First, an offender's religious worldview is often shaped by his or her cultural background, and this impacts treatment. Second, the language an offender speaks will affect his or her ability to understand the content of the treatment program. Third, language is steeped in cultural understandings. Fourth, the cultural background of the therapist affects the client–therapist relationship and rapport. Fifth, in many criminal justice systems across the world, minorities tend to be overrepresented proportionally. For all these reasons, it is useful to incorporate cultural aspects into rehab programs.

Dr. Thakker discussed the programs in Canada (e.g., The Tupiq Program for Inuit Sexual Offenders), Australia (e.g., The Indigenous Family Violence Offender Program), and New Zealand (e.g., The Te Piriti Special Treatment Unit). She makes the point, however, that culture-based and culture-sensitive treatments programs are limited in number, findings are tentative, and conclusions are speculative. This is mainly due to small sample size issues, low base rates for recidivism in some offender groups, and the fact that the large majority of studies have been conducted within 'in-house' government departments. There is much future scope to incorporate cultural issues into treatment approaches.

---

[20] She defines 'a cultural group is one that shares a set of norms, values, concepts, beliefs, and practices, which, in part, differentiates them from other cultural groups'.

5.12.2 *Cultural Approaches to Treatment: 'In Search of Your Warrior' (ISYW) Program*

The Correctional Service of Canada (CSC) provides a continuum of culturally appropriate interventions that address the specific needs of First Nations, Métis, and Inuit offenders in a way that contributes to building safe and healthy communities (Djamila, 2013). CSC has created eight healing lodges across Canada. Here are some of the key features of the program:

- The program's name comes from the Aboriginal vision of the warrior. It speaks of a spiritual warrior who fights for justice and strengthens values and ethics in the community;
- The program was made in collaboration with community Elders and people in charge;
- Offenders learn about their own culture all over again, go back to their spiritual roots, and after their conditional release, live with a better self-image;
- Living and housing units: These are rearranged in a circle to represent the circles of influence, unity, and social interaction. From the top, the unit resembles the shape of an eagle, symbolizing life and vigilance against evil. The bright colours of the place represent the Aboriginal heritage of its residents — red for the east, yellow for the south, blue for the west, and white for the north. This architectural design is the outcome of consultations between architects and Cree Elders;
- The ISYW consists of 75 activities accompanied by spiritual cleansing ceremonies. The program's facilitators choose activities according to the offenders' individual needs. The course length is generally from 6 to 10 weeks. The lodge's Elder is always involved in the activities;
- The Cleansing Ceremony: The day often begins with a spiritual ceremony in a peaceful meeting room in dim light. The facilitator and inmates burn sweet grass, each of them running their arms through the smoke and wafting it over their heads. Then, each participant holds the eagle feather (symbolizing respect for the truth) and, without inhibition, gives free rein to thoughts, feelings,

and hopes. The facilitator respects their silence if they choose not to speak. Facilitators remind them of their identity, to make them aware that they have a culture they can be proud of; their heritage, to teach them the concept of the tepee, and tell them personal stories which prompt them to open up.

- The Mask-making Ceremony: Offenders create their own masks and this includes the smallest details of their features. Then, they paint the masks according to how they see themselves, and select colors that reveal their feelings. Later, they move to a solitary location with the mask, to think about who they really are. After self-reflection, the offender may decide to throw away the mask or simply burn it because it symbolizes the bad person from the past that they want to forget.

- Sweat Lodges: Some activities involve the use of 'sweat lodges'. This process is similar to detoxification and cleansing, but it also induces relaxation. One offender had remarked: "When I'm inside the sweat lodge, in the dark where I can't see anyone else, alone before my Creator, hearing only the hiss of the water on the burning stones, I feel close to my Creator, to my grandparents, so I dare to speak, to confess. I pray from the bottom of my heart for forgiveness." (Djamila, 2013, p. 23).

THINKING ACTIVITY

How can cultural aspects be incorporated into violent offending programs in Singapore (or in Asian contexts) and in which aspects can it be used? Discuss the psychological mechanism involved.

5.13 Crime Prevention

Preventing homicide and other violent crimes is no easy task, given the diversity of violent incidents. Nevertheless, if prevention approaches are to be employed, then Brookman (2005) suggests that a sensible approach will be to approach this from a primary, secondary, and tertiary approach. Primary prevention would refer to the direct prevention of the crime event of the offences of homicide. Secondary approaches would involve combatting motivation before people get involved in crime or addressing the at-risk populations. Tertiary prevention involves targeting those already involved in the crime, i.e., using punishment and treatment approaches. Drawing on this, Table 5.7 shows some of the possible approaches, which could be taken to prevent homicide and violent crimes.

Table 5.7:   Examples of Preventive Measures

Approach	Crime prevention examples
Primary prevention (Targeted at masses)	o Situational Crime prevention measures o Reduce opportunities: Reducing the supply of lethal weapons (e.g., guns)
Secondary prevention (Targeted at-risk groups)	o Monitor at-risk hot spots o Programs which keep young people off the streets, e.g., 'Do not join gangs' programs o MARACs (see the following section)
Tertiary prevention (Targeted at those already involved)	o Punishment and custodial regimes o Prisons rehabilitation programs o Probations programs o Anger Management programs/VOTPs

5.13.1 *Preventing Homicide Using Multi-Agency Risk Assessment Conference (MARAC)*

Family violence can result in murder. Recognizing this in many parts of the world, agencies have come together to discuss the needs of high-risk families and victims. MARAC is an example of a meeting where information is shared on the domestic abuse cases with the highest risk, between representatives of police, probation, health, child protection, housing authority, and other specialists from voluntary sectors. MARACs are useful because no single agency can see the complete picture of the life of a victim, but all may have insight into the individuals concerned. After sharing all information they have about a victim, the members discuss options for increasing the safety of the victim and turn these into a coordinated action plan. The primary focus of the MARAC is to safeguard the victim. The

MARAC will make links with others to safeguard the children who may be involved.

In Singapore, there are family violence specialist centers that may arrange meetings, and these are organized by Family Violence Specialist Centres such as PAVE, TRANS-SAFE Centre, and Care Corner Project Start. The Ministry of Social and Family Development (MSF) and the Family Service Centre (FSC) offer arrangements of 'Temporary Shelter' for victims of family violence.

As far as legal measures are concerned, individuals who are concerned for their safety can approach the Family Court to ask for a 'Protection Order' to stop family violence, an 'Expedited Order' if there is imminent danger of family violence being committed against a person or their family member, and/or a 'Domestic Exclusion Order' to prevent the perpetrator from entering someone's home. A person can request for the order as long as he/she is 21 years old and above.[21]

5.13.2 *Specific Crime Reduction Strategies*

As explained earlier, there are many types and sub-types of violence, and it is difficult to be comprehensive on all types in an introductory book. However, Professor Fiona Brookman highlights several major categories worth discussing and provides useful recommendations for the under-mentioned types:

o *Domestic partner homicides:* Approaches have evolved to deal with this type of violence and these include prosecution of perpetrators of domestic violence, training the police to be aware of the signs of domestic violence, anti-stalking legislations, offender treatment programs, and looking into services for the safety of partners and children.

o *Killing of children and infants:* Proven approaches to deal with this revolve around education for young parents. These include

---

[21] (https://www.msf.gov.sg/policies/Strong-and-Stable-Families/Supporting-Families/Family-Violence/Pages/default.aspx).

preparation for parenthood, better antenatal advice, how to cope with crying babies and sleep deprivation, improving diagnosis and identification of infant and child abuse, recognizing sudden infant death syndrome, and better coordinated responses to child abuse cases. The last includes better coordination between police, health care professionals, forensic pathologists, and social services.

o *Street homicide and alcohol-related homicide*: These recommended approaches include managing physical and social environment around licensed premises, controlling the social atmosphere, training for 'door staff' of pubs and clubs, reduction of loud music, managing problematic premises, and injury-reduction programs such as the use of plastic drinking cups, removal of glassware, and weapon searches.

5.14 Summary

- The most serious type of violence among individuals is the kind that results in homicide.
- There are complexities in how societies have come to define and construct the notion of 'homicide'.
- One interesting way of examining aggression is to look at *instrumental* and *expressive* aggression.
- There was a discussion on characteristics of violent crimes and homicide as they occur globally, the causes of violence, and characteristics of homicide offenders.
- The legal aspects of homicide are important and can differ country by country.
- The forensic psychologist must appreciate the forensic science aspects of homicide to examine if there is consistency between the forensic and behavioral evidence.
- It is useful to appreciate the psychological aspects of violence risk, especially in relation to threat assessment. There are established tools to assess the risk of violent offending.
- Today, there are good guidelines for the structure of violence offending treatment programs. However, more is to be done to incorporate cultural dimensions into such programs. The idea is

to figure out what works, for whom, when, how, and in which settings.

- Finally, there was a discussion on situational crime prevention measures for major types of violent offending. Once again, the solutions for these programs would involve matching crime prevention programs to various violent offending sub-types.

Relevant Journals

Journal of Interpersonal Violence
Journal of Family Violence
Aggression and Violent Behaviour
Journal of School Violence
Violence and Victims
Journal of Gender Based Violence
Journal of Religion and Violence

E-Resources

Hare Psychopathy Checklist. http://www.hare.org/scales/pclr.html
HCR-20 Version 3. http://hcr-20.com/
Threat Assessment in Schools. https://www2.ed.gov/admins/lead/safety/threatassessmentguide.pdf
Violence Risk Screening 10. http://www.forensic-psychiatry.no/violence_risk/index.html
Workplace Violence Risk Assessment. https://workplace-violence.ca/tools/workplace-violence-risk-assessment-wvrat/

Some Relevant Legal Cases

PP v Thenegaran a/l Murugan (2013) 3 MLJ 328 (Culpable Homicide Not Amounting to Murder)
PP v Lim Poh Lye & Anor (2005) 4 SLR (R) 582 (Section 300 (c))
Balasubramaniam Palaniappa Vaiyapuri v PP (2002) 1 SLR (R) 138 (Defence of Intoxication)

Tan Chor Jin v PP (2008) 4 SLR 306 (Defence of Private Defence)
PP v Wang Zhijan (2012). SGHC 238 (Diminished Responsibility)
Mohammad bin Kadar & Anor v PP (2011) (Diminished Responsibility)
G Krishnasamy Naidu v PP (2006) 4 SLR 474 (Diminished Responsibility)
T Paramasparan v PP (2012) 2 MLJ 545 (Defence of Sudden Fight)

Sample Essay Titles

- What are the main causes of violence in the world?
- Is it possible to develop a profile of a violent person?
- Does culture play a role in violence attitudes and behaviors?
- How would you go about designing a violent offender treatment program for violent offenders involved with street gangs?

References

Australian Institute of Criminology (2017). *National Homicide Monitoring Program report.* Retrieved at http://www.aic.gov.au/publications/current%20series/mr/21-40/mr23.html.

Andrews, D.A. (2012). The risk-need-responsivity (RNR) model of correctional assessment and treatment. In J.A. Dvoskin, J.L. Skeem, R.W. Novaco, & K.S. Douglas (Eds.), *Using Social Science to Reduce Violent Offending* (pp. 127–156). New York, NY: Oxford University Press.

American Psychological Association (2005). *APA calls for reduction of violence in interactive media used by children.* Retrieved from http://public.psych.iastate.edu/caa/abstracts/2005-2009/05apa.pdf.

Andrews, D.A., Bonta, J., & Wormith, S.J. (2010). The Level of Service (LS) assessment of adults and older adolescents. In R.K. Otto & K.S. Douglas (Eds.), *Handbook of Violence Risk Assessment* (pp. 199–225). New York, NY: Routledge.

AWARE (n.d.). Retrieved from http://www.aware.org.sg/information/dealing-withfamily-violence/getting-a-personal-protection-order/.

Bartol, C. & Bartol, A. (2008). *Introduction to Forensic Psychology* (2nd ed.). Singapore: Sage Publications.

Brookman, F. (2015). *Understanding Homicide.* Singapore: Sage Publications.

Brookman, F. & Innes., M. (2013). The problem of success: What is a 'good' homicide investigation? *Policing and Society, 23*(3).

Bryant, W. & Cussen, T. (2015). Homicide in Australia: 2010–11 to 2011–12: National Homicide Monitoring Program report. *Australian Institute of*

Criminology. Retrieved http://www.aic.gov.au/media_library/publications/mr/mr23/mr23.pdf.

Bush, J. (1995a). *Cognitive Self-Change: A Program Manual*. Burlington, Vermont: Department of Corrections.

Bush, J. (1995b). Teaching self-risk management to violent offenders. In J. McGuire (Ed.), *What Works: Reducing Reoffending — Guidelines from Research and Practice* (pp. 139–154). Chichester: Wiley.

Campbell, M.A., French, S., & Gendreau, P. (2009). The prediction of violence in adult offenders: A meta-analytic comparison of instruments and methods of assessment. *Criminal Justice and Behavior*, 36, 567–590.

Center for Disease Control and Prevention (n.d.). *Intimate Partner Violence*. Retrieved from https://www.cdc.gov/violenceprevention/intimatepartnerviolence/index.html.

Chong, S.A. (2015, September 1). The fine line between duty of care and duty to report. *The Straits Times*.

Corcoran, M.H. & James S.C. (2008). *Violence Assessment and Intervention: The Practitioner's Handbook* (2nd ed.). New York, NY: CRC Press.

Craig, L., Dixon, L., & Gannon, T.A. (2013). *What Works in Offender Rehabilitation: An Evidence-Based Approach to Assessment and Treatment*. Hoboken: Wiley.

De Becker, G. & Associates (2000). *Domestic violence method* (DV MOSAIC). Retrieved from www.mosaicsystem.com.

Department of Justice Canada (2004). *The Development of the Brief Spousal Assault Form for the Evaluation of Risk (B-Safer): A Tool for Criminal Justice Professionals*. Canada: Author.

Devon, L.L., Polaschek, & Collie, R.M. (2004). Rehabilitating serious violent adult offenders: An empirical and theoretical stocktake. *Psychology, Crime and Law*, 10(3).

Djamila, A. (2013). Let Talk: In search of your inner warrior. *Correctional Service Canada*, 30(4).

Douglas, K.S. (2014). Version 3 of the Historical-Clinical-Risk Management-20 (HCR20V3): Relevance to Violence Risk Assessment and Management in Forensic Conditional Release Contexts. *Behavioral Sciences and the Law*, 32(5), 557–576.

Douglas, K.S., Nicholls, T.L., & Brink, J. (2009). Reducing the risk of violence among persons with mental illness: A critical analysis of treatment approaches. In P.M. Kleespies (Ed.), *Behavioral Emergencies: An Evidence-Based Resource for Evaluating and Managing Risk of Suicide, Violence, and Victimization* (pp. 351–376). Washington, D.C.: American Psychological Association.

Douglas, K.S., Hart, S.D., Webster, C.D., Belfrage, H., Guy, L.S., & Wilson, C.M. (2014). Historical-Clinical-Risk Management-20, Version 3 (HCR-20V3):

Development and Overview. *International Journal of Forensic Mental Health*, *13*(2), 93–108.

Doyle, M. & Dolan, M. (2006). Predicting community violence from patients discharged from mental health services. *The British Journal of Psychiatry*, *109*, 520–526.

Eisner, M. (2012). *What Causes Large-scale Variation in Homicide Rates?* (Working Paper, July 2012). UK: University of Cambridge, Institute of Criminology.

Fazel, S., Singh, J.P., Doll, H., & Grann, M. (2012). Use of risk assessment instruments to predict violence and antisocial behaviuor in 73 samples involving 24,827 people: Systematic review and meta-analysis. *BMJ*, *345*.

Fazel, S. & Grann, M. (2004). Psychiatric morbidity among homicide offenders: A Swedish population study. *American Journal of Psychiatry*, *161*, 2129–2131.

Gray, N.S., Fitzgerald, S., Taylor, J., MacCulloch, J., Snowden, M.J., & Robert, J. (2007). Predicting future reconviction in offenders with intellectual disabilities: The predictive efficacy of VRAG, PCL-SV and the HCR-20. *Psychological Assessment*, *19*, 474–479.

Gray, N.S., Taylor, J., & Snowden, R.J. (2008) Predicting violent reconvictions using the HCR-20. *The British Journal of Psychiatry*, *192*, 384–387.

Gray, N.S., Fitzgerald, S., Taylor, J., MacCulloch, J., Snowden, M.J., & Robert, J. (2007). Predicting future reconviction in offenders with intellectual disabilities: The predictive efficacy of VRAG, PCL-SV and the HCR-20. *Psychological Assessment*, *19*, 474–479.

Howitt, D. (2009). *Introduction to Forensic and Criminal Psychology*. Harlow: Pearson Education.

Holtzworth-Munroe, A. & Stuart, G. (1994). Typologies of male batterers: Three subtypes and the differences among them. *Psychological Bulletin*, *116*, 476–497.

Holtzworth-Munroe A. & Meehan, J. (2004). Typologies of men who are maritally violent: Scientific and clinical implications. *Journal of Interpersonal Violence*, *19*, 1369–1389.

Johnson, M. (1995). Patriarchal terrorism and common couple violence: Two forms of violence against women. *Journal of Marriage and Family*, *57*(2), 283–294.

Johnson, M. (2000). Conflict and control: Images of symmetry and asymmetry in domestic violence. In A. Booth, A.C. Crouter, & M. Clements (Eds.), *Couples in Conflict*. Hillsdale: Lawrence Erlbaum.

Kevin, H., Day, A, Bubner, S., Jauncey, S., Williamson, P., Parker, A., & Heseltine, K. (2002). *Anger Management and Violence Prevention: Improving Effectiveness*. Australian Institute of Criminology.

Koh, K.G.W.W., Gwee, K.P., Chan, Y.H., & Koh, K.W.B. (2005). Are homicide offenders psychiatrically different from other violent offenders? *Psychiatry, Psychology and Law, 12*(2).

Koh, K.G.W.W., Gwee, K.P., & Chan, Y.H. (2006). Psychiatric aspects of homicide in Singapore: A five-year review (1997–2001). *Singapore Medical Journal, 47,* 297–304.

Large, M., Smith, G., & Nielssen, O. (2009). The relationship between the rate of homicide by those with schizophrenia and the overall homicide rate: A systematic review and meta-analysis. *Schizophrenia Research, 112,* 123–129.

Lum, S. (2018, February 15). Spurned man found guilty of stabbing student nurse. *The Straits Times.*

Ministry of Social and Family Development (n.d.) Retrieved from https://www.msf. gov.sg/policies/Rehabilitation-of-Offenders/Community-based-Rehabilitation-ofChildren-and-Youth/Court-Ordered-Options-for-Offenders/Probation-Order/Pages/default.aspx.

McCauley, C. (2000). *Some Things Psychologists Think They Know About Aggression and Violence.* US: Bryn Mawr College.

Mullen, P.E., Pathé, M., Purcell, R., & Stuart, G.W. (1999). Study of stalkers. *American Journal of Psychiatry, 156,* 1244–1249.

National Institute of Justice (2011). *Death Investigation: A Guide for Scene Investigators.* US: Department of Justice.

Nevin, R. (2007). Understanding international crime trends: The legacy of preschool lead exposure. *Environmental Research, 104*(3), 315–336.

Nielssen O. & Large, M. (2010). Rates of homicide during the first episode of psychosis and after treatment: A systematic review and meta-analysis. *Schizophrenia Bulletin, 36*(4), 702–712.

Polaschek, D.L. & Collie, R.M. (2004). Rehabilitating serious violent adult offenders: An empirical and theoretical stocktake. *Psychology, Crime and Law, 10*(3), 321–334.

Prahlow, J. (2010). *Forensic Pathology for Police, Death Investigators, Attorneys, and Forensic Scientists.* New York, NY: Springer Science and Business.

Quinsey, V.L., Harris, G.T., Rice, M.E., & Cormier, C.A. (2006). *Violent Offenders: Appraising and Managing Risk* (2nd ed.). Washington, DC: American Psychological Association.

Robinson, D. (1995). *The Impact of Cognitive Skills Training on Post-release Recidivism among Canadian Federal Offenders* (No. R-41). Ottawa: Correctional Service of Canada.

Roth, R. (2009). *American Homicide*. Cambridge, MA: Belknap Press.

Spierenburg, P. (2012). Long-Term Historical Trends of Homicide in Europe. In M.C.A. Liem & W.A. Pridemore (Eds.), *Handbook of European Homicide Research* (pp. 25–38). New York, NY: Springer.

Straus, M.A. (1979). Measuring intra-family conflict and violence: The Conflict Tactics Scale. *Journal of Marriage and the Family, 41*, 75–88.

Sheridan, L., Blaauw, E., & Davies, G.M. (2003). Stalking known and unknowns. *Trauma, Violence, & Abuse, 4*(2), 148–162.

Tan, O.B. (1995). Body parts case — Martin guilty. *The Straits Times*.

United Nations Office on Drugs and Crime [UNODC] (2011). *Global Study on Homicide Trends, Contexts, Data*. Retrieved on http://www.unodc.org/documents/data-and-analysis/statistics/Homicide/Globa_study_on_homicide_2011_web.pdf.

United Nations Office on Drugs and Crime [UNODC] (2013). Global Homicide Trends. Retrieved from https://www.unodc.org/documents/gsh/pdfs/2014_Global_Homicide_Book_web.pdf.

Violence Policy Center (2016). *When Men Murder Women: An Analysis of 2014 Homicide Data*. Retrieved http://www.vpc.org/studies/wmmw2016.pdf.

Vines, S. (1995). Murder on the tourist trail — and a killer with a death wish. *Independent*.

Verkko, V. (1967). Static and dynamic "laws" of sex and homicide. In M. Wolfgang (Ed.), *Studies in Homicide*. New York, NY: Harper and Row.

Ward, T., Melser, J., & Yates, P.M. (2007). Reconstructing the Risk Responsivity Model: a theoretical elaboration and evaluation. *Aggression and Violent Behavior, 12*, 208–228.

Weerasekera, P. (1996). *Multi-perspective Case Formulation: A Step Towards Treatment Integration*. Malabar, FL: Kriege.

Witt, K., van Dorn, R., & Fazel, S. (2013). Risk Factors for Violence in Psychosis: Systematic Review and Meta-Regression Analysis of 110 Studies. *PLoS ONE, 8*(2).

Yuen, S. (2018, January 2). Workplace deaths fall to a 13-year low. *The Straits Times*.

CHAPTER 6
RESPONDING TO CRIME

Punishment is not for revenge, but to lessen crime and reform the criminal.

Elizabeth Fry
English Prison Reformer

6.1 Introduction

How do we respond to crime? Should we prevent or react to crime? Experts have argued that prevention is better than cure. If that is so, what is 'crime prevention' exactly? Academics have struggled to define the term for decades without much success because there are so many dimensions to consider and yet, societies continue to use this term. A good starting definition can be that 'crime prevention' is any action that causes a reduction in the level of criminal activity and the resulting harm (Tilley, 2005).

Crime prevention can be broken down into three levels: *primary, secondary,* and *tertiary* prevention, or PST (Australian Institute of Criminology, 2004). This model was developed by Brantingham and Faust (1976), who adapted a medical model of prevention (i.e., PST) for crime prevention. While this model is not without its critics, it is simple enough as a guide to organising crime prevention initiatives. This framework guided crime prevention thinking in both academic and the criminal justice systems for 30 years.

Primary crime prevention is directed at stopping the problem before it arises. These are risk-reduction or risk-removal measures. They are usually undertaken to address larger groups, the masses, or the environment surrounding the crime. This could involve reducing opportunities for crime and strengthening community and social structures. Primary prevention focuses on both *social* and *situational* factors. *Social crime prevention* involves person-centred measures, which address factors that influence an individual's likelihood of committing a crime such as poverty and unemployment, poor health, and low educational performance. Examples include school-based and community-based programs. *Situational crime prevention* addresses the environment, for example, target hardening in the design of buildings and landscapes.

Secondary crime prevention focuses on intervention, typically with those at high risk of embarking on a criminal career or criminal victimization. Techniques involve rapid and effective early interventions (for example, youth programs) and addressing the situation in high-risk neighbourhoods (for example, having neighbourhood dispute centres to address disputes). It may also involve targeting at-risk areas or hot-spots.

Tertiary crime prevention focuses on dealing with offending, after it has occurred, with a view to prevent re-offending. The primary focus is on intervention with known offenders in an attempt to prevent re-offending and recidivism. Some examples include community-oriented youth conferencing schemes, punishment schemes, incapacitation, community-based sanctions and treatment, and rehabilitation interventions.

Table 6.1 shows a pictorial summary of the various initiatives under the PST model of crime prevention.

Table 6.1: The Primary-Secondary-Tertiary Model Crime Prevention Approach

	Primary crime prevention	Secondary crime prevention	Tertiary crime prevention
General foci of these programs	Crime prevention by environmental design Crime prevention education (posters, crime watch television show)	Early intervention programs Pre-delinquent screenings At-risk targeted programs (people and places) Neighborhood programs	Punishment, treatment and rehabilitation Training Community interventions
Time Horizon	Long-term	Short- to medium-term	Short-term and immediate

Source: Adapted from Martin and Greg (2008).

6.2 Primary Crime Prevention Measures

This section discusses *situational crime prevention*. Situational crime prevention (SCP) has two strategies: *people-oriented* strategies and *place/environmental-oriented* strategies.

6.2.1 *Crime Prevention through Social Development*

The *people-oriented strategy* of crime prevention is known as Crime Prevention Through Social Development (CPSD). CPSD involves long-term actions that deal with the root causes of crime (Canadian Council of Social Development, 1989). Typically, CPSD work tends to be longitudinal in nature. Its aim is to reduce risk factors that start children and youth on the road to crime, and to build protective factors that may mitigate risks. CPSD tends to be proactive and it is concerned about preventing crime before it happens. It is a long-term measure as it aims to improve the quality of life of those most at risk. Finally, CPSD is guided by social and economic factors. Some examples are child abuse, drug addiction, alcohol misuse, school behavioural problems, teenage pregnancy, poverty, and unemployment. The CPSD approach suggests that police patrols are useful but reactive, and they do not have a lasting impact on crime rates as they do not address the root causes of crime such as poor parenting, poor police–community engagement, and distrust.[1] The advocates of CPSD explain that the police should have a community-oriented style of policing.[2] CPSD projects typically involve many agencies in the government, private businesses, and social agencies (Canadian Council of Social Development, 1989). Examples of programs include the following:

- *Projects in the Family, Community and School,* such as:
  - Child care services to prevent child abuse,
  - Parent training programs (e.g., to prevent infanticide),
  - Respite care programs for single parents,
  - Family violence prevention and intervention programs,
  - Positive parenting programs in schools and the community,
  - Avoiding concentration of disadvantaged families in one housing area, and
  - Relevant recreational programs.

- *Projects for School Programs that Deal with Disadvantaged and At-Risk Youth.* Some examples are:
  - Modifying school curricula to include information on life skills, parenting, sexual behaviour, and assertiveness, to meet the needs of children from disadvantaged families, and

---

[1] This is truer in other countries, rather than in Singapore. In Singapore, the levels of trust with the police appear to be quite high. In a 2016 survey which involved 4,800 Singaporeans and permanent residents, 90% believed the police were ready to deal with any major law and order incident, and were well prepared to respond to future security needs (Seow, 2017).

[2] Singapore adopts the community policing approach and this is discussed in the later section of this chapter.

o Developing employment projects that will involve youth from disadvantaged families.

Many of these projects are targeting risk factors and promoting protective factors, which were discussed in Chapter 1 (e.g., family risk, parenting, leisure, employment, etc.).

6.2.2 *Crime Prevention through Environmental Design*

Place-oriented strategies are known as Crime Prevention Through Environmental Design (CPTED). CPTED considers the built environment which can be targets of criminal activity or the location where crime takes place. CPTED approaches consider proper design, effective use, and maintenance of the built environment. CPTED is complementary to CPSD strategies as people live in the built environment and the built environment influences how people behave. CPTED is based on the idea that much of crime is opportunistic and contextual. There are four key CPTED design principles:

- *Natural access control*: The design of buildings and spaces influences the flow of people, and can be used to naturally maximize control and surveillance (e.g., landscaping, lighting, movement of people, etc.)
- *Natural surveillance*: The idea is to design buildings and spaces to maximize visibility. Users can observe and monitor activities around them in a formal and/or casual manner (e.g., office or flat windows with sightlines to parking areas).
- *Territoriality*: The design of the environment should extend a sense of territory. People taking ownership of their surroundings make it more difficult for offenders to carry out crimes or disorder.
- *Maintenance*: Enhancement, maintenance, and management of the built environment encourage the users of the area to respect their surroundings (e.g., removing graffiti and litter, avoiding overgrowth of hedges, fixing broken lighting, installing good locks, etc.)

The National Crime Prevention Council (Singapore) produced a CPTED Guidebook arguing that the community, homeowners, planners, developers, and architects could play a greater role in protecting the community and themselves from crime, by integrating CPTED principles and concepts into the design of the physical environment. The four CPTED principles can be translated into various planning and design strategies that could enhance security. As shown in Table 6.2, these strategies can be categorised as follows:

Table 6.2   Principles of CPTED

Principles of CPTED	Some examples
1. *Allow for clear sight lines* Design visibility into environment	• Columns and walls can be tucked into the built design, as protrusions can hinder visibility. Visibility can be improved through modification such as creation of windows and openings in otherwise blank walls. • Residential apartments with windows overlooking car park and parks can allow for clear sight lines and improve visibility.
2. *Provide adequate lighting* Enhance visibility or reduce duration of gatherings	• Lighting of different wattage, colour temperature and rendition may be used to make certain public areas 'less hospitable' for gathering for long periods. • Lighting should take into account vegetation, such as mature trees and obstructions that would cause light to be blocked off.
3. *Minimize concealed and isolated routes* An attacker can predict where pedestrians will end up once they are on the path	• If there is a need for concealed or isolated routes within the environment, they should be designed to incorporate visibility. If a pedestrian cannot see what is on or at the end of a concealed or predictable route, visibility should be improved by lighting and/or the use of a reflective mirrors.
4. *Avoid entrapment* e.g., lifts, tunnels or bridges, enclosed and isolated stairwells.	• If elimination of an entrapment area is not possible, it should be locked or closed after operating hours. • It is preferable to have natural surveillance, if an entrapment area is unavoidable (e.g. lifts with see through doors).

(*Continued*)

Table 6.2: (*Continued*)

Principles of CPTED	Some examples
5. *Reduce isolated area* Most people feel insecure in isolated areas especially if people judge that signs of distress or yelling will not be seen or heard.	• In isolated areas, have telephones, emergency telephones or signs to indicate the location of panic alarms. • Video cameras and patrols can help monitor areas. • Money withdrawal places such as banking facilities can be located near pedestrian activities, to reduce sense of isolation.
6. *Promote land use mix*	• Locating residential developments with in a main street, a town square, day-care centres or shops to increase natural surveillance as the local business people 'watch' the street.
7. *Use of activity generators*	• 'Activity generators' are facilities that attract people, create activities and add life to the street or space and reduce the opportunities for crime, for e.g. recreational facilities in a park, placing housing in the central business district or adding a restaurant to an office building.
8. *Create a sense of ownership through maintenance and management* Sense of ownership or territoriality makes a place safer	• Offensive graffiti should be removed. • Response to litter. • Repairs should be prompt as a well-maintained space gives an impression of 'ownership' and 'care'. • Use vandal resistant materials for street furniture and common facilities.
9. *Provide signs and information*	• Well-designed, strategically located signs and maps contribute to a feeling of security. • Signs should be standardized to give clear, consistent, concise and readable messages from the street. • Having addresses lit up at night will make them even more visible.
10. *Improve overall design of the built environment.*	• The design of the environment influences human behaviour. A barren, sterile place surrounded with security hardware will reinforce fear, while a vibrant and beautiful place conveys confidence and care.

Source: Adapted from CPTED, National Crime Prevention Council Singapore, n.d.

6.2.3 *25 Crime Prevention Techniques: Combining People and Environment Strategies*

Inspired by the work and success in CPSD and CPTED, British criminologists Ronald Clark and Patricia Mayhew at the U.K. Home Office developed the idea of combining place and persons to develop crime prevention techniques. Solutions may include increasing the effort required to commit a crime, making it less attractive, increasing the risk of being caught, reducing the potential rewards of crime, reducing provocations and temptations, and removing excuses for committing crime.

Take the example of situational crime prevention to deal with intoxicated people leaving bars and getting involved in fights. Situational solutions may include education for club staff and customers about responsible drinking, regulations addressing the number, size, and location of clubs and their closing times, police presence near clubs at closing times, random spot checks, and availability of public transport.

As a framework, SCP has a classification system of 25 situational prevention techniques (with examples shown in Table 6.3).

These 25 SCP techniques were premised on three main theoretical foundations. These were briefly discussed in Chapter 1 but will be explained again here.

First, the *Rational Activity Theory* (Cohen & Felon, 1979) argues that for a crime to be committed, three things are needed: (1) a motivated offender, (2) a suitable and desired target, and (3) the lack of a capable controller. There are three types of controllers: (1) intimate handlers, (2) guardians, and (3) place managers/monitors. *Intimate handlers* could be people who have direct personal influence over an offender (parents, teachers, coaches, friends, or employers). *Guardians* include friends (as when three women decide to run together in a park in order to protect each other) as well as formal authority such as private security guards. *Place managers* (such as apartment managers and lifeguards) regulate behaviour at the locations they control. This theory posits that crime is normal, to be expected, and is dependent on opportunities. If a target is not sufficiently protected, and if the reward

Table 6.3:   25 Techniques of Crime Prevention

Increase the effort for crime	Increase the risks of crime	Reduce the rewards of crime	Reduce emotional provocation	Remove excuses of criminal
Target Hardening	*Extend Guardians*	*Conceal targets from offender*	*Reduce frustration for those involved*	*Set rules so expected behaviour is clear*
Steering locks Ignition locks Anti-robbery screens	Crime occurs when there are no guardians Go out in groups Leave signs of occupancy (when house is vacant)	Use unmarked armour trucks for money transport from banks	More seating Provide soothing music	Rental agreement (premise cannot be used for criminal purposes) Hotel registration
Control the access	*Assist natural surveillance*	*Remove targets from sight (so crime would not occur)*	*Avoid disputes*	*Post clear instructions*
Entry phones at apartments, Electronic card access into buildings and office	Improved street lighting (could reduce robbery, sex crimes) Support whistle blowers	Women's shelters to protect women from abusers	Separate seats for members from different teams in football matches Fix cab fares, so there are no arguments	'No parking' signs 'Private property' 'This place is being monitored by CCTV'

Toughen exits/ Escape	*Reduce anonymity*	*Identify property*	*Reduce temptation and arousal*	*Raise conscience*
Ticket needed for exit points	Taxi drivers have identity disclosed	Property marking	Control pornography	Signatures for customs declarations
Clothing tags	School uniforms	Car marking	Prohibit racial slurs	Roadside speed reminders
		Phone		

Deflect offenders	*Use place monitor*	*Disrupt markets*	*Neutralize peer pressure*	*Assist compliance*
Street closures, Separate toilets for women	CCTV for double deck buses	Monitor pawn shops	Teach that it is okay to say 'no'	Easy library checkout
		Monitor chemicals imported		Litter receptacles

Control tools	*Strengthen formal surveillance*	*Deny benefits*	*Discourage imitation*	*Control drugs and alcohol*
Smart guns	Red light cameras	Ink merchandise tags	Censor details of crime in media	Breath analyzers in bars
Restrict spray paint sales from juveniles	Burglar alarm	Graffiti cleaning		
		Disable stolen phone		

is worth it, crime will happen. The basic idea of routine activity theory is that most crimes are petty theft which go unreported to the police. Crime is neither spectacular nor dramatic, and it happens all the time. This is a macro theory, which explains how changes in society expand or contract opportunities for crime. These opportunities are affected by the supply of suitable crime targets and the availability of capable guardians (for example, shop assistants, custodians, parents, and teachers) who can protect these targets. Examples of suitable crime targets could be light-value or lightweight goods, such as mobile phones and laptops, which are often targets of theft. So, the higher the availability of mobile phones in society, the more we can expect a rise in mobile phone theft, unless there is also a rise in capable guardians. This theory argues that crime is less affected by social causes such as poverty, inequality, and unemployment. For instance, after World War II, there was an economic boom in many Western countries (i.e., poverty was reduced), but crime also rose significantly during that time. This is because the prosperity of society offers opportunities for crime — there is much more to steal. The routine activity theory is controversial among sociologists who believe in the social causes of crime. However, only several types of deviance can be adequately explained by the routine activity theory. This includes copyright infringement (e.g., illegal downloading of songs and movies), employee theft, and corporate crime.

The second is *crime pattern theory* (Brantingham & Brantingham, 1993), developed by Canadian environmental criminologists Patricia and Paul Brantingham. This theory has a neighbourhood and community focus. It sought to explain how offenders were looking for, and stumbled across opportunities for committing crime, in the course of their everyday 'patterned' lives. They discussed the concept of 'activity spaces', which was central to crime pattern theory. Starting with a triangle, offenders go from home to work to recreation. Around each of these three nodes (except a buffer zone where they might be recognized by others), offenders look for crime opportunities. It is easier to commit crimes during the course of their daily routine, than by making a special journey out of this pattern to do so. The term 'edges' refers to the boundaries of areas where people live, work, shop, or seek entertainment. Some crimes such as racial attacks, robberies, or shoplifting are more likely to occur at these edges because this is where people from different neighbourhoods who do not know each other cross paths.

The third theory is the *rational choice theory* (micro theory) which argued that certain decision-making processes resulted in an offender choosing to be involved in certain specific crimes. The rational choice theory (Cornish & Clarke, 1986) is based on the idea that criminals consider their decisions before they took the opportunity to commit a crime. The decision to commit a crime is constrained by time, cognitive ability, and information, resulting in 'limited' reasoning for the offender. This theory highlighted that an offender will commit a crime because of the benefits received from the act. The decision to commit a crime is based on the thinking that the *benefits* of committing a crime are greater than the *cost* of the crime. This bounded reasoning (although not necessarily rational) assists the offender in determining the risks of being detected. The rational choice crime prevention theory focuses on an offender's decision-making process, thus providing a framework to prevent crime through deterrence (e.g., effective urban planning and improved surveillance that can increase the likelihood of detection). This analyses the offenders' perspective and how they use the environment, rather than just looking at what motivates the offender.

6.2.4 *Other Primary Prevention Measures*

6.2.4.1 *Closed Circuit TV (CCTV)*

Closed Circuit TV (CCTVs) prevent crime by increasing surveillance. Criminals are less likely to commit crimes if they feel that they are being observed.[3] This is the idea behind increasing police patrols, using park

---

[3] You will realize that many prisons were built with a very similar philosophy; that is, that someone is watching over your behaviour or the concept of guardianship. Think about how prisons in the past typically had tall watchtowers with guards in them. These days however, modern prisons use CCTV technology. In a similar vein, some shopping centres use the idea of an 'eye' (literally a picture of big eye) or reflective mirrors watching over shoppers to deter shoplifting.

rangers, and bus conductors; someone may be watching (Joyce, 2012). This increases 'guardianship' (as discussed earlier) and creates the idea that someone bothers to guard or look after the target (i.e., the explanation behind the "broken windows" concept). The use of CCTV is a technological advancement of this older idea. CCTVs may be used to protect property or businesses. However, the key factor determining the effectiveness of CCTVs is not the increased guardianship, but whether CCTVs can aid in crime detection (Arrington, 2007), since offenders will still offend if they know that they are being observed but will not be caught. The Singapore Police Force (SPF) has invested heavily into the use of CCTVs and, since 2012, more than 52,000 police cameras have been installed in 8,600 housing blocks. Political leaders have noted that housing blocks with CCTV cameras do seem to have fewer unlicensed moneylender harassment cases involving property damage. The number of such cases reported at 2,152 blocks with police cameras plummeted from 1,617 in 2013 before the installation of cameras to just 426 in 2014 (Heng, 2016). Armitage (2002) explained that surveillance seeks to persuade individuals not to engage in criminal behaviours and encourages individuals to 'police their own behaviour'. However, deterrence is not the only value of CCTVs, they are also used for detection and investigation (this means that their value goes beyond primary prevention to secondary investigation) and tertiary prevention (i.e., proving a case in court). According to reports, authorities in Malaysia are also looking to expand the use of CCTVs in public areas to trains, buses, and MRT stations, and these cameras will be linked to police stations. These CCTVs would also be equipped with facial recognition software (*The Star*, 2017). The same report mentioned that CCTV use is common in Britain, China, and Australia.

6.2.4.2   *Neighbourhood watch scheme*

'Neighbourhood watch' is an extension of situational crime prevention. The idea is that the community defends itself and engages in its own surveillance to keep its own place safe. This idea was first introduced to the City of Seattle in 1974. It relies on neighbours looking out for one another and for each other's properties. They note anything suspicious and would inform the police if they think something is amiss. Neighbourhood watch schemes are useful when they result in people who live amongst each other getting to know and looking out for one another. This approach works well when a community member recognizes a stranger loitering around their district, but does not work as well when the crime is committed by someone within the community (Joyce, 2012). In Singapore, the Neighbourhood Watch Zone (NWZ) Scheme was launched on 27 April 1997. NWZs were formed under the Residents' committees (RCs) and Neighbourhood Committees (NCs). The NWZ scheme aims to develop closer police–citizens relationships in the community to help prevent and detect crime and help develop a community spirit so that citizens look out for one another's homes and properties.

6.2.4.3 *The National Crime Prevention Council*

A citizens' committee called the National Crime Prevention Council (NCPC) was created in 1981 with a mandate to promote public awareness of and concern about crime, and to propagate the concept of self-help in crime prevention (Sim & Khader, 2017). Minister of Home Affairs, Mr. Chua Sian Chin, inaugurated it in 4 July 1981. It was set up as an impartial, independent, voluntary, and non-profit organization (Koh, 2016). The council hoped to work closely with both private and people sectors to encourage them to take more responsibility in crime prevention. Being a non-profit organisation, it also had to work hard to raise its own funds from the public and business community. NCPC worked on initiatives such as the NWZs and the Community Safety and Security Program. In general, the NCPC studied crime problems and made preventive recommendations. Coordinating committees were formed at each constituency to spread the word about crime prevention. The NCPC started several projects, including working with committees and businesses, commissioning crime prevention buses that toured factories, and organizing outreach activities in schools (Koh, 2016). This approach is not unique to Singapore, and many countries have similar projects, e.g., Force Watch in the U.K.[4] and Neighbourhood Watch in Australia.[5]

6.2.4.4 *Community policing*

There are several factors that made community policing possible for Singapore. First, there was strong police–public trust and relationships. Second, policing styles had changed over the years from watchman, to legalistic, to service orientation. Community policing is service-oriented. Third, although crime was lower in Singapore than in many other countries in the 1970s and 1980s, it had seemed to be on the rise with a booming economy and new towns. There was thus a need for a new policing strategy, which could incorporate the public's assistance through crime prevention awareness activities. Fourth, with the success of the Housing and Development Board's plans, there were many new towns, which were being developed in the 1980s. The police could not rely on their method of 'vertical patrolling' of high-rise apartments and instead, had to plan a decentralized presence with neighbourhood-based police posts in new towns. Fifth, manpower was limited and there was a need to utilize it effectively. Finally, the success of the Japanese Koban system, where clearance rates were high, convinced the Singaporean authorities of the need to start something similar that would bring about high degrees of trust and cooperation between the police and the public (Quah, 1992).

In 1981, the Minister of Home Affairs, Chua Sian Chin led a team to Japan to study the Japanese system of community policing. In Japan, reports showed that there was a high crime clearance rate of 60% and this was due to the public trust of the Japanese police. Statistics indicated that 80% of the Japanese public *readily* provided information to help the police with arrests (Singh, n.d.). With the desire to learn from the Japanese, community policing as the new

---

[4] See https://www.ourwatch.org.uk/force-level-association
[5] See http://nhw.com.au

policing strategy was born. In the 1980s, it was a timely move as the SPF thought that there was a need to re-orient its patrol strategy from *fast-car vehicle response* to *community-oriented patrols.* There were several conceptual differences between the traditional policing approach and the community policing approach as shown in Table 6.4.

Table 6.4: Differences Between Traditional and Community Policing

Traditional policing	Community policing
Reactive to incidents	Pro-active in solving community related problems.
Roles of police officers are limited to incident response	Roles of police officers are broadened to include identification and solving of problems.
Random patrols in cars to respond to crimes. Focus on internal resources	Visible patrols to interact with the community, i.e., foot patrols, bicycle patrols, scooter patrols.
Some though limited linkages with the community. Information from the community is limited	Leverage strongly on community resources. Police work with extensive co-operative links with the community. Information from the community comes from many sources.
Supervision is control-oriented; authoritative command and control	Decentralization of authority and autonomy given to front-line officers.
Rewards based on solving of cases	Performance evaluation rewards based on service activities; crime prevention, satisfaction and sense of safety of the community

Source: Adapted from Singh (n.d.).

The police felt that community policing could create a heightened sense of police presence to deter crimes and build closer police-community ties. The Neighbourhood Police Post (NPP) system, which was adapted from the Japanese Koban System, was introduced in 1983. The first NPP was launched in the Khe Bong constituency in "B" division, in Toa Payoh. The idea was that every policeman would be a friend, helper, and protector of his precinct (Koh, 2016). People would see policemen as friends who would mingle with members of the community and understand their concerns, and prevent larger problems from surfacing. In October 1997, the SPF made a move to re-design the NPP system. The Neighbourhood Policing Centres (NPCs) system was introduced as an extension of the NPP system to enhance the community policing approach further. The NPC system was a one-stop total policing center providing the full range of policing services and had more efficient pooling of manpower resources to serve the community.

6.2.4.5 *New developments in policing*

What does the long-term future portend for policing across the world? There are foreseeable trends. First, experts view that police roles are becoming more similar to social services work, as there is a need to be service-oriented, working with social and community agencies, and becoming more oriented to human problems (Coomber *et al.*, 2015). Second, experts expect strong public scrutiny of and accountability over police work. There may be more questions about 'who polices the police'. Thankfully, in Singapore, there is a high level of trust in this area (Seow, 2017). Third, the roles of the police have expanded largely because of technology and wider enforcement. CCTVs, police databases, police body-worn cameras, video recorded investigations and sophisticated command and control systems, all of which means better policing, but also entails more scope and complexity in police work. This is the promise that more will be done, and done well, which creates a stressful working situation. However, there is pressure to be savvy and cost-effective, and police forces worldwide are drawing on three ways to optimise resources. First is reducing bureaucracy so that police officers can do police work rather than administrative work. Second, using civilians in key civilian roles such as personnel management, logistics, human resources, and public affairs, so as to deploy police to operational roles. Thirdly is using private commercial providers who provide security services. Fourth, retired police officers can help in certain job areas. Each of these solutions can be useful; the only question remains as to whether the public could be comfortable with these options (Coomber *et al.*, 2015). Responsibility, after all, cannot be delegated.

6.3 Secondary Crime Prevention Measures

Secondary crime prevention refers to preventive techniques focused on 'at-risk' situations. Some examples of 'at-risk' groups are youth who are at risk of dropping out of school or at risk of getting involved in gangs. It targets 'at-risk' neighbourhoods or 'hot-spots' where crime rates are high. While primary prevention tends to target a wider audience and wider issues, secondary prevention is more targeted at at-risk persons, groups, or situations.

6.3.1 *Engaging 'At-Risk' Youths*

One of the ways in which Singapore deals with youths who are at risk is by setting up a whole of government (WOG) entity called the National Committee on Youth Guidance and Rehabilitation (NYGR). This is a committee that examines youth delinquency and crime. The committee recognizes that youths have potential and should not be criminalized as far as possible, unless necessary (i.e., diversionary programs). Set up in 2010, the NYGR has agencies from education, community, and social services, healthcare, the police force, prisons, the narcotics department, the National Youth Council (NYC), the Attorney-General's Chamber (AGC), and the Courts. There are also representatives from the academia and ethnic self-help groups. The aim of the NYGR is to develop policies and strategies across the entire (youth) offending spectrum, to conduct research into evidence-based programming, and to be a platform for information sharing. The main targeted youths are those from 12 to 21 years old. The committee's oversight includes a wide range of interventions as shown in Table 6.5 (Tan, 2012).

Table 6.5:   Examples of Programs Addressing Potential Youth Delinquency

Young age	'At-risk' children/youths	Post offence management
• ComCare GROW Pillar • Programs that focus on the developmental needs of children from needy families • Student Care Centres • Educational Financial Assistance Scheme • Learning Support Programme (LSP) • Child Protection Programs	• Beyond Parental Control • Honorary Voluntary Special Constabulary (VSC) (School) Scheme • NPCC Youth Crime Prevention Ambassadors (PYA) Programme • Youth Crime Prevention Roadshow (YCPR) • Prison Visit Education Programme for Schools (PVEPS) • Youth Hanging Out Late (YHOL) Letters • Youth employment programs • Delta League Football program	• Guidance Programme • Probation • Juvenile Homes • StreetWise Programme

6.3.2 *The Delta League Story*

The Delta League is a youth engagement program designed to meaningfully occupy youths during their school holidays with football to steer them away from crime. This started when youth groups were playing *ad hoc* football games with the officers from Clementi Police Division. Then Division Commander of Clementi Police HQ, Melvin Yong who noted visible benefits from his officers' informal interaction with these young footballers, suggested taking this further. The youths enjoyed football and responded well to the mentorship of the police officers. This gave him the idea for a new way for the Singapore Police Force to engage with youths, and this was extended further to become a national league. The league has more than 700 youths participating each year,[6] and the program has been extended to

---

[6] This wider outreach means it is no longer just a secondary prevention measure, but a primary prevention measure which is aimed to build better public-police trust levels.

include international schools. The idea seems potentially useful since it involves harnessing the energy of youths, steering youths away from crime, developing in them a sense of responsibility, and encouraging personal development. According to reports, a detailed systematic program evaluation is being conducted (Kasim, 2016). This notion of using sports as a way of steering kids away from crime is consistent with most international best practices. For example, the UNODC has launched a global youth crime prevention initiative that builds on the power of sports as a tool for peace. The initiative aims to promote sports related activities to prevent crime and to build resilience in 'at-risk' youths. Strengthening the life skills of youths is a key objective, because it minimizes risk factors and maximizes protective factors related to crime, violence and drug-use (UNODC, n.d.).

6.3.3 *Hot Spots Policing*

The idea in hot spots policing is that crime does not occur evenly over space and land. Some are 'hot spots', which carry higher risk. In Minneapolis, Minnesota, 3% of the city's addresses accounted for 50% of 'calls for service' to the police. In Jersey City, New Jersey, about 4% of streets and intersection areas generated nearly half of the city's narcotics arrests and 42% of the disorder arrests (Weisburd *et al.*, 2000). These studies reported that crime tended to concentrate at certain times. For example:

- Assaults occurred most frequently between 3.00 a.m. and 7.00 a.m. This was when streets are largely vacant;
- Residential burglaries occurred mostly during daytime hours. This was when residents were not home; and
- Incidents of driving under the influence occurred more frequently in areas with a large number of bars or liquor stores.

In Singapore, ex-Commissioner Ng Joo Hee in 2014 remarked (after the Little India Riot in 2013) that there were hot spots in Singapore where there was a clear need for more hot spots policing (Husain, 2014). The traffic police also deploy speed cameras in places where speeding is prevalent (Cheong, 2016).

How do we identify a hot spot? Experienced police officers know about these through their professional instinct, because they have developed sharp powers of observation, street intelligence, and simply because they are on the ground often and long enough. So they know about the usual (and hence also unusual activity) patterns in malls, street corners, apartment surroundings, and warehouses. The modern technological tools used these days are Geographic Information Systems (GIS) and statistical tests. Analysts can develop density maps to show where crimes occur. GIS programs can combine street maps with data about schools, clubbing spots, and mass crowding spots, revealing hot spots.

Data mining and business analytics may yield interesting findings for hot spots. For example, Professor Fei Da Zhu, Professor Kam Ting Seong Zhu, and their student collaborators at the Singapore Management University (SMU) reported a study, which employed data mining to examine Singaporean crime trends. Using geospatial data, they looked at descriptions of crime, including the time and location of occurrence for more than 5,000 records in the year 2000. They found that much of crime patterns recorded had occurred in the Geylang area, most were residential in nature, were about residential burglaries, and that crime occurred during the afternoon (and not during the night) and often during weekends as well. They explained that these findings had implications for the operational area coverage of police stations (e.g., some new towns that were not adequately covered by existing police stations), on the role of the housing authority in building design to reduce burglary, and also the optimal deployment of police resources at various times of day through the week (He *et al.*, 2010).

6.3.4 *Big Data and Predictive Policing*

There is a discussion presently about whether big data can be of use in policing. Broadly speaking, it refers to an analytical process in which a large amount of data points are processed to produce a product. The purpose of this product is to solve problems. Ironically, big data is not defined in terms of data set size but the capacity to search, aggregate, and cross-reference data sets (Boyd & Crawford,

2012). Many commercial organizations use it to determine their pricing, inventory control, and advertising. Global Positioning System (GPS) systems use it to provide real-time traffic information and healthcare systems use it to improve care and save lives. In policing worldwide, big data has been used in the collection and storage of DNA information, mass surveillance, and predictive policing. Babuta argued that DNA information is the easiest to manage since it is more straightforward, i.e., stored as numbers (Babuta, 2017). He explained further that the ability of the police to trawl large amounts of data is more limited, since data sizes are unmanageable. Predictive policing appears to show some promise since it is about taking data from sources, analyzing them, and using results to anticipate, prevent, and respond to future crime (Pearsall, 2010). This is not new, as the New York Police Department has been using quantitative analysis for some time.

Despite all this potential, big data has limitations. First, data does not interpret itself. The data cleaning process during which the relevance and usefulness of data is judged is a subjective procedure. Second, much of the data used for analysis is unreliable, since it is gleaned from very diverse sources and often from the Internet. This means the potential for error and false positives increases.[7] Third, the data size is so big that most organizations will find it difficult to store. 'Data lakes', which are centralised data storage, are needed. This means there is a need to work with third-party vendors in dealing with sensitive police data, which is not desirable from a security angle. Fourth, there are ethical and legal constrains of using big data and the major concerns over privacy.

A related technique is *predictive analytics*. Advanced analytics enables the development of predictive crime mapping tools that use statistical models to predict areas which are at risk of experiencing crime, based on past criminal events (Babuta, 2017). This is based on

---

[7] A well-known example was that of statistician David Leinweber who made an excellent point about this using a regression model that predicted a stock index using three inputs: cheese production in the U.S., butter production in the U.S. and Bangladesh, and the sheep population in the U.S. and Bangladesh (Babuta, 2017).

the idea that *repeat victimisation* accounts for a large proportion of crime (Pease, 1998). Furthermore, Babuta explained that crime is often contagious (2017), and the risk of victimisation increases in an area's surroundings in the aftermath of a crime (Bowers *et al.*, 2004). Predictive mapping software is significantly more effective in predicting the location of future crimes, than traditional policing methods.

A recent development called Predpol is a crime prediction tool developed by the University of California, Los Angeles (UCLA) and Santa Clara University, in collaboration with the Los Angeles Police Department (LAPD) and Santa Cruz Police Department. The developers used 'self-exciting point process modelling' (a time series model in which occurrence of past points makes occurrence of future points more probable) to develop the tool. The program, which is easy to use, pinpoints small boxes that indicate the time and places where crime is most likely to occur. Boxes are generated for each police patrol shift, and officers respond to potential crime locations. Typical crime data would include the type of offense, the time of day it was committed, and the day of the week. Emerging predictive methods may include wider scope of data variables. See Table 6.6 for potential data variables which may be considered in predictive analytics.

Table 6.6:   Types of Variables Used in Predictive Policing

Spatial	Temporal	Social network
Areas with Potential Victims/Targets	Payday schedules	Kinship
Shopping malls	Time of day	Friendship
Properties of value	Weekend vs. weekday	Affiliation with an
Hotels	Traffic patterns	organization
Tourist spots	Sporting and	Financial transaction
	entertainment	Offender/victim
Area demographics	events	
Population density	Festivals	
Residential instability		
Escape Routes		
Highways		
Bridges		
Tunnels		

(*Continued*)

Table 6.6:   (*Continued*)

Spatial	Temporal	Social network
Public transportation		
Dense foliage		
Criminal Residences (or places linked		
to criminals)		
Bars and liquor stores		
Fast food restaurants		
Bus stops		
Public health information (alcohol		
and drug use records)		
Areas with physical decay		

Source: Adapted from Bachner (2013).

Predpol has been effective in reducing burglary. Santa Cruz PD reported a 14% decrease in burglaries after using Predpol. The LAPD Foothill police reported a 20% reduction in predicted crimes. In the U.K., Kent Police has found the program to be 10 times more effective than random patrolling (Babuta, 2017). This program nonetheless has some limits too. First, it creates boxes, which are grid-based predictions that are not geographically oriented and therefore hard to use. Second, the algorithm is simple — past events are used to predict future ones. They do not take into account the complex dynamic environmental factors which affect crime. According to Babuta, the "interplay between routine behavioural patterns and the physical geography of urban environments is equally important, as past crimes, when examining the distribution of hotspots" (2017, p. 22). Third, as with computerized systems, there are larger concerns about the overreliance on technology. As Berkeley Law Professor David Sklansky explains: "A fixation on technology can distract attention from the important parts of the process, the parts that rely on imagination and judgment. It can distract attention, too, from other critical parts of the contemporary policing agenda: building trust and legitimacy..." (Sklansky, 2011, p. 63). Additionally, there is concern that officers may value *dispassionate analysis* at the expense of investing in community policing, such as building neighborhood partnerships. As officers spend more time analyzing real-time density maps, they spend less time interacting with the community (Bachner, 2013).

In summary, as Bachner (2013) asserts, one could make a strong case for predictive analytics policing for a few reasons. First, it may be cost-effective in a policing climate where resources are limited. Second, it is useful when it complements officers' judgment and intuition, but it should not be a substitute for operational police judgement. Finally, she mentions that it is most useful when geographic and demographic information is considered together and when data is timely and accurate.

6.3.5 *Clubs Against Drugs Campaign*

If poorly managed, clubs could be 'at-risk' areas and hot spots, especially because of the dangers of alcohol use and drug overdose. Recreational drug use in the nightlife setting carries the risk of many negative consequences such as violence, injuries, drink-driving, and sexual risk-taking. The nightlife arena is a high-risk setting for drug use. In a recent study in Norway, researchers Nordfjærn and colleagues (2016) studied 1099 patrons entering or exiting 12 popular licensed premises. Participants had to complete an anonymous self-administered questionnaire and their blood alcohol concentration (BAC) levels were measured. Results of this study showed that the average Blood Alcohol Content levels were high for both males and females. A total of 67% reported having used illicit drugs: 43% reported using them last year, 25% used them last month, and 14% used them during the last 48 hours. High-risk groups included young patrons (16 to 20 years), of which 50% also reported illicit drug use in the last year. In a related study, the same author (Nordfjærn, 2017) investigated the role of substance use characteristics and its relationship with nightlife violence; 10% reported that they had been involved in physical violence when they consumed alcohol in the nightlife setting during the last 12 months. The prevalence of illicit substance use in the year before was high, especially in the violence-involved group.

In Singapore, knowing that clubs can be a high-risk area, the Clubs Against Drugs (CAD) Campaign was launched in 2000 by the

National Council Against Drug Abuse (NCADA) in Singapore, with the support of the Central Narcotics Bureau (CNB) to address the possible issue of drug abuse in clubs. This joint effort carried an anti-drug message to patrons of nightlife establishments and raised awareness of the dangers of drugs.

6.3.6 *Anti-Drug Abuse Campaign and 'Danceworks'*

An anti-drug dance competition has attracted tens of thousands of participants each year, since its first run in 1999 in Singapore. The theme aims to remind youths not to experiment with drugs and that they can work towards their dreams. Through the competition, NCADA and the CNB hoped that youths could have a platform to express themselves and pursue their passion for dance in a positive manner and stay away from drugs. This idea is not unique to Singapore. In New York, this year's Electric Zoo dance-music festival required all attendees to watch a two-minute video encouraging them not to use drugs. The New York event has instated a slew of new anti-drug policies in response to incidents last year in which two people died and several were hospitalised after taking MDMA.[8] *Come to Life* is the name of Electric Zoo's anti-drug campaign (Micheals, 2014).

6.3.7 *Deterring Young People through Meetings with Reformed Inmates*

To deter young people from a life of crime, many criminal justice systems arrange for at-risk teens to meet reformed inmates (see Table 6.12 for Singapore's own examples). The Hong Kong Correctional Service has been running the Personal Encounter with Prisoners Scheme (PEPS) since 1993 (Chung, 2010). Under this scheme, youths visit correctional institutions and have personal discussions with reformed prisoners. The idea here is to have the participants to think about the

---

[8] According to National Institute of Drug Abuse (U.S.), MDMA is 3,4-methylenedioxy-methamphetamine, a 'synthetic drug that alters mood and perception. It is similar to both stimulants and hallucinogens, producing feelings of energy, pleasure, emotional warmth, and distorted sensory and time perception. It is also known as Ecstasy or Molly'.

consequences of committing crimes. Another purpose is to spread the message of offender rehabilitation. This has several other benefits since prisoners can build up their own confidence through these experience-sharing sessions. Since 1993, PEPS has invited students and youth groups to visit several institutions, which include three maximum-security prisons, and a detention center.

The Hong Kong Correctional Service started the Green Haven Scheme to promote anti-drug messages as well as the importance of environmental protection among young people. Under the scheme, participants visit the drug information centre at the Drug Addiction Treatment Centre on Hei Ling Chau. There, they meet young inmates to learn about the harmful effects of drug abuse. They also make vows to support rehabilitated persons and the environment (Chung, 2010).

6.4 Tertiary Crime Prevention: Punishment and Treatment

6.4.1 *Imprisonment and Punishment*

THINKING EXERCISE

What is the purpose of prisons? Does it help the individual reform and reflect, or make him/her worse off because he/she is mixing with 'bad company'?

Imprisonment has been a main feature in tertiary prevention efforts. Early prison reformers were driven by religious ideals (e.g., Elizabeth Fry). The idea was that prison would allow an offender to reflect on his or her behaviour, and combined with religious teachings, the person would reform. Faith-based approaches exist today all over the world. On the other hand, there is a secular school of thought, which argued that crime was an irrational act and that the role of prisons was to reform a person so that he or she would think rationally. Related to this was the idea that government-run prisons should be secular and not religious.

Jeremy Bentham was a reformer who wrote *The Panopticon*, within which he drew a blueprint of a prison layout that could bring about the transformation of inmate behaviour. He introduced the *principle of surveillance*, which proposed that if inmates perceived that they were in constant surveillance, there would be conformity and compliance, because they would not know when they were being watched and, hence, had to be on good behaviour all the time. To achieve this, he proposed that prisons be built with a central tower housing the observers, and rows of single cells arranged in tiers. This is one of the reasons why many prisons were built in this fashion.[9] Over time, the purpose of prisons became more defined and refined. Scholars now believe that imprisonment serves several purposes such as a) *retribution* (you pay for your past bad deeds); b) *incapacitation* (prevent future reoffending); c) *deterrence* (having offenders think before offending because of the consequences); d) *reform and rehabilitation* (altering the offenders thinking and behaviours so that they do not re-offend in the future); e) *signalling* (demonstrating to others that this behaviour is disapproved of) (Putwain & Sammons, 2002). All of these are a part of tertiary crime prevention.

Two other related concepts in prisons regimes are the concepts of *separate* and *silent* systems. The *separate system* separated prisoners from each other during the initial phases of imprisonment so that they could reflect on their actions and become more open to religious teachings. The downside of this isolation approach, however, was that many prisoners developed long-term psychological issues, such as depression and mood disorders. The *silent system*, on the other hand, disallowed all forms of communications between prisoners, to stop prisoners learning from one another or influencing one another negatively. Most prison regimes incorporate these two considerations to various degrees for various programs.

6.4.2 *Rehabilitation and Treatment Programs*

While earlier thinking on prison regime in the yesteryears proposed to create harsh conditions for inmates, this has progressed over time with

---

[9] With technology and CCTVs, this concept may have changed since it is possible to convey the idea that prisoners are being observed with CCTVs.

changing social mores. In 1896, Herbert Gladstone argued in a governmental report that offenders were sent to prisons 'as punishment' and not 'for punishment'. Reduction of liberties, he explained, was bad enough and there was no need to further punish. The report explained that the role of prisons was to reform the person to become a better man or woman (Joyce, 2012). This led to the 'rehabilitative' idea.

Prenzier and Sarre (2009, pp. 260–261) defined rehabilitation as

"...one of the key objectives of criminal justice systems and [it] aims to bring about positive behavioural changes within offenders, encouraging a cessation of offending. The individual is thus transformed in the public and/or private perception from having the identity or image of a criminal to that of a non-criminal or 'normal' citizen. In contemporary rehabilitation programs, offenders participate in a range of therapeutic interventions such as employment and skills programmes and drug and alcohol counselling, either in the community or in prison".

Thus, an important role of prisons is to rehabilitate. Good rehabilitation is crime prevention, since the offender stops committing crimes. This is another tertiary element of crime prevention. So, in this sense, it is not philosophically different from police crime prevention programs which try to prevent offending behaviour. Prisons regimes all over the world seek to secure the rehabilitation of offenders by offering programs that hope to tackle the root causes/ needs of offending behaviour. These include programs that tackled alcohol and abuse, anger management, and specialized programs such as treatment for sex offending and violent offending. Comprehensive programs address issues such as community reintegration, education, and vocational training. Proponents of rehabilitation believed that it could improve individual offenders, increase social participation by making offenders employable, and reduce or eliminate re-offending (Robinson, 2008).

Rehabilitative programs need to be based on a proper understanding of the needs of prisoners or *criminogenic needs* (as discussed earlier in Chapter 1) and a key idea related to this is the 'RNR' framework.

6.4.2.1 *Risks, Needs, and Responsivity Framework (RNR)*

The Risks, Needs, and Responsivity (RNR) framework forms the main thinking behind the modern rehabilitative framework (Andrews *et al.*, 1990). Interventions delivered along the framework proposed by RNR have been empirically validated to be effective at reducing recidivism in high-risk offenders (Andrews & Dowden, 2006). The RNR framework argues that the following are important:

- *Risk*: Certain risk factors are likely to predict criminal behaviour and these factors are associated with specific criminogenic needs. The idea is that we should match program intensity with offender risk. High-risk offenders should be enrolled in a more intense program while low-risk offenders should get minimal intervention.
- *Needs*: Criminogenic needs are functionally related to the crime. Find out what these needs are and attempt to change them. Targeting the wrong needs doesn't change the behaviour that caused the criminal behaviour.
- *Responsivity*: We should take into account individual differences of offenders to consider different motivations and learning styles of offenders.

6.4.2.2 *Understanding 'Risk'*

'Risk' focuses on understanding the likelihood of re-offending and how it can be reduced (Andrews & Bonta, 2006). Knowledge of what constitutes risk and how it can be measured is important as it will help decide who needs help and the level of help they need. Risk factors are either *static* or *dynamic*. *Static factors* relate to a person's prior history. *Dynamic factors* are changeable factors, which can be reduced through treatment. The higher the offender scores on risk factors, the higher their overall risk profile, and in turn, chance of re-offending. Andrews and Bonta (2006) expressed risk in a framework known as the 'Central Eight' (as discussed in Chapter 1, but will be repeated here for the convenience of readers, see also Table 6.7).

Table 6.7: Central 8 and Their Indicators

Factor	Elaboration
Anti-Social Behaviour	Early current involvement in a number and variety of anti-social acts in a variety of settings
Anti-Social Personality	Impulsive, adventurous, pleasure-seeking, restlessly aggressive and irritable, may break laws, shows deviance, not law abiding
Anti-Social Cognitions	Attitudes, values, beliefs and rationalization of deviant behaviour
Anti-Social Associates	Has criminal friends, is isolated from pro-social others (who may prevent him/her from trouble)
Substance Abuse	Abuse of alcohol and/or drugs
Family/Marital Relationships	Inappropriate parental monitoring and disciplining, poor family relationships, weak relationships with partner
School and Work	Poor performance at school or work, low levels of satisfaction
Lacks Pro-Social Recreational Activities/ Leisure	Lack of involvement in pro-social hobbies and sports

THINKING QUESTIONS

Think about the following offenders and their possible criminogenic needs.

Offence/Crime Scenario	What Criminogenic Need?
1. A drug abuser who breaks into a car, steals the cash and cash-card, and sells it for money.	
2. Someone who hacks into a website and leaves a sinister message on the website.	
3. Someone who takes 'up-skirt photos' on the MRT and train station.	
4. Someone who repeatedly slaps and hits 3 random persons on the street and arranges for his friend to record these incidents. They upload it onto the Internet and they all have a good laugh about it.	
5. Someone who breaks into a house then steals all the jewelry and electronics and sells them.	

6.4.2.3 *Understanding 'Needs'*

The *'needs'* principle focuses on targeting criminogenic needs. Each risk factor has specific needs that can be targeted. On the other hand, targeting needs like low self-esteem or personal distress is unlikely to lead to any reductions in recidivism (Ward *et al.*, 2007). This is because these factors are not directly related to crime. See Table 6.8 for needs and possible interventions to address those needs.

Table 6.8: Criminogenic Needs and Possible Interventions to Address Needs

Criminogenic needs	Possible interventions and response in treatment
Anti-social behaviour/current anti-social behaviour	E.g., provide non-criminal alternative behaviour
Anti-social personality	E.g., build problem-solving skills, teach self-management, anger management, coping skills, impulse control
Anti-social cognition/attitudes	E.g., recognize risky thinking and feelings, adopt alternative thinking patterns
Anti-social peers/associates	E.g., reduce association, avoid mixing with 'bad company', enhance contact with 'better people'/pro-social others
Family and relationship stressors	E.g. teaching problem solving in relationship contexts, communications skills
Poor performance in school/work	E.g., increase employability skills, give employment stability, provide education, keep person in education system
Substance use	E.g., reduce/prevent use of substances, increase alternative coping techniques

6.4.2.4 *Understanding Responsivity*

The *'responsitivity'* principle is about delivering services that take into account individual differences, motivations and learning styles. Responsivity can be broken down into *general responsivity* and *specific responsivity*. *General responsivity* emphasizes the style and structure of delivery. A useful style adopts counselling techniques such as being warm and respectful, and establishing a working alliance. *Specific responsivity* acknowledges the need to account for an individual's strengths and personality factors. For example, someone who is depressed may need medical treatment and more time to focus on the key messages conveyed in treatment. Another who has lowered cognitive functioning may need the messages in the rehabilitation program to be simpler and concrete, rather than abstract and theoretical.

THINKING QUESTIONS

Think about the following responsivity issues:

1. How would men differ from women, in terms of responsivity?
2. How would elderly offenders differ from young offenders?
3. How would you see cultural factors influencing responsivity?

6.4.2.5　*RNR instruments*

Andrews and colleagues have developed several instruments, which have been useful in the RNR framework, and these include the following:

- *The Levels of Service Inventory-Revised* (Andrews & Bonta, 1995). This is an older version before the arrival of the LS/CMI.
- *The Level of Service/Case Management Inventory* (LS/CMI) (Andrews *et al.*, 2004) is an assessment and management tool. It covers risk, needs, and responsivity factors. It measures the risks and needs of late adolescent and adult offenders (aged 18 years and older). It is a case management tool. The key areas measured are criminal history, education and employment, family and marital, leisure/recreation, companions, alcohol and drug problem, attitudes/orientation, criminogenic/non-criminogenic needs, and responsivity and case management.
- *The Youth Level of Service/Case Management Inventory* (YLS/CMI) (Hoge & Andrews, 2002). The YLS/CMI is used for young offenders below 21 years old in prison.

In Singapore, the RNR framework has been used for offender rehabilitation in the Singapore Prisons Service (SPS), as well as the Ministry of Social and Family Development (MSF) (Chu *et al.*, 2012;

Chua *et al.*, 2014; Leong, 2012). In the SPS, the LS/CMI is used for inmates who are sentenced for more than a year (Leo, n.d.). Neo (2009) developed norms for male youth offenders within the Singapore context, and Chu and colleagues (2013) have shown that the YLS/CMI (the youth version of the LSI-R) has moderate predictive validity for general recidivism for Singaporean youth offenders. In a study in 2014, Chu and colleagues showed the predictive validity of the YLS/CMI-SV for violent, non-violent, and general recidivism in a sample of 3,264 youth offenders within a Singaporean context. Their results showed that the YLS/CMI-SV was predictive of general, violent, and non-violent recidivism for male youth offenders, although there were mixed results for female youth offenders (Chu *et al.*, 2014).

The RNR framework has been subject to some criticisms. First, without *treatment integrity*, there is likely to be a program 'drift' which diverts from the treatment focus and this, in turn, reduces the effectiveness of the treatment. This could be due to poor delivery fidelity and poor treatment integrity (Goggin & Gendreau, 2006). Second, critics like Ward and Maruna (2007) have argued that the RNR framework is too deficit-focused and negative, and not strengths-focused. They explained that the Good Lives Model (GLM) is better as a strengths-focused approach towards rehabilitation. The GLM takes into account the rights of the offenders as human beings. Third, risk factors are not the same for men and women, although both genders share some similar ones. Men and women both have criminal histories, anti-social attitudes, antisocial friends, substance abuse, and employment/financial factors as common risk factors. However, research is increasingly showing that the predictive risk factors for women appear to be depression/anxiety, unhealthy relationships, psychosis, anger, child abuse, adult abuse, housing safety, and parental stress. The protective factors for women appear to be self-efficacy, family support, educational assets, and parental involvement (National Resource Center on Justice Involved Women, n.d.). Findings suggested that women are more engaged when prison officers use a relationship-based therapeutic approach.

6.4.2.6 *The Good Lives Model for Rehabilitation*

The Good Lives Model (GLM) is premised on the idea that we need to build strengths to reduce re-offending. Interventions should add to an individual's personal functioning, rather than merely removing problem behaviour. According to the GLM theorists, people offend because they are trying to obtain something that they value in their lives. Unfortunately, the desire manifests itself in anti-social behaviours, due to a range of weaknesses within the offender. Following an extensive review of research, Ward and colleagues (Ward & Brown, 2004; Ward & Marshall, 2004) first proposed nine classes of primary valued goods, which was extended to 11 classes as shown in Table 6.9.

Table 6.9:   11 Primary Goods According to the GLM

1	Life	Healthy living and functioning
2	Knowledge	How well-informed one feels about things that are important to them
3	Play	Hobbies and recreational pursuits
4	Work	Mastery experiences
5	Agency	Autonomy, power, and self-directedness
6	Inner Peace	Freedom from emotional turmoil and stress
7	Relatedness	Including intimate, romantic, and familial relationships
8	Community	Connection to wider social groups
9	Spirituality	In the broad sense of finding meaning and purpose in life
10	Pleasure	Feeling good in the here and now
11	Creativity	Expressing oneself through alternative forms

Source: Good Lives Model (2016).

The GLM assumes that all humans seek out all the primary goods to some degree. The weightings an individual gives to specific primary goods reflect an offender's values and priorities at that time. Instrumental goods, or secondary goods, on the other hand, provide means of securing primary goods (Ward *et al.*, 2006). Ward and colleagues explain that completing an apprenticeship might meet the primary goods of knowledge, whereas joining a sports team might satisfy the primary good of being part of a community and having a sense of belonging.

In applying the GLM in practice, assessment is done by identifying the weightings given to the primary goods. This is achieved by:

- Asking about an offender's core commitments in life. What does he or she value on a day-to-day basis? In terms of activities and experiences?
- Identifying the goals and values that were evident in an offender's offence-related actions
- Once an offender's concept of what constitutes a good life is understood, future-oriented secondary goods are formulated collaboratively with the offender and
- Finally, a good lives rehabilitation plan is formulated.

As critics to the GLM model, RNR proponents explained that there is a need to ensure that the focus on criminogenic needs and risk factors are not lost, as these are directly related to reoffending. They explained that the focus of criminal justice agencies should really be on preventing re-offending rather than on the broader humanist goals of achieving primary goods. Moreover, they argue that the latter should be the focus of broader human service institutions such as mental health providers, educational providers, or social service providers (Andrews & Dowden, 2007).

6.4.3 *Corrections in Singapore: The Singapore Prisons Service*

The first jail in Singapore was situated along Bras Basah Canal and the first prison arrived on 18 April 1825 (Singapore Prisons Service, November 2016). Prisoners were housed in temporary huts. A Civil Jail at Pearl's Hill was built later, but it had an overcrowding problem. The British built the maximum security Changi Prison in 1936. Deterrence meant punitive measures rather than rehabilitation. As it presently stands today, the Singapore Prisons Service (SPS) runs several prison and drug rehabilitation centres in Singapore. Its responsibilities encompassed the safe custody, rehabilitation, aftercare of offenders, and preventive education. It remains one of the world's top correctional institutions with low rates of recidivism. The vision of the SPS reads, "As Captains of Lives, we inspire everyone, at every chance, towards a society without re-offending". On its mission, SPS explains, "As a correctional agency, we enforce secure custody of offenders and rehabilitate them, for a safe Singapore". Singapore's current recidivism rate is considered low in comparison with other nations. See Tables 6.10 and 6.11 for inmate population rates and the recidivism[10] rates.

Table 6.12 shows the various programs offered by the Singapore Prisons Service both in care and in the community.

Table 6.10:   Year by Inmate Population

Year	Inmate population[11] (Total convicted penal population)
2010	11,154
2011	10,028
2012	9,901
2013	10,042
2014	9,754
2015	9,602
2016	9,502
2017	8885

Table 6.11:   Recidivism Rates for A New Offence within Two Years of Release

Release cohort year								
2007	2008	2009	2010	2011	2012	2013	2014	2015
26.5%	27.3%	26.7%	23.6%	27.4%	27.6%	25.9%	26.5	25.9

---

[10] The recidivism rate is defined as the percentage of local inmates detained, convicted and imprisoned again for a new offence within two years from their release.

[11] 11 Females were in the range of 8% to 10% of the male inmate population. For example, in 2017, there were 8,051 males and 834 female inmates while in 2016 there were 8,623 males and 879 females.

Table 6.12: Programs by the Singapore Prisons Service

Programs offered during incarceration

Core Skills Programmes	This seeks to equip inmates with the relevant coping skills and to help them adapt to incarceration.
Education	Education programs allow inmates to do their studies within prison.
Work Vocational Training	This is a program where inmates are given vocational training programs to equip them with job skills. Singapore Prisons works with SCORE (See Chapter 1 for SCORE's role) to provide a range of skills training that will prepare inmates for future employment. These include electronics, food preparation, work place literacy and IT skills. The SPS reported that about 4,653 inmates were trained in these programs in 2017 (Singapore Prisons Service News Release, 2018).
Specialised Treatment	These programmes are given to inmates to address their criminogenic needs (e.g., drug addictions).
Family-Focused Programme (FFP)	SPS works with community agencies to provide family-focused programmes to enhance bonding between offenders and their families.
Religious Programme	Inmates are given opportunities to attend religious programs. These programs are delivered by major religious organizations.

Programs offered in the community

Community Reintegration Programme	Delivered just before release, this program seeks to equip inmates with relevant skills and knowledge, so as to prepare them for their release from prison. Topics covered includes employment, family, and community reintegration.

(*Continued*)

Table 6.12: (*Continued*)

Community Education Programmes	Community education programs create awareness on the consequences of criminal behaviour and drug abuse. Visits to prisons and Drug Rehabilitation Centres are facilitated.
Preventive Drug Education (PDE) DRC Visit Programme	Under this program, visits to Changi Prison (coordinated by the CNB) are arranged for youths at risk, who are arrested for drug abuse. The idea is to create awareness amongst students about the consequences of drug abuse and the strict regime that they will undergo if they are incarcerated for drug use.
Prison Visit Education Programme for Schools (PVEPS)	The Singapore Police Force (SPS) and the Ministry of Education jointly arrange this. Schools identify potential participants. They are usually male students between the ages of 13 to 19 years old, who have been identified as 'at-risk' of offending.
Streetwise Programme (SWP)	This is a six-month developmental program, coordinated by the Ministry of Social and Family Development (MSF) and the Secret Societies Branch of CID. It aims to reduce juvenile delinquency by catering to youths who have drifted into street corner gangs.
Probationers' Prison Visit Programme	Probation is a community-based program administered by the Ministry of Social and Family Development for offenders. Participants are probationers with poor progress under supervision and are identified by the Probation Service Branch of MSF. They are mandated by the Juvenile Courts to attend the program.
Conditional Remission System and Mandatory Aftercare Scheme	In the past, the remission system allowed for offenders to be released with no conditions, after serving two-thirds of their sentence. This new Conditional Remission System (CRS), subjected some types of offenders (e.g. drug offenders and serious crime officers) to conditions upon their release. A selected group of ex-offenders will have mandatory aftercare conditions imposed. The Mandatory Aftercare Scheme (MAS) is a structured aftercare regime that provides enhanced community support, counseling and case management with tight supervision.

Source: Adapted from the Singapore Prisons Service Website.

6.4.4 *New Penologies*

How will punishment regimes change in the future? Cohen (1985) explained that the four 'D's of new penologies are *D*epenalisation, *D*iversion, *D*einstitutionalization, and *D*ecarceration.

- *Depenalisation* refers to the efforts taken to widen the range of non-imprisonable offences. The idea is to make prisons the last resort for the courts. This effort includes reducing the scope of criminal law and attempting to address offenses with civil remedies.
- *Diversion* diverts offenders from formal punishment. Some examples are police warnings and cautions, and family conferences.
- *De-institution* is the idea of seeking alternatives to prisons and institutions. These may include probations, suspended sentences, or community service orders.
- *Decarceration* is about reducing the time spent in prison environments. Some examples include parole, day-leave, and conditional release (Coomber *et al.*, 2015).

Some of the above-mentioned measures are discussed in the sections to come.

6.4.5 *Treatment at the Ministry of Social and Family Development (Centre of Forensic Mental Health)*

At the Ministry of Social and Family Development (Centre for Forensic Mental Health), services are offered in the area of assessment and treatment for youth and adults with sexual and violent offending behaviours. Some of the programmes include:

- *Positive Adolescent Sexuality Treatment* (PAST): This is a cognitive-behavioural group treatment program for adolescents who have committed sexual offences,

- *Positive Psychotherapy Group* (PPG): This is a cognitive-behavioural group treatment program for adult men who have committed sexual offences,
- *Basic Education and Sexuality Treatment* (BEST): This is a specialised treatment program for adolescents and adult males with special needs (e.g., intellectual disability) who have committed sexual offences, and finally
- *Violence Prevention Programme* (VPP): This is a cognitive-behavioural group treatment program for adolescents who have committed violent offences or engaged in serious or chronic aggression (Ministry of Social and Family Development, n.d.).

6.4.6 *Community-based Corrections and Treatments*

Prison regimes distinguish between serious and less serious offences. Serious offences require the offender to be removed from society and imprisoned. Less serious ones require the offender to serve some penalty, while remaining in the community. In England, community-based sentences include some of the following: (a) unpaid work, (b) program attendance, (c) prohibition of activity, (d) curfew, (e) residence requirement, (f) mental health treatment, (g) drug rehabilitation, and (h) supervision (Joyce, 2012). The Probation Service in most parts of the world have been set up as a way of administering community sentences. Singapore follows many of these practices as well. Explaining the Singapore approach, the previous Attorney General, V.K. Rajah explained:

> "Criminal law must not be enforced for its own sake, but for the greater good of society...not every offender is a hardened criminal and there can be extenuating circumstances. We have a framework for assessing such matters. So, sometimes, after taking into consideration the factual matrix, we are prepared to consider issuing advisories or proceeding on reduced charges"
>
> (Vijayan, 2016)

He explained that punishment is not always the main consideration when a prosecution is pursued. Prosecutors will therefore ask the court to consider giving out community sentences in appropriate cases (Vijayan, 2016).

The Singapore Community Court sees a variety of cases. They include offenders aged 16–18 years, offenders below 21 years old who have been accused of theft, violence, sex, gambling, or drug-related offences, offenders with mental disorders, attempted suicide cases, family violence cases, cruelty to animal cases, cases which impact race relations, persons who are 65 years old and above, and cases involving chronic addiction problems, and shop theft cases.

Community-Based Sentencing (CBS) was introduced in 2010 in Singapore. The Courts are given more 'graduated sentencing options' for minor offences.

The Community Court Secretariat supports the Community Court. The Secretariat has psychologists, social workers, and administrative staff who help in the assessment, referral, management, and coordination of cases. They work closely with community agencies in Singapore to provide rehabilitation services and treatment options for offenders.

There are several community-based sentencing options such as:

(a) Mandatory Treatment Order (MTO), through the Institute of Mental Health (for offenders suffering from psychiatric conditions),
(b) Community Service Order (CSO) for offenders to make amends to the community by performing unpaid community service,
(c) Day Reporting Order (DRO) administered by the Singapore Prison Service (to report to a day reporting centre for monitoring, counselling, and rehabilitation), and
(d) Short Detention Order (SDO), where offenders can be detained in prison for a period not exceeding 14 days.

If the CBS is successfully completed, the criminal record will be rendered spent, i.e., the offender is deemed to have no record of that conviction (State Courts, n.d.).

Does research show that community sentences are effective? Community sentences do have some advantages. For example, they reduce the burden on prisons. Also, they are reform- and rehabilitation-focused. These is evidence that community sentences are more effective in changing behaviour compared to short-term prison sentences (Joyce, 2012). From a financial angle, they are less expensive as prison custody costs a lot more. On the other hand, critics have argued that community sentencing has limitations. The public does not view these sentences as sufficiently harsh. Sometimes, rehabilitation officers or probation officers may not want to escalate difficult cases who fail to comply with order or breach their agreements, because they worry that the offender will be penalized in a harsher manner. Hence, the offender might not really reform and may re-offend. One other concern by critics is the concept of *net-widening*. Before community sentencing was introduced, a police officer may warn an offender and let him off or threaten further action if he does not behave. With community sentencing, low-level offenders are entered into the criminal justice machinery at an early stage and will not be able to break away from future monitoring from government machinery (Joyce, 2012). Worall (1997) argued that the net of control encompasses a larger area of the community, its thinner mesh widened to entrap even smaller fish. Once caught in the net, disciplinary intervention penetrates deeper.

6.4.7 *Other Criminal Justice Concepts*

6.4.7.1 *Restorative Justice*

Another community-oriented response to crime is the concept of Restorative Justice (RJ). It has been defined as consisting of values, aims, and processes that aim to repair the harm caused by criminal behaviour (Young & Hoyle, 2003). RJ involves activities such as:

- *Victim offender reconciliation* is a one-to-one mediation meeting facilitated by a mediator and sometimes involves both mediation and conferencing.
- *Family group conferencing* is for young offenders. This started early in New Zealand and is based on Maori methods of conflict

resolution. This is similar to peacemaking circles. The idea is to bring parties together in a dialogue which allows the victim to share how the crime has impacted him or her personally, and for the perpetrator to explain him/herself and 'repair the harm done', and

- *Reintegrative shaming* is another process used in RJ. The process of shaming is used as a tool to secure reconciliation of members of the community that crime has brought into conflict.

The central idea behind restorative justice was for the offender to avoid formal systems of justice and to use the neighbourhood, communities and family groups to deal with the issue. This not only reduces the strain on the formal criminal justice system, it helps the offender reintegrate better. When families and social systems are involved, it signals that the many parties have a shared responsibility for crime (which was the point made in Chapter 1, see Section 1.7.3).

The philosophy of the Youth Courts in Singapore is based on restorative justice, which recognizes the potential for reform in young offenders. In the Youth Courts, the youths are made accountable for their offending behaviour and will take responsibility for their behaviour by making reparations to society, whether through community work, restitution, compensation, or apology to the victim. Parents of the offender/delinquent youth are provided the opportunity to take responsibility for their child's behaviour (Family Justice Courts, n.d.).

Does restorative justice work? Well, the key issue is how the perpetrator reacts to the process. Will he or she take personal responsibility or blame someone else (e.g., parents, harsh childhood)? Will shaming work or will it result in the offender feeling humiliated? It has been argued that shaming may work for more communalistic societies like Japan, as opposed to Western societies, which lean towards a more individualistic culture. Another critique is whether the offender is able to express himself or herself meaningfully to repair the damage, because if he/she does not do it well, things may get worse. Of course, the important issue to consider in mediation meetings is whether the victim is comfortable enough to want to see the perpetrator (Joyce, 2012).

6.4.7.2   *Therapeutic Jurisprudence (TJ)*

Proponents of Therapeutic Jurisprudence (TJ) argue that the behavioural sciences can be used to minimize the negative impact of laws, legal processes, and institutions on its participants (Wexler, 2000). The work of TJ has had a great influence in justice systems as evidenced by the development of family violence courts, community courts, juvenile courts, and courts relating to mental health issues. TJ values should not dominate over the other values of the justice system. Instead, its role is to augment the other values of the legal system. For example, when a decision which seems anti-therapeutic is made, TJ may suggest some solutions to mitigate the negative impact of hard decisions. For example, Judge David Letcher of the North Liverpool Community Justice Centre explained that when he imposes a jail sentence, he would send the offender a letter explaining the reasons for his decision (King & Wexler, 2010). Some areas of application in TJ are in:

- Offender rehabilitation,
- Studying the impact of criminal victimization,
- Studying the effects of court processes on witnesses,
- Studying the effects of family law processes on parents and children, and
- Studying the effect of civil law processes on parties involved in a dispute.

TJ has been described as humanistic and a psychologically optimal way of problem-solving in human societies; but, it has also been viewed in a larger sense as a movement towards non-adversarial justice (Daicoff, 2000; Freiberg, 2007).

6.5   Summary

- We can respond to crime by looking at it from primary, secondary and tertiary prevention lens. All three are important and play different roles within the criminal justice system.
- We should try to deal with the roots of criminal behaviour before it surfaces (primary prevention); but when it does, we should address

those persons and situations that are most 'at-risk' (secondary prevention), and if this fails, address the person or issue such that it does not reoccur or repeat (tertiary prevention).

- As a key primary prevention effort, much can be done by managing behaviour using situational crime prevention efforts, especially though situational crime prevention (e.g., the 25 SCP measures). It may be far more practical to *manage* behaviour, rather than *change* behaviour.
- This should not mean that primary prevention efforts though social development should take a back seat, since every nation should endeavour to create conditions for its citizens where crime and security is a low concern. It is the foundation for everything else: wealth generation, happy families, and personal aspirations. Moulding individual and societal behaviour is, however, effortful and it takes a longer time, even though it remains an important social endeavour to create a better society.
- Secondary prevention measures are critical, even though it takes more to figure who and which situations are worth focusing on. Secondary prevention is about providing the evidence-base behind the 'what works, when, why, and for whom'.
- When we examine tertiary measures, it is useful to consider evidence-based practices, especially in the area of rehabilitation. All in all, there is evidence that rehabilitation is generally successful in reducing re-offending and it does improve offenders. Many report better employment, education, and improved family relationships. On the other hand, there are others who believe some rehabilitative options, especially those that allow for discretionary power in courts and parole boards, and in extra judicial specialists such as counsellors, psychologists, and parole officers, could result in the net-widening effect. When it works well, good rehabilitation results in recidivism and it is, in fact, effective crime prevention.

Relevant Journals/Books

Crime Prevention and Community Safety
Security and Crime Prevention

Crime Prevention and Reduction Programs
Journal of Scandinavian Studies in Criminology and Crime Prevention

Local Books

'Policing Singapore in the 19th–20th centuries'. Peer M. Akbur. 2002.
'Friends in blue: the police and the public in Singapore'. Stella R. Quah, and Jon S.T. Quah. 1987.
'Making Singapore safe: thirty years of the National Crime Prevention Council'. Sim, Susan, 2011.
'Setia dan Bakti: 50 stories of loyalty and service'. Susan Sim, chief editor & writer; Francis Chan, editor & writer. 2015.
'Home at Mount Pleasant: the Senior Police Officers' Mess of the Singapore Police Force'. Editorial consultant & writer, Koh Buck Song and photography, Desmond Wang. Koh, Buck Song. 2007.
'In the service of the nation'. John Drysdale. 1985.
'Protect your home and property: a police guide to crime prevention' Singapore Police Force. Singapore. Police Force., 1978.
'Singapore: A Police Background' (First Edition) by Rene Onraet. Book, 1945–1947.
'The making of captains of lives: prison reform in Singapore', 1999 to 2007. Chua, Chin Kiat, 2012.
'Captains of lives: a Singapore Prison Service special'.
Book, 2006.
'Dare to strike: 25 years of the Central Narcotics Bureau' Singapore. Central Narcotics Bureau. 1996.

E-Resources and Books

Police Life Monthly (Singapore)
Everyday Guardians: 50 years of National Service in the Home Team. Koh Buck Song.
Sentencing Principles in Singapore. Kow Keng Siong. Academy Publishing, pp. 2–9.

Statistics, Singapore Police Force. https://www.police.gov.sg/news-and-publications/statistics

SG SECURE. https://www.police.gov.sg/sgsecure

Yellow Ribbon Project. http://www.yellowribbon.org.sg/

Delta League (on Facebook). https://m.facebook.com/DeltaLeague2018/

DanceWorks (CNB Initiative). https://www.cnb.gov.sg/newsandevents/events

Data on Crime. https://data.gov.sg/dataset/overall-crime-cases-crime-rate

World Prison Brief. http://www.prisonstudies.org/country/singapore

Singapore Prisons Service, Annual Statistics Release. http://www.sps.gov.sg/news-about-us/in-the-news/2016-singapore-prison-service-annual-statistics-release

Prison Annual 2016. http://www.sps.gov.sg/docs/default-source/publication/sps_annuals_2016_lowres.pdf

Department of Statistics Singapore (on Crime). https://www.singstat.gov.sg/statistics/browse-by-theme/culture-recreation-and-public-safety

Some Legal Cases of Interest

PP vs Kwong Kok Hing (2008). 2 SLR 684, CA (Factors to be considered in sentencing)

PP vs Vitria Depsi Wahyuni (alias Fitriah) (2013). 1 SLR 699, CA (Sentencing Considerations)

PP vs Mohammad Al-Ansari bin Basri (2008) 1 SLR 449 (Young Young offender considerations)

PP vs Adith Sarvotham (2014) SGHC 103 (Young offender considerations)

Sample Research Essay Titles

- Describe the main differences between primary, secondary, and tertiary crime prevention.
- You are asked to design a situational crime prevention program using the 25 techniques to address the rising trend of cyber scams. How would you go about doing it?

- Should 'deterrence' be the main principle of sentencing someone?
- Compare the RNR framework and the GLM model.
- The Commissioner of Prisons asks you to design a sex offender treatment program for young offenders. How would you do it and what would you include in the program?

References

Andrews, D. & Dowden, C. (2007). The Risk–Need–Responsivity Model of Assessment and Human Service in Prevention and Corrections: Crime-Prevention. Jurisprudence. *Canadian Journal of Criminology and Criminal Justice, 49*(4), 439–464.

Andrews, D.A., Zinger, I., Hoge, R.D., Bonta, J., Gendreau, P., & Cullen, F.T. (1990). Does Correctional treatment work? A psychologically informed metaanalysis. *Criminology, 28,* 369–404.

Andrews, D.A. & Dowden, C. (2005). Managing correctional treatment for reduced recidivism: A meta analytic review of program integrity. *Legal and Criminological Psychology, 10,* 173–187.

Andrew, D.A. & Dowden, C., (2006). Risk principle in case classification in correctional treatment: A meta analytic investigation. *International Journal of Offender Therapy and Comparative Criminology, 50,* 88–100.

Andrew, D.A. & Bonta, J. (2006). *The Psychology of Criminal Conduct* (4th ed.). Newark, NJ: LexisNexis.

Armitage, R. (2002). *To CCTV or Not to CCTV? A Review of Current Research into the Effectiveness of CCTV Systems in Reducing Crime.* London: NACRO. Community Safety Practice Briefing.

Arrington, R. (2007). *Crime Prevention: The Law Enforcement Officers' Practical Guide.* Sudbury, MA: Joes and Bartlett.

Australian Institute of Criminology (2004). *Approaches to understanding crime prevention.* May 2003, No 1. Retrieved from http://www.aic.gov.au/media_library/publications/crm/crm001.pdf on 11/18/2016.

Babuta, A. (2017). *Big Data and Policing: An assessment of law enforcement requirements, expectations and priorities.* Occasional paper. Royal United Services Institute for Defence and Security Studies.

Bachner, J. (2013). *Predictive Policing Preventing Crime with Data and Analytics.* IBM Centre for the Improvement of Government: Improving performance series.

Bonta, J., Law, M., & Hanson, R.K. (1998). The prediction of criminal and violent recidivism among mentally disordered offenders: A meta-analysis. *Psychological Bulletin, 123,* 123–142.

Bottomley, K. & Pease, K. (1986). *Crime and Punishment: Interpreting the Data*. Milton Keynes, Open University Press.

Bowers, K.J., Johnson, S.D., & Pease, K. (2004). Prospective hot spotting in the future of crime mapping? *British Journal of Criminology, 44*(5).

Brantingham, P.L. & Brantingham, P.J. (1993). Environment, routine, and situation: Toward a pattern theory of crime. In R.V. Clarke & M. Felson (Eds.), *Routine Activity and Rational Choice. Advances in Criminological Theory*, Vol. 5. New Brunswick, NJ: Transaction Publications.

Canadian Association of Chiefs of Police (2002). *Resolution on community safety, health and wellbeing*. Retrieved from www.cacp.ca/english/resolutions/past5/2002.pdf.

Canadian Council of Social Development (1989). *Crime Prevention Through Social Development A Discussion Paper for Social Policy Makers and Practitioners*. Retrieved from http://www.ccsd.ca/resources/CrimePrevention/pdf/cptsd1984.pdf.

Carrington, K. (1993). *Offending Girls: Sex, Youth and Justice*. Sydney: Allen and Unwin.

Cheong, D. (2016, May). Warning: better slow down at these hot spots. *The Straits Times*.

Chesterman, S. (2014, May 24). Tinkering with the machinery of death. *The Straits Times*.

Chu, C.M., Lee, Y., Zeng, G., Yim, G., Tan, C. Y., Ang, Y., & Ruby, K. (2013). *Assessing Youth Offenders with the YLS/CMI in a non-Western context*. Manuscript submitted for publication.

Chu, C.M., Teoh, J., Lim, H.S., Long, M., Tan, E.E., Tan, A., & Puay, L.L. (2012). *The implementation of the Risk, Needs, Responsivity framework across the youth justice services in Singapore*. Presented at the Australian and New Zealand Association for Psychiatry, Psychology, and Law Congress.

Chu, C.M., Yu, H., Lee, Y., & Zeng, G. (2014). The utility of the YLS/CMI-SV for Assessing Youth Offenders in Singapore. *Criminal Justice and Behaviour, 41*(12), 1437–1457.

Chua, J.R., Chu, C.M., Yim, G., Chong, D., & Teoh, J. (2014). Implementation of the Risk–Need–Responsivity Framework across the Juvenile Justice Agencies in Singapore. *Psychiatry, Psychology and Law, 21*(6), 877–889.

Chung, M. (2010). *Effective Resettlement of Offenders by Strengthening 'Community Reintegration Factors*. Retrieved from www.unafei.or.jp/english/pdf/RS_No82/No82_08PA_Chung.pdf.

Clarke, R.V. (1995). Situational crime prevention in Building a Safer Society: Strategic Approaches to Crime Prevention. In M. Tonry & F. David (Eds.), *Chicago: Crime and Justice*, Volume 6. The University of Chicago Press.

Clarke, R.V. & Felson, M. (Eds.) (1993). *Routine Activity and Rational Choice. Advances in Criminological Theory*, Vol. 5. New Brunswick, NJ: Transaction Books.

Clark, R.V. (2005). Seven misconceptions of situational crime prevention. In N. Tilley (Ed.), *Handbook of Crime Prevention and Community Safety* (pp. 39–70). Willan Publishing.

Cohen, S. (1985). *Visions of Social Control: Crime, Punishment and Classification.* Cambridge: Polity.

Cohen, L.E. & Felson, M. (1979). Social change and crime rate trends: A routine activity approach. *American Sociological Review, 44*, 588–605.

Cornish, D. & Clarke, R. (1987). Understanding crime displacement: An application of rational choice theory. *Criminology, 25*(4), 933–947.

Coomber, R., Donnermeyer, J.F., McElrath, K., & Scott, J. (2015). *Key Concepts in Crime and Society.* Los Angeles, CA: SAGE.

Durrant, R. (2013). *An Introduction to Criminal Psychology.* New York, NY: Routledge.

Goldblatt, P. & Lewis, C. (1998). *Reducing Offending: An Assessment of Research Evidence on Ways of Dealing with Offending Behaviour.* London: Home Office.

Eysenck, H.J. & Gudjonsson, G.H. (1989). *The Causes and Cures of Criminality.* New York, NY: Plenum Press.

Family Justice Courts (n.d.). *Youth Court Matters, Philosophy: Restorative Justice.* Retrieved from https://www.familyjusticecourts.gov.sg/Common/Pages/YouthMatters.aspx.

Felson, M. (1986). Linking criminal choices, routine activities, informal control, and criminal outcomes. In D. Cornish & R.V. Clarke (Eds.), *The Reasoning Criminal: Rational Choice Perspectives on Offending.* New York, NY: Springer-Verlag.

Felson, M. (1994). *Crime and Everyday Life: Insight and Implications for Society.* Thousand Oaks, CA: Pine Forge Press.

Garland, D. (1996). The limits of the sovereign state: strategies for crime control in contemporary society. *British Journal of Criminology, 36*(4), 445–471.

Garrido, V. & Redondo, S. (1993). The institutionalisation of young offenders. *Criminal Behaviour and Mental Health, 3*(4), 336–348.

Good Lives Model (2016). *The Good Lives Model.* Retrieved from http://www.goodlivesmodel.com/

Groth, A.N., Hobson, W.F., & Gary, T.S. (1982). The child molester, clinical observations. In J. Conte & D. Shore (Eds), *Social work and Child Sexual Abuse.* New York, NY: Harworth.

Joyce, P. (2012). *Criminology: A Complete Introduction.* London: Hodder & Stoughton.

Hesseling, R. (1994). Displacement: A review of the empirical literature. In R.V. Clarke (Ed.), *Crime Prevention Studies*, vol. 3. Monsey, NY: Criminal Justice Press.

Heng, J. (2016, March 9). Network of CCTV cameras proving effective. *The Straits Times.*

He, G.S., Ponnuru, V., & Chow, E. (2010). *Crime data analysis* (Professor Fei Da Zhu). Data Mining and Business Analytics Project. Singapore: Singapore Management University.

Hollin, C.R. (2013). *Psychology and Crime: An Introduction to Criminological Psychology* (2nd ed.). London: Routledge.

HM Inspectorate of Constabulary (2000). *Beating Crime.* London: Home Office.

Husain, A. (March 2014). More officers needed to better patrol hot spots: Police chief. *Today.* Retrieved http://www.todayonline.com/singapore/more-officersneeded-better-patrol-hot-spots-police-chief?singlepage=true.

Kasim, A. (2016). *Delta League: Changing Lives Through Football.* National Crime Prevention Council. Singapore: Marshall Cavendish.

Koh, B.S. (2016). *Our Guardians.* Singapore: The Straits Times Press.

Leo, T.H.S. (n.d.). *Current evidence-based practices in the Singapore prisons.* Retrieved http://www.unafei.or.jp/english/pdf/RS_No88/No88_14VE_ Leo_Current. pdf

Leinweber, D.J. (2007). Stupid data miner tricks: Over fitting the S&P 500. *Journal of Investing, 16*(1), 15–22.

Leong, L. (2012). *The Story of the Singapore Prisons Service: From Custodians to Captain of Lives: A Case Study.* Singapore: Singapore Civil Service College. Retrieved from http://www.pgionline.com/wp-content/uploads/2015/08/ The-Story-ofthe-Singapore-Prison-Service.pdf

Martin, A.A. & Greg, W.J. (2008). Crime Prevention and the Science of Where People Are. *Criminal Justice Policy Review, 19*(2), 164–180.

Micheals, S. (2014). Dance festival to make attendees watch an anti-drugs video. *The Guardian.*

Ministry of Foreign Affairs, Singapore (2014, September 25). Transcript of Statement by Minister for Foreign Affairs and Minister for Law K Shanmugam at the High-Level Side Event at the 69th Session of the United Nations General Assembly, "Moving Away from the Death Penalty: National Leadership".

Ministry of Social and Family Development (n.d.). Retrieved from https://www.msf.gov. sg/about-MSF/our-people/Divisions-at-MSF/Social-Development-andSupport/ Rehabilitation-and-Protection-Group/Clinical-and-Forensic-Psychology-Service/ Pages/Centre-for-Forensic-Mental-Health-(CFMH).aspx.

Muncie, J. & McLaughlin, E. (2001). *The Problem of Crime.* Sage

National Crime Prevention Council (n.d.). *Crime Prevention Through Environmental Design Guidebook.* Singapore: National Crime Prevention Council.

National Centre for Justice Involved Women (n.d.). Retrieved from http://cjinvolvedwomen.org/

National Institute of Justice (2010, May 25). *How to identify hot spots.* Retrieved from http://www.nij.gov/topics/law-enforcement/strategies/hot-spot-policing/pages/identifying.aspx.

Neo, L.H. (2009). *A retrospective study of factors predicting breach and reoffending in local young offenders under the purview of RPRSD.* RPRSD (MCYS). Unpublished manuscript.

Nordfjærn, T., Bretteville-Jensen, A.L., Edland-Gryt, M., & Gripenberg, J. (2016). Risky substance use among young adults in the nightlife arena: An underused setting for risk-reducing interventions? *Scandinavian Journal of Public Health, 44*(7), 638–645.

Nordfjaern, T. (2017). Violence involvement among nightlife patrons: The relative role of demographics and substance use. *Aggress Behavior, 43*(4), 398–407.

Office of the Surgeon General (2001). *Youth Violence: A Report of the Surgeon General.* Washington, DC: U.S. Department of Health and Human Services, Office of the Secretary, Office of Public Health and Science, Office of the Surgeon General. Retrieved from www.surgeongeneral.gov/library/youthviolence.

Oxford Dictionary of National Biography (2004). *Fry, Elizabeth (1780–1845).* Oxford University Press.

Painter, K. & Farrington, D.P. (1997). The crime reducing effect of improved street lighting: The dudley project. In R.V. Clarke (Ed.), *Situational Crime Prevention: Successful Case Studies* (2nd ed.). Guilderland, NY: Harrow and Heston.

Pease, K. (1998). *Repeat Victimisation: Taking Stock.* Crime detection and prevention series, Paper 90. London: The Stationery Office.

Pease, K. (1991). The Kirkholt Project: Preventing Burglary on a British Public Housing Estate. *Security Journal, 2,* 73–77.

Pearsall, B. (2010). *Predictive policing: the future of law enforcement.* National Institute of Justice. No. 266.

Prenzler, T. & Sarre, R. (2009). The criminal justice system. In H. Hayes & T. Prenzler (Eds.), *Introduction to Crime and Criminology* (pp. 259–273). Sydney: Pearson Education Australia.

Quah, J.S.T. (1992). Crime prevention Singapore style. *Asian Journal of Public Administration, 14*(2), 149–185.

Robinson, G. (2008). Late-modern rehabilitation: The evolution of a penal strategy. *Punishment and Society, 10*(4), 429–445.

Rutter, M. (1987). Psychosocial resilience and protective mechanisms. *American Journal of Orthopsychiatry, 57*(3), 316–331.

Reppetto, T.A. (1976). Crime prevention and the displacement phenomenon. *Crime and Delinquency, 22*(2), 166–177.

Siegel, L.J. (2010). *Criminology: Theories, Patterns, Typologies.* Singapore: Wadsworth.

Sherman, L., Buerger, M., & Gartin, P. (1989). *Repeat Call Address Policing: The Minneapolis RECAP Experiment.* Final Report to the National Institute of Justice. Washington, DC: Crime Control Institute.

Sherman, L.W., Farrington, D.P., Welsh, B.C., & MacKenzie, D.L. (2002). *Evidence Based Crime Prevention.* New York, NY: Rutledge.

Sim, S. & Khader, M. (2017). *The Ostrich, The Ah-Long, The Con Man and the Creepy Guy. The Story of Crime Prevention in Singapore.* Singapore: National Crime Prevention Council Singapore.

Singh, J. (n.d.). *Community policing in the context of Singapore.* Retrieved from http://www.unafei.or.jp/english/pdf/PDF_rms/no56/56-11.pdf.

State Court (n.d.). *Community Courts.* Retrieved https://www.statecourts.gov.sg/CriminalCase/Documents/Community%20Court.pdf

Tan, H.S. (2012). *Youth at Risk in Singapore.* Retrieved from https://www.nac.gov.sg/naccorp/dam/jcr:1d8343b2-1434-4d15-ac45-a7c4dc0e53e1.

Tang, S. (2010). *Effective Rehabilitation and Reintegration of Offenders.* Retrieved http://www.unafei.or.jp/english/pdf/RS_No82/No82_07VE_Tang.pdf.

The Straits Times (2016). *Warning: Better Slow Down at These Hot Spots.* Retrieved from http://www.straitstimes.com/singapore/transport/warning-better-slow-down-atthese-hot-spots.

The Star (2017). *Nur Jazlan Moots CCTV Surveillance Plan.* Retrieved from https://www.thestar.com.my/news/nation/2017/09/11/nur-jazlan-mootscctv-surveillance-plan/.

Tilley, N. (2005). *Handbook of Crime Prevention and Community Safety.* Cullompton, UK: Willan Publishing.

Seow, B.Y. (2017, March 4). Singapore police seen as world-class crime fighters: Survey. *The Straits Times.*

Singapore Prisons Service (2016). *The Prisons Story.* Retrieved from http://www.sps.gov.sg/about-us/prison-story/.

Singapore Prisons Service News Release (2018). *Statistics.* Retrieved from http://www.sps.gov.sg/Data/Editor/Documents/SPS%20Annual%20Stats%20Release%20for%202017_SG%20Press%20Centre.pdf.

Sklansky, D.A. (2011, March). The Persistent Pull of Police Professionalism. *New Perspectives in Policing.*

Ward, T. & Marshall, W.L. (2004). Good lives, aetiology and the rehabilitation of sex offenders: A bridging theory. *Journal of Sexual Aggression, 10*, 153–169.

Ward, T. & Brown, M. (2004). The good lives model and conceptual issues in offender rehabilitation. *Psychology, Crime, & Law, 10*, 243–257.

Ward, T., Vess, J., Gannon, T., & Collie, R. (2006). Risk management or goods promotion: The relationship between approach and avoidance goal in the treatment of sex offenders. *Aggression and Violent Behaviour, 11*, 378–393.

Weisburd, D. & Mazerolle, L.G. (2000). Crime and disorder in drug hot spots: Implications for theory and practice in policing. *Police Quarterly, 3*, 331–334.

Wilson, D.B., Gallagher, C.A., & MacKenzie, D.L. (2000). A meta-analysis of corrections-based education, vocation, and work programs for adult offenders. *Journal of Research in Crime and Delinquency, 37*(4), 347–368.

Weigend, T. (1988). The legal and practical problems posed by the difference between Criminal Law and Administrative Penal Law. *Revue Internationale de Droit Pénal, 59*, 67–86.

Winfree, L.T. & Abadinsky, H. (2003). *Understanding Crime, Theory and Practice* (2nd ed.). Singapore: Thomson Learning.

Winn, R. (1999). *Running the Red: An Evaluation of Strathclyde Police's Red Light Camera Initiative — Research Findings.* Scottish Government Office.

Worall, A. (1997). *Punishment in the Community. The Future of Criminal Justice.* London: Harlow.

UNODC (n.d.). *Youth Crime Prevention through Sports Preventing Youth Crime Through Sports-Based Programmes and Life Skills Training.* Retrieved from https://www.unodc.org/documents/dohadeclaration/Sports/infosheet/Info_sheet_Sports_EN.pdf.

Vijayan, J. (2016, January 11). Attorney General calls for more community-based sentencing options for less serious crimes. *The Straits Times.*

Young, R. & Hoyle, C. (2003). Restorative Justice and Punishment. In S. McConville (Ed.), *The Use of Punishment.* Cullompton, Devon: Willan Publishing.

CHAPTER 7
TERRORISM AND VIOLENT EXTREMISM

"With guns you can kill terrorists, with education you can kill terrorism."

Malala Yousafzai
Pakistani activist for female education, and the youngest Nobel
Prize laureate

7.1 Introduction

Not all terrorism acts are religiously motivated, even though much of what we read about in the news seems so. Therefore, it would be interesting to start this chapter with an example of right-wing terrorism. Read the case study below to discover more.

CASE STUDY:
The Norway Attack

When people think of Norway, the impression of an idyllic Scandinavian country with picturesque scenery of mountains and coastal fjords comes first to mind, *not* terrorism. The 2011 Norway terror attacks, however, was the deadliest attack in Norway since World War II. Anders Behring Breivik (ABB) claimed 77 lives and injured many. The attacks on 22 July 2011 started off in Oslo, the capital of Norway. A car bomb was detonated in Regjeringskvartalet, central Oslo, outside the executive government quarter which housed the Office of the Prime Minister and the Ministry of Justice. ABB had driven a white Volkswagen van to the front of the government buildings, initially coming to a halt, with hazard light warnings for a few minutes. He parked the van in front of the building and left the vehicle for another car he had prepared for his escape. When

---

(*Continued*)

(Continued)

the bomb in the van went off, it killed eight people, and injured more than 200 people. The bomb, which was composed of a mixture of fertilizer and fuel oil, resulted in fires. The resultant blast shattered all the windows in the vicinity. The whole area was filled with glass and debris.

ABB, who was dressed as a policeman, managed to flee the crime scene without attracting much attention, save for a passer-by noticing a policeman with a face shield getting into an unmarked vehicle. Unimpeded, ABB was on the move and was about to carry out the second part of his plan. The second attack was deadlier. ABB had obtained two guns (a semi-automatic rifle and a pistol) a few years prior to the attacks. He began a mass shooting at Utøya island, which hosted about 600 teenagers who were there for the annual Norwegian Labour Party's AUF youth camp. ABB had taken a public ferry to the island, again, posing as a policeman. After shooting the camp organiser and a security officer, ABB searched for people around him and opened fire into the crowd indiscriminately. It was a scene of terror as ABB killed and wounded numerous people. He even used hollow-point bullets as ammunition to increase tissue damage to his victims. In the middle of the shooting, ABB called the Norwegian emergency number twice to surrender but hung up both times, and the police was unable to contact him after each time. Curiously enough, when the police arrived at the scene in Utøya, ABB willingly surrendered in spite of having unused ammunition.

On the day of the attacks, ABB electronically distributed a text titled *2083: A European Declaration of Independence*, describing his ideology. In it, he discusses his opposition to Islam and advocates for the deportation of all Muslims from Europe (McIntyre, 2011).

The ABB incident is an example of right-wing terrorism. Right-wing terrorism includes neo-nazism, racism, xenophobia, and opposition to immigration. This type of terrorism tends to be sporadic, with little or no international organization (Moghadam, 2006; Mudde, 2010). Presently, some countries in Europe seem to be affected by this brand of terrorism. Dr. Jessica Stern, a terrorism expert from Boston University, explains that Germany's domestic intelligence agency estimates that there were 22,150 right-wing terrorists in Germany alone in 2012, and almost half of them are violence-prone. These terrorists are also growing in number in Sweden and Norway (Stern, 2014).

This chapter will attempt to elaborate on terrorism and the main issues and debates surrounding the study of terrorism.

7.1.1 *Defining Terrorism*

Terrorism experts, Drs. Alex Schmid and Albert Jongman provide a comprehensive definition of terrorism. According to *Political Terrorism: A Research Guide to the Concepts, Theories, Databases and Literature* (Schmid & Jongman, 1988), they argue that:

1. Terrorism refers to a tactic of fear-generating, coercive political violence, and a conspiratorial practice of calculated, direct violent action without legal or moral restraints, targeting mainly civilians and non-combatants, performed for its propagandistic and psychological effects on audiences;
2. Terrorism as a tactic is employed in three main contexts: (i) illegal state repression, (ii) propagandistic agitation by non-state actors in times of peace, and (iii) as an illicit tactic of irregular warfare employed by state- and non-state actors;
3. It is physical violence or threat employed by terrorist actors which involves single-phase acts of lethal violence (such as bombings); dual-phased life-threatening incidents (like kidnapping, and hostage-taking for coercive bargaining) as well as multi-phased sequences of actions (such as in 'disappearances' involving kidnapping);
4. The terrorist initiates threat-based communication processes whereby, on the one hand, conditional demands are made to individuals, groups, governments, societies or sections, and on the other hand, the support of specific constituencies (based on ties of ethnicity, religion, political affiliation and the like) is sought by the terrorist perpetrators;
5. Terrorism is about 'terror' which instills fear, dread, panic or mere anxiety;
6. The main direct victims of terrorist attacks are the public in general, not the armed forces. These are civilians, non-combatants or innocent and defenceless persons;
7. The direct victims are not the ultimate target (as in a classical assassination) but serve as 'message generators', more or less

unwittingly helped by the news values of the mass-media to reach various audiences;

8. The sources of terrorist violence can be individual perpetrators, small groups, diffused transnational networks, as well as state actors or state-sponsored clandestine agents (such as hit teams); and

9. While showing similarities with methods employed by organized crime and war crimes, terrorist violence is predominantly political.

Terrorism has been a contested and politicized term as 'one man's freedom fighter is another man's terrorist' (Schmid, 2013). The type of definition reflects the priorities and interests of the governing agency or countries (Dedeoglu, 2003). The reality is that people would surely know a terrorist act when they saw one; yet, it is an act whose nature is hard to define academically (Weinberg *et al.*, 2004).

7.1.2 *Types of Terrorism*

There are many genres of terrorism, as discussed below.

Religion-Based Terrorism

Religion itself does not promote terror. Terrorist groups, however, have been using religious ideologies to justify their actions for a long time. Unscrupulous leaders distort religious concepts to justify their violence and aims. Al-Qaeda and the Islamic State of Iraq and Syria (ISIS) are the most prominent groups that can be characterized today as religious terrorists. However, there have been other terrorist groups using Buddhism (Hodal, 2013) and Christianity (Rice, 2007) to justify their violent and extreme deeds.

Right-Wing Terrorism and Left-Wing Terrorism

This type of terrorism aims to combat liberal governments but champions neo-nazism, xenophobia, and opposition to immigration (Martin, 2006). Modern right-wing terrorist groups include the Klu Klux Klan (KKK). Many groups are present not only in the U.S., but also in Europe. Another field of terrorism is left-wing terrorism.

Left-wing terrorism is concerned about the injustice caused by the threat from capitalist societies. Seger (2001) explains that left-wing terrorism developed from working-class movements seeking to eliminate class distinctions. Leftist terrorists have been responsible for three-fourths of the acts of terrorism in America in the 1980s, and they are still active today. For example, the German police are still concerned about the activity of the Red Army Faction terrorists who were implicated in several robberies in 2017 (Deutsche Welle, 2017).

Biological and Chemical Terrorism

The U.S.'s Centres for Disease Control and Prevention (CDC) explains that the term 'bioterrorism' refers to the use of biological agents as weapons for political or individual agendas. It explains that bioterrorism differs from other forms because the materials needed to make a biological agent are readily available, require little specialized knowledge, and are inexpensive (CDC, n.d.). Biological agents can be spread easily through the air, water, or in food, and can be disseminated using bacteria such as Anthrax, viruses such as Smallpox, and toxins such as Ricin (National Child Traumatic Stress Network, n.d.). Chemical attacks are just as dangerous. The National Child Traumatic Stress Network (NCTSN) explains that chemical terrorism involves the use of chemicals to cause physical and psychological damage. These affect the nervous system (nerve agents), the respiratory system (choking agents), the circulation system (blood agents), and the skin (blister agents). Chemicals like the nerve-agent sarin are odourless, while others have a smell. The use of chemical agents is not new. Japan experienced two mass-casualty terrorist events involving chemical releases; the 1994 Matsumoto sarin attack (600 injured and seven dead) and the 1998 Wakayama arsenic incident (67 injured and four dead) (Asai & Arnold, 2003).

Agro-terrorism

This form of terrorism involves the deliberate introduction of an animal or plant disease. The goal here is to generate fear, causing economic losses, and in the longer term, social instability. Terrorists may kill farm animals, contaminate vegetation, and disrupt supplies of natural resources to bring about economic damage (Govern, 2009).

Cyber-terrorism

This is when terrorism meets the cyberspace. Cyber-terrorism refers to attacks and threats against cyber networks to intimidate a government or its people. Cyberattacks may not equate to cyber-terrorism; and an attack should result in violence against persons or property, or at least cause terror, to qualify as the latter (Denning, 2000; Nouri & Whiting, 2014). In December 2014, ISIS launched a spear-phishing attack on citizen media groups sympathetic to the Syrian government (Scott-Railton & Hardy, 2014). In another attack, ISIS also used spear-phishing to gain access to the U.S. Military Central Command's (Centcom) Twitter and YouTube accounts. Another hacker group, the Syrian Electronic Army (SEA), with links to Syria, Iran, and Hezbollah, hacked the Twitter account of the Associated Press (AP) (Prigg, 2015).

7.1.3 *Distinguishing Terrorism, Extremism, and Radicalisation: Conceptual Challenges*

There are many definitions of the terms 'radicalization', 'terrorism', and 'extremism'. Here are some common ones and they often overlap:

- According to Schmid (2011, p. 86), the revised academic consensus of the definition of terrorism is:

    "Terrorism refers to a doctrine about the presumed effectiveness of a special form or tactic of fear-generating, coercive political violence and, on the other hand, to a conspiratorial practice of calculated, demonstrative, direct violent action without legal or moral restraints, targeting mainly civilians and non-combatants, performed for its propagandistic and psychological effects on various audiences and conflict parties."

- The European Commission's 'Expert Group on Violent Radicalisation' defined *violent radicalization* as "socialisation to extremism which manifests itself in terrorism" (European Commission's Expert Group on Violent Radicalisation, 2008).
- The Danish intelligence services (PET), on the other hand, describes *violent radicalization* as a "process by which a person, to an increasing extent accepts the use of undemocratic or violent means, including terrorism, in an attempt to reach a specific political/ideological objective" (PET, 2009, p. 1).
- The Norwegian government in its 'Action Plan against Radicalisation and Violent Extremism' defines *radicalization* to be a "process whereby a person increasingly accepts the use of violence to achieve political, ideological or religious goals. Violent extremism is understood here to be activities of persons and groups that are willing to use violence in order to achieve their political, ideological or religious goals" (Norwegian Ministry of Justice and Public Security, 2014, p.7).
- The Prevent Strategy of the British Government provides the following definitions of radicalisation, extremism and violent extremism. *Radicalization* is defined as "the process by which a person comes to support terrorism and forms of extremism leading to terrorism." *Extremism*, on the other hand, is "vocal or active opposition to fundamental British values, including democracy, the rule of law, individual liberty and mutual respect and tolerance of different faiths and beliefs" and, finally, *violent extremism* means the "endorsement of violence to achieve extreme ends" (HM Government, 2011).

Taking this all together, there are several salient points to consider:

- First, there is confusion about the terms. The relationship between 'radical', 'radicalization', and 'terrorism' is a complex one. Not every radical becomes a terrorist, and not every terrorist holds radical views (Schmid, 2013).
- Next, radical attitudes alone may not be a good indicator of radicalization. A radical belief does not always lead to radical

actions (National Consortium for the Study of Terrorism and Responses to Terrorism, 2010).

- Confusing 'radicalization' with 'terrorism' and 'violent extremism' has practical implications for understanding these terms. How something is defined can shape how it is put into practice. There is no clear or unequivocal causal relationship between the concepts of radicalization, terrorism, and violent extremism. Yet, many of the models developed to deal with these assume there is a direct relationship between being a 'radical' or holding radical views or perceived as being on a pathway to radicalisation, and being a terrorist. This is not to say there is no relationship. Clearly, in many cases, there are some. As Bjørgo's (2009) work underscores, some people drift into terrorism for a host of reasons that have nothing to do with ideology or radical views. Some simply find it fun, a way of doing what they perceive as humanitarian work, akin to having an adventure, or a way to escape boredom.
- Finally, phase-based radicalization frameworks, which demonstrate a developmental pathway, may shed some insights on how an individual would gradually gravitate towards the use of violence as a means to an end. Some of these frameworks are discussed in the later part of this chapter.

7.2 Pathways of Radicalisation

What are the pathways to radicalization? What follows in this section are some models and frameworks. They are summarized as an introduction. Interested readers are advised to read the original reports and papers.

Randy Borum's Four-Stage Model (2003)

Professor Randy Borum (2003) postulated a four-stage model for the terrorist mindset and these were:

1. *Grievance*: 'It's not right'; a sense of dissatisfaction with one's condition

2. *Injustice*: 'It's not fair'; perceptions of illegitimate inequality and injustice
3. *Target attribution*: 'It's your fault'; referring to the attribution of injustice to a targeted group, and finally
4. *Distancing/devaluation*: 'You are evil'; negatively stereotyping the targeted group and justification of one's actions.

One of the strongest aspects of Borum's model is that it begins with the focus on *grievance* and *injustice*. Borum (2003) mentioned that the model was developed as a conceptual, rather than as an empirical model, and it provides a reasonable starting point for understanding radicalization.

Aarhus University Research of Eight-Stage Radicalization (2005)

Dr. Michael Taarnby at the Centre for Cultural Research, University of Aarhus, produced a report titled *Recruitment of Islamist Terrorists in Europe* (Tarnby, 2005). Taarnby's eight-stage recruitment process includes the following stages:

1) Individual alienation and marginalization,
2) Seeking a spiritual quest,
3) Going through a process of radicalization,
4) Meeting with like-minded people,
5) Going through gradual seclusion and cell formation,
6) Mental acceptance of violence as a legitimate political means,
7) Connection with a "gatekeeper" (i.e., a militant who is personally connected to a terrorist network), and finally
8) Doing the terrorist act.

While being quite informative, Taarnby focuses mainly on the recruitment practices in the global Jihad movement in Europe, and this may not directly apply to radicalization in other parts of the world.

FBI's Model

In a report titled *The Radicalization Process: From Conversion to Jihad*, the Federal Bureau of Investigations (FBI) Counter-Terrorism

Division (2006) explained that the radicalization cycle has four steps: (1) Pre-radicalization, (2) Identification, (3) Indoctrination, and (4) Action. Each is distinct, and a radicalized person may never reach the final step. The first stage, pre-radicalization, is unique to each individual but four motivations have been identified — 'jilted believers', 'protest-converts', 'acceptance-seekers', and 'faith-interpreters'. People could be pre-radicalized in mosques, prisons, universities, and places of employment. In the identification stage, the 'us-versus-them' categorization is created, where the individual is separated from his former life and affiliates with like-minded individuals, strengthening his dedication to religious beliefs in an attempt to prove his worth. In the indoctrination stage, the individual is convinced that action is required to support and further the cause but is unsure of or unfamiliar with how to participate. At this stage, the person's loyalty is tested. This is done to gauge the recruit's willingness to participate in an attack, and it allows the recruit to test his own resolve. In the final stage, action can be accomplished through several means including participation in a terrorist attack, facilitation, recruitment, or financing. While this model was useful, it was based on assessments made on individuals arrested by the FBI in the U.S.[1] and may not be representative of other terrorists across the world.

The New York Police Department's (NYPD) Model of Radicalization

Developed based on case studies, the New York Police Department (NYPD) produced a research report on the radicalization process (Silber & Bhatt, 2007). It consists of four stages: (1) Pre-Radicalization, (2) Self-identification, (3) Indoctrination, and (4) Jihadization. Pre-radicalization describes an individual's lifestyle prior to radicalization.

---

[1] Understanding the local context in which terrorism breeds is important, as terrorism is both a global and local phenomenon. So, as discussed in the earlier chapter, in the CLIP framework, there is a need to understand the "L" (in CLIP) or the 'local considerations'. In another section of this chapter, it is later explained that in Singapore's case, whilst there were no aggravating circumstances for those who became involved in terrorism, they were influenced by charismatic leaders.

Self-identification is when an individual begins to explore Salafi[2] Islam; these ideology and values begin to influence the individual's identity formation. Indoctrination is when the individual intensifies his beliefs from the self-identification stage and takes actions to fulfil them. Jihadization is when individuals accept their duty to participate and decide to commit in jihad as "holy warriors". This will eventually lead them to plan for a terrorist attack. The NYPD explained that anyone who begins the radicalization process does not necessarily pass through all the stages. They can stop at different points. They argued that the stages are not in a linear progression. While this NYPD model is insightful, these stages are found not to be discrete or progressive, but rather intertwined.

Moghaddam's Staircase to Terrorism Model

In this model, a stairway to radicalization is described (Moghaddam, 2006). At the 'Ground Floor', there is psychological interpretation of material conditions, and these are perceptions of relative deprivation and unfairness. The 'First Floor' is where there are perceived options to fight unfair treatment. At the 'Second Floor', there is displacement of aggression and readiness to displace anger onto out-groups. The 'Third Floor' is where there is moral engagement, which encourages disengagement from mainstream society. At the 'Fourth Floor', there is categorical thinking and the perceived legitimacy of the terrorist organization. Terrorism is seen as justifiable. On the 'Fifth Floor' is where we see the terrorist act. The staircase model is useful in that it provides an explanation as to why a very small minority end up committing acts of terrorism, even though there are large numbers of disgruntled people in society. Moghaddam argues that although many people feel deprived and unfairly treated, most remain on the 'Ground Floor', but some do climb up and are eventually recruited into terrorist organizations. These individuals are encouraged by leaders

---

[2] The ideology of Salafism and Wahhabism is built upon a narrowly defined religious text. Methodologically, they are literalist and puritanical in their approaches to Islamic theology and law (Mohamed *et al.*, 2016).

and become socialized to see terrorist organizations as legitimate and out-group members as evil. This model is interesting because Moghaddam argues that the current policy of focusing on individuals already at the top of the staircase brings only short-term gains, and that the best long-term policy against terrorism is prevention. However, a problematic assumption of this model is that it assumes that those who may potentially be radicalized are disgruntled, but this may not be the case.

Marc Sageman's Four-Stage Process

Marc Sageman (2004, 2007) argues that radicalization consists of four 'prongs'. First, a sense of 'moral outrage' arising from the killings of Muslims. Second, there is a specific 'interpretation of the world', for example, that there is 'war against Islam'. Third, there is 'resonance with personal experiences' — the interpretation of a Western war against Islam that meshes with perceptions of social, political, economic, and religious discrimination. These feelings are made worse because of unemployment and boredom, which drive participation in radical activities and finally the 'mobilization stage'. Sageman says that these processes are not necessarily sequential.

Wiktorowicz's Model of Radicalization

Quintan Wiktorowicz conducted fieldwork observing the al-Muhajiroun group in London. He identified four processes that enhanced the likelihood of an individual being drawn to a radical group (Wiktorowicz, 2005). Al-Muhajiroun supports the use of violence against Western interests and argues for the establishment of an Islamic state through military coup. Wiktorowicz argued that the stages of radicalization were:

1. *Cognitive Opening*: Where a person becomes receptive to the possibility of new ideas and world views;
2. *Religious Seeking*: Where a person seeks meaning through a religious framework;

3. *Frame Alignment*: Where the ideas by the radical group 'makes sense' to the seeker and attracts their interest; and
4. *Socialization*: Where a person experiences religious instruction that facilitates indoctrination, identity-construction, and value changes.

The interesting point about this model is Wiktorowicz's idea that a crisis can produce a 'cognitive opening'. This idea refers to the individual's receptiveness to the possibility of alternative views. He explains that the specific crisis that results in this varies across individuals. These could be economic ones (e.g., losing a job and blocked mobility), sociocultural ones (e.g., sense of cultural weakness, racism, and humiliation), political crises (e.g., repression, torture, and political discrimination), and personal crises (e.g., a death in the family, victimization by crime, and family feuds).

The Home Team Behavioural Sciences Center's RECRO Model

The Home Team Behavioural Sciences Centre (HTBSC) proposed a five-phase model called RECRO (Neo, 2016). Adapted from Weimann and von Knop's (2008) work, this model outlined the phases in which a potential violent extremist chooses to desist from or continue on the path to radicalization. The phases of the RECRO model are:

- *Reflection* phase: This is the period during which an individual's propensity to seek out alternative belief systems may increase as a result of one's vulnerabilities, needs, and/or inept worldviews. This is the phase where person-specific factors and social milieus interact to create the motivation for individuals to 'open up' and initiate the search online for alternative rhetoric to fulfil their needs.
- *Exploration* phase: The individual starts to explore alternative belief systems. An individual's likelihood of becoming receptive to radical narratives largely hinges on how these online narratives relate to his/her sense of self and life experience.

- *Connection* phase: The individual connects with like-minded people. These communities enable the individual to find support and reinforce his/her worldviews with other like-minded individuals.
- *Resolution* phase: The individual gains the momentum to translate his or her radical beliefs into action. It is essential to note that the act of internalizing radical narratives into one's belief systems does not necessarily precipitate the act of violence; most people with radical ideas would never act on them. Rather, there is a need for the individual to be 'retriggered' and coerced into action.
- *Operational* phase: The individual is mentally and/or operationally prepared to commit violence to further his/her radical objectives.

Summary of Phase-Based models

Several points are worth emphasizing. First, there is no single clear pathway to terrorism. Each explanation is different (McCauley & Moskalenko, 2011). People do not necessarily proceed in a straight line or in a conveyer-belt style. Second, not every person who holds on to and embraces radical ideas will actually engage in any terrorist activity (Aly *et al.*, 2014).

7.3 Levels of Explanations for Terrorism

When discussing different explanatory models of the causes and factors for terrorism and radicalization, scholars advocate the use of different levels of analysis: *macro, meso,* and *micro* (Schmid, 2013). Some of the major thinking has been summarized in Table 7.1.

When examining these levels, what can we conclude? First, because these levels discuss possible conditions that lead to terrorism, therefore the solutions must necessarily follow in the same manner. There ought to be macro, meso, and micro level solutions. Second, it is important to ensure that the solutions at one level do not lead to problems in another level. For example, macro level solutions (e.g., foreign policy) should not lead to new problems at the micro level, and there is a need to ensure the levels are broadly consistent.

Table 7.1: Levels of Explanations for Terrorism

Levels of explanation	Concepts
Macro level explanations for terrorism	Environmental and Political Conditions • Unhappiness with the role of government at home and abroad, e.g., foreign policies and policies towards integration of immigrants (Institute for Safety, Security and Crisis Management [ISSCM], 2008) • The radicalization of public opinion and tense majority–minority relationships, etc. (Schmid, 2013) • Structural causes within society, e.g., demographic imbalances, globalisation, rapid modernization, transitional societies, relative deprivation, and class structure (Bjørgo, 2005) • Political reasons, e.g., poor integration, perceived marginalization, discrimination, and the feeling that the world is at war with your own religion • Cultural reasons, e.g., modernization, identity clash between Muslims living in Western countries and the host society, and conflicts between radical and moderate strands of Islam (ISSCM, 2008)
Meso level explanations for terrorism	Social Factors • Social identification, social interaction (Veldhuis & Staun, 2009) • Threat to the in-group, network dynamics, homophily, social influence, social rules, friendship bonds (ISSCM, 2008) • Group polarization: Individual opinions tend to become more extreme in a group • Groupthink: The phenomenon in which the desire to reach consensus in the group becomes stronger than arriving at the best and most rational decision • In-group/out-group bias: Holding a much more positive view of individuals inside one's group and a much more negative view of others outside • Diminished sense of responsibility: Individuals feel less responsible for actions that have been taken in a group context or in the name of the group • (Perceived) rewards and benefits: Individuals join groups in order to receive something, be it material goods like food or shelter, or perceived benefits such as companionship, sense of belonging, etc.

(Continued)

Table 7.1: (*Continued*)

Levels of explanation	Concepts
	• Group norms and rules: The conducts of individuals within the group is regulated (Borum, 2011)
	Catalysts
	• Mobility, technology, transportation, publicity, weapons, weak state control of territory (Neumann, 2012; Veldhuis & Staun, 2009; Weimann, 2007)
	• Role of the Internet: Network and opinion formation (ISSCM, 2008)
	• Role of prisons (ISSCM, 2008)
Micro explanations for terrorism	Distal Micro factors
	• Personal identity problems (Schmid, 2013)
	• Feelings of alienation by host country, marginalization, discrimination, relative deprivation, humiliation, stigmatization and rejection, often combined with moral outrage and feelings of (vicarious) revenge (Schmid, 2013)
	• Individual level psychological characteristics, e.g., depression, anxiety, violence, identity seeking, impulsive, sensitive to humiliation, etc. (ISSCM, 2008)
	• Personal experiences that lead to the adoption of radical ideology (ISSCM, 2008)
	• Motivations for joining radical groups (ISSCM, 2008)
	Proximal/Immediate Micro Factors
	• Motivational causes: The actual grievances that people experience at a personal level motivating them to act (Borum, 2014; Bjørgo, 2005)
	• Triggering causes, e.g., a political calamity, an outrageous act committed by the enemy, or some other events that call for revenge or action (Bjørgo, 2005)
	• Personal life experiences (Veldhuis & Staun, 2009)
	• Precipitants or trigger causes, e.g., call for revenge or action such as violence against in-groups, police brutality, contested elections, but also provoking acts committed by hostile out-groups (Crenshaw, 1981)

7.4 Psychological Characteristics of Terrorists

Researchers have long tried to figure out terrorists. In the 1970s when plane hijacks were common, a Dallas psychiatrist with training in psychoanalysis, David Hubbard, identified in his book, *The Skyjacker: His Flights of Fantasy*, five traits of skyjackers by looking at the profile of both successful and failed skyjackers (Hubbard, 1971). He explained that they: (1) had a violent, alcoholic father; (2) had a deeply religious mother; (3) were sexually shy, timid, and passive; (4) had younger sisters toward whom the terrorist acted protectively; and (5) had poor social achievement. Hubbard's study dispelled the image of the "average" skyjacker as being a rugged 'Che Guevara' revolutionary-type, fighting against 'capitalist' oppression. Instead, they are reported to be shy, timid, sexually passive, and generally apolitical, and always failed in everything — marriage, sex, business, and social activity. Hubbard reported that they were helpless, except for the few exhilarating moments when they seized control of the aircraft. He completed this analysis based on his theoretical psychoanalytic formulations.

Ferracuti and Bruno (1981), also studied 908 right-wing terrorists in Italy, and they claimed to have identified nine typical characteristics: (1) ambivalence toward authority, (2) defective insight, (3) adherence to convention, (4) emotional detachment from the consequences of their actions, (5) sexual role uncertainties, (6) magical thinking, (7) destructiveness, (8) low education, and (9) an adherence to violent subculture norms and weapons fetishes.

In another article by Post *et al.* (2003) titled *The Terrorists in Their Own Words*, the authors described the semi-structured interviews that they conducted with 35 incarcerated Middle Eastern terrorists, including 21 Islamic religious terrorists from Hamas, as well as 14 secular terrorists from Fatah. They found that most had a high school education. The sub-group of suicide bombers among the Palestinians was between 17 to 22 years of age, uneducated, unemployed, and unmarried. Most came from respected families that supported their activism. Peer influence was the major reason for joining a group, and joining a group increased one's social standing within society.

Members identified with the group's collective identity and goals. Imprisonment did not help as prison experience strengthened group commitment for most terrorists. Anger and hatred without remorse were often expressed, but there was little interest in obtaining weapons of mass destruction. The limitations with this study were that the method of subject selection, the circumstances of the interviews, and the methods of interviewing were not described (Victoroff, 2005).

Even though these are just a couple of selected studies, taking these findings altogether, there is no clear consensus on the characteristic of terrorists. Each study is heavily influenced by convenience samples and the biases of each researcher. Characteristics vary a lot. Given this heterogeneity, it appears that broad types of profiling may not work well. If anything, the composition of terrorist groups is remarkable for its diversity. In recent years, terrorist psychology is no longer just about the question of why someone becomes involved, but it appears to be making way for exciting developments that encompass the entire 'arc' of terrorism — from involvement to engagement, to disengagement; and this line of analysis can identify behavioural characteristics that terrorists may exhibit based on in-depth interviews and case study analysis of past terror attacks (Horgan, 2017).

7.4.1 *Do Terrorists Have Mental Health Issues?*

Friedland (1992) argued that there was no compelling evidence that terrorists are abnormal, insane, or match a unique personality type. In a detailed discussion in an interesting paper, *Cheshire-Cat Logic: The Recurring Theme of Terrorist Abnormality in Psychological Research*, Professor Andrew Silke (1998, p. 20) also concludes:

"While the attraction to view terrorists as being abnormal is understandable, for now, the evidence allows only one conclusion: terrorists are normal people. Without doubt, while the individual actors may be generally normal, the activity itself most certainly is not. This is the heart of the...argument, that normal people can do abnormal things".

With more cases being analyzed by researchers in recent times, and the fact that we understand more about terrorist thinking through their own publicly available publications, this position may be changing.

For instance, in a recent paper by Patrick Andres James and Daniela Pisoiu titled *Mental Illness and Terrorism*, the authors argued that most terrorists are psychologically normal (START, 2016). This is because terrorist group leaders tend to emphasize the importance of ideological and religious knowledge, and the ability to acquire combat, logistical, and propaganda skills. They explained that traditional terrorist groups like Al-Qaeda have not been recruiting mentally unstable individuals, since they were deemed unreliable and uncontrollable. ISIS, on the other hand, is less particular. Anyone, any person, and any type of attack will do. The authors argued that ISIS made use of social media campaigns and attractive magazines (e.g., Dabiq, Rumiyah), and promoted 'do-it-yourself' approaches; hence, the mental health status of the individual is not important as long he/she does the terror act in the name of ISIS (James & Pisoiu, 2016). This attracts lone wolves, and there are some suggestions that lone wolves may have some adjustment problems (Corner *et al.*, 2016).

Take the case of Norway's Brevik (the case discussed in the opening of this chapter). Professor Ulrik Fredrik Malt of Oslo University told the court that Breivik might have had Asperger's Syndrome, Tourette's Syndrome, and a narcissistic personality disorder. Support for his diagnoses included the lack of emotion that Breivik showed when he discussed those he killed. Also, there were other factors, such as his memory for details, his obsession with numbers, his hypergraphia (obsessive writing), his monotonous tone of voice, and his difficulties in understanding social signals. Professor Ulrik's hypotheses seemed intriguing but do not explain Breivik's behaviors totally, since many individuals with these conditions do not resort to mass slaughter in this manner.

As a result of the link with autism, another article discussed the linkages between Autism Spectrum Disorders (ASD) and terrorism. It was mentioned that having a diagnosis of ASD does not explain how someone proceeds along the path toward terrorism. The author hints that coming to quick conclusions based on anecdotal evidence can be risky, and that by identifying the risk factors systematically, victimization of individuals with ASD can be minimized (Al-Attar, 2016). Autism cannot create terrorists.

Emily Corner and colleagues in an article titled *Mental Health Disorders and the Terrorist: A Research Note Probing Selection Effects and Disorder Prevalence* explained that mental health does play a role in lone wolf terrorism, although it may not be the main factor (Corner *et al.*, 2016). They say that studies now highlight that mental disorder is more common in lone-actor terrorists than group-linked individuals (Corner & Gill, 2015). There appears to be three disorders that have a higher prevalence in the lone-actor population: (1) schizophrenia, (2) delusional disorders, and (3) ASD. Prevalence of mental illness among lone wolves was 13.49 times higher than members of violent extremist groups (Corner & Gill, 2015). This does not mean that everyone with these disorders or disabilities is vulnerable. It merely means that there is an increased risk for a mentally-ill individual to engage in terrorist acts, if influenced by radical thought. They explained that mental disorder is rarely attributed as a *direct cause* of violence, but rather creates vulnerability. One needs to be careful not to attribute too much weightage to mental health factors, since Corner and Gill (2015) demonstrated that lone-actor terrorists with a mental health disorder were just as likely to engage in a range of rational attack planning behaviors, as those without mental health disorders.

7.4.2 Assessing the Risk and Protective Factors for Violent Extremists

The National Institute of Justice (NIJ) of the U.S. Department of Justice hosted a conference that brought together practitioners working on countering violent extremism (CVE) programs in the

U.K., Canada, and the U.S. They looked at studies on the process from radicalization to violent extremism. Their discussions found that the main facilitators of radicalization were the connections with violent extremists in an individual's social network, identity processes, violent extremist narratives, group dynamics, the connections with violent extremist material via the Internet and social media, and grievances. Researchers explained that radicalization is complex and cannot be explained by any one factor alone. There are multiple facilitators that may vary by individual, group, type of belief systems, and context. They recommended: (1) high-level models that can be used as general guides to help users identify the specific factors at work in a particular situation or context, and (2) specific models focused on different individuals, groups, types of violent extremist belief systems, and contexts. The main risk and protective factors they discussed are shown in Figure 7.1.

Risk Factors For Individual Radicalising To Violent Extremism

- Individual factors: experiencing family conflict, feeling there is no meaning in life, wanting to belong, desiring action or adventure, experiencing trauma*, having mental health issues, having little religious knowledge, having strong belief beliefs, having grievances, feeling under threat, having a 'us' versus 'them' mentality, justifying violence as a solution to problems*, having engaged in previous criminal activity*.
- Contextual factors: stressors (family crisis), societal discrimination, exposure to violent extremist groups, exposure to violent extremist narratives, family member or others in violent extremist network*.

Protective Factors Against Individual Radicalising To Violent Extremism

- Individual factors: Having self esteem, Having strong ties with community*, having a nuanced understanding of religion and ideology
- Contextual factors: Parental involvement in an individuals life. Exposure to non violent belief systems and ideology, a diversity of non-violent outlets for addressing grievances, societal inclusion and integration, resources to address trauma and mental health issues.

Figure 7.1:   Risk and Protective Factors of Violent Extremism

Source: Adapted from 'Radicalisation and Violent Extremism, Lessons from Canada, the UK and the USA' (National Institute of Justice, 2015).

7.5 Forensic Science Considerations

The forensic science and criminalistics considerations in a terror attack would vary depending on the kind of method used during the attack (e.g., assassination by gun, knifing, truck attack, plane hijack, suicide bombing, and so on). Therefore, it would be difficult to narrow down all possible specific forensic science considerations. Most police forces today, however, have specialized investigation teams to look into this to analyze the attack or incident. Typically, these include scene management, evidence preservation, scene integrity, photography and video analysis, identification, and victim interviews. Interested readers should look up *A Guide for Explosion Bombing Scene Investigation,* by the U.S. National Institute of Justice, Department of Justice (National Institute of Justice, 2000). For an example of some of the issues involved, please read the following research article by the Office of Chief Medical Examiner, New York, relating to the 9/11 incident in New York.

RESEARCH ARTICLE OF INTEREST
The 9/11 Attacks: The Medico-legal Investigation
of the World Trade Center Fatalities

In an article by the Office of Chief Medical Examiner in New York, examining the 9/11 World Trade Center (WTC) attack, the authors discussed the forensic science and medico-legal considerations involved. They explained that internal bodily examinations were not done, because the cause and manner of death were apparent. Nearly 90% of victims were fragmented. The paper discussed that 1,466 people died in the north tower of the WTC and 624 people in the south tower. There was a removal of 1.7 million tons of debris and recovering of 19,964 remains.

The team involved medical examiners, forensic anthropologists, medico-legal investigators, forensic biologists, odontologists, medical students, and support staff. The forensic anthropologists focus was on the determination of human versus non-human remains. Remains were photographed, personal effects were registered, and samples of tissue for DNA were collected. Much of the remains had post-mortem changes

(Continued)

(*Continued*)

with the addition of heat and fire. Skeletal remains were the norm. The authors reported that non-clotted blood, skeletal muscle (deep), or bone were preferred for DNA analysis. For decomposed remains, the preferred samples were deep muscle, bone, and teeth.

The paper mentions that a Family Assistance Center (FAC) was set up to provide information to family, friends of the deceased, the injured, and the missing. Families were asked to bring in personal effects of the victims (e.g., hairbrush, razor, undergarment, toothbrush) for DNA comparisons. From the start of the ante-mortem collection, a decision was made to collect DNA samples from family members of all victims, regardless of whether the decedents could be identified via photos, dental records, or fingerprinting. Several family members did not feel comfortable working with the Office of Chief Medical Examiner.

Another important aspect was 'identification'. Identification included personal recognition, fingerprints, dental, radiographic, and unique marks (e.g., tattoos) or items (e.g., unique wedding band), and a victim identification profile (V.I.P.) questionnaire was completed by the next of kin. By December 2008, there were 1,625 (59%) identifications. Of these, 996 were identified by a single means, which included DNA analysis in 877 (88%) followed by dental comparisons in 52 (5%).

Another aspect of these investigations was 'death certification'. The cause of death for most was blunt injury (1,566). Asphyxia by debris accounted for 11 deaths and combinations of injury (blunt/thermal/ smoke inhalation) caused 17 deaths. A death certificate is usually needed by the next of kin for various reasons (e.g., insurance companies claims, social security benefits for dependents, estates issues). Practically, there was a concern about the vast amount of DNA analysis that would be needed for the majority of identifications. Therefore, a plan was implemented to help families quickly obtain death certificates in order to facilitate their needs. The authors explained that there is a law in New York State that allowed for the determination of death without physical remains (which will not usually be allowed in normal death situations). This law enabled the issuance of death certificates before the identification of remains, which was helpful for some families.

Source: James R. Gill, Mark Desire, T. Dickerson, and Bradley J. Adams. In *Forensic Pathology Reviews*, Volume 6, Elizabeth E. Turk, (Editor). Humana Press, 2011, 181–195.

7.6 Terrorism: The Singapore Experience

Terrorism is not unknown to Singapore and, in the past, we have had several significant incidents:

- 10 March 1965: A bomb explosion at the MacDonald House along Singapore's Orchard Road, which killed three and injured 33. This was during Konfrontasi (1963–1966), which was a campaign launched by Indonesia's President Sukarno to oppose the formation of the Federation of Malaysia, which Singapore was a part of from 1963 to 1965 (Daniel, 2015). The choice of the MacDonald House was significant as it was near the Istana and, at the time, also the tallest building in Orchard Road (Nirmala, 2014).
- 31 January 1974: Four men armed with submachine guns and explosives attempted to storm the Shell oil refinery complex on Pulau Bukom. They comprised two Japanese nationals from the Japanese Red Army and two Arabs from the Popular Front for the Liberation of Palestine (PFLP). A PFLP spokesman mentioned that the attack was a warning to all monopolising oil companies and imperialism — especially the oppression of the Arab masses in the Middle East (Ong, 2002). They hijacked a ferryboat named "Laju", which was intercepted by marine police boats and navy gunboats. Following days of negotiations, the terrorists agreed to release the crewmembers they were holding hostage, in exchange for a party of guarantors for their safe passage (Ong, 2002).
- 26 March 1991: Singapore Airlines (SIA) flight SQ117 took off from Subang Airport in Kuala Lumpur, Malaysia, with 129 passengers and crew on board. Four passengers who claimed to be members of the Pakistan People's Party (PPP) took control of the aircraft. They demanded the release of PPP members who were in detention. They also asked for the plane to be refuelled, so that they could fly to Australia. They later threatened to kill one passenger every 10 minutes if their demands were not attended to. The incident was resolved when several commandos[3] entered the

---

[3] This shows that it is not just the police who undertake security and terrorism operations. In several past incidents, our military has been part of several effective and successful counter-terrorism responses.

plane, killed the four Pakistani hijackers, and freed all 118 passengers and nine crewmembers (National Security Coordination Centre, 2004).

7.6.1 *The Jemaah Islamiyah Threat*

One major incident we faced in Singapore was the threat of the Jemaah Islamiyah (JI) in late-2001.[4] This was discovered when the Internal Security Department (ISD) arrested 15 persons in December 2001. Thirteen were members of a group, Jemaah Islamiyah, which means "Islamic community". They had been planning to conduct bomb attacks in Singapore. JI and its affiliated groups had close ties with Al-Qaeda, the organization responsible for the U.S. 9/11 attacks (Ministry of Home Affairs, 2003).

A White Paper was written on the threat of the JI. It explained that JI is a Southeast Asian terrorist group, which aimed to create a "Daulah Islamiyah" (Islamic caliphate) within Southeast Asia. It would be based mainly in Indonesia, but covered Malaysia, southern Philippines, and Singapore. This vision was spelt out in a JI manual known as "*Pedoman Umum Perjuangan Jemaah Islamiyah*" (PUPJI, or "General Guidelines of the Struggle of Jemaah Islamiyah") (Ministry of Home Affairs, 2003).

The Singapore JI branch started in the 1990s when its leader, IM, was appointed. By conducting religious classes which appealed to those who were keen to find out more about Islam, IM began recruiting members into JI. IM was a charismatic leader who won many followers, and spoke several languages including Arab, Malay, and English. IM conducted surveys with selected JI members to gauge their willingness to carry out various tasks for the *jihad* cause in Afghanistan. Many of the members of the JI were veterans from Afghanistan; they were high-risk individuals as they had received training in the use of AK-47 guns, mortars, and military tactics. Members of the Singapore JI branch did not attend the local mosques,

---

[4] The Singapore Ministry of Home Affairs 'Jemaah Islamiyah Arrests and the Threat of Terrorism' (Ministry of Home Affairs, 2003) is an excellent read on this subject.

as they did not believe in the local schools, mosques, or local preachers (Ministry of Home Affairs, 2003).

JI had three well-developed attack plans. The first was to attack a shuttle-bus that conveyed U.S. military personnel and their families in the Sembawang area to the Yishun MRT station. The second plan was to use truck bombs to attack targets in Singapore, including the U.S. and Israeli Embassies, the Australian and British High Commissions, and commercial buildings housing U.S. firms. There were steps taken to procure 17 tons of ammonium nitrate for the manufacture of truck bombs. The third plan was to attack U.S. naval vessels in Singapore (Ministry of Home Affairs, 2003).

7.6.2 *Psychological Characteristics of JI Members*

Were there any salient characteristics for these members? The Singapore Ministry of Home Affairs White Paper on the Jemaah Islamiyah detailed the psychological characteristics of the members. Teams of psychologists interviewed a total of 31 detainees (Ministry of Home Affairs, 2003). Some characteristics noted were:

- All JI members, except two, were assessed to have "average" or "above average" intelligence levels. About one-third had intelligence levels above the population norm, including two individuals with 'superior level' of intelligence;
- As a group, most regarded 'religion' as their most important personal value. The second highest value they held was "economic", i.e., having material comforts and material wealth. The next few were "spiritual" and "social values", such as concern for the wellbeing of others and being good Muslims to help the "ummah", or Muslim community;
- The psychologists found the organizational and socialization techniques used by JI to promote the acceptance of JI ideology and belief systems to be highly sophisticated.
  - ○ *Characteristics:* Psychological assessments showed that the JI members had high levels of "compliance", were low in "assertiveness", were low in the "questioning of religious values",

and were high in levels of "guilt and loneliness". They needed a sense of belonging. Some were "altruistic" and wanted to help fellow Muslims.

o *Recruitment and selection*: The JI's recruitment process had two stages. The first stage involved religious classes organized for mass audiences. The potential recruit was recommended to join these classes by their own friends, relatives, and colleagues.[5] JI teachers would also employ the tactic of inserting quotations from religious scriptures, including discussions on the concept of jihad, and why it was important to every person. They talked about the plight of suffering Muslims worldwide to appeal to the students.[6] The second stage involved identifying those who were captivated enough to find out more about the plight of Muslims in other regions such as the Malukus, Bosnia, and Mindanao. JI leaders would then identify potential members from those who were curious enough to remain after classes to enquire further. Teachers and leaders engaged students' interests and finally invited those they deemed suitable to join JI.

o Socialisation: The White Paper explained that the JI socialisation process involved:

- *Secrecy*: 'JI language' was used. Military-like code-names, for instance, resulted in a strong sense of 'in-group' superiority identity. Even other Muslims who did not subscribe to militant jihad concepts were seen as infidels (disbelievers).

- *Manipulation*: Members were manipulated when they were asked to take the *bai'ah*, which was the pledge of allegiance. This was a powerful compliance-generating mechanism.

- *Psychological contracting*: After a fiery speech when the audience's emotions had been stirred up, leaders would give out surveys to members to fill up. Members were required to indicate their preferred capabilities such as 'contributing ideas' or even 'dying for the cause'. Having signed their names on the survey, members found it difficult to back out

---

[5] This made them unguarded about the authenticity of these classes.
[6] This is consistent with several phase-based frameworks that were discussed earlier.

from the plan later. Although a few members had misgivings about their reconnaissance missions, they felt they could not withdraw as they were already "in too deep". The members were promised martyrdom if they died for the cause of *jihad* (Ministry of Home Affairs, 2003).

- *Indoctrination*: The concept of jihad was one of the main teachings by JI. They were taught that Jihad *Nafs* (desire) is the struggle against one's own desire or basal instincts (*nafs*). Military Jihad or Jihad war is a defensive military struggle against one's aggressor. The JI trainers argued that the latter was the 'greater jihad' and quoted selected verses from the holy book to support their claims to 'go to war'[7] (Ministry of Home Affairs, 2003).

Summary of the Singapore Experience

Is the Singapore experience consistent with earlier discussed radicalization frameworks? Broadly speaking, many factors appear consistent. For example, the idea of creating an 'us-versus-them' mindset in the socialization processes, the levels of secrecy, and the levels of manipulation seem to be consistent. The belief in political entities and ideals is also a consistent feature. The dynamics of building a strong sense of belonging is another. On the other hand, there are differences. For example, the arrested members were not

---

[7] This was misleading. The Religious Rehabilitation Group (RRG) (led by volunteer Singaporean religious leaders and religious counsellors) explained: "The word jihad is derived from the root '*juhdor jahd*' (*jahada*), which means to exert the most effort. The definition of jihad in the Quran is a general one; an individual can exert effort in a variety of areas, from work and study to striving towards the peace and security of the humankind. Jihad is divided into two levels — *akbar* (major level) and *asghar* (minor level). The major level of jihad is *jihad al-nafs* or the internal struggle against one's self and its lustful desires in order to seek self-improvement. The minor level of jihad is *jihad al-qitalor*, armed struggle that is subjected to strict rules and regulations in the Islamic law. The concept of jihad in Islam is widely misunderstood and has been manipulated to the extent that it is now often associated with terrorism and violence. The term 'holy war' has also become synonymous to jihad. Terrorists often exploit the concept of jihad to justify their violent acts...". (Religious Rehabilitation Group, n.d.)

disenfranchised or disadvantaged in any way. There was no known unhappiness against the nation or against the Singapore government. This suggests that while terrorism is global in its influence, there is no 'one-size-fits-all' understanding. How terrorism manifests itself within each country would depend on the issues it faces and the regional and global influences.

7.7 Understanding Other Terrorism Concerns

7.7.1 *ISIS or Daesh*

The Islamic State of Iraq and Syria (ISIS) is known as the Islamic State, or Daesh. ISIS seized large pieces of land stretching from central Iraq to northern Syria. In 2014, the group declared the establishment of a 'caliphate' which is governed according to Sharia law. ISIS controlled a number of lucrative oil fields in Syria. ISIS has a strong social media and propaganda campaign to recruit fighters from other parts of the world, including the U.K. and Europe (Carter *et al.*, 2014; Saltman & Winter, 2014). The main leader behind ISIS is Iraqi Sunni cleric, Abu Bakr al-Baghdadi. ISIS has been successful in mobilizing many foreign fighters to join them. ISIS has claimed responsibility for the terror attacks in Paris in 2015, and the suicide bombings in Brussels in March 2016. However, of late, ISIS has been losing ground due to military interventions by The Global Coalition Against Daesh.

The real danger today is how ISIS has decentralized its efforts urging individuals to attack using their name. This may result in the rise of 'lone-wolf attacks' that we are seeing across the world. ISIS has migrated online to what many have called the 'cyber caliphate'; because governments and vigilante groups have actively targeted them. There is also a side concern with other terrorist groups that are being overlooked, as most countries are currently solely concerned about ISIS. These overlooked terror groups include the re-emergence of Al-Qaeda (with the next generation of leaders) and a plausible coalition between terror groups (e.g., Al-Qaeda and ISIS).

There is a real concern about ISIS in Southeast Asia. According to reports, about 700 Indonesians, 100 Malaysians, 100 Filipinos, and a handful of Singaporeans are believed to have joined ISIS (Chan, 2015). Commentators are concerned that ISIS has embarked on a campaign to set up a province (referred to as a '*wilayat*') in Southeast Asia. Some analysts have argued that terrorist entities in Mindanao such as the Bangsamoro Islamic Freedom Fighters and Abu Sayyaf Group, may be reorganizing themselves in this part of the world for terror attacks (Singh & Muhammad Haziq, 2016). Singapore is concerned with how terrorism can continue to pose a threat. We have had, in the past, several notable arrests of individuals influenced by global terror groups. These are:

- Cases of self-radicalized individuals: Mr ABAK was a 28-year-old former lawyer detained in 2007. He went to top schools in the country before graduating from university. He practised law at a top firm and became a polytechnic lecturer. The Internet shaped his views and, in 2006, he left for a Middle Eastern country to learn Arabic for the purpose of communicating with 'mujahidin' fighters. He bought a plane ticket to Pakistan, where he planned to get training for militant jihad, and wanted to join the Taleban in Afghanistan (Chang, 2015).
- Bangladeshi Foreigner workers: 27 male Bangladeshi nationals working in Singapore were planning to take part in terrorist activities in other countries, including their homeland Bangladesh, before they were arrested in 2015. Twenty-six of them were members of a closed religious study group that supported the armed jihad ideology of terrorist groups like Al-Qaeda and ISIS. Most subscribed to extremist beliefs and the teachings of radicals like Anwar al-Awlaki. Found in the men's possessions were radical material including books and videos of young children undergoing military training with the ISIS flag. They shared material which showed images on how to attack and kill someone. One such document was titled *Techniques of Silent Killing* (Hussain, 2016).

- Maids and foreign domestic workers: Nine maids had been radicalized whilst in Singapore. One was a 25-year-old who intended to travel to Syria with her foreign boyfriend to join ISIS. Another was a 28-year-old who had worked in Singapore for two years. Both appeared to be ISIS supporters, radicalized through social media. Although none had plans to carry out acts of violence in Singapore, the Singapore government does not condone support for any radical ideologies, whether by locals or foreigners, because of the potential threat to Singapore (Chia, 2017).
- Singaporean in Islamic State Video: The first known ISIS video featuring a fighter from Singapore appeared on social media. He was identified as M.S.A.S, aged 39. It is said that he left Singapore in 2014 to work in the Middle East, where he may have been radicalized. He appeared as a fighter dressed in desert fatigues and identified himself as "Abu Uqayl from Singapore" (Cheong, 2017).
- Marina Bay terror attack plan: Indonesia's counter-terror police detained six suspected militants on the suspicion of planning to launch a rocket attack on Singapore's Marina Bay from Batam. These men were members of Katibah Gigih Rahmat, a little-known terrorist group that helps Indonesian militants travel to Syria. Indonesian police believe that they may have received funds from Bahrun Naim, an Indonesian fighting with ISIS. Naim has also been linked to a suicide bombing outside police headquarters in the City of Solo, Indonesia (*The Guardian*, 2016).

Many are taken in by the ISIS message. Why do people find the message of ISIS so attractive? In a research article by the Ministry of Home Affairs Singapore, it was explained that ISIS's aggressive promotion of fighting in Syria has resonated with a handful of Singaporeans for a few reasons (Hu, 2016). There were five psychological drivers that have contributed to the radicalization process. They are: (1) justifying violence, (2) romanticizing the notion of a utopian 'truly Islamic' state, (3) a desire to be a 'good' Muslim, (4) escaping the 'unbearable present' world, and (5) existential anxiety in relation to end-times prophecies (Hu, 2016).

CASE STUDY:
ISIS Beheading of JF

In August 2014, the world was shocked by the release of a video on YouTube by ISIS. In the video, an American was seen dressed in orange prison garb in a desert, kneeling by the feet of a man dressed in black. The American delivered a long message critiquing the foreign policy of the U.S. and criticizing U.S. military operations in the Middle East. Then, in an unexpected twist and without warning, the American was beheaded. The video went viral, despite efforts to contain its dissemination, and rattled the online community. Many social media websites were rife with panic and anxiety about the rise of ISIS. The group was seen to be declaring war against Americans by targeting the U.S. military regime. What was worse was that ISIS and its supporters were active on numerous popular social media platforms, ranging from Twitter to Facebook to YouTube. The brutal decapitation of J.F. heralded the start of many more beheading videos from ISIS.

Experts speculated that one of ISIS' goals for releasing these graphic images was to demonstrate their power, by showing the world their ability to capture and kill anyone. These atrocious crimes were committed in the name of religion, with the ultimate aim of establishing an Islamic caliphate. ISIS's show of power presented a warning to the global community, hoping to force countless others into doing their bidding.

Video analysts reported that the videos were produced in a slick manner and they garnered many online hits. These videos almost made war seem dramatic and glamorous, presenting viewers with a chance to be part of a performance that many people have only seen in movies. In short, these gory videos romanticized terror. With a slew of videos that dramatized terrorism, ISIS managed to attract a large pool of recruits who were willing to give their lives to the cause. Compared to its predecessors like Al-Qaeda, ISIS is adept at using social media to garner the support of the online community.

Source: Adapted from Taylor (2014). "From Daniel Pearl to James Foley: The modern tactic of Islamist beheadings". *Chicago Tribune*. Retrieved September 21, 2014.

7.7.2 Violence in Myanmar (969 Movement)

Controversial monk, Ashin Wirathu, spearheads the campaign against the Rohingya and Muslims in Myanmar. He is the leader of an ultranationalist group called the 969 Movement, which is against the growth of Islam in Myanmar. Wirathu has warned against · an impending Muslim takeover of Myanmar. The clash between the Rohingya Muslims and Rakhine Buddhists has led to more than 125,000 Rohingya and other Muslims displaced. Wirathu justified the violence saying the Rohingya were planning to establish an Islamic state in Rakhine. He has since urged non-Muslims and Buddhists to boycott Muslim shops and avoid doing business with Muslims (Hallowell, 2013).

7.7.3 The Concern with Lone Wolves

A 'lone wolf' is someone who operates on their own and is not part of a group, network, or directed by an outside organization (Byman, 2017). While this definition seems simple, like the earlier definitions of terrorism, there is little consensus on what exactly the term signifies. There are some broad features nonetheless, according to a good review by the Royal United Services Institute (RUSI) for Defence and Security Studies (Pantucci *et al.*, 2015). First, there is the lack of direction from a wider terrorist group. There is no clear command and control, and this separates lone wolves from networked terrorists. Next, the lone actor may be inspired by the ideology of a terrorist group. The authors explain that lone actors often emerge from a milieu,[8] inspired by a group, but are not under the command

---

[8] David Rapoport argued that terrorism has occurred in waves. Each one characterized by a common driving ideology or objective, and with similar activity undertaken by groups within different countries. He identifies four waves. First, the anarchists originated in 1880s in Russia. Then, anti-colonial terrorists followed the First World War. Then, the New Left terrorists who emerged in the 1960s. And finally, the religious wave which dominates the current threat landscape. The RUSI report explains that lone actors have been active during each wave (cited in Pantucci, Ellis & Chaplais [2015]).

of any other person, group, or network. The main conclusion seems to be that although lone wolf terrorists are, by definition, not tied to any established terrorist group, this is not to say that at any one time they might not have been a member or affiliate of some type of terrorist organization. While there is an absence of direction (from a wider group), this does not mean an absence of inspiration. To be influenced, we do not need interaction; and most of us can be influenced to change our behaviors by things we read or advertisements that we watch.

Byman (2017) questions if the year 2016 was the year of the 'lone wolf terrorist'. Byman makes two interesting points. First, he says that this phenomenon is not new at all. Islamist groups, right-wing white supremacists, abortion foes, and separatists have all used this tactic before. Lone wolfs have killed presidents and prime ministers in their campaign to overturn what they saw as oppressive governments. For example, the deadliest terrorist attack on the U.S. in 1993 was by white supremacists Timothy Mcveigh and Terry Nichols, who bombed the Murrah Federal Building in Oklahoma City. Second, Byman challenges the notion of the true loner. He says that the San Bernardino terror killers were married, and the perpetrator of the Nice (France) truck attack was in contact with a range of radicals.

In an earlier analysis, Spaaji (2010) analysed the main patterns of lone wolf terrorism in 15 countries. He found it to be more prevalent in the U.S. than in the other countries. The cross-national analysis suggested that while in the U.S., lone wolf terrorism has increased markedly in the last 30 years, this is not the same for the other countries. He reported that casualty numbers from lone wolf terrorism have been limited, and there is no evidence of the increase in lethality. Interestingly, he reports that the rates of psychological disturbance and social ineptitude are relatively high among lone wolf terrorists. He reports that lone wolves tend to create their own "ideologies that combine personal frustrations with broader political, social, or religious aims. In this process, many lone wolf terrorists draw on the communities of belief and ideologies of validation generated and transmitted by extremist movements" (Spaaji, 2010, p. 854).

Pantucci *et al.* (2015) make the case that while there are no major consistent patterns, emerging literature suggests some possible features. They reported the following:

- There appears to be no dominant ideologies. However, there appears to be four stands of influence: (1) those driven by right-wing ideology, (2) those driven by Anwar al-Awlaki's thinking, (3) those persuaded by their own idiosyncratic ideology, and (4) those influenced by ISIS' ideology instigating those who are radicalised to attack their own governments (Pantucci *et al.*, 2015);
- The average age was higher than in comparable studies of terrorist groups (this may change, becoming younger with the influence of social media) (Gill *et al.*, 2014);
- Most tend to be male (Gill *et al.*, 2014);
- Many appear to have past convictions — history of incarceration, prior arrests, or are known to the criminal justice system;
- They appear *not* to be economically or socially disadvantaged (and *not* be from the lower class and may likely to be employed);
- A good number may have high school or tertiary education;
- About 25% appear to have military backgrounds;
- About 50% were single or never married;
- About 40% seem to be mentally ill (Gruenewald *et al.*, 2013) (compared to group/networked terrorists). A lone actor is 13.49 times more likely to have a mental illness than an actor within a terrorist group (Corner & Gill, 2015);
- They appear to have personality and social issues and do not 'work and play well with others'. Studies have suggested that these result in social isolation and exclusion, even though many may want to be a part of a social network or group; and
- They appear to have current, past grievances, and personal maladjustment crises. (Clark & Moskalenko, 2014). Experts argue that lone wolves are often developing their own delusions and ideologies, combining their unhappiness with religion, society, or politics with personal frustration.[9]

---

[9] Joel Brynielsson *et al.*, 'Analysis of Weak Signals for Detecting Lone Wolf Terrorists', European Intelligence and Security Informatics Conference, 2012, p. 198.

Given the multiple variables involved and the complexity of how they may vary considerably, experts contend that lone wolves can come in any shape, size, or ideology, and hence, it is difficult to develop a one-mould profile. While we have some early suggestions of the behavioural patterns involved, it remains early days to conclude anything definitively (Pantucci *et al.*, 2015).

7.8 Developing Effective Counterterrorism Measures

There are many counter-terrorism measures undertaken by countries worldwide today. These measures include policy and tactical solutions. Others cover macro and micro solutions. We will discover that many of these are related to the root conditions and needs which appear to explain for the rise of terrorism (see the earlier section on 'levels of analysis'). Listed below are some commonly accepted measures that are used in many countries, and many Singapore examples are mentioned here as well.

Developing strategic frameworks

In any broad plan, there is a need for a strategy. The strategy then outlines the plans.

The United Nations (UN):
The UN developed a "Global Counter-Terrorism Strategy" in the form of a resolution composing of four pillars. These are: (1) addressing the conditions conducive to the spread of terrorism, (2) measures to prevent and combat terrorism, (3) measures to build the capacity of states to prevent and combat terrorism, and to strengthen the role of the UN system in that regard, and finally (4) measures to ensure respect for human rights for all and the rule of law as the fundamental basis in the fight against terrorism (UN Global Counter Terrorism Strategy, 2016).

The United Kingdom:
The U.K. developed CONTEST. The aim of this strategy is to reduce the risk of terrorism to the UK and its interests overseas, so

that people can go about their lives freely and with confidence. CONTEST is split into four work streams that are known as 4 'P's':

o **P**revent: Preventing people from becoming terrorists or supporting terrorism
o **P**ursue: Stopping terrorist attacks
o **P**rotect: Protection against a terrorist attack, and
o **P**repare: Mitigating the impact of a terrorist attack (HM Government, 2011).

The United States:
The U.S. Department of State and USAid developed a "Joint Strategy on Countering Violent Extremism" document that was published in May 2016. It had the following aims:

1. Expand international political will, partnerships, and expertise to better understand the drivers of violent extremism and mobilize effective interventions;
2. Encourage and assist partner governments to adopt more effective policies and approaches to prevent and counter the spread of violent extremism, including changing unhelpful practices where necessary;
3. Employ foreign assistance tools and approaches, including development, to reduce specific political, social, or economic factors that contribute to community support for violent extremism in identifiable areas, or put particular segments of populations at high risk of violent extremist radicalization and recruitment to violence;
4. Empower and amplify local credible voices that can change the perception of violent extremist groups and their ideology among key demographic segments;
5. Strengthen the capabilities of government and non-governmental actors to isolate, intervene with, and promote the rehabilitation and reintegration of individuals caught in the cycle of radicalization to violence (Department of State USAID, 2016).

Singapore:

The National Security Coordinating Centre outlined Singapore's approach. It involves three aspects:

1. *Prevention*: Entails an integration of effective diplomacy, good intelligence work, and strong border controls.
2. *Protection*: Involves the need to harden Singapore with a layer of strong, protective measures. Some examples would be the protection of maritime, aviation, and land transport security.
3. *Response*: Being ready to respond to attacks by undertaking realistic exercises, simulations, and preparing the community to be resilient (to an attack) (National Security Coordination Centre, 2004).

One major initiative in this regard is the SGSecure movement, which is a national movement to sensitize, train, and mobilize the community to play a part in preventing and dealing with a terrorist attack. SGSecure explains that the cornerstone of Singapore's counter-terrorism strategy must be the strengthening of community vigilance, cohesion, and resilience. SGSecure emphasizes the need to "Stay Alert, Stay Strong and Stay United", in the event of a terror attack.[10]

Combine International Efforts

Corsi (2008) argued that a signature element of countermeasures against terrorism involved reaching out to the international community for assistance. Citing Singapore as an example, Corsi mentioned that Singapore worked within the UN framework, and helped pass the landmark United Nations Security Council Resolution 1373 of 2001, which established a legal foundation for international action against terrorism. Singapore also signed the UN Convention for the Suppression of the Financing of Terrorism in December 2001, ratifying it the

---

[10] See https://www.sgsecure.sg/Pages/default.aspx for more details.

following year. Singapore was the first Asian country to implement the U.S. Container Security Initiative (CSI) in January 2003 (Corsi, 2003). The CSI aims to screen high-risk containers before they arrive at U.S. ports. Another example of international level arrangements was the Global Coalition against Daesh, of which Singapore is a participating country. It was formed in September 2014 and consists of 74 members that are committed to tacking Daesh (i.e., ISIS) on all fronts.[11]

Develop Legal Frameworks

Laws explicate what a terrorist offence is, and what is within the purview of law enforcement. Here are some laws[12] to manage terrorism. Readers should be mindful that there could be amendments to these laws and these examples also are not exhaustive in any way.

In the United Kingdom:

The Terrorism Act of 2006 was introduced to tighten the laws in the U.K., following attacks on London in July 2005. The Act amends the definition of terrorism, increases the penalties available, extends the grounds for detention, and extends the period of detention. Significantly, the 2006 Terrorism Act extends the period in which a terrorist suspect may be held in detention without charge to 28 days. A High Court must authorize the extension of detention (Pathania, 2012).

In Australia:

Australia's offences are contained in the Criminal Code Act 1995. In Australia, the police can detain people under preventative detention orders where there is a threat of an imminent terrorist attack or immediately after a terrorist attack. Individuals can be detained if it is necessary to prevent an imminent terrorist act or if it is likely that vital evidence will be lost. Under the Commonwealth Law, the maximum amount of time a person can be preventatively detained is 48 hours.

---

[11] See http://theglobalcoalition.org/en/home/for more details.
[12] Laws and regulations for each country change and readers should be mindful of this. It is good practice to check up on the latest amendments to these laws.

Under State and Territory laws, a person can be detained for up to 14 days. Australia's financial intelligence unit, the Australian Transaction Reports and Analysis Centre (AUSTRAC), is a member of the Egmont Group of Financial Intelligence Units, and it has worked closely with Southeast Asian countries in developing a profile of the financial characteristics of foreign fighters (U.S. Department of State, 2016).

In Singapore:

There are several pieces of legislation to combat terrorism. For example, Singapore has ratified the United Nations' International Convention for the Suppression of Acts of Nuclear Terrorism (ICSANT), which punishes a person who commits a fatal act of terrorism using radioactive material or nuclear explosive devices. Another important piece of legislation is the Terrorism (Suppression of Financing) Act, Chapter 325 (TSFA), which is concerned about addressing terrorism financing. Another important legislation used to deal with the terrorist threat is the Internal Security Act (ISA). The ISA provides powers to deal with threats to security (Pathania, 2012). This Act also provides the detainee with certain rights, which must be given to him. An Advisory Board (AB) chaired by Supreme Court Judge reviews all detentions under the ISA. There are safeguards of the ISA, as follows[13]:

○ A person cannot be held for more than 30 days from the date of arrest in order to facilitate investigation before a decision has to be made. A decision has to be made to detain him under an Order of Detention (OD), which is not exceeding two years, or issue him with a Restriction Order (RO) which is also not exceeding two years, or release him unconditionally, and if the decision is to serve an OD or an RO, the President's assent must be sought,

○ Each OD and RO must be reviewed by the independent AB, which comprises a Supreme Court Judge and two qualified citizens appointed by the President,

---

[13] These points made are purely for academic purposes and readers may want to seek legal advice on actual cases.

- o The AB has all the powers of a court of law to summon and examine witnesses, compel the production of documents and evidence it deems relevant, examine a detainee's representation within three months of the date of his OD, and can also make its recommendation to the President,
- o The AB is required to review every OD and RO at intervals of no more than 12 months,
- o A detainee must be told of the grounds of detention and allegations against him,
- o He has the right to make representations against his OD to the AB. He is free to engage a lawyer or anyone of his choosing, to assist him in his representations,
- o And over and above these, an important check on the use of the ISA is the veto power of the President (Pathania, 2012).

More recently, Singapore has introduced new laws to tackle terrorism, in light of the recent trends in attacks across the world. A law will make it an offence for people to film or take photographs of what is taking place in the vicinity of a terror attack, if a stop order is issued, and if the authorities deemed that such footage might undermine security operations. This is the Public Order and Safety (Special Powers) Act. The law gives police the powers to take down or disable unmanned aircraft and autonomous vehicles and vessels. It involves stopping and questioning people, and making it an offence if they refuse to give information, and directing building owners to take actions such as closing their premises (Seow, 2018).

In Indonesia:
Indonesia plans to introduce new laws to tackle terrorism. Those who join terrorist groups overseas will face a maximum of 15 years' jail term under the anti-terrorism laws expected to be passed in 2018. The new laws will enable authorities to crack down on Indonesians who return after fighting with ISIS or in the Philippines (Topsfield & Rompies, 2017). The proposed draft suggested criminalizing individuals "who deliberately

disseminate speeches, thoughts, behaviours, or writings that could lead others to commit violence, anarchy and other actions which adversely impact other people/communities or degrade certain individual's or community's dignity through intimidation, which leads to terrorism crimes. Conviction would result in a 3- to 12-year prison term" (Hwang, 2017).

In Malaysia:
Malaysia has the Prevention of Terrorism Act 2015 (POTA), which is an anti-terrorism law enacted on 7 April 2015. It enables the Malaysian authorities to detain terror suspects without trial for a period of two years. Malaysia became a full member of the Financial Action Task Force (FATF) in February 2016, and is also a member of the Asia/Pacific Group on Money Laundering. In September 2015, FATF published its Mutual Evaluation Report on Malaysia's anti-money laundering (AML) and countering the financing of terrorism (CFT) measures, and it gave Malaysia positive ratings (US Embassy in Malaysia, 2016).

Successful Intelligence Coordination across Countries

Accurate intelligence allows authorities to disrupt terror plots and arrest key operatives, before attacks can be launched. Singapore has worked closely with other Southeast Asian countries in sharing intelligence with hopes of arresting key terrorists within the region. For example, Thailand arrested and repatriated a senior member of the Singapore JI cell (National Security Coordination Centre, 2004). Additionally, Indonesia arrested and handed over to Singapore Mas Selamat, a Singapore JI cell leader. The Malaysian Special Branch and Singapore's ISD worked very closely to recapture Mas Selamat when he escaped from Singapore in February 2008. Japan has also worked closely with ASEAN in countering terrorism. In November 2004, the ASEAN–Japan Joint Declaration for Cooperation in the Fight against International Terrorism was adopted at the Japan–ASEAN Summit that placed emphasis on enhancing the cooperation on counter-terrorism issues (National Security Coordination Centre, 2004).

Effective Border Controls

Stringent border control measures are necessary to prevent the entry of foreign terrorist elements and materials. Recognizing the need to create a coordinated border control system, the Singapore government merged the border control functions of the Customs and Excise Department and the Singapore Immigration and Registration to form the Immigration and Checkpoints Authority (ICA) on 1 April 2003. The ICA is responsible for monitoring and regulating the movement of goods and people across Singapore's borders. Some of the border control measures included screening facilities at border points (e.g., at ports and airports); the use of x-ray machines to scan containers; the deployment of 'sniffer' dogs; and naval escorts for tankers and high value and vulnerable vessels (National Security Coordination Centre, 2004). This reorganization and new capability proved useful in later years, as the ICA officers detected four Indonesian ISIS supporters when they arrived at the Singapore Changi Airport in February 2016 (Hussain, 2016).

'Whole-of-Government' Response

A 'whole of government' response is important in the fight against terrorism, because terrorist organizations are nimble and adaptable, while governments are generally bureaucratic organizations. Singapore recognized the need for the government to work as a united whole to ensure that there is proper command and control of any major incident. Several governmental processes are in place. In Singapore, there is the Home Front Crisis Ministerial Committee, which will be set up during times of crisis. There is also the Home Front Crisis Executive Group (HCEG), led by senior government officials to provide policy guidance on the management of major crises. Many international governments have similar arrangements, although, in bigger countries, federal agencies play a major role in working closely with state agencies (National Security Coordination Centre, 2004).

Protection of Critical Infrastructure

There are multiple ways of hardening targets to prevent terrorists from being successful. Some of the main domains to consider could be land transport security, aviation security, maritime security, protective security, and quick response forces (National Security Coordination Centre, 2004).

Terrorism Forensics and Investigations

As discussed in the earlier chapters with the CLIP model, an important element in countering terrorism is to understand terrorism forensics and post-blast investigations. Singapore works closely with other countries to train its officers on these issues (Chen, 2012). Forensics for bomb blast will include issues such as understanding the ingredients used in a bomb, the modus operandi involved in the bomb-making, and the bomb or the attack itself, the similarity of the bomb used with other kinds of bombs used in other parts of the world.

Outreach and Counter-Messaging

Ideas do not always lead to trouble. However, some extreme ideas do incite violence. Eidelson and Eidelson (2003), for example, discuss how five dangerous ideas (i.e., superiority, injustice, vulnerability, distrust, and helplessness) can lead to conflict if they are not addressed. Thus, there is a need for counter-messaging to mitigate the negative effects of dangerous ideas. Several countries have developed outreach initiatives to counter the messages of terrorists. For example, Indonesian 'cyber warriors' has been sending out messages promoting a moderate form of Islam in Indonesia. Some 500 members of the Nahdlatul Ulama (NU), one of the biggest Muslim organizations in Indonesia, are seeking to counter the radical messages of ISIS. They aim to showcase their particular brand of the Muslim faith, known as

'Islam Nusantara' (or, Islam of the Archipelago), to counter ISIS' radical interpretation (Cochrane, 2015). According to NU, their message of tolerance is at the heart of the group's campaign against ISIS, which will be carried out online, and in hotel conference rooms and convention centers from North America to Europe to Asia. Governments can also encourage counter narratives initiatives from the community such as 'Average Mohammad' or 'Abdullah-X'. In Singapore, the Majlis Ugama Islam Singapura (MUIS) set up a network of religious teachers and youth groups to counter radical ideology online.

The U.S. has its own Digital Outreach Team (DOT) to counter misinformation and explain government positions surrounding U.S. foreign policies through direct engagement on the Internet and social media. The activities of the DOT are threefold: (1) contest the space, (2) redirect the conversation, and (3) confound the adversary. The DOT is composed of approximately 20 staff, including 10 Arabic-, 5 Urdu-, and 2 Somali-speaking writer–analysts, who aim to proactively contrast "objective facts and analysis with the often emotional, conspiracy laden arguments of U.S critics in hopes that online readers will take a fresh look at their opinions of the U.S." (Counterterrorism.org, n.d.). The DOT uses a multi-platform approach, operating on a variety of mainstream news platforms, social networking, and micro-blogging platforms through overt engagements (QAISS, 2013).

Law enforcement agencies could also learn from ISIS' messaging strategies to develop narratives that appeal to the audience. Firstly, agencies should introduce more evidence that undermine the credibility of the arguments put forth by ISIS and its supporters. In fact, based on a review by the United Nations Counterterrorism Implementation Task Force (CTITF), it was highlighted that:

"While terrorist argumentation often shows weakness in content and logic, the counter-narrative that points these out needs more substance to sustain itself. Secondly, the counter-narratives should provide a moderate perspective that resonates with the viewers and offers alternative mainstream resources. For example, Aly, Weimann-Saks, and Weimann (2014) note that: 'One of the most significant challenges to an effective counter narrative is that traditional structures of religious authority in Islam are increasingly undermined and delegitimised by the Internet. Religious authority therefore becomes a matter of individual agency as individuals are able to assemble their own religious guides accepting those that conform to a certain world view and rejecting those that do not.'"

(CTITF, 2011, p. 45).

Prepare the Community for a Possible Attack

The notion here is that everyone has a role to play during an emergency. Immediate help by friends and families to those wounded emotionally or physically can be faster than formal emergency response systems such as the police or medical services. Law enforcement and emergency services can take time, especially when there are multiple incidents and multiple casualties. Singapore has taken the position of "it is not if, but when". As mentioned earlier, Singapore has started the SGSecure movement to prepare its citizens for terror attacks. It is a movement to sensitize, train, and mobilize the community to prevent and deal with a terrorist attack. There are three limbs of SGSecure and they are: (1) community vigilance, (2) community cohesion, and (3) community resilience. The movement includes 'Staying Alert' (being vigilant, looking for threats and calling the police), 'Staying United' (building ties with the community and enhancing community cohesion), and 'Staying Strong' (knowing what to do in an emergency, e.g., first aid). Under the idea of staying strong is the notion of "Run, Hide, Tell" during a terror incident. These are as follows:

- *Run*: Run away from any danger or threat. SGSecure explains that you should not attempt to negotiate with the terrorists or attempt to surrender. However, if escape is not possible then,

- *Hide*: Find cover and stay hidden. Be quiet and switch your communication devices to silent mode.
- *Tell*: Call "999" (the police) or SMS to "71999" if you are not able to talk. Provide important details to the police on the location, description of attackers.

Other useful ideas promulgated are the Improvised-First Aid Skills, or I-FAS, which lists out what you could do when you are a victim of an attack (Press-Tie-Tell). Readers will find very useful information in the SGSecure portal.

Many countries have developed similar messages to educate their citizens on what to do in the event of a terror attack. For example, the French government has developed a card detailing "Flee, Hide, Alert". The city of Houston, Texas, on the other hand, has developed a guide called "Run, Hide, Fight".

Early Intervention and Rehabilitation

How can we rehabilitate terrorists? Members of Singapore's Muslim community formed the Religious Rehabilitation Group (RRG). The RRG is a voluntary group consisting of Islamic scholars and teachers. Initially, RRG's primary objective was to rehabilitate detained JI members and their families through counselling, but it has now broadened its scope to include countering misinterpretations promoted by self-radicalized individuals and those in support of ISIS. The RRG believes that there is no need for cases to always be dealt with by the law, and the early detection of potential terrorists can help. They cited examples of how they reached out and helped individuals early. They provided an example of a school student who had written pro-ISIS slogans after being exposed to radical online material. This alarmed his father who took the boy for counselling at the RRG. Counsellors were able to help the teenager. As the Minister of Muslim Affairs, Dr. Yaacob Ibrahim had remarked, "Reporting those who have been radicalised are the best and only way to help a loved one before it is too late" (Toh, 2017).

As the detainees' ideology often affects their family members, RRG counsels the latter as well to disrupt the vicious ideological cycle. Another important feature of the rehabilitation programme is to stimulate the minds of the detainees to understand Islam within the Singapore context. The program aims to show that living as a Muslim in Singapore is practicable and not at odds with Islamic principles. Besides its primary counselling and rehabilitation work, the RRG is committed to building social resilience in the community through its outreach programmes.

The research article below by the ISD discusses several interesting issues relating to rehabilitation and treatment. It provides a rare insight into the stages of psychological change seen in Singaporeans detained for involvement with regional terrorist groups, from disengaging from radical ideologies to finally renouncing the use of violence. It explains that the Singapore rehabilitation programme consists of three components. These are 'psychological rehabilitation', 'social rehabilitation', and 'religious rehabilitation'. Psychologists who provided psychological counselling and assessment visited detainees regularly. They would look at the detainee's ability to cope with the mental stressors, their psychological reasoning, propensity for hatred and violence, and vulnerability to radical influence.

RESEARCH ARTICLE:
The Stages of Change in the Rehabilitation of Terrorist Operatives: The Singapore Experience

The article explains that there are seven broad stages. These stages do not necessarily follow a fixed pattern. They may develop in different directions for different individuals, feed off one another in a mutually reinforcing way, or strengthen one another as they interact as shown in the Figure 7.2.

This paper discusses the case of 'Former JI member, D', who was introduced to the JI class by acquaintances made at a religious class. D wanted to enhance his religious knowledge. He found that the JI class was initially conducted like any other religious classes, but the teachers gradually began to discuss global events and turmoil in countries such as

(Continued)

(*Continued*)

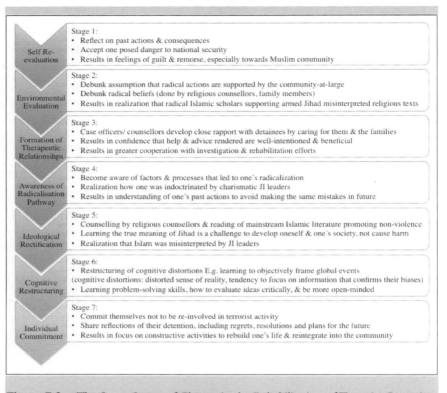

Figure 7.2:   The Seven Stages of Change in the Rehabilitation of Terrorist Operatives

Afghanistan and Palestine. D participated in the JI activities because he sympathised with its cause. He brought several people to join the JI and went to the Philippines to undergo weapons training.

Whilst in detention, D felt distressed. His children could not accept his detention and asked his wife for the reason behind his involvement. He found his four years in detention to be very difficult. He lost his freedom, and was separated from his family. He regretted his past actions. He began to recognise that what he did was wrong, and treated the entire episode as a lesson learned. In detention, D was well treated. He had time to exercise, and spent the rest of his time reciting the Quran and reading

(*Continued*)

(Continued)

books. He also underwent counselling. Each week, his family would visit him faithfully.

As a whole, the article suggested that the results of the rehabilitation programme have been very encouraging. A good number of the detainees have been released. They continue to maintain close rapport with their case officers, religious counsellors, and psychologists. They have also reintegrated well into society among friends, at work and at home.

Source: Counter-Terrorism Operations Division, Internal Security Department, *Home Team Journal*, Issue No. 5 (2014).

Exit Programs

Finally, in rehabilitation, there is the need to address deradicalization and exit programs. After all, a violent extremist who is not reformed can still remain a threat. According to Ramalingam and Tuck (2014) in a paper titled *The Need for Exit Programmes*, they recommended that to be successful, the exit programs should have the following characteristics:

- They must be run by trained and experienced intervention providers with a proven track record of running such programs.
- Ideally, they should be voluntary, as evidenced from countries where these programs exist; programs are most effective when they are voluntary.
- The personal commitment of participants is vital, and no direct financial incentives should be offered.
- They should seek to change ideology (partially or completely).
- They should involve 'former' extremists. However, this should be done only where they would have an impact on the individual and could offer mentorship. 'Formers' themselves should pass rigorous security checks, and should always meet with the individual in the presence of the main intervention provider.
- They should be internally and externally evaluated. These programs should be constantly refined in approach and methodology, based on evidence about what is, and what is not working in rehabilitation.

- They should consider providing support to families and social networks of participants. Exit programs should generally be integrated into wider social support system.
- They should require at least two years of funding. Exit programmes are most successful when backed by long-term, sustainable financial support.

7.9 Summary

- There are major challenges in defining the term 'terrorism'. It is often confused with radicalism and extremism.
- Our major challenge is with the violent person and not just the radical mind. Radicals may actually be useful for society, especially when they question the existing norms and society innovates. We cannot police every radical mind because such a society would be unbearable to live in. On the other hand, history has also shown that *some* radical minds may possibly turn to violent extremism under some circumstances. Therefore, they cannot be ignored entirely.
- While it is challenging to pinpoint a terrorist profile, there are many useful explanatory developmental pathways. Even though there are no models which can explain everything, most pathway models suggest that there are common elements.
- Terrorism has several levels of explanations ranging from macro, meso, and micro level explanations. From this, we know that terrorism is *both* a global and local phenomenon. The solutions therefore must also follow in the same manner.
- Terrorists as a group (nomothetic profiles) do not appear to have mental illness or adjustment disorders. On the other hand, some lone wolves (idiographic profiles) do appear to have some kind of adjustment issues. This does not mean that mental illness or mental disability causes terrorism.
- Terrorism (in its various forms) has been with Singapore for many years, and security ministries including the Ministry of Home Affairs (MHA) and Ministry of Defense (MINDEF) have dealt with these challenges effectively.

- The threat of terrorism remains high. The SGSecure Movement is a movement to empower the Singapore community to respond in the aftermath of a terror attack.
- There are counter measures. These range from strategic measures (macro and meso) to tactical and community-based (micro) measures.
- Another way of looking at these measures is to use the CLIP model, for example, the legal measures, the local considerations (e.g., the role of RRG and Islam as it is practiced in Singapore); criminalistics considerations (e.g., terrorism forensics); investigative and enforcement considerations (e.g., detention and arrests processes), and psychological considerations (e.g., risk assessment, behavioral characteristics, role of mental illness, and rehabilitation).

Relevant Journals

Studies in Conflict Terrorism
Terrorism and Political Violence
Journal of Terrorism Research
Behavioral Sciences of Terrorism and Political Aggression
International Journal of Cyber Warfare and Terrorism
Journal of Policing, Intelligence and Counter Terrorism
International Journal of Intelligence and Counterintelligence

E-Resources

United Nations Office of Counter-Terrorism. http://www.un.org/en/counterterrorism/index.shtml
911 Commission Report. https://9-11commission.gov/report/911Report.pdf
US Department of State. Bureau of Counter-Terrorism. https://www.state.gov/j/ct/
Department of Homeland Security. Planning ahead of Disasters. https://www.ready.gov/
National Child Traumatic Stress Framework. http://www.nctsn.org/trauma-types/terrorism

Global Terrorism Database. START. University of Maryland. http://www.start.umd.edu/research-projects/global-terrorism-database-gtd

SG SECURE. https://www.sgsecure.sg/Pages/default.aspx

MINDEF Counter-Terrorism Page. https://www.mindef.gov.sg/web/portal/mindef/defence-matters/defence-topic/defence-topic-detail/counter-terrorism

Singapore Police Force. Prevent Terrorism. https://www.police.gov.sg/resources/prevent-terrorism/guarding-against-terrorism-pamphlet

International Center for Political Violence and Terrorism Research (Singapore). http://www.rsis.edu.sg/research/icpvtr/

Southeast Asia Regional Center for Counter-Terrorism. http://www.kln.gov.my/web/guest/dd-searcct

Jakarta Center for Law Enforcement Cooperation. https://www.jclec.org/

Australian Federal Police. Counter-Terrorism. https://www.afp.gov.au/careers/graduate-program/eligibility-qualifications-and-business-area/counter-terrorism.

Sample Research Essay Titles

- What is 'terrorism'?
- What are the causes and correlates of terrorism?
- Is there a profile of a terrorist?
- What main strategies should be adopted to counter and manage terrorism?

References

Australian Government (n.d.). *Australia's counter-terrorism laws.* Produced by Attorney Generals Department.

Bandura, A. (1973). *Aggression: A Social Learning Analysis.* New York, NY: Prentice Hall.

Bandura, A. (1998). Mechanisms of moral disengagement. In W. Reich (Ed.), *Origins of Terrorism: Psychologies, Ideologies, Theologies, and States of Mind* (pp. 161–192). Washington, DC: Woodrow Wilson Center Press.

BBC News (December 2004). Retrieved from http://bbcspain.localizer.co/news/world-uscanada-30401100

Bjørgo, T. (2009). Processes of disengagement from violent groups of the extreme right. In T. Bjørgo & J. Horgan (Eds.), *Leaving Terrorism Behind: Individual and Collective Disengagement* (pp. 30–48). Abingdon: Routledge.

Borum, R. (2004). *Psychology of Terrorism*. Tampa, FL: University of South Florida.

Borum, R. (2014). Psychological vulnerabilities and propensities for involvement in violent extremism. *Behavioral Sciences and the Law, 32*, 286–305.

Byman, D.L. (2017). *Can lone wolves be stopped?* Retrieved from https://www.brookings.edu/blog/markaz/2017/03/15/can-lone-wolves-be-stopped/.

Chang, R. (2015, May 29). Self-radicalised Singaporeans who were previously detained. *The Straits Times*.

Chen, S. (2012, March 16). Investigating a bomb from the past. *Home Team News*.

Chia, L. (2017, July 4). Nine radicalised maids repatriated from Singapore since 2015: Desmond Lee. The Second Minister for Home Affairs said two more foreign maids have been detected since January. *Channel News Asia*.

Cheong, D. (2017, September 14). ISIS posts video of Singaporean fighter in Syria, security agencies monitoring his activities. *The Straits Times*.

Centers for Disease Control and Prevention (n.d.). *Bio-terrorism*. Retrieved from https://www.cdc.gov/healthcommunication/toolstemplates/entertainmented/tips/Bioterrorism.html.

Chan, F. (2015, November 22). Returning ISIS militants a growing menace to S-E Asia. *The Straits Times*.

Channel News Asia (2016). *27 Bangladeshi nationals arrested in Singapore and repatriated for terror links*. Retrieved from http://www.channelnewsasia.com/news/singapore/27-bangladeshi-nationals-arrested-in-singapore-and-repatriated-f-8221840.

Cochrane, J. (2015, November 26). From Indonesia, A Muslim Challenge to The Ideology of The Islamic State. *The New York Times*.

Corner, E. & Gill, P. (2015). A false dichotomy? Mental illness and lone-actor terrorism. *Law and Human Behavior, 39*(1), 23–34.

Corner, E., Gill, P., & Mason, O. (2016). Mental health disorders and the terrorist: A research note probing selection effects and disorder prevalence. *Studies in Conflict and Terrorism, 39*(6), 560–568.

Corsi, V. (2008). Singapore's Terrorism Countermeasures. Retrieved from http://crimeandterrorism.org/sites/default/files/Singapore_CT_Efforts_Corsi.doc.

Counterterrorism.org (n.d). Retrieved from https://www.counterextremism.org/resources/details/id/404/center-for-strategic-counterterrorism-communicationscscc.

Crayton, J.W. (1983). Terrorism and the psychology of the self. In L.Z. Freedman & Y. Alexander (Eds.), *Perspectives on Terrorism* (pp. 33–41). Wilmington, DE: Scholarly Resources, Inc.

Crenshaw, M. (1986). The psychology of political terrorism. In M.G. Hermann (Ed.), *Political Psychology* (pp. 379–413). San Francisco: Jossey-Bass.

Crenshaw, M. (1992). How terrorists think: What psychology can contribute to understanding terrorism. In L. Howard (Ed.), *Terrorism: Roots, Impact, Responses*. New York, NY: Praeger.

Daniel, W.B. (2015). Konfrontasi: Why It Still Matters to Singapore. *RSIS Commentary*.

Dedeoglu, B. (2003). Bermuda triangle: comparing official definition of terrorist activity. *Terrorism and Political Violence, 15,* 81–110.

Department of State and US Aid (2016, May). Department of State & USAID Joint Strategy on Countering Violent Extremism.

Deutsche Welle (2017, September 15). Left-*wing extremism: 'German police step up search for former RAF terrorists'*. Retrieved from http://www.dw.com/en/left-wingextremism-german-police-step-up-search-for-former-raf-terrorists/a-41356234.

Denning, D.E. (2000). *Testimony before the Special Oversight Panel on Terrorism, Committee on Armed Services.* U.S. House of Representatives. Retrieved from https://web.archive.org/web/20140310162011/http://www.cs.georgetown.edu/~denning/infosec/cyberterror.html.

Dollard, J., Doob, L.W., Miller, N.E., Mowrer, W., & Sears, R.R. (1939). *Frustration and Aggression.* New Haven, CT: Yale University Press.

Eidelson, R.J. & Eidelson, J.I. (2003). Dangerous ideas. Five beliefs that propel groups toward conflict. *American Psychologist, 58*(3), 182–192.

European Commission's Expert Group on Violent Radicalisation (2008). *Radicalisation Processes Leading to Acts of Terrorism.* Retrieved from http://www.rikcoolsaet.be/files/art_ip_wz/Expert%20Group%20Report%20Violent%20Radicalisation%20FINAL.pdf.

Friedland, N. (1992). Becoming a terrorist: Social and individual antecedents. In L. Howard (Ed.), *Terrorism: Roots, Impact, Responses.* New York, NY: Praeger.

FBI Counterterrorism Division (2006). *The Radicalization Process: From Conversion to Jihad.* Federal Bureau of Investigation Intelligence Assessment.

Ferracuti, E. & Bruno, E. (1981). Psychiatric aspects of terrorism in Italy. In *The mad, the bad and the different: Essays in honor of Simon Dinitz.*

Gill, P. (2015). *Seven Findings on Lone-Actor Terrorists.* International Center for the Study of Terrorism (ICST). Retrieved from http://sites.psu.edu/icst/2013/02/06/seven-findings-on-lone-actorterrorists/.

Gill P., Horgan J., & Deckert P. (2014). Bombing alone: Tracing the motivations and antecedent behaviors of lone-actor terrorists. *Journal of Forensic Science, 59*(2), 425–435.

Govern, K.H. (2009, January). *Agroterrorism and Ecoterrorism: A Survey of IndoAmerican Approaches Under Law and Policy to Prevent and Defend Against the Potential Threats Ahead*. Retrieved from https://www.law.upenn.edu/live/files/2299-governagroterrorism-and-ecoterrorism.

Gruenewald, J., Chermak, S., & Freilich, J.D. (2013). Distinguishing "loner" attacks from other domestic extremist violence: A comparison of far-right homicide incident and offender characteristics. *Criminology and Public Policy, 12*(1), 65–91.

Gurr, T. (1970). *Why Men Rebel*. Princeton, NJ: Princeton University Press.

Hacker, F.J. (1983). Dialectic interrelationships of personal and political factors in terrorism. In L.Z. Freedman & Y. Alexander (Eds.), *Perspectives on Terrorism* (pp. 19–31). Wilmington, DE: Scholarly Resources, Inc.

Handler, J.S. (1990). Socioeconomic profile of an American terrorist: 1960s and 1970s. *Terrorism, 13*, 195–213.

Hallowell, B. (2013). Punk rockers take on 'Buddhist bin laden' and radical monks who are sparking violence against Muslims. *The Blaze*. Retrieved from http://www.theblaze.com/stories/2013/08/05/punk-rockerstake-on-buddhist-bin-laden-and-radical-monks-who-are-sparking-violenceagainst-muslims/.

HM Government (2011). *CONTEST: The United Kingdom's Strategy for Countering Terrorism*.

Hodal, K. (2013, April 18). Buddhist monk uses racism and rumours to spread hatred in Burma. *The Guardian*.

Hubbard, D.G. (1971). *The Skyjacker: His Flights of Fantasy*. New York, NY: Macmillan.

Hussain, Z. (2016, January 21). 27 radicalised Bangladeshis held under ISA. *The Straits Times*.

Hussain, Z. (2016). How ISIS supporters passing through Singapore were nabbed. *The Straits Times*.

Hwang, J.C. (2017, October 1). The Unintended Consequences of Amending Indonesia's Anti-Terrorism Law. *Lawfare*.

Hu, W. (2016). Psychological effects of the threat of ISIS: A preliminary inquiry of Singapore case studies. In M. Khader, L.S. Neo, G. Ong, E. Tan, & J. Chin, (Eds.), *Countering Violent Extremism and Radicalisation in the Digital Era*. Hershey, PA: IGI Global.

International Centre for the Study of Radicalisation (2014). *ICSR Insight: Who inspires the Syrian foreign fighters?* Retrieved from http://icsr.info/category/icsr-news/insights/.

Institute for Safety, Security and Crisis Management (ISSCM) (2008). *Radicalisation, Recruitment and the EU Counter-radicalisation Strategy*. Brussels: European Commission.

Jäger, H., Schmidtchen, G., & Süllwold, L. (Eds.) (1981). *Analyzen zum Terrorismus 2: Lebenslaufanalysen*. Darmstadt, Germany: DeutscherVerlag.

James, P.A. & Pisoiu, D. (2016, July 6). *Mental Illness and Terrorism*. Retrieved from http://www.start.umd.edu/news/mental-illness-and-terrorism.

Kebbell, M.R. & Porter, L. (2011). An intelligence assessment framework for identifying individuals at risk of committing acts of violent extremism against the West. *Security Journal, 25*(3), 212–228.

Kellen, K. (1979). *Terrorists — What Are They Like? How Some Terrorists Describe Their World and Actions*. Santa Monica, CA: RAND.

Levine, S. (1999). Youths in terroristic groups, gangs and cults: The allure, the animus, and the alienation. *Psychiatric Annals, 29*, 342–349.

Lezak, M.D. (1995). *Neuropsychological Assessment* (3rd ed.). New York, NY: Oxford University Press.

Lifton, R.J. (2000). *Destroying the World to Save It: Aum Shinrikyo and the New Global Terrorism*. New York, NY: Holt.

McCauley, C. & Moskalenko, S. (2011). *Friction: How Radicalization Happens to Them and Us*. UK: Oxford University Press.

McCauley, C. & Moskalenko, S. (2014). Toward a profile of lone Wolf terrorists: What moves an individual from radical opinion to radical action. *Terrorism and Political Violence, 26*(1), 69–85.

Martin, G. (2006). *Understanding Terrorism: Challenges, Perspectives, and Issues* (2nd ed.). Thousand Oaks: Sage Publications.

McIntyre, J. (2011, July 25). Anders Behring Breivik: a disturbing ideology. *The Independent*.

Ministry of Home Affairs (2003). *The Jemaah Islamiyah Arrests and the Threat of Terrorism*.

Moghadam, A. (2006). *The Roots of Terrorism*. New York, NY: Chelsea House.

Mudde, C. (2010). *The Ideology of the Extreme Right*. Oxford: Manchester University Press.

Mohamed, B.A, Muhammad, S., & Alam, S.B.S. (2016). Salafis and Wahhabis: Two Sides of the Same Coin? *RSIS Commentaries*.

National Child Traumatic Stress Network (n.d.). *Chemical Terrorism*. Retrieved from http://www.nctsn.org/trauma-types/terrorism/chemical.

National Consortium for the Study of Terrorism and Responses to Terrorism (2010). *Community Level Indicators of Radicalization: A Data and Methods Task Force*. Report to Human Factors, Behavioral Sciences Division, Science and Technology Directorate, U.S. Department of Homeland Security.

National Institute of Justice (2000). *A Guide for Explosion Bombing Explosion Bombing Scene Investigation*. Department of Justice.

National Security Coordination Centre (2004). *The Fight Against Terror: Singapore's National Security Strategy*.

Nasser-Eddine, M., Garnham, B., Agostino, K., & Caluya, G. (2011). *Countering Violent Extremism (CVE) Literature Review*. Edinburgh, Australia: Australian Government, Department of Defence, Command and Control Division, Defence Science and Technology Organisation (DSTO).

Neo, L.S. (2016). An Internet-mediated pathway for online radicalisation: RECRO. In M. Khader, L.S. Neo, G. Ong, E. Tan, & J. Chin, (Eds.), *Countering Violent Extremism and Radicalisation in the Digital Era* (pp. 197–224). Hershey, PA: IGI Global.

Nirmala, M. (2014, February 13). MacDonald House attack still strikes home in S'pore, *The Jakarta Post*.

Norwegian Ministry of Justice and Public Security (2014). *Action plan against Radicalisation and Violent Extremism*.

Nouri, J.L. & Whiting, A. (2014). Understanding, locating and constructing cyberterrorism. In T. Chen, L. Jarvis, & S. Macdonald (Eds.), *Cyberterrorism: Understanding, Assessment and Response* (pp. 25–41). New York, NY: Springer.

Olsson, P.A. (1988). The terrorist and the terrorized: Some psychoanalytic consideration. *Journal of Psychohistory*, 16, 47–60.

Oots, K.L. & Wiegele, T.C. (1985). Terrorist and victim: Psychiatric and physiological approaches. *Terrorism: An International Journal*, 8(1), 1–32.

Ong, K.S. (2002). 1974 — The Laju Incident 07 Jan 2002, 0900 hours. Retrieved from https://www.mindef.gov.sg/oms/imindef/about_us/history/overview/birth_of_saf/v06n01_history.html.

Pathania, S.R. (2012). Preventive detention of terrorists: A review of law in commonwealth countries. *TMC Academic Journal*, 7(1), 28–39.

Pantucci, R., Ellis, C., & Chaplais, L. (2015). Countering Lone-Actor Terrorism. Series No. 1, Royal United Services Institute for Defence and Security Studies Lone-Actor Terrorism Literature Review.

PET (2009). Center for Terroranalyse (CTA) *'Radikalisering og terror'*. Retrieved from http://www.pet.dk/upload/radikalisering_og_terror.pdf.

Prigg, M. (2015). The tweet that cost $139 billion: Researchers analyse impact of hacked 2013 message claiming President Obama had been injured by White House explosion. *The Daily Mail*. Retrieved from http://www.dailymail.co.uk/sciencetech/article-3090221/The-tweet-cost-139-BILLION-Researchersanalyse-impact-hacked-message-claiming-President-Obama-injured-WhiteHouse-explosion.html.

Post, J.M. (1984). Notes on a psychodynamic theory of terrorist behavior. *Terrorism*, 7, 241–256.

Post, J.M., Sprinzak, E., & Denny, L.M. (2003). The terrorists in their own words: Interviews with thirty-five incarcerated Middle Eastern terrorists. *Terrorism and Political Violence*, 15, 171–184.

Ramalingam, V. & Tuck, H. (2014). *The Need for Exit Programme. Why Deradicalisation and Disengagement Matters in the UK's Approach to Far Right Violence.* Institute of Strategic Dialogue.

Rice, X. (2007). Background: The Lord's resistance army. *The Guardian.*

Religious Rehabilitation Group (RRG) (n.d.). *Jihad: Jihad and its correct interpretation.* Retrieved from https://www.rrg.sg/jihad/.

Robins, R.S. & Post, J.M. (1997). *Political Paranoia: The Psychopolitics of Hatred.* New Haven, CT: Yale University Press.

Sageman, M. (2004). *Understanding Terror Networks.* Philadelphia: University of Pennsylvania Press.

Sageman, M. (2006). *Islam and al Qaeda, Root Causes of Suicide Terrorism.* London, NY: Routledge.

Sageman, M. (2007). *Radicalization of Global Islamist Terrorists.*

Sandler, T. & Lapan, H.E. (1988). The calculus of dissent: An analysis of terrorists' choice of targets. *Synthése, 76,* 245–261.

Sandler, T., Tschirhart, J.T., & Cauley, J. (1983). A theoretical analysis of transnational terrorism. *American Political Science Review, 77,* 36–54.

Schmid, A.P. (Ed.) (2011). *The Routledge Handbook of Terrorism Research.* New York and London: Routledge.

Schmid, A.P. & Jongman, A.J. (1988). *Political Terrorism* (2nd ed.). Oxford: North-Holland.

Schmid, A.P. (2013). *Radicalisation, De-radicalisation and Counter-radicalisation: A Conceptual Discussion and Literature Review.* The Netherlands: International Centre for Counter-Terrorism (ICCT): The Hague. States Senate Committee on Homeland Security and Governmental Affairs.

Scott-Railton, J. & Hardy, S. (2014, December 18). Malware attack targeting Syrian ISIS critics. *Citizenlab.* Retrieved from https://citizenlab.org/2014/12/malware-attack-targeting-syrian-isis-critics.

Seger, K.A. (2001). *Left-Wing Extremism: The Current Threat. Center for Human Reliability Studies.* Oak Ridge, TN: Oak Ridge Institute for Science and Education.

Seow, B.Y. (2018, February 28). Bill to give police more powers in a terror attack. *The Straits Times.*

Shell, A. (2013). This stocks gyrate wildly after fake terror tweet. *USA Today.* Retrieved from http://www.usatoday.com/story/money/markets/2013/04/23stocks-gyrate-wildly-after-fake-terror-tweet/2107089.

Silber, M.D. & Bhatt, A. (2007). *Radicalization in the West: The Homegrown Threat.*

Silke, A. (1998). Cheshire-Cat Logic: The recurring theme of terrorist abnormality in psychological research. *Psychology, Crime, and Law, 4*(1), 51–69.

Singh, J. & Muhammad Haziq, B.J. (2016, April 12). United front needed to counter ISIS growing campaign in SEA. *The Straits Times*.

Spaaij, R. (2010). The enigma of lone wolf terrorism: An assessment. *Studies in Conflict and Terrorism, 33*(9), 45–53.

Stern, J. (1999). *The Ultimate Terrorists*. Cambridge, MA: Harvard University Press.

Stern, J.E. (2014). X: A case study of a Swedish Neo-Nazi and his reintegration into Swedish society. *Behavioral Sciences and the Law, 32*(3), 440–453.

Strentz, T. (1988). A terrorist psychosocial profile: Past and present. *FBI Law Enforcement Bulletin, 57*, 13–19.

The Straits Times (2015). *6 things to do in a terror attack: Advice from experts*. Retrieved from http://www.straitstimes.com/world/europe/6-things-todo-in-a-terror-attack-advice-from-experts.

The Straits Times (2016). *Indonesia's Muslim 'cyber warriors' take on terrorists*. Retrieved from http://www.straitstimes.com/asia/se-asia/indonesiasmuslim-cyber-warriors-take-on-terrorists.

Tarnby, M. (2005). *Recruitment of Islamist Terrorists in Europe*. Trends and Perspectives, Research Report funded by the Danish Ministry of Justice.

Taylor, M. & Quayle, E. (1994). *Terrorist Lives*. London: Brassey's.

Taylor, M. & Ryan, H. (1988). Fanaticism, political suicide and terrorism. *Terrorism, 11*, 91–111.

The Guardian (2016, August 16). *Plot to launch Singapore rocket attack foiled, say Indonesian police*.

Toh, Y.C. (2017, June 24). Case studies show value of detecting radicals early. *The Straits Times*.

Topsfield, J. & Rompies, K. (2017). Indonesia cracks down on terrorism with new laws and joint patrols. *Sydney Morning Herald*.

U.S. Department of Homeland Security (2004). *Homeland Security Centers (HS Centers) Program Broad Agency announcement: Homeland Security Center for Behavioral and Social Aspects of Terrorism and Counter-terrorism*. Washington, DC: University Programs, Office of Research and Development, Science and Technology.

US Department of State (2016). *Country Reports*. East Asia and Pacific, Australia.

US Embassy in Malaysia (2016). *Country Reports on Terrorism 2016 (Malaysia)*. Retrieved from https://my.usembassy.gov/crt2016_ms_eng-072017/.

United Nations Counterterrorism Implementation Task Force (CTITF) (2011). *Use of the Internet to counter the appeal of extremist violence*. UN: Working Group on use of the Internet for terrorist purpose.

Victoroff, J. (2005). The mind of the terrorist: A review and critique of psychological approaches. *Journal of Conflict Resolution, 49*(1), 3–42.

Weinberg, L. & Eubank, W.L. (1994). Cultural differences in the behavior of terrorists. *Terrorism and Political Violence, 6*, 1–28.

Weinberg, L., Pedahzur, A., & Hirsch-Hoefler, S. (2004). The challenges of conceptualizing terrorism. *Terrorism and Political Violence, 16*, 777–794.

Weimann, G. & von Knop, K. (2008). Applying the notion of noise to countering online terrorism. *Studies in Conflict and Terrorism, 31*(10), 883–902.

Whitaker, B. (1972). *The Fourth World: Victims of Group Oppression: Eight Reports From the Field Work of the Minority Rights Group.* New York, NY: Schocken.

Wilson, M.A. (2000). Toward a model of terrorist behavior in hostage-taking incidents. *Journal of Conflict Resolution, 44*, 403–424.

Wiktorowicz, Q. (2005). A genealogy of radical Islam. *Studies in Conflict and Terrorism, 28*(2), 75–97.

Winter, C. (2015). *The Virtual 'Caliphate': Understanding Islamic State's Propaganda Strategy.* London: Quilliam Foundation.

Zetter, K. (2015). Central command's Twitter account hacked...As Obama speaks on cybersecurity. *Wired.com*. Retrieved from http://www.wired.com/2015/01/centcoms-twitter-hack.

CHAPTER 8

APPLYING FORENSIC PSYCHOLOGY IN LEGAL SETTINGS

"There are nearly as many intersections between law and psychology...
conflict resolution and negotiation; judgment and decision-making
capacity; prejudice and stereotyping; criminal responsibility; competency;
assessment of evidence, including the reliability of eyewitnesses, and lie
detection; hedonics; developmental psychology and educational policy;
addiction and drug policy — these are just a few of the frontiers open
to scholars and practitioners educated in both law and psychology."

Stanford Psychology–Law Program

8.1 Introduction

This chapter is about the application of forensic psychology in legal settings. This is about the interdisciplinary work between law and psychology. In many parts of the world, this field is growing rapidly, even though its developments are slower in Singapore. Much of this fascinating work has been systematically discussed in journals such as *Law and Human Behaviour*, *Psychology*, *Public Policy and Law*, *Psychology, Crime, and Law*, and *Journal of Psychiatry, Psychology and Law*.

In addition, there are many professional societies today, which discuss this interdisciplinary work. The American Psychological Association, for example, has Division 41, in which the American Psychology–Law Society "promotes the contributions of psychology to the understanding of law and legal institutions, the education of psychologists in legal matters and law personnel in psychological matters, and the application of psychology in the legal system."[1] In Europe, there is the European Association of Psychology and Law.[2] In Australia and New Zealand, there is the Australia and New Zealand Association of Psychiatry, Psychology and Law (ANZAPPL).[3] Within Asia, there are several annually held conferences between Japan, Korea, and China, at a meeting called the East Asian Psychology and Law Conference. In Singapore, the Singapore Psychological Society is beginning to collaborate with the Singapore Law Society, but it is still in its early days.

8.1.1 *Roles of a Forensic-Legal Psychologist*

In Chapter 1, it was discussed that there are four sub-types of forensic psychologists (forensic-enforcement, forensic-clinical, forensic-academic, and forensic-legal). This final chapter provides a deeper

---

[1] http://www.apa.org/about/division/div41.aspx
[2] https://eapl.eu/
[3] https://anzappl.org/new-zealand/

treatment of the final sub-type. There are several roles of the forensic-legal psychologist, and these are as follows:

Academia

Many forensic-legal psychologists work as professors in university psychology departments, criminal justice departments, or law schools. Like other professors, they generally conduct and publish empirical research, teach classes, and mentor graduate and undergraduate students.

Expert witnesses

Psychologists specifically trained in legal issues can be called by legal parties to testify as expert witnesses on issues such as crime victim reactions, eyewitness memory, and competence to stand trial. Psychologists who focus on clinical issues often testify specifically about a defendant's behavior, competence, intelligence, suggestibility, and trauma.

Policy and law making

Psychologists employed in the public service may be called to undertake research to support legislative policy and laws, which are introduced through Bills in Parliament.

Amicus briefs or Amicus Curiae

Usually seen in other countries, namely America, psychologists provide an 'amicus brief' to the Court as an *amicus curiae* ('friend of the court'). An *amicus curiae* is usually a person with interest in or views on the subject matter. Such *amicus curiae* briefs are commonly filed in matters of broad public interest (Bersoff, 2013). Amicus briefs are a means for educating legal decision-makers about social science data relevant to the issues. The American Psychological Association (APA) has provided briefs concerning mental illness, battered woman syndrome, child abuse, and retardation.

Visit this link for a listing of amicus briefs by the APA: http://www.apa.org/about/offices/ogc/amicus/index-issues.aspx.

Trial consulting

In America, psychologists work in trial consulting. Trial consultants perform a variety of services for lawyers, such as performing 'mock trials', organising testimony, and preparing witnesses to testify (for example, managing their stress, anxiety, and credibility).

Private practice

Some psychologists in private practice are hired by lawyers to evaluate their clients. These opinions may entail assessments and reports on whether a defendant has a mental disability or disorder that prevents him or her from going on trial, or what a person's mental state might have been at the time of an offense (Novotney, 2017).

Civil law cases

Forensic psychologists may be involved in evaluating plaintiffs in workers' compensation cases, as well as in divorce and custody cases.

Forensic neuropsychologists

These professionals are asked to assess the validity of claims such as amnesia during an alleged offense, and to evaluate whether or not a defendant can be neuro-psychologically able to have competence to stand trial, particularly when conditions such as dementia might be present. Neuropsychologists may provide personal injury and fitness-for-duty evaluations, looking at the impact, for example, of a traumatic brain injury on functioning (Novotney, 2017).

8.2 Special Topics in Criminal Law Applications

There are many specialized topics in legal psychology, and this introductory book cannot possibly cover every important issue. Therefore, only some of the main issues have been selected and will be discussed.

8.2.1 *Eyewitness Testimony*

Eyewitnesses are not infallible. They make mistakes. However, we use them a lot in legal settings. The number one contributor to false confessions in the criminal justice system is error in eyewitness testimony evidence. There are factors that affect eyewitness accuracy. In order to appreciate the factors involved, we have to consider the role of memory.

Experts often make the point that memory does not function like a digital device that records things permanently nor accurately. Memory is constructed and reconstructed. There are three aspects to memory: (1) acquisition or encoding of information, (2) retention, and (3) retrieval of stored information. Many factors affect these aspects (Brown & Campbell, 2010).

During the crime event itself, the viewing and encoding conditions affect the level of details provided and the accuracy. They are divided into characteristics of the crime scene, witness factors and perpetrator factors, and they are as follows:

Crime scene (or situation) characteristics matter (Brown & Campbell, 2010). For example:

- Recall accuracy is affected by the amount of light at the crime scene;
- The greater the exposure to the event, the greater the opportunity to attend to more details and the greater the accuracy of recall (MacLin *et al.*, 2001). However, people overestimate short events (a few seconds were estimated as being minutes) and underestimate long events;
- Large objects appeared to move slower than small objects, even when they were moving at the same speed (Scialfa *et al.*, 1991);
- Facial identification accuracy rates were poorer when observations are made at a distance of 15 meters or more, and illuminations less than five lux (Wagenaar & van der Schrier, 1996);
- Highly emotional events are well retained in memory but less central and peripheral events are poorly retained (Christianson, 1992). The most salient aspects such as a weapon, knife, or danger signals are most attended to and remembered, and often

at the expense of other details, such as the offender's face (Steblay, 1992);

- There is a strong cross-race effect. There is better identification of the same race than other race situations, and more mistakes made in other race/cross-race identifications (Meissner & Brigham, 2001).

'Witness factors' matter as well:

- Age is an important witness factor. Young preschool children tend to recall fewer details than older ones;
- Younger children are also more susceptible to suggestions;
- Children are however not *more* suggestible than adults when it comes to meaningful events (King & Yuille, 1987); and
- Older witnesses (60- to 80-year-olds) show more impairment in their accuracy of suspect descriptions (Yarmey, 2000). They show greater tendencies to choose someone from target-absent line-ups, resulting in false identifications (Memon & Gabbert, 2003).

'Perpetrator factors' that affect eyewitness testimony include the following:

- Changes in hairstyle and removal of perpetrators' eyeglasses will influence accuracy of facial recognition and witnesses may be less accurate (Patterson & Baddeley, 1977);
- Changes in perpetrators' hairline by the wearing of a hat or something similar could result in inaccuracy of identification;
- Faces that are changed or disguised are less easily recognized (Cutler *et al.*, 1987); and
- Perpetrators with distinctive faces are more easily recognized (Light *et al.*, 1979).

In conclusion, most of the time, eyewitness descriptions can be accurate, but we need to also appreciate that, at times and under some conditions, they can also be mistaken and inaccurate. There are many individual and contextual factors to consider. All of this has serious implications, especially in the misidentification of innocent persons.

Therefore, it is good for the courts and police officers to be aware of the research on the psychological factors that affect eyewitness testimony.

8.2.2 *False Memories*

While memory works most of the time, it is, at times, vulnerable to suggestions. Leading questions by interviewers can affect memory and plant ideas into people's minds. Conversations with co-accused/ co-witnesses can also affect memory accuracy. The 'misinformation effect' happens when misleading information (presented after an event) is incorporated into an individual's memory (Davis & Loftus, 2006). When psychologists conduct experiments to show this effect, they create a mock crime scene and instruct people to observe, then arrange for the participants have a conversation with another (staged) person. The participants who spoke to the other staged person tended to remember the details incorrectly, despite having personally witnessed it! The control group participants who witnessed the same mock scene but did not have a conversation with the actor actually did better in recalling scene details. For example, in these studies, participants would remember the Eiffel Tower as the Leaning Tower of Pisa. Others would recall details about broken glass which was not there at all! (Laney & Loftus, 2010). This has real-world implications since witnesses would talk to other witnesses about the incident/crime which they saw or were involved in, and then report this later to police officers and lawyers (Powell *et al.*, 2005).

There is debate about 'recovered memory'. Some clinicians believe that memory is immune to distortion, especially memories of a traumatic nature, such as child abuse. They believe that these memories can be held or repressed for years before they surface to consciousness again years later (Brown *et al.*, 1998; Terr, 1991). Terr (1991) explained that repeated traumas such as child abuse are repressed, because these children develop skills that dissociate themselves from their experiences of abuse and this hence 'protects' them. While this idea sounds plausible, there is a problem with the way these studies have been done. Most are retrospectively conducted. Experimenters ask individuals who had been abused, if they remember periods of time when they could *not* remember the abuse, and most replied in the positive. The main issue is — if a person knew there was abuse, is it at all possible to fully repress it (Laney & Loftus, 2010)? Also, very few prospective studies seem to provide scientific evidence for this 'repression'. There are reasons why people do not recall this abuse. The reasons do not have to be repression. For example, some victims were very young, others could not really tell if they were being abused or not, as they could not recognise inappropriate touching or violation as sexual abuse due to their age. Sometimes, victims failed to report an event or cannot recall an event, and this cannot be taken as repression (Garaerts *et al.*, 2005). The question remains that if people are not repressing these memories, then where do false memories come from? Well, there is evidence that memories can be implanted in others! For example, Loftus and Pickrell (1995) did an early study where participants were showed three true childhood events and one traumatic childhood event which was false (the false event planted was 'being lost in a shopping mall'). From these studies, 25% of participants reported being 'lost in the mall' when their parents confirmed that this did not actually happen. Similar studies seem to have convinced people that they had overnight hospitalisation, were bitten by a dog, or had a serious indoor accident (Hyman *et al.*, 1995; Porter *et al.*, 1999).

Taking these findings together, it seems that people can believe in things that actually *did not* happen. Also, they can have strong emotional reactions when they are told about this. McNally *et al.* (2004) found that those who felt that they were 'space alien abductees' were very genuinely upset that people did not believe them, since they felt that these experiences were real.

How do we address these memory issues? Good investigative interviewing is one useful solution. However, there are many other useful solutions, including training the police to appreciate the challenges of memory limitations, using good police line-up procedures, and training the police to appreciate how mistaken identification occurs.

ACTIVITY
Inducing False Memories

Spend a minute memorizing the words below. After that, cover the list and write down as many of the words as you can remember.

Table	Desk	Swivel
Sit	Recliner	Stool
Legs	Sofa	Sitting
Seat	Wood	Rocking
Couch	Cushion	Bench

The *Deese-Roediger-McDermott* list-learning paradigm is one way of inducing the false memories. The idea here is that the list learning is semantically related to a common associate. The common associate as a result tends to be recalled. For instance, in the above list, most people recall seeing 'Chair', when it was not in the word list!

Source: Roediger & McDermott (1995). Roediger, Henry L. and McDermott, *Journal of Experimental Psychology: Learning, Memory, and Cognition*, Vol. 21(4), Jul 1995, 803–814.

8.2.3 *Investigative Interviewing*

Investigative interviewing concerns interviewing people within the investigative process and may involve the accused, the witness, and victims. The idea here is that the process of interviews should obtain good quality and accurate information from interviews. Most times, the idea behind a good interview is to find out what, when, and how something happened, and who did it (Milne & Bull, 1999). The problem with interviews in many parts of the world appears to be poor preparation for the interview, assumption of guilt, repetitiveness, poor interviewing techniques, persistent questioning, failure to establish facts, and putting undue pressure on the suspects (Baldwin, 1992).

In the U.K., there are some very good practices that have evolved as a result of the pressure to get investigative interviewing right after several major cases of miscarriages of justice. These are as follows:

(1) Obtain accurate and reliable information from suspects, witnesses, and victims, in order to discover the truth;

(2) Approach everyone with an open mind. Information from the person should always be tested against what the officer already knows;

(3) When questioning anyone, act fairly;

(4) You are not bound to accept the first answer given. Repeated questioning is not necessarily unfair or oppressive questioning;

(5) Even when the person's right of silence is exercised,[4] the officer may still have the right to ask questions;

(6) When conducting an interview, the police are free to ask questions in order to establish the truth; and

(7) Treat vulnerable people, whether victims, witnesses, or suspects with due consideration at all times.

(Adapted from Milne & Powell, 2010)

The PEACE interviewing approach

Since 1993, the U.K. uses the 'PEACE' interviewing approach which stands for Planning and Preparation, Engaging the interviewees and Explaining the ground rules for the interview, obtaining an Account of what happened and Closure of the interview. Finally, the process has to be Evaluated. The final part involves evaluating the skills and development of the interviewer (Centrex, 2004). This model showed promise but there has been criticism. There was an evaluation in 2001 by Clarke and Milne for the U.K. Home Office and they reported several. First, there was poor transfer of information and skills from the classroom to the workplace. For example, the research found poor use of interviewing techniques for obtaining an interviewee's account, little evidence of routine supervision of interviews, and misunderstandings about the PEACE model. Furthermore, the evaluation found that the interviewing of victims and witnesses

---

[4] This applies more to the UK context.

was not done as well as the interviewing of suspects. The review found that this was because there was a lack of guidelines, the perception of a lesser 'status' for witness interviews (compared to suspect interviews), and the distractions present when the person is interviewed. Most importantly, Clarke and Milne recommended tape-recording all interviews with 'event-relevant' victims and witnesses. Following this early work, Milne and Powell (2010) explained that two models of interviewing seem to have emerged as useful models. These are called 'Conversation Management' (Shepherd, 1991) which is useful for resistant suspects, and the 'Cognitive Interview', which is useful for cooperative suspects (Fisher & Geiselman, 1992).

The Cognitive Interview

The Cognitive Interview (CI) is a misnomer because it is not really an 'interview' *per se*. It is four techniques to be used with cooperative witnesses (Geiselman & Fisher, 1985). These are:

(1) *Report everything* (RE): The witness is asked to report everything about the incident;
(2) *Reverse the order* (RO): The witness is asked to recall in a variety of chronological sequences. For example, the account of what had occurred could be narrated from beginning to end, or in reverse order, or forward and then backwards;
(3) *Change perspective* (CP): Here, the witness is asked to look at the event from a different perspective (e.g., from the point of view of someone else at the scene);
(4) *Context reinstatement* (CR): the witness is asked to focus his or her mind on the context (e.g., features of the physical environment, his or her thoughts and feelings at the time, and so on).

The CI was enhanced for use in the field and re-labelled as the Enhanced Cognitive Interview (ECI), which was the CI embedded within an interview framework (Kebbell *et al.*, 1999; Milne, 2004).

Conversation Management

The Conversation Management (CM) technique was developed for unwilling and resistant interviewees (Milne & Bull, 1999). In these interviews, the interviewer has to take control. During the Account stage of the interview, the interviewer must be able to manage varying levels of interviewee resistance, sometimes through more directive and firm (though non-oppressive) approaches. Although CM was developed specifically for police officers to elicit information from resistant and reluctant subjects, its use is not widespread (Clarke & Milne, 2001).

The Reid Technique

Some interviewing models are viewed as coercive in nature (Gudjonsson & Pearse, 2011). Researchers have argued that one such model is the 'Reid Technique' used to elicit confessions (Inbau *et al.*, 2001). This technique has not been grounded in science. The technique follows two stages. The first stage is the non-accusatory and non-coercive 'behavioral analysis interview', where trust and rapport are built up between the interviewer and suspected offender. If the interviewing officer believes the person has not been honest or is deceptive, the second stage begins that involves a 'nine-step (interrogative) process', where interviewing officers can lie to suspected offenders about the nature and strength of the evidence against them.

The 'Nine Steps Technique' involves the following:

1. The direct positive confrontation: The interrogator firmly advises the suspect that the investigation clearly indicates that he is responsible for the commission of a crime. This may not be true. However, to persuade a guilty suspect to tell the truth, the investigator must often exaggerate his or her confidence.
2. Development of themes that psychologically justify the crime: The investigator offers moral or psychological excuses for the suspect's criminal behaviour. The theme is not designed to plant new ideas in the suspect's mind, but merely to reinforce the justifications that

already exist in the guilty suspect's mind (e.g., that it was an accident, any man would respond that way if she dressed that way).

3. Steps 3 and 4 address statements the suspect makes during theme development. The investigator discourages (by forcefully interrupting) the suspect from offering denials or explanations for incriminating evidence.

4. Interrogator keeps speaking, thus not allowing the suspect to offer any factual or emotional objections.

5. Ensuring the suspect is paying attention to the theme (and does not withdraw). At this stage, the investigator may move his chair in closer to the suspects.

6. Responding to the suspect's passive mood. The investigator condenses theme concepts to one or two central elements and shows sympathy and understanding and urges the suspect to cooperate. He/she moves into the next step designed to elicit the initial admission of guilt.

7. Presenting an alternative question: This is a question that presents two choices to the suspect concerning some aspect of his crime. The choices generally contrast a positive and a negative choice (e.g., "Have you done this many times before or was this just the first time?") Accepting either choice, of course, results in an admission of guilt.

8. Developing the oral confession.

9. Converting the oral confession into a court admissible document.

(Adapted from Schollum, 2005)

Looking at the stages of the Reid Technique, it would not be surprising to most that it has been linked to false confessions (Leo, 1996), as it relies heavily on the psychological manipulation of the suspect (Kassin & Gudjonsson, 2004). Readers are advised not to use the Reid technique in their interviews.

As a summary to this section, the field and research relating to investigative interviewing seems to converge towards the conclusion that the most important skill for the skilled investigative interviewer is the 'information gathering and rapport-based interviewing' approach rather than the 'accusatory' one. The use of non-leading and open-ended questions is very useful because they maximize the accuracy and detail of the interviewee's account, minimise confusion, contamination (see the earlier section on false memories), and misunderstanding (Milne & Powell, 2010).

In Singapore, there has been a move to make sure the interviews are done ethically. One important move by the government has been the introduction of 'video recorded interviews' (VRIs) which may help prevent false confessions. The Singapore Ministry of Law proposed some changes under the Criminal Justice Reform Bill and Evidence (Amendment) Bill. The Ministry explained that under the current law, law enforcement agencies taking statements under the Criminal Procedure Code could only do so in writing. With the new Bill, statements may be taken via video recording. It was explained that this new Bill and Act will allow the Courts to take into account the interviewee's demeanour when deciding the weight to be accorded to statements. Secondly, video recordings provide an objective account of the interview, to assist the Court in deciding on any allegations made about the conduct of the interview. In the first phase of implementation, the Ministry makes it mandatory to conduct VRIs for suspects in rape offences (Ministry of Law, 2018).

Another important legal matter for readers to take note of is that all interviewers must be very careful about doing interviews without any 'promise, threat, and inducement'. In a judgement made in PP v. Nagenthran (2011), the Court concluded the following:

> "The law on the operation of threat, inducement, promise and oppression in respect of voluntariness of statements made by accused persons is fairly well settled. First, there must objectively be a threat, inducement or promise and second this subjectively must operate on the mind of the accused."

> Chai Chien Wei Kelvin v. PP [1999] 1 SLR 25.

8.2.4 *Psychological Impact of Criminal Victimisation*

The criminal justice system can be a difficult process for victims of crime. Victims perceive that police do not respond fast enough, even when the police do respond. When the police arrive, victims feel that the police are not sensitive enough. Victims cannot appreciate why their property cannot be returned to them during the process of investigation. They are shocked when they hear that their aggressors have been released on bail.

In the U.S., there have been many provisions to mitigate the impact of victimization. First, most states have laws requiring 'notification' of victims of various stages, during the process of investigation and prosecution. This is especially so if the perpetrator is about to be released on bail, released from jail, or escaped from prisons. Second, in the U.S., victims sometimes have the right of 'allocution', which refers to their right to speak up during certain proceedings, such as bail hearing or sentence hearing. This can be done in person or prepared in writing, and then presented to the court. In many jurisdictions, pre-sentence reports also include 'victim impact statements'. In these statements, the victim may explain, for instance, that he or she has bad nightmares, wakes up in cold sweat, or avoids the place of the attack. Third, in several U.S. states, there is 'compensation' as well. Victims are compensated for medical expenses, psychological counselling, funeral bills, and stolen property. This is often paid for by the state or sometimes even the offenders themselves. Many states disallow criminals to write books about their crimes while in prisons and gain from the sales profits of these books. This is called the 'Son of Sam' laws. Next, there are also 'Shield laws' which protect victims from being asked about their sexual history.

What are the *psychological effects* of criminal victimization? Psychological trauma may be more troubling to the victim than the physical injury itself in many cases. Reactions can range from mild to severe, including sleep disturbances, irritability, worry, and health concerns (Markesteyn, 1992). Severe reactions may include depression, anxiety disorders, alcohol and drug overuse, and suicide ideation (Walker & Kilpatrick, 2002).

One of the most common reactions to criminal victimisations is post-traumatic stress disorder (PTSD). Several studies have documented this[5]:

---

[5] This list is non-exhaustive. We have just selected some examples of studies here for illustration.

a. Kilpatrick *et al.* (1985) found that the *offence of rape* causes the most trauma, with 19% of victims having attempted suicide, 44% reporting suicide ideation, and 16% reporting that they had a nervous breakdown. Resnick *et al.* (1993) found that 32% of rape victims met the criteria for PTSD at some point of their lives. It is important to appreciate that rape victims may also be impacted physically. Another study found that rape victims might suffer significantly more from sexual dysfunction and pelvic floor dysfunction when compared with non-traumatized controls. This was true even when there was provision of treatment for PTSD for them. In a cross-sectional study by Postma *et al.* (2013), a group of 89 young women aged 18- to 25-years-old who were raped in adolescence was compared to a group of 114 non-victimized controls. Three years post-treatment, rape victims were 2.4 times more likely to have a sexual dysfunction (lubrication problems and pain) and 2.7 times more likely to have 'pelvic floor' dysfunction (symptoms of provoked vulvodynia, general stress, lower urinary tract, and irritable bowel syndrome) than non-victimized controls. The authors argued that it could be possible that physical manifestations of PTSD have been left unaddressed in treatment. They concluded that future treatment protocols should consider incorporating (physical and psychological) treatment strategies for sexual dysfunction into trauma exposure treatments.

b. Short-term reactions to non-domestic assaults such as *robbery* and *assaults* experienced by 40% of victims include anger, difficulty sleeping, confusion, denial, and fear (Markestyn, 1992). In the same sample, about 20% to 40% reported depression, helplessness, loss of appetite, nausea, and malaise, sometimes lasting for up to three weeks.

c. For *homicide victims*, the impact appears to be very intense when a loved one is murdered. The process of mourning is longer, intense, and complex (Markestyn, 1992). Grief reactions are deep, and include rage and vengefulness. There is long-lasting anxiety and phobic reactions (Amick-McMullun *et al.*, 1989).

d. In the case of *child sexual abuse*, victimization produces long-term psychological problems such as depression, guilt, and feelings of inadequacy, substance abuse, suicidality, anxiety, fears, and phobias. Children feel responsible for the abuse, if no force or threat was used. A history of childhood abuse is linked to greater risk of mental health issues in adulthood (Briere, 1988).

e. *Burglary*, while officially classified as a property crime, carries a very interpersonal angle to it (Merry and Harsent, 2000). Victims feel traumatized beyond physical loss. They feel violated at a place where they are supposed to feel safe. The distress tends to be more pronounced when the invasion occurs in places which are personalized sectors of the home, such as the bedroom or private closets and drawers. It is common for homeowners to react by installing alarms, getting guard dogs, and often moving to a new house.

To conclude this section, readers should note that the level of criminal impact is *not* equal for everyone. It is a matter of degree of impact and Markesteyn (1992) proposes that victim recovery may be mediated by three factors: 1) pre-victimization characteristics of the victims, such as his/her socioeconomic status, ethnicity, religious beliefs, gender, and age; 2) post-victimization ability to cope, and 3) factors related to the crime event itself, such as the degree of violence involved and location of crime (Bartol & Bartol, 2008).

8.3 Special Topics Under Civil Law

8.3.1 *Child Custody Evaluations*

One difficult area of work for the family courts is divorce and child custody. Studies have estimated that children are involved in 40% of divorce cases (Horvath *et al.*, 2002). This field of work come under a subfield of forensic psychology called 'Family Forensic Psychology'.[6] Psychologists (private and court-appointed) are sometimes asked to provide an opinion on the capacity of parents to provide a safe and

---

[6] This is an area of work where family psychology and family law overlap (Grossman & Okun, 2003).

positive environment for children. Usually, the main concern is whether the parent can provide the 'right parenting support' that will meet the physical, emotional, social, intellectual, and cultural needs of the child. The role of the psychologist is really to make an assessment, which is in the best interests of the child, and the assessment has to be fair and independent.

There are different legal standards used to determine child custody. The earliest standard was called the 'Tender Years Doctrine', which suggested that young children, and particularly girls, are best left under the care of the mother. In more recent years, this doctrine has been replaced by the BIC standard ('Best Interests of Child'), and it does not make any assumption as to which parent is better for the child. It looks at what is in the best interests for the *child*. Krauss and Sales (2000), however, explain that a better standard might be the 'least detrimental alternative standard', which suggests that the least harm done to the child might be the better standard. The idea was to 'screen out' harmful arrangements for the child, rather than examine which parent would be better for the child.

Common methods used for child custody evaluations include interview data, home visitations, and assessments, and useful instruments such as the Care Index and the Home Inventory. Readers should look up the American Psychological Association's 'Guidelines for Child Custody Evaluations for Family Law Proceedings' (2009). There are no well-established standardized protocols, but the research seems clear that merely relying on parent interviews would be risky for the child. Usually, the assessment involves interviewing the child, the parents, significant others, and home visitations, to look into various dimensions such as the following (Puckering, 2010):

a. *Child's own development needs*: Self-care, identity, emotional development, education and health needs, stability in child's education, family and community life, mental and psychological health of child, child's sibling relationships, past and present abuse, well-reasoned preference of the child based on child's maturity;

b. *Parent capacity*, which refers to the parental duties performed by each party: The ability to ensure safety, provide emotional warmth, mental stimulation, guidance, and boundaries; the mental and psychological health of parents, including history of alcohol and drug abuse; attempts by parent to turn the child against the other parent; which party is more likely to attend to the daily physical, emotional, developmental, educational and special needs of the child; the level of conflict between the parents and willingness to cooperate;

c. *Family and Environmental factors*: Income, employment, housing, wider family network and extended family, community resources, family and social integration, and religious and cultural observances.

In making the overall assessment, psychologists have to be careful not to make the decision for the courts. The courts will be the main decision-makers. Psychologists, however, may evaluate possible options for the child, childcare, and contact. It is always useful to provide more than one option in this respect in making the assessment in the best interests of the child.

8.3.2 *Work-Related Stress*

Another area in civil law towards which forensic-legal psychologists can contribute to is work-related stress. In the U.K., the courts have developed a set of principles which they expect to be addressed when discussing workplace stress litigation. The main issues are the following:

- That there should be some identifiable psychological stress injury and that this injury could have been *foreseen* by the employer,
- That the employer should have done their *duty of care* in a reasonable way and,
- That any psychological injury could have been *attributable* to a cause in the workplace.

The main issue in the U.K. workplace stress litigation appears to be the 'principle of foreseeability' (Campbell, 2010). As you can imagine, making out a case for psychological injury due to workplace stress may not be such an easy thing to do.

In making an assessment in totality, there is a need to assess the workplace environment, and determine if there were psychosocial hazards in workplace settings, whether the individual was involved, and whether there was 'reasonable care' shown by the employer. It may be legally challenging to establish that the workers' psychological state was a result of workplace stressors or factors. As for the issue of 'reasonable care', while it is clear that there might have been 'duty of care', it is less clear what this care should entail and whether it is reasonable. For example, is it enough to provide a critical incident stress debriefing session after a major stressful and traumatic event?

In Singapore, the main laws of relevance would be the Employment Act, which regulates employment and welfare issues. The Workplace Safety and Health Act (WSHA) focuses on the safety and health issues of employees. The WSHA covers several matters, including minimum health and safety workplace standards; medical and hygiene monitoring of employees; implementation of a safety and health management system; provision of first aid boxes and first aiders at workplaces; regular inspections to uncover safety or health lapses at the workplace; and the elimination of foreseeable risks to employees at the workplace. The Work Injury Compensation Act (WICA) also spells out the conditions of compensation to employees for any injury or illness suffered in the course of work (Rajah & Tann, n.d.)

8.3.3 *Assessment of Personal Injury*

Personal injuries are damages to the physical person rather than to a person's property. This relates to the law of Tort, and a tort is an act which causes harm to a person, whether intentionally or not. Such harm could, for example, result from an employer not having 'duty of care' or 'negligence' during a medical procedure, for example. The result of personal injury on another person can give rise to a claim for personal injuries, which is settled by an award of damages, as compensation. Powell and Powell (2010) explained that the tort of negligence requires that the claimant establish: (1) that there was a 'duty of care' issue, (2) the defendant owed the plaintiff a 'duty of care', (3) the defendant breached that 'duty of care' because he or she was careless or negligent, and (4) the breach caused the plaintiff some damage.

According to Barton (1990), the role of the forensic psychologist is to examine the nature of the injury within the domain of psychology. There are several issues for consideration, when undertaking an assessment:

a. What is the reason for the evaluation?
b. Use psychological interviews: how is examinee doing now? What effects has the injury had? What is the mental status and behavioural observations? What was his/her pre-morbid clinical, psychological, and physical history like (i.e., medical history, family history, prior injuries, etc.)?
c. Use personality testing, neuropsychological testing, pain inventories, tests for post-traumatic disorder, and tests of malingering. Working with psychiatrists and physicians, you may also want to study blood panels and imaging results. There may be a mental health disorder or issue resulting from the injury. Some examples may be experiencing depression or post-traumatic stress, or stress symptoms such as phobia, trauma, or anxiety. In some cases, there could be loss of intellectual functioning or cognitive impairment that may affect his/her work. There could also be emotional or behavioral issues which may occur.
d. Undertake collateral interviews with those who may have useful information. These may be family members, medical professionals, co-workers, and supervisors. Confidentiality is important here.
e. The main issue in assessment and report writing is to make the 'chain of causality' clear (e.g., a facial injury or scar due to a work injury, which affects an actress's potential future earnings or a model's earning in the future). Experts concur that when conducting the assessment, there are three important assessment challenges. First, the 'thin eggshells' issue. This is a pre-existing vulnerability that makes the claimant more susceptible to the disabling effects of the injury (Barton, 1990; Taylor, 1997).

Research has found that it is common for individuals who report a disproportionate amount of disability from minor injury to have prior histories of traumatic events or emotional vulnerability. The second issue pertains to 'multiple causation'. This is a situation where the event results in more than one type of injury. This is seen in auto-accidents and workplace injuries (Miller, 1998). The plaintiff may complain of pain, cognitive impairment, and post-traumatic stress — the 'big three' of personal injury cases (Miller, 1999). Here, the psychologist or expert may have to isolate and identify the causative factors of the disability. The third issue is that of 'malingering'. Plaintiffs may want to prove something, get back at the organization or simply obtain generous cash settlement. Experts are of the view that a credible independent report should always make an assessment of malingering and especially the exaggeration of existing symptoms (Miller *et al.*, 2011).

In the case of Singapore's laws, the laws of negligence are employed for personal injury cases including injury due to medical negligence. The Singapore Academy of Law has a detailed description of how the law of negligence in employed and interested readers should look this up at: http://www.singaporelawwatch.sg/.

8.3.4 *Assessment of Sexual Harassment*

Sexual harassment occurs within a context. It is important therefore to appreciate the contextual issues involved. Bowers and O'Donohue (2010) explained, for example, that sexually explicit jokes told by male colleagues may seem like sexual harassment, but might not be so if first told by the claimant herself. So, what constitutes sexual harassment depends on the context. There are several core features when thinking about sexual harassment. These include the following (Bowers & O'Donohue, 2010):

a. The sense that one is working in a 'hostile environment', or an environment that is sexualized and a person feels offended. For example, constant sex jokes, leering, and fondling. The issue here is that the conduct and behavior must be offensive (to the reasonable person standard);[7]

b. The idea of *quid pro quo*, or that the employee feels that he/she must explicitly or implicitly engage in or endure sexualized behaviours in order to retain the job or progress on the job or prevent the loss of their job or to obtain a job promotion;

c. Work setting is *negative* and *sexualised*;

d. *Welcome-ness* refers to whether the accuser welcomed the target behaviour. Sexualized behavior that is welcome is not usually considered sexual harassment. This issue is difficult to assess since whether someone feels welcomed or not is hard to assess, and there is a need for corroborative evidence. Bowers and O'Donohue provide interesting examples of how difficult this assessment can be. They explain that sometimes the accuser may appear to welcome sexual comments and advances just to fit in or appear cool and get along with other colleagues. In other instances, the accuser may initiate sexual contact at work and then claim that similar reciprocal sexual behavior was unwelcomed. All these scenarios make assessment complex and difficult.

The psychological impact on sexual harassment can be emotionally and psychologically challenging to victims. Studies have noted that victims experience depression, post-traumatic stress, anxiety, anger, somatic, and physical problems. Bowers and O'Donohue point out that the presence of symptoms cannot be taken as evidence that sexual harassment took place, and symptoms could be due to the misunderstanding of certain events.

In sexual harassment suits, the alleged victim may be asked to undergo a psychological or psychiatric evaluation. An established instrument to assessing sexual harassment is the Sexual Experiences Questionnaire (SEQ) (Fitzgerald & Shullman, 1985). It lists 29

---

[7] Some courts would prefer the 'reasonable woman' standard on the premise that men may not fully appreciate the effects of sexual harassment on women. On the other hand, because men may also be victims, most courts prefer the 'reasonable victim' standard.

specific behaviors and five types of harassments that are measured, including: 'gender harassment', 'seductive behavior', 'sexual bribery', 'sexual coercion', and 'sexual imposition'. A related issue in making an assessment is the consideration of 'false allegations'. In some cases, the victim may not fully understand what sexual harassment is or is not; for example, a female office worker may complain of sexual harassment because her male supervisor criticizes her work performance. Also, the alleged victim may unintentionally distort events and believe events to be of a sexual nature. Reports have suggested that those with borderline disorder or histrionic personality disorder may unintentionally distort the events. All of these issues make these kinds of assessments challenging.

8.4 Summary

- This chapter discussed several roles of the forensic–legal psychologist.
- It discussed several areas of application of forensic–legal psychology in investigative issues. These included a discussion on eyewitness testimony, false memories, interviewing, and the impact of victimization.
- In the area of civil law applications, this chapter contained discussions on child custody evaluations, workplace stress, sexual harassment, and personal injury.

E-Journals and Books

Law and Human Behaviour
Psychology, Public Policy and the Law
Psychology, Crime and Law
Psychiatry, Psychology and Law
Psychology and Law: A Critical Introduction. Andreas Kapardis (2009)
Handbook of Psychology and Law. Editors: Kagehiro, Dorothy K., Laufer, William S. (Eds.) (2013)
The Psychology of Law: Human Behavior, Legal Institutions, and Law By Bruce D. Sales, PhD, JD, and Daniel A. Krauss, JD, PhD. (2015).

Some Relevant Legal Case Studies

Mohd Sairi bin Suri v PP [1997] SGCA 57 (Duress)
PP v Ng Pen Tine [2009] SGHC 230 (Duress)
PP v Nagaenthran [2011] 4 SLR 1156 (Duress)

Sample Research Essay Titles

- Compare and contrast the disciplines of psychology and law.
- What roles do forensic–legal psychologists have?
- When are eyewitnesses accurate?
- How do we enhance investigative interviewing?

References

American Psychological Association (2009). *Guidelines for Child Custody Evaluations in Family Law Proceedings*. Washington D.C.: Author.

Amick-McMullen, A., Kilpatrick, D.G., & Resnick, H.S. (1991). Homicide as a risk factor for PTSD among surviving family members. *Behavioral Modification*, 15, 545–559.

Baldwin, J. (1992). *Videotaping of Police Interviews with Suspects: An Evaluation*. Police Research Series Paper No 1. London: Home Office.

Barton, W.A. (1990). *Recovering for Psychological Injuries*. Washington DC: ATLA Press.

Bartol, C. & Bartol, A. (2008). *Introduction to Forensic Psychology: Research and Application*. Singapore: Sage Publications.

Bersoff, D. (2013). APA's amicus briefs: Informing public policy through the courts. *The Monitor*, 44(6).

Bowers, A. & O'Donohue, W. (2010). Sexual harassment. In J. Brown and E. Campbell (Eds.), *The Cambridge Handbook of Forensic Psychology* (Cambridge Handbooks in Psychology). Cambridge: Cambridge University Press.

Briere, J. (1988). The long-term clinical correlates of long term childhood sexual victimisation. In R.A. Prentky and V.L. Quinsey (Eds). *Human Sexual Aggression: Current Perspectives*. New York: New York Academy of Sciences.

Brown, J. & Campbell, B. (Ed.) (2010). *The Cambridge Handbook of Forensic Psychology* (Cambridge Handbooks in Psychology). Cambridge: Cambridge University Press.

Brown, D., Scheflin, A.W., & Hammond, D.C. (1998). *Memory, Trauma Treatment and the Law*. New York: W.W. Norton.

Campbell, E. (2010). Work place stress. In J. Brown and E. Campbell (Eds.), *The Cambridge Handbook of Forensic Psychology* (Cambridge Handbooks in Psychology). Cambridge: Cambridge University Press.

Centrex (2004). *Practical Guide to Investigative Interviewing.* London: Central Police Training and Development Authority.

Christianson, S. (1992). Emotional stress and eyewitness memory: A critical review. *Psychological Bulletin, 112*(2), 284–309.

Clarke, C. & Milne, R. (2001). *National Evaluation of the PEACE Investigative Interviewing Course.* Home Office: U.K., Research Award Scheme, Report No. PRSA 149. Retrieved from http://www.homeoffice.gov.uk/peace_interviewcourse.pdf.

Crittenden, P. M. (1991). Strategies for changing parental behavior. *APSAC Advisor*, Spring, 9.

Cutler, B.L., Penrod, S.D., & Martens, T.K. (1987). The reliability of eyewitness identification: The role of system and estimator variables. *Law and Human Behaviour, 11*(3), 233–258.

Daicoff, S. (2000). The role of therapeutic jurisprudence within the comprehensive law movement. In D.P. Stolle, D.B. Wexer, and B.J. Winick (Eds). *Practicing Therapeutic Jurisprudence*, pp. 465–467. Durham, NC: Carolina Academic Press.

Davis, D. & Loftus, E.F. (2006). Internal and external sources of misinformation in adult witness memory. In M.P. Toglia, f.D. Read, D.F. Ross, and R.C.L. Lindsay (Eds.) *The Handbook of Eyewitness Psychology, Vol. 1: Memory for Events*, pp. 95–237. London: Erlbaum.

Fisher, R.P. & Geiselman, R.E. (1992). *Memory Enhancing Techniques for Investigative Interviewing: The Cognitive Interview.* Springfield, IL: Charles C. Thomas.

Geraerts, E., Smeets, E., Jelicic, M., Heerden, J.V., & Merckelbach, H. (2005). Fantasy proneness, but not self-reported trauma is related to DRM performance of women reporting recovered memories of childhood sexual abuse. *Consciousness and Cognition, 14*(3), 602–612.

Grossman, N.S. & Okun, B.F. (2003). Family psychology and family law: Introduction to the special issue. *Journal of Family Psychology, 17*(2), 163–168.

Gudjonsson, G. (2010). Interrogative suggestibility and false confessions. In J. Brown and E. Campbell (Eds.) (2010), *The Cambridge Handbook of Forensic Psychology* (Cambridge Handbooks in Psychology). Cambridge: Cambridge University Press.

Horvath, L.S., Logan, T., & Walker, R. (2002). Child custody cases: A content analysis of evaluations in practice. *Professional Psychology: Research and Practice, 33*(6), 557–565.

Hyman, I.E., Husband, T.H., & Billings, F.J. (1995). False memories of childhood experiences. *Applied Cognitive Psychology, 9*(3), 181–197.

Fitzgerald, L.R. & Shullman, S.L. (1985). *Sexual Experiences Questionnaire*. Kent, OH: Kent State University.

Gudjonsson, G.H. & Pearse, J. (2011). Suspect interviews and false confessions. *Current Directions in Psychological Science, 20*(1), 33–37.

Inbau, F.E., Reid, J.E., Buckley, J.P., & Jayne, B.C. (2001). *Criminal Interrogation and Confessions* (4th ed.). Sudbury, MA: Jones & Bartlett.

Layney, C. & Loftus, E. (2010). False Memory. In J. Brown and E. Campbell (Eds.), *The Cambridge Handbook of Forensic Psychology* (Cambridge Handbooks in Psychology, pp. 202–207). Cambridge: Cambridge University Press.

Leo, R.A. (1996). Inside the interrogation room. *The Journal of Criminal Law and Criminology, 86*, 266–303.

Light, L.L., Kayra-Stuart, F., & Hollander, S. (1979). Recognition memory for typical and unusual faces. *Journal of Experimental Psychology: Human Learning & Memory, 5*(3), 212–228.

Loftus, E.F., Loftus, G.R., & Messo, J. (1987). Some facts about "weapon focus." *Law and Human Behavior, 11*(1), 55–62.

Kassin, S.M. & Gudjonsson, G. (2004). The psychology of confessions. *Psychological Science in the Public Interest, 5*(2), 33–67.

Kebbell, M.R., Milne, R., & Wagstaff, G.F. (1999). The cognitive interview: A survey of its forensic effectiveness. *Psychology, Crime and Law, 5*, 101–115.

Kilpatrick, D.G., Best, C.L., Veronen, L.J, Amick, A.E., Villepontreaux, L.A., & Ruff, G.A. (1985). Mental health correlates of criminal victimisation. A random community survey. *Journal of Clinical and Consulting Psychology, 53*, 866–873.

King, M. & Wexler, D. (2010). Therapeutic Jurisprudence. In J. Brown and E. Campbell (Eds.), *The Cambridge Handbook of Forensic Psychology* (Cambridge Handbooks in Psychology) (2010). Cambridge: Cambridge University Press.

King, M.A. & Yuille, J.C. (1987). Suggestibility and the child witness. *Children's Eyewitness Memory*, pp. 24–35.

Krauss, D.A. & Sales, B.D. (2000). Legal standards, expertise, and experts in the resolution of contested child custody cases. *Psychology, Public Policy, and Law, 6*(4), 843–879.

Maclin, O.H., Maclin, M.K., & Malpass, R.S. (2001). Race, arousal, attention, exposure and delay: An examination of factors moderating face recognition. *Psychology, Public Policy, and Law, 7*(1), 134–152.

Markesteyn, T. (1992). *The Psychological Impact of Nonsexual Criminal Offences on Victims*. Ottawa: Ministry of Solicitor General of Canada, Corrections Branch.

Mcnally, R.J., Lasko, N.B., Clancy, S.A., Macklin, M.L., Pitman, R.K., & Orr, S.P. (2004). Psychophysiological responding during script-driven imagery in people reporting abduction by space aliens. *Psychological Science, 15*(7), 493–497.

Meissner, C.A. & Brigham, J.C. (2001). Thirty years of investigating the own-race bias in memory for faces: A meta-analytic review. *Psychology, Public Policy, and Law, 7*(1), 3–35.

Memon, A., Hope, L., & Bull, R. (2003). Exposure duration: Effects on eyewitness accuracy and confidence. *British Journal of Psychology, 94*(3), 339–354.

Memon, A. & Gabbert, F. (2003). Improving the identification accuracy of senior witnesses: Do prelineup questions and sequential testing help? *Journal of Applied Psychology, 88*(2), 341–347.

Merry, S. & Harsent, L. (2000). Intruders, pilferers, raiders and invaders: The interpersonal dimension of burglary. In Canter, D.V. & Alison, L.J. (2000), *Profiling Property Crimes*. Aldershot: Ashgate.

Miller, L. (1998). *Shocks to the System: Psychotherapy of Traumatic Disability Syndromes*. New York: Norton.

Miller, L. (1999). Mental stress claims and personal injury. Clinical neuropsychological and forensic issues. *Neurolaw Letter, 8*, 39–45.

Miller, L., Sadoff, R.L., & Dattilo, F.M. (2011). Personal injury: The Independent Medical Examination in Psychology and Psychiatry. In *Handbook of Forensic Assessment: Psychological and Psychiatric Perspectives*.

Milne, R. & Bull, R. (1999). *Investigative Interviewing: Psychology and Practice*. Chichester: Wiley.

Milne, R. (2004). *The Enhanced Cognitive Interview — A Step-by-Step Guide*.

Milne, B. & Powell, M. (2010). In J. Brown and E. Campbell (Eds.), *The Cambridge Handbook of Forensic Psychology* (Cambridge Handbooks in Psychology). Cambridge: Cambridge University Press.

Ministry of Law, Singapore (2018). *Second Reading Speech by Ms. Indranee Rajah, Senior Minister of State for Law and Finance, on Criminal Justice Reform Bill and Evidence (Amendment) Bill*. 19 March 2018.

Novotley, A. (2017). *Helping courts and juries make educated decisions*. Retrieved from http://www.apa.org/monitor/2017/09/courts-decisions.aspx on 12 March 2018.

Pansky, A., Koriat, A., & Goldsmith, M. (2005). Eyewitness recall and testimony. In N. Brewer and K.D. Williams (Eds). *Psychology and Law: An Empirical Perspective*. pp. 93–150. New York: Guildford.

Patterson, K.E. & Baddeley, A.D. (1977). When face recognition fails. *Journal of Experimental Psychology: Human Learning & Memory, 3*(4), 406–417.

Porter, S., Yuille, J.C., & Lehman, D.R. (1999). The nature of real, implanted, and fabricated memories for emotional childhood events: Implications for the recovered memory debate. *Law and Human Behaviour, 23*(5), 517–537.

Postma. R., Bicanic. I., van der Vaart. H., & Laan, E. (2013). Pelvic floor muscle problems mediate sexual problems in young adult rape victims. *Journal of Sexual Medicine, 10,* 1,978–1,987.

Powell M.B., Fisher R.P., & Wright R. (2005). 'Investigative interviewing'. In N. Brewer and K. Williams (Eds.), *Psychology and Law: An Empirical Perspective.* (11–42). New York: Guilford.

Powell, G.E. & Powell, C. (2010). Personal injury. In J. Brown and E. Campbell (Eds.), *The Cambridge Handbook of Forensic Psychology* (Cambridge Handbooks in Psychology). Cambridge: Cambridge University Press.

Pozzulo, J.D. & Lindsay, R.C. (1998). Identification accuracy of children versus adults: A meta-analysis. *Law and Human Behaviour, 22*(5), 549–570.

Puckering, C. (2010). Parenting capacity and consent. In J. Brown and E. Campbell (Eds.), *The Cambridge Handbook of Forensic Psychology* (Cambridge Handbooks in Psychology, pp. 202–207). Cambridge: Cambridge University Press.

Rajah & Tann (n.d.). *The Singapore Employer's Duty of Care on Workplace Safety and Health when Employees Travel.* Retrieved from https://www.internationalsosfoundation.org on 23 December 2018.

Resnick, H.S., Kilpatrick, D.G., Dansky, B.S., Saunders, B.E., & Best, C.L. (1993). Prevalence of civilian trauma in PTSD in a representative national sample of women. *Journal of Consulting and Clinical Psychology, 61,* 984–991.

Roediger, H.L. & McDermott, K.B. (1995). 'Creating false memories' remembering words that were not presented in lists. *Journal of Experimental Psychology: Learning, Memory and Cognition, 21,* 803–814.

Schollum, M. (2005). *Investigative Interviewing: The Literature.* The New Zealand Police. Office of the Commissioner of Police.

Shepherd, E. (1991). Ethical interviewing. *Policing, 7*(1), 42–60.

Steblay, N.M. (1992). A meta-analytic review of the weapon focus effect. *Law and Human Behaviour, 16*(4), 413–424.

Taylor, J.S. (1997). *Neurolaw: Brain and the Spinal Cord.* Washington D.C.: ATLA Press.

Terr, L. (1991). Childhood traumas: An outline and an overview: A prospective study. *American Journal of Psychiatry, 148,* 10–20.

Tuckey, M.R. & Brewer, N. (2003). The influence of schemas, stimulus ambiguity, and interview schedule on eyewitness memory over time. *Journal of Experimental Psychology: Applied, 9*(2), 101–118.

Wagenaar, W.A. & Schrier, J.H. (1996). Face recognition as a function of distance and illumination: A practical tool for use in the courtroom. *Psychology, Crime & Law*, *2*(4), 321–332.

Walker, S.D. & Kilpatrick, D.G. (2002). Scope of crime/historical review of the victims' rights discipline. In A. Semour, M. Murray, Sigmon, M. C. Edwards, M. Gaboury and G. Coleman (Eds). *National Victims Academy Textbook.* Washington, DC: US Department of Justice, Office of Victims of Crime.

Wright, D.B. & Sladden, B. (2003). An own gender bias and the importance of hair in face recognition. *Acta Psychologica*, *114*(1), 101–114.

Yarmay, A.D. (2000). 'The older witness'. In M.B. Rothman, B.D. Dunlop and P. Entzel (Eds). *Elders, Crime and the Criminal Justice System: Myths, Perceptions and Reality in the 21 Century.* pp 127–148. New York: Springer.

Yarmay, D. (2012). 'Eyewitness testimony'. In J. Brown and E. Campbell (Eds.), *The Cambridge Handbook of Forensic Psychology* (Cambridge Handbooks in Psychology, pp. 177–186). Cambridge: Cambridge University Press.

EPILOGUE

In closing, what can we expect for crime in the future?

First, crime will always exist. Its form may differ but its essence should remain the same. Human motives do not change much over time, places and people. Dr. Tom Keenan who works at the University of Calgary and is Adjunct Professor of Computer Science was known to have said the following:

> "Criminals of the future will probably have many of the same motives as today's crooks...greed, lust, and revenge...but the ways in which they carry out their crimes may be radically different. With technology now into development, a criminal will be able to invade your home using computer links, telephone and two-way video taps. He or she may attack you with psychological harassment or mind manipulation techniques, demanding protection money to stay out of your brain. New technology will make all these things possible, even likely".

> Tom Keenan (1984)
> Transcript of the CBC "Ideas"

With greater wealth, rising digital use, global travel, higher mortality, technology, more information stored in smaller devices and the Internet of Things (IoT), there is more to take and to be easily taken as well. There will be more opportunity for crime. On the other hand, while we mature physically, our cyber maturity does not seem commensurate. We are already seeing a surge in cybercrimes globally, much of it a result of greater opportunities in cybercrimes and cyber-enabled crimes. In the beginning of this book, there were examples of cyber scams, which exemplified this trend. The solutions for this have been to develop cybercrime and cyber security expertise. However, this is only half of the solution — a systems and technical solutions. These solutions often do not consider the 'human element'. The other half would be enabled by the development of the human focus: cyber psychology, cyber cognition, and behavioral research on digital resilience and digital maturity.

Second, countries are beginning to realize that future work needs to understand 'what works, when, for whom, and why'. I believe that this will be true for Singapore and for Asian countries. There is already a *Handbook of Asian Criminology*,[1] and the *Asian Journal on Criminology*, which is a great start in this right direction. Other useful professional groupings have been the East Asia Psychology Law Meetings, the Asia Pacific Association of Threat Assessment Professionals, and the Asian Conference of Criminal and Operations Psychology. We might expect some theoretical differences in our thinking about crimes. For example, Liu *et al.* (2017) are of the view that there is some evidence that some Western theories such as the General Strain Theory and the Routine Activities do not work all the time in all Asian societies. Liu explains that the goal of criminal justice systems differ in Asian settings. He explains:

> "From an Asian perspective, there are difficulties in accepting the assumptions in Western criminal justice systems. This is partly because justice is understood more broadly than the relationship between the individual and state... In Asian societies, there is a different objective than punishment. The purpose of the justice system is to heal society, provide compensation and restore harmony in social relations."

> (Liu *et al.*, 2017, p. 26)

Liu explains that there are four relationship aspects of Asian communities. The first is importance of *attachment to families and*

---

[1] Liu, J., Jou, S., and Hebenton, B. (Eds.) (2012). *Asian Handbook of Criminology*. New York: Springer.

communities. Individuals cannot bear disapproval from social groups. The second is that both the individual and groups are concerned with *honour.* The Chinese, Korean, and Japanese family will seek to maintain its reputation as a high priority. Western researchers sometimes refer this to as the need to save 'face'. Muslim societies may be concerned about community and religious shame. The third is the concern with *harmony and conflict avoidance*, and the concern is restoring harmony to groups, rather than just seeking to rehabilitate or discipline individuals. The fourth aspect is a *preference for holistic thinking rather than analytical thinking.* Holistic thinking is about an orientation to the context as a whole, including attention to relationships between a focal object and the field. Putting all this together, the point is that there is much scope for the development of crime psychology and criminology in Asian settings.

A final area of future development is to work towards greater interdisciplinary synergies between criminal psychology, psychiatry, criminology, forensic sciences, and the law. The slant of this book has already been multidisciplinary, but with a focus on psychology (since it is the expertise of this author). Hopefully, this book may be a catalyst towards more interdisciplinary work since no one field has a monopoly over wisdom.

In conclusion, we have to acknowledge that the psychology of crime is a complex subject. An introductory text cannot possibly cover all types of crimes. In fact, there were many that were missed here, including property crimes, cybercrimes, and white-collar crimes. It is hoped that researchers would study these further, especially with the Singaporean and Asian lens. More research is needed for another reason. Criminals are a heterogeneous intra-group and inter-group. Complexity should not be an excuse for complacency. It should be the impetus to study these issues further, to advance our societies to keep them safe.

Reference

Liu, J. (2017). The new Asian paradigm: A relational approach. Chapter 2. In *Comparative Criminology in Asia*. Liu, J., M. Traver, and L.Y.C. Chang (Eds.), Switzerland: Springer Publishing.

ABOUT THE AUTHOR

 A forensic and criminal psychologist, Dr A. Majeed Khader is Chief Psychologist (Senior Consultant) at the Singapore Ministry of Home Affairs (MHA), and Director of the Home Team Behavioural Sciences Centre, Singapore. He was a police psychologist for 26 years and was the first home-grown officer to obtain a doctorate. He has been teaching criminal psychology at the Nanyang Technology University (NTU), Singapore, for over a decade, and has been guest lecturer at the National University of Singapore and James Cook University.

Obtaining degrees from the National University of Singapore (NUS) with an Honours in Psychology and the University of London (UOL) with an Honours in Sociology, he then completed a Masters in Forensic Psychology (with Distinction) at Leicester University, U.K., and a doctorate in crisis leadership and personality at the University of Aberdeen, Scotland. He has conducted international briefings at the Federal Bureau of Investigation (FBI), the Royal Canadian Mounted Police, Bramshill Police College, the Hongkong Police Force, previous National Crime Faculty, U.K., the Serious Organised Crime Agency (U.K.), the U.K. Home Office, the U.S. State Department, National Criminal Investigation Service, and the Ministry of Foreign Affairs, Japan.

During his career, he has trained large numbers of law enforcement officers and leaders, and has been involved in several operations such as the Jemaah Islamiyah arrests, the Little India Riot, the crash of Silk

Air MI185 and SQ006, and the Asian Tsunami. A trained hostage negotiator, his previous duties included being the ex-Deputy Commander and Head Training at the Singapore Police Force. In his career, Majeed has overseen the development of psychological services in the areas of profiling, crime prevention, victim support, negotiation, crisis leadership, threat assessment, and operational resilience. He has been instrumental in the early development of forensic-legal psychology, having been an invited speaker at the Singapore Law Society, and the Criminal Law Conference.

For his work, he was awarded the National Day Public Administration Award (Bronze) in 2006, and again the Public Administration Award (Silver) in 2014 by the President of Singapore.

Majeed has published widely in scientific journals and has been editor/co-editor of *Combatting Violent Extremism in the Digital Era*, *The Ostrich, The Ah Long, The Con Woman, And The Creep Guy: The Story Of Crime Prevention In Singapore*, and *Learning from Violent Extremist Attacks: Behavioural Sciences Insights for Practitioners and Policymakers*. He has been the Chairman of several conferences held in Singapore, titled the 'Asian Conference of Criminal and Operations Psychology'. He is the Asian Director of the U.S.-based Society of Police and Criminal Psychology and a member of the Asia Pacific Association of Threat Assessment Professions. Majeed is an Adjunct Senior Fellow at the NTU S. Rajaratnam School of International Studies (RSIS), a member of the Temasek Polytechnic School's Advisory Board, a member of Rainbow Centre's School Committee, and a Director at the Special Needs Trust Company.

His vision is to use psychology to make Singapore the safest place in the world. His strategy? To understand the criminal mind. For past opportunities to be able do this, he is grateful for the support of the Singapore Police Force and the Ministry of Home Affairs.